Happy

Mays

Love

Val a John

2006

Motto

Honour to God
Loyalty to the Throne,
Service to the Country,
Through Country Women,
For Country Women,
By Country Women

Aim of the Association

The Aim shall be to improve the well-being of all people, especially those in country areas by promoting courtesy, cooperation, community effort, ethical standards and the wise use of resources.

"Homes"

So long as there are homes to which men turn at close of day,
So long as there are homes where children are, and women stay,
If love and loyalty and faith be found across those sills,
A stricken nation can recover from its greatest ills.

So long as there are homes where fires burn, and there is bread,
So long as there are homes where lamps are lit, and prayers are said,
Although a people falter through the dark, and nations grope,
With God Himself back of these little homes we have sure hope.

By permission from "The Queensland Council Letter" of the C.W.A.

THE C.W.A. COOKERY BOOK AND HOUSEHOLD HINTS

Compiled by a committee led by Mrs. Agnes Barnes from the favourite and tried recipes and hints contributed by members and published under the direction of

THE COUNTRY WOMEN'S ASSOCIATION OF WESTERN AUSTRALIA (INCORP.)

NON SECTARIAN AND NON PARTY POLITICAL

HEAD OFFICE: 1174 HAY STREET, WEST PERTH

Foreword

Good food and family around the table are the essence of The Country Women's Association of Western Australia, which is currently celebrating 80 years of service to the community. During these years many changes in lifestyle, community needs and cooking trends have occurred, but CWA has always happily met the challenge.

It is with confidence and pride we again present a new edition of our famous cookery book which retains the universal appeal it has enjoyed since the 1st edition in 1936.

We have pleasure in inviting you to enjoy using this, the 52nd edition of *The CWA Cookery Book and Household Hints.*

Margaret Sullivan JP
State President
2003

Glossary

Basic Recipe:	Foundation recipe from which other recipes may be developed.
Blend:	To mix two or more ingredients together.
Cream:	To mix together to the consistency of cream.
Parboil:	To cook until just tender.
Saute:	To brown in frying pan with a small amount of fat.
Simmer:	To boil gently.

Notes

Some of the recipes in the book are more than 60 years old, and modern methods of cooking can be used. The following suggestions are made:

Oven temperatures:

If oven temperature is not mentioned, then use a moderate oven.
A "quick" oven means a hot oven.
Where the word "fire" is used, this means heat.

Ingredients:

Flour, unless otherwise stated, means plain flour.
Fat for frying, substitute a good vegetable oil.
"Household" pastry is short pastry.
"Burnt" sugar means caramelise the sugar.

Utensils:

For a kerosene tin, substitute a large cooking pot.

Simple Home Remedies:

Some ingredients included in these remedies, in the hands of children, could be dangerous. Due care must be taken.

Contents

Contents

Measures and Equivalents

The metric teaspoon is — 5 ml
The metric tablespoon is — 20 ml
The metric cup is — 250 ml

Quantities for metric recipes are likely to be a little larger than the old recipes, but they will still fit into the same cooking utensils.

CUP MEASURES

	Metric	*Imperial*
1 cup flour	155 g	5 oz.
1 cup sugar (crystal or castor)	250 g	8 oz.
1 cup brown sugar, firmly packed	185 g	6 oz.
1 cup icing sugar, sifted	185 g	6 oz.
1 cup shortening (butter, margarine, etc.)	250 g	8 oz.
1 cup honey, golden syrup, treacle	375 g	12 oz.
1 cup fresh breadcrumbs	60 g	2 oz.
1 cup packaged dry breadcrumbs	155 g	5 oz.
1 cup crushed biscuit crumbs	125 g	4 oz.
1 cup rice, uncooked	220 g	7 oz.
1 cup mixed fruit or individual fruit such as sultanas, etc.	185 g	6 oz.
1 cup nuts, chopped	125 g	4 oz.
1 cup coconut, dessicated	90 g	3 oz.

OVEN TEMPERATURES

	Fahrenheit °F	*Celsius* °C
Electric		
Very slow	250	120
Slow	300	150
Moderately slow	325-350	160-180
Moderate	375-400	190-200
Moderately hot	425-450	220-230
Hot	475-500	250-260
Very hot	525-550	270-290
Gas		
Very slow	250	120
Slow	275-300	140-150
Moderately slow	325	160
Moderate	350	180
Moderately hot	375	190
Hot	400-450	200-230
Very hot	475-500	250-260

Note: Where carbonate of soda is mentioned in recipes this refers to bi-carbonate of soda.

Time to Cook

MEATS

Ham	25 mins. per 500 gr, 20 mins. over
Bacon	15 mins. per 500 gr, 15 mins. over
Corned Beef	35 mins. per 500 gr, 30 mins. over
Beef, Roast, Rib or Sirloin ..	20 mins. per 500 gr
Mutton, Leg	20 mins. per 500 gr
Mutton, Shoulder	20 mins. per 500 gr
Mutton, Boiled	20 mins. per 500 gr
Veal, Roasted	25 mins. per 500 gr
Pork, Roasted	25 mins. per 500 gr
Tongue, Boiled	3 to 4 hours

POULTRY

Chicken, Boiled	20 mins. per 500 gr, 20 mins. over
Chicken, Roasted	20 mins. per 500 gr, 20 mins. over
Fowl, Roasted (old)	35 mins. to 500 gr
Goose, Roasted	$1\frac{3}{4}$ to 2 hours according to size
Turkey, Roasted	3 to $3\frac{1}{2}$ hours for $3\frac{1}{2}$-4 kg turkey
Fowl (old), Steamed	4 hours
Duck (full grown), Roasted	30 mins. per 500 gr, 30 mins. over
Duck (young), Roasted ..	30 mins. per 500 gr, 30 mins. over

GAME

Rabbit, Roasted	1 hour
Rabbit, Braised	$1\frac{1}{2}$ hours

CATERING

Catering for 50 People

MEAT

5 fowls
2 tongues
medium ham
3 kg (6 lb.) corned beef

SAVOURIES

6 dozen sausage rolls
4 dozen small pies
2 tins salmon made into patties
6 dozen cheese straws or similar cheese savoury
6 dozen savouries
500 gr (1 lb.) devilled almonds
2 dozen savoury eggs
cocktail onions—cheese

SALADS

500 gr (1 lb.) carrots
1 head celery
1 kg (2 lb.) tomatoes
1½ kg (3 lb.) beetroot (jellied)
5 large lettuce
1 large tin peas (jellied)
3 oranges

SWEETS

9 trifles
11 tins fruit
1 kg (2 lb.) apples
1¼ dozen oranges (for fruit salad)

MISCELLANEOUS

500 ml (1 pint) cream
6 dozen lamingtons
3 dozen fancy small cakes
6 dozen bread rolls
1-1¼ kg (2-2½ lb.) butter
2 kg (4 lb.) sugar
250 gr (½ lb.) tea
500 ml (1 pint) salad dressing
2 litres (½ gallon) milk

Afternoon Tea at Fete

SANDWICHES

6 long sandwich loaves
2 kg (4 lb.) butter
1 kg (2 lb.) cooked meat cut thin
1 bottle mock chicken spread
375 gr (12 oz.) cheese
2 white onions grated with cheese
other fillings as desired

MISCELLANEOUS

24 dozen small cakes
6 large cakes
12 dozen scones
500 gr (1 lb.) butter
1½ kg (3 lb.) tea
3 kg (6 lb.) sugar

Allow 2 sandwiches, 2 pieces of cake and ½ scone per person.

QUANTITIES

1 large sandwich loaf makes 13 rounds of sandwiches.

Allow 250 gr (½ lb.) butter per loaf.

Allow 375 gr (¾ lb.) pressed beef, ham or cheese per loaf. 500 gr (1 lb.) cuts 16 slices.

Allow 250 gr (½ lb.) tea and 500 gr (1 lb.) sugar for 50 people.

Allow 500 ml (1 pint) milk for 20 cups of tea.

Wedding Breakfast for 100 Guests

Menu: Cold meat, salad, trifles etc. Savouries.

MEAT

4 gobblers (1 gobbler equals 4 fowls)
6 kg (12 lb.) ham
2 tongues
6 kg (12 lb.) pork (to bake) or 6 kg (12 lb.) silverside corned beef

SALADS

3 kg (6 lb.) tomatoes
9 lettuce
500 gr (1 lb.) carrots
1 bottle gherkins
3 kg (6 lb.) beetroot (jellied)
2 large tins peas (jellied)

TRIFLES

6 sponges
2 tins pineapple
12 litres (3 gals.) egg custard (custard powder may be used instead of eggs)
1 bottle sweet sherry
6 jellies
almonds and cream
(16 dishes)

FRUIT SALAD

3 tins pears
3 tins peaches
3 tins apricots
2 kg (4 lb.) Granny Smith apples (or any other variety in season)
3 tins pineapple
2 dozen oranges
3 dozen passionfruit
(16 dishes)

FURTHER ADDITIONS TO TABLE

9 dozen small bread rolls
1 kg (2 lb.) butter
12 dozen sausage rolls
12 dozen savouries
12 dozen cheese straws
12 dozen fancy small cakes

BEVERAGES

250 gr (½ lb.) tea
1½ to 2 large bottles coffee essence 250 gr (or ½ lb.) jar Nescafe
3 kg (6 lb.) sugar
20 litres (5 gals) separated milk or 12 litres (3 gals.) whole milk and 8 litres (2 gals.) water

These suggestions can be varied according to personal taste and availability of requirements.

Soup and entree may be served if required.

Other beverages as directed by parties concerned.

Wedding Cake: A 1 kg (2 lb.) each fruit mixture makes a 2 tiered cake.

Catering for a Public Stock Sale

To serve approximately 300 adults with lunch consisting of cold meat and salad with sweet to follow.

MEAT

2 whole sheep (legs corned or baked—rest boned, rolled and stuffed)
6 pressed ox tongues. Pressed beef.

SALADS

35 kg (5 stone) potatoes
7 kg (14 lb.) tomatoes
3 heads celery
3 kg (6 lb.) carrots
18 lettuce
4 kg (8 lb.) beetroot

MISCELLANEOUS REQUIREMENTS

1½ kg (3 lb.) tea
4½ kg (9 lb.) butter
3 kg (6 lb.) sugar
6 long loaves bread
2 litres (½ gallon) salad dressing

SWEETS

large baked custard
2 large trifles
2 cases apples
6 tins fruit
2½ kg (5 lb.) pastry

Sweets may be varied according to availability of material (i.e. cream, fruit etc.).

Potato Salad (for 100 People)

3½ kg (½ stone) potatoes
500 gr (1 lb.) white onions
1 tin peas
1 litre (2 pints) salad dressing
chopped parsley or mint
salt and pepper to taste

Pea Soup (for Approx. 120)

Use 28 litre (7 gallon) boiler and half fill with bones (including ham bones). Boil one day, set and take off fat. Strain stock and add:

5 kg (10 lb.) split peas
1½ kg (3 lb.) onions
½ head celery
1 cup vinegar
1 teaspoon ground cloves (or to taste)
salt and pepper to taste

Vegetable Soup

Prepare stock as for pea soup excluding ham bones. Strain stock and add:

1 kg (2 lb.) barley
1½ kg (3 lb.) grated carrots
1 kg (2 lb.) onions
1½ kg (3 lb.) white turnips
½ head celery
salt and pepper to taste

Curry (for 50 People)

6 kg (12 lb.) topside steak
1 kg (2 lb.) brown onions
1 kg (2 lb.) carrots
1 kg (2 lb.) apples
½ tin plum jam
1 kg (2 lb.) bananas (optional)
small tin pineapple
250 gr (½ lb.) sultanas
250 gr (½ lb.) shelled almonds (optional)
1 small tin curry powder
500 gr (1 lb.) margarine

Dice onions and fry in margarine. Add curry powder, meat, vegetables, apple, pineapple, and jam, salt and pepper to taste. Cover with water, simmer gently, stirring frequently. Serve with rice, using 2 kg (4 lb.) rice.

BREAKFAST

Pour boiling water over wheatmeal for porridge, and cook in a double saucepan, or in a basin over a saucepan of water. Leave at the side of the stove all night. In the morning the mixture will be a thick jelly, and will require the addition of more boiling water. The longer the cooking the better the porridge.

After serving the breakfast porridge, put 500 ml (1 pint) of boiling or very hot water in the saucepan, put the lid on tightly and stand the saucepan away from the fire.

When bacon is too salt, instead of parboiling it, fry in the usual way. Then put it in a deep plate or pie-dish and pour boiling water over it. Take out and serve at once. Bacon so treated is delicious and retains its flavour.

To cook bacon appetisingly, cut the rashers into three parts, place them in milk and water and leave for about half an hour. Then roll in flour and fry in boiling fat until brown.

PORRIDGE

3 Tablespoons Wheatmeal or Oatmeal
3 cupsful water
water for soaking meal
salt to taste

Soak the meal overnight in enough cold water to cover it. Bring water to the boil, add soaked meal and salt. Stir until boiling and simmer for half an hour or longer.

APPLES AND BACON

Good Cooking Apples
ham or bacon
sugar

Fry some slices of ham a nice brown. Slice some good cooking apples, place them in a pan, sprinkled well with sugar, and fry till evenly browned and cooked through. Serve very hot with the bacon.

BATTER FOR FRITTERS

1 Large Tablespoon Flour
1 yolk of egg
1 tablespoon butter
2 tablespoons tepid water
1 white of egg
salt

Sift flour into a basin, make a well in the centre, and into this drop the egg yolk. Add a pinch of salt, then the water

BATTER FOR FRITTERS—*continued*

gradually, working in the flour from the centre. Mix smoothly, add melted butter. Cover the basin and let it stand for one hour. When ready to use, whisk the egg white very stiffly and mix it lightly with the batter.

BATTER FOR FRYING MEAT

125 gr (¼ lb.) Flour
1 egg
1 cup milk
salt

Rub the salt through the flour, make a well in the centre and drop in the egg, unbeaten. Beat thoroughly with a little of the milk, and finally add the rest of the milk. Allow to stand for 1 hour before using.

BATTER (FRENCH) FOR FRUIT, MEAT OR VEGETABLES

60 gr (2 oz.) Butter
scant 125 ml (¼ pint) boiling water
375 ml (¾ pint) of cold water
375 gr (12 oz.) finely sifted flour
whites of 2 eggs
pinch of salt

Cut butter into pieces, pour on to it the boiling water; when dissolved add the cold water, so that it shall be just warm. Mix by degrees, smoothly, with the flour and salt. Use extra salt if the batter is to be used for meat or vegetables. Before using stir into the batter the whites of eggs beaten to a stiff froth. Previous to adding eggs add a little more water if batter is too thick. This is excellent for frying vegetables and for fruit fritters.

EGGS (ANCHOVY)

2 Eggs
anchovy paste
30 gr (1 oz.) butter
salt and pepper
2 slices toasted bread

Spread the toasted bread, while very hot, with anchovy. Make butter hot, break eggs into it, add seasoning and stir quickly. Heap on toast and serve at once.

EGGS (BOILED)

Have sufficient boiling water in a saucepan to cover completely the eggs to be cooked. Using a spoon, slip eggs carefully into the water. Boil for three to four minutes according to taste.

EGGS (FRIED)

Have some fat hot in a frying pan. Break egg into a saucer, slip it into the hot fat, and fry until set. Baste with hot fat while cooking. Lift out carefully with a slice. Serve with bacon, chops or steak.

EGG AND ONION CURRIED

Toast
eggs
hot water
onions
1 tablespoon butter
1 dessertspoon curry powder
1 dessertspoon flour

Prepare a round of toast for each person and butter. Cut onions in circles and fry in deep fat, and place on toast. Fry one egg for each slice of toast, and place on the onion. Then pour over a thick sauce made as follows:—Melt tablespoonful of butter, mix in the curry powder, then the flour, and add sufficient hot water to thicken nicely, and cook for a few minutes. Delicious for a breakfast change, and the children love it.

EGGS (POACHED)

Break egg to be poached into saucer. Have ready some salted boiling water, and add to it a few drops of vinegar or lemon juice. Stir the water well and drop egg carefully into it when fast boiling. Cook gently until set. Lift out with a slice and place on buttered toast.

EGGS (SCRAMBLED)

Allow one dessertspoonful of butter and two tablespoonsful of milk to two eggs, with pepper and salt to taste. Make milk and butter hot in a small saucepan. Drop in the eggs without beating and stir them with a fork. When the mixture begins to thicken, keep it well beaten, and mix in any egg adhering to the sides of the pan. Remove from the fire while still soft, when thickening and cooking will continue. Serve on buttered toast.

Any left over remnants of cooked vegetables can be added to scrambled eggs, and make a nice change.

OMELETTE

6 Eggs
1 tablespoon butter
3 tablespoons milk
seasonings

Beat the eggs, whites and yolks separately until very light. Mix and add milk and seasoning. Have a pan very hot with butter, pour in the egg mixture, keep shaking and moving the pan until the omelette begins to thicken, allow to brown. Slip a slice under the omelette and fold over. Serve on a hot dish. Garnish with lemon or parsley. Omelettes should not be cooked until just before they are required and should be served immediately they are ready.

OMELETTE (AMERICAN)

¾ Cup Milk	1 heaped teaspoon chopped shallots
1 tablespoon butter	1 breakfast cup breadcrumbs
1 dessertspoon chopped parsley	¾ teaspoon salt
4 eggs	

Bring milk to the boil, pour it over the breadcrumbs, add butter and stir well, and add salt, parsley and shallots. Beat the yolks of eggs and mix well into breadcrumb mixture, fold in stiffly beaten whites and pour into a well-buttered, hot frying pan. Brown well, then cut in sections and turn and brown the other side.

OMELETTE ECONOMICAL

3 Eggs	salt and pepper
small cup of milk	butter to fry
1 teaspoon cornflour	

Beat the eggs well, blend the cornflour with the milk and add to eggs, season to taste. Melt butter in frying pan, pour in the mixture and cook a light brown. Loosen round edge of omelette. While cooking cut in sections, turn and brown on the other side. Serve on buttered toast or with bacon or steak.

TOMATOES

3 Tomatoes (Large)	butter
2 eggs	pepper and salt
toast	parsley

Take tomatoes, slice and put in a stewpan with a little butter, pepper and salt. Allow all to cook for a few minutes, then add eggs and stir till the eggs set. Serve on buttered toast with a little finely chopped parsley sprinkled over, or some chopped ham can be added.

SOUP

STOCK MAKING AND GENERAL HINTS

Most soups are improved by having the stock (or foundation liquid) prepared the day before the soup is required. For ordinary soup any meat and bones, cooked or uncooked, if fresh and wholesome, may be utilised for stock. Specially useful are trimmings from joints, remains of cooked meat, vegetables, gravies or sauces (not containing milk), bacon rinds and pieces, ham bones, etc. Celery seed or dried celery tops are excellent for flavouring. About one teaspoonful of salt to 500 gr (one pound) of meat, etc., roughly, will be required, with pepper added to taste. Peppercorns, cloves, a blade or two of mace, a bay leaf and some onion, preferably stuck with cloves, also are suitable flavourings. Water in which a joint, fish or vegetables have been boiled may be used for soup or gravy.

For rich, brown soups dark stock is necessary. Beef is the best meat for making brown soup. It should be cut into small pieces and the bones broken, so as to secure the marrow. Gelatine greatly improves the nourishment value of soup, and a few herbs are an agreeable addition.

For giving body and variety to soups made from ordinary stock, rice, sago, tapioca, vermicelli, haricot beans, pearl barley or lentils may be used. Fresh vegetables, finely diced and simmered in the soup for $\frac{1}{2}$ an hour, also add to its nutritive value, and make simple soup made from stock more appetising.

When milk is used, do not boil soup after milk is added.

Save your celery leaves, dry in the sun, crush, and add a seasoning of salt. Place in air-tight bottle. Useful for flavouring soups, stews, etc.

CARROT SOUP

6 Young Carrots
warm milk
salt
1 stick celery
butter, size of walnut
pepper

Scrape carrots and cut into thin rings. Boil in water until tender with salt and celery (cut finely). Drain pulp through a sieve. Season with pepper and return to saucepan, adding one cupful of the water in which the carrots were boiled. Re-heat, and add one cupful warm milk in which butter has been melted. Serve very hot, sprinkled with chopped parsley.

CELERY CREAM SOUP

1 Head of Celery
1 onion
2 tablespoons butter
750 ml (1½ pints) of milk
flour and seasoning
2 tablespoons sweet cream

Cut celery into small pieces, and stew in water until soft enough to pass through a fine sieve. Bring the milk, with a grated onion, to boiling point, thicken with plain flour, and allow to simmer for a few minutes before adding the celery. Boil gently for 15 minutes, then season with salt and pepper. Just before serving add butter and cream. Serve very hot.

CHICKEN BROTH

1 Boiling Fowl or Chicken
1 tablespoon rice
½ teaspoon salt
1 onion
parsley, mace and seasoning

Cut up the fowl after it has been drawn, and attend to the giblets (the gizzard and feet should be scalded and skinned, the crop cleaned and the other parts washed). Place all in a saucepan and cover with cold water; add the salt, finely chopped onion and seasoning, and simmer slowly for 3 hours; then pour off the liquid, add the rice and chopped parsley, and boil for 20 minutes. The liquid in which any boiled fowl is cooked should always be used for making chicken broth.

CHEESE SOUP

30 gr (1 oz.) Butter
125 gr (¼ lb.) cheese
500 ml (1 pint) milk
30 gr (1 oz.) flour
2 eggs
seasoning
chopped parsley

Make some white sauce with butter, flour and milk. Allow to cool and add beaten yolks of eggs, grated cheese and seasoning. Whisk egg whites very stiff, add chopped parsley and pour over heated liquid. Serve at once.

CREAM OF BARLEY SOUP

1 Teacup Pearl Barley
1 onion
2 egg yolks
mace
2 litre (2 quarts) white stock
30 gr (1 oz.) butter
250 ml (½ pint) milk.
cinnamon

Wash the barley and put into a saucepan with the stock, an onion, cut finely, and a small piece each of mace and cinnamon. Let all simmer for two or three hours, strain through a sieve, and return to the saucepan to boil. Add the butter. Beat the yolks of eggs, and add to them the milk. Mix well, then add gradually, a tablespoon at a time, sufficient of the hot soup to warm it. Pour the warmed egg and milk into the soup, season, and serve.

CREAM OF MUSHROOM SOUP

250 gr (½ lb.) Mushrooms
1 litre (1 quart) chicken or veal broth
1 slice of onion
2 tablespoons butter
2 tablespoons flour
1 cup cream
salt and pepper

Chop mushrooms, add to chicken soup with onion, cook 20 minutes and rub through a sieve. Re-heat. Put butter in saucepan and add flour. When it bubbles add 2-3 cups mushroom and soup liquid. Stir in the remainder and then add the cream and seasonings.

FISH SOUP

1 litre (1 quart) Fish Stock
30 gr (1 oz.) butter
250 ml (½ pint) milk
60 gr (2 oz.) flour
30 gr (1 oz.) butter
2 tablespoons cooked fish
salt and pepper

Fry butter and flour without browning, add stock, cooked fish, finely diced, and boil 10 minutes. Then add milk and seasoning, and serve hot, sprinkled with a little finely chopped parsley.

GIBLET SOUP

1 Set Giblets (liver, gizzard, heart, legs (skinned) and neck)
1 litre (1 quart) stock
1 small onion
medium carrot
celery
rice for thickening
salt and pepper to taste

Add giblets to stock, dice vegetables and bring to boil. Add rice and simmer until tender.

JULIENNE SOUP

1½ litre (3 Pints) Good Meat or Vegetable Stock
60 gr (2 oz.) carrot
60 gr (2 oz.) turnip
½ lettuce
½ head celery
30 gr (1 oz.) onion
60 gr (2 oz.) leek

Cut all vegetables evenly into fine shreds about an inch long, using only the reddest part of the carrot and the whitest of the celery and leek. Boil these separately in boiling water to which a little salt has been added. Shred the lettuce finely and boil it, too, for a few minutes, adding a small piece of soda to keep it a good colour. Drain the vegetables, and put them in the tureen. Pour the boiling stock, which should be clear, over the vegetables.

KIDNEY SOUP (No. 1)

1 Small Ox Kidney, or 6 Sheep's Kidneys
60 gr (2 oz.) boiled macaroni
1 teaspoon ketchup
30 gr (1 oz.) flour
1 onion
1 litre (1 quart) stock
30 gr (1 oz.) butter or dripping
chopped parsley
lemon juice, salt and pepper to taste
1 large teaspoon Worcester sauce

Skin the kidney, remove fat from centre, and cut into dice. Dredge the pieces with flour, season and brown with the onion in a saucepan in which the butter or dripping has been made hot. Then add the stock, bring gently to the boil, skim well, and simmer for an hour. Have the macaroni boiled in salted water and cut into small pieces. Add it, with the ketchup, sauce and seasoning. Just before serving, add a little lemon juice and chopped parsley, or omit the macaroni and thicken to taste with butter and flour (30 gr (1 oz.) of each) mixed well and fried till brown.

KIDNEY SOUP (No. 2)

1 litre (1 Quart) Stock from Soup Bones
1 ox kidney
2 onions
1 tablespoon sharp sauce
1 carrot
1 turnip
parsley
seasonings

Cut the kidney in several places, and pour over it enough boiling water to cover. Allow to remain in the water for 1 hour, remove and cut into small pieces, and add to the stock. Cut the vegetables into very small pieces, and add, bring to the boil, and then simmer for 3 to 3½ hours. Add parsley, sauce and seasoning just before serving.

LEEK SOUP

1 Leek
1 tablespoon butter
30 gr (1 oz.) flour
1 litre (1 quart) good stock
pepper and salt

Wash the leeks and cut into short lengths. Fry them lightly in butter, add flour and mix well. Add a little stock, bring to boil and put into a saucepan with the rest of stock, salt and pepper. Boil until leeks are very tender, strain and serve very hot.

MILK SOUP

1 Small Carrot
1 onion
water
1 dessertspoon butter
1 potato
500 ml (1 pint) milk (or more)
pepper and salt
1 dessertspoon flour
grated nutmeg

Cut up vegetables finely and put into saucepan with pepper and salt and sufficient water to cover. Cook until tender, then add milk and bring to boil. Mix butter and flour thoroughly, add a little cold milk and stir into boiling milk. Add a little nutmeg, boil for a minute or two and draw to one side of stove to keep hot until required. To vary this soup, parsnip, macaroni, or vermicelli could be used in place of carrot.

MULLIGATAWNY SOUP

1½ kg (3 lb.) Raw Meat
2 sour apples, sliced
¼ cup celery, cut in cubes
1 teaspoon curry powder
1 teaspoon salt
1 cup tomato, strained
⅛ teaspoon mace
1 teaspoon sugar
4 litres (4 quarts) cold water
¼ cup onion, sliced
¼ cup carrot, cut in cubes
1 tablespoon flour
2 cloves
½ green pepper, chopped finely
1 teaspoon chopped parsley
a little pepper
¼ cup butter or dripping

Cook vegetables and meat in the fat until browned; add flour, curry powder, cloves and other ingredients, and cook slowly until the meat is tender. Remove meat and cut into small pieces. Strain the soup and rub the vegetables through a sieve. Add the meat, season and serve hot, with boiled rice.

NOODLES

1 Egg
pinch of salt
3 tablespoons flour
lard for frying

Whisk the egg with the salt till it froths. Work in as much sifted flour as it will take (about three tablespoons will be found ample) and knead to a firm, smooth paste. Roll out this dough on a lightly floured board as thin as possible, and cut into rounds with a very small cutter—a thimble does very well. The paste may be placed so that two rounds are cut at a time. Have ready a pan of boiling lard, drop in the noodles, and they will swell into golden balls in a minute. Skim them out, drain on to butter paper and add to soup when ready to be sent to the table.

ONION SOUP (BROWN)

250 gr (½ lb.) Brown Onions
1 dessertspoon flour
60 gr (2 oz.) grated hard cheese
stale bread
1 dessertspoon butter or margarine
750 ml (1½ pints) brown stock—this may be made with 750 ml (1½ pints) water and 2 dessertspoons of vegetable extract

Fry onions in butter until golden brown and add flour. Stir well and still stirring add stock slowly. Bring to the boil and simmer 20 minutes. To serve, top with bread which has been cut into triangles, topped with grated cheese, and brown in a hot oven or under a griller.

OX TAIL SOUP

1 Ox Tail
1 carrot
1 stick celery
½ cup barley
1 slice of ham (uncooked)
1 onion
pepper and salt
1 litre (1 quart) cold water

Cut up the tail into joints and simmer over a slow fire with the ham, carrot and onion (finely chopped), seasoning and celery. When well browned add cold water and bring slowly to the boil. Skim off all grease and strain after stock has boiled for about an hour. Add barley and cook till tender. Serve very hot.

OYSTER SOUP

2 Cups Milk
1 tablespoon butter
1 tin oysters
½ teaspoon salt
pepper to taste

Warm a little of the milk and put in the oysters with liquid and butter. Heat until the edges of the oysters curl. Add the rest of the milk, hot, and seasoning. Cook one minute and serve at once.

PEA SOUP

250 gr (½ lb.) Split Peas
1 onion
3 litres (3 quarts) stock or water
1 dessertspoon salt
chopped dried mint
1 carrot
2 sticks celery
ham bones or bacon rind
2 tablespoons flour
fried bread diced
salt and pepper

Wash peas and soak overnight, or soak them in hot water with a pinch of bi-carbonate of soda for half an hour. Peel and cut vegetables up roughly. Put peas, vegetables, seasoning, ham bones and water into a saucepan. Simmer for three hours. Remove bones, pass soup through a sieve, rubbing peas and vegetables well through. Return to saucepan. Mix flour to a smooth paste with a little cold water and stir into soup; boil three minutes. Turn soup into a hot tureen, sprinkle with finely chopped dried mint, and serve with cubes of fried bread.

POTATO SOUP

750 gr (1½ lb.) Potatoes
1 litre (1 quart) mutton stock
1 stick celery
45 gr (1½ oz.) butter
2 small onions
parsley
pepper and salt

Slice potatoes, onions and celery, and boil in the stock for one hour. Strain and rub through a sieve. Add butter, milk and seasoning to taste. Re-heat and add parsley chopped very fine. Cook about 10 to 15 minutes.

PUMPKIN SOUP

1 kg (2.2 lb.) pumpkin
2 onions
pepper and salt
1 pkt. cream of chicken soup
1 cup cream

Place pumpkin, peeled and diced, and onions chopped finely, on a saucepan covered with water. Cook till pumpkin is very soft, remove from stove. Put through sieve (or puree in an electric blender), return to stove, add chicken soup mixed with cup of water, pepper and salt to taste, lastly blend in cream, heat and serve.

PUREE

1 Cupful Good Stock
a little water
2 tablespoons chopped onion or shallot
1 cupful grated carrot and turnip or swede
a little gravy
2 tablespoons pearl barley
salt and pepper

Boil above ingredients until tender and strain through sieve. Make to quantity required by adding sufficient fresh milk, thickened with flour and lastly adding ½ cup chopped parsley. The vegetables, except onion, can be left out.

RABBIT SOUP

2 Rabbits
2 or 3 onions
a pinch of sugar
salt and pepper
2 slices of fat bacon
1 cupful breadcrumbs
250 ml (½ pint) water
parsley, thyme, mace
2 litres (2 quarts) stock from mutton or marrow bone, skimmed of all fat

Put the rabbits, cut-up, on to stew in about 250 ml (half a pint) of water, add bacon, onions, parsley, thyme, mace, and stew slowly for an hour or more, then add the stock and let all boil gently for an hour. Take out the rabbits, strain the liquid, add the breadcrumbs and some of the rabbit chopped very finely. Add a little salt and pepper and a pinch of sugar. Simmer for 10 minutes.

RICE AND TOMATO SOUP

500 ml (1 Pint) Tinned or 500 gr (1 lb.) Fresh Tomatoes
1 litre (1 quart) water or stock (vegetable water is good)
15 gr (½ oz.) butter or margarine
1 onion
salt, pepper and a pinch of sugar
60 gr (2 oz.) rice

Chop onion finely and fry lightly in butter. Remove the skins from tomatoes by pouring boiling water on them and leaving for a few minutes, then cut into dice. Add to the onion and washed rice, and pour on the stock or vegetable water. Simmer gently until cooked. Time: From half to three quarters of an hour. A little meat extract can be added with advantage if water is used for this soup.

SHEEP'S HEAD SOUP

1 Sheep's Head
2 large carrots
pinch of mixed herbs
2 large onions
5 medium-sized potatoes
salt and pepper

Soak the head in salt water to remove blood, cut vegetables into small dice, remove the skin from the brains, then place head, tongue and brains into a large pot with enough water to cover. Bring to the boil and remove scum. Add vegetables, pepper and salt, and simmer gently for two or three hours. Before dishing, add a pinch of mixed herbs, skin the tongue and serve meat with the soup.

TOMATO SOUP

1 kg (2 lb.) Tomatoes
250 ml (½ pint) milk
250 ml (½ pint) water
½ tablespoon sago
1 onion
½ slice bacon
salt and pepper

Peel and slice onion and cut up tomatoes. Put into saucepan with water, salt, pepper and bacon. Bring to boil and simmer until tender. Rub through sieve and return to saucepan with pulp. Bring to boil, add sago, and cook until clear. Remove from fire and add hot milk.

VEGETABLE SOUP

500 gr (1 lb.) Neck of Mutton
1 onion
1 grated carrot
60 gr (2 oz.) washed rice
2 potatoes
1 litre (1 quart) water
pepper, salt and parsley

Place mutton in pan with water, bring to boil, skim. Add finely cut onions and potatoes, carrot and salt to taste. Allow to cook slowly for one hour. Add rice and pepper. Simmer until rice is cooked. Remove the meat and serve soup very hot. The boiled meat can be served with white sauce and mashed potatoes.

WHITE VEGETABLE SOUP

9 Potatoes
2 leeks
60 gr (2 oz.) dripping
250 ml (½ pint) milk
2 onions
2 sticks of celery
125 gr (4 oz.) rice
1 tablespoon chopped parsley
pepper and salt to taste

Prepare the vegetables and cut into dice. Fry them in dripping for 20 minutes, then cover with boiling water and allow to simmer until vegetables are tender. Pass all through a sieve, then add rice and boil the soup for 30 minutes. Pour in milk, season to taste and bring to the boil again. Sprinkle parsley over and serve hot. For a health soup, omit the rice and dripping and do not fry the vegetables, nor pass through a sieve. Serve the vegetables in the soup.

FISH

FRYING FISH

Prepare fish, wash and dry in a cloth. Dip in batter or egg and breadcrumb and place in a pan of boiling fat, enough to cover the fish. Brown on one side, then lift and turn over with a slice and brown other side. Lift from pan with a fish slice, drain and place on paper to absorb surplus fat. Serve very hot.

Dry stale bread in the oven, and grind in the mincer for crumbs for fish, cutlets, etc.

BREAKFAST DISH

750 gr (1½ lb.) Fish (Small, Whole Fish is best)
1 dessertspoon butter
1 cup milk
2 teaspoons of flour
pepper and salt

Place the fish in a saucepan and just cover with boiling water, milk, butter and seasoning. Simmer for 20 minutes; take out the backbone, thicken with the flour, made into a fine paste with a little cold water and serve very hot.

TASTY SALMON DISH

1 Tin Salmon
1 tablespoon flour
potatoes
capers
a good sized piece of butter
1 cup of milk
1 hard-boiled egg
salt and pepper

Remove all skin and bone from the salmon, and pull into flakes. Melt the butter in a saucepan, dredge in the flour and stir until smooth. Pour in the milk gradually, season with salt and pepper, and stir over the fire until it thickens, then put in the salmon and leave till quite hot. Arrange a wall of mashed potatoes on a hot dish, place the fish and sauce in the centre and strew with chopped capers and slices of hard boiled egg.

BAKED FISH CUTLETS

Fish Cutlets
seasoning
butter
flour

Place cutlets in baking pan and sprinkle very lightly with flour, pepper, salt and a small piece of butter. Wrap the baking pan up in greased paper, and bake for about ½ an hour; then lift cutlets out of pan, thicken the gravy, and flavour with anchovy sauce. Sauce can be served separately or poured around cutlets.

BAKED SCHNAPPER

500 gr (1 lb.) Schnapper Cutlets — **3 tomatoes**
30 gr (1 oz.) butter — **pepper and salt**

Put a layer of sliced tomatoes in a pie-dish, place the cutlets on top, put a dab of butter on each and another layer of tomatoes. Season second layer, cover with another pie-dish and bake $\frac{3}{4}$ of an hour in a moderate oven. A casserole is useful for this dish.

BAKED SALMON

1 Tin Salmon — **4 potatoes**
$\frac{1}{2}$ teaspoon anchovy sauce — **salt and pepper**
lemon juice to taste

Remove bones from the salmon, cook and mash the potatoes, mix together, add salt, pepper, anchovy and lemon juice. Turn into a hot, greased pie-dish, smooth over the top and glaze with milk. Bake in moderate oven 20 minutes.

BAKED SARDINES

1 Large Tin Sardines — **1 cup milk**
15 gr ($\frac{1}{2}$ oz.) flour — **lemon juice**
1 egg — **breadcrumbs**
a pinch of cayenne — **pepper and salt**
30 gr (1 oz.) butter

Melt butter in a saucepan, blend in the flour, then the milk and beaten egg. Add the sardines (boned) and mix well; add a little lemon juice, salt, pepper and cayenne. Put into a small pie-dish, cover with breadcrumbs and bake a nice brown.

BOILED FISH WITH MACARONI

Macaroni — **1 dessertspoon butter**
cold boiled fish — **salt**
pepper — **stock**

Boil the quantity macaroni required, equal quantities of macaroni and fish. Cut the macaroni into small pieces and mix well into the fish, season and add butter chopped into small pieces, and just a little of the stock the fish was boiled in. Put mixture into a buttered pie-dish, and bake in a good oven until nicely browned. Serve hot.

BOILED LOBSTER

Kill the lobster either by chilling it in the freezer or by covering with cold fresh water for a few minutes. Bring sufficient water to the boil to cover the lobster. A small amount of salt may be added. When it boils fast, drop the lobster in. From the time it boils fast again, 12 minutes is sufficient to cook a lobster of 500–750 gr. Remove from the water and rinse off under cold water to clean the shell. Place lobster head down to drain.

CRAYFISH MORNAY

1 Crayfish
salt and pepper
butter
white sauce
½ cup grated cheese

Make white sauce per recipe under Sauces, add salt and pepper. Add cut up crayfish. Mix well, put in pie-dish, cover with grated cheese and dot with butter. Bake until browned.

Tuna Mornay can be made in the same way.

CURRIED FISH

250 gr (½ lb.) Flaked Fresh Haddock or Schnapper
185 ml (1½ gills) milk or fish stock
30 gr (1 oz.) butter or margarine
curry powder
15 gr (½ oz.) flour
1 tablespoon lemon juice
boiled rice
salt to taste

Melt butter in a saucepan. Stir in the flour and beat till smooth. Stir in curry powder and salt to taste. Add milk or stock gradually. Simmer for 5 minutes, stir carefully. Cook fish till tender and add to sauce, then add lemon juice. Serve surrounded with boiled rice.

FISH BALLS

1 Cup Cold Fish
½ cup mashed potatoes
1 tablespoon parsley
½ cup boiled rice
1 egg
salt and pepper

Chop the fish finely, removing the bones. Mix the potatoes and rice together, add fish and parsley. Season well and moisten with egg, well beaten. Shape into balls, roll in flour, and fry a nice brown in deep, boiling fat.

FISH CAKES

1 Small Tin Salmon, or any Cooked Fish
1 egg
3 medium potatoes, boiled and mashed
seasoning

Mash up fish, removing bones, add potatoes and seasoning, mix with egg, form into balls and dip into a mixture of flour, pepper and salt, or egg and breadcrumbs. Fry in boiling fat, and serve very hot with white sauce. A little chopped parsley or boiled onion lends variety to the sauce.

FISH CURRY

375 gr ($\frac{3}{4}$ lb.) Cooked Fish or Tin Salmon
2 or 3 hard boiled eggs
1 cup boiled rice
1 dessertspoon curry powder
1 dessertspoon chutney
60 gr (2 oz.) flour
30 gr (1 oz.) butter
$\frac{1}{2}$ lemon
250 ml ($\frac{1}{2}$ pint) milk
salt

Remove all skin and bone from fish, break in pieces and have rice plainly boiled as for curry. Melt butter in a saucepan, stir in flour and mix well. Add chutney, salt, curry powder and milk, and stir till boiling. Put in the prepared fish, rice and eggs. Mix all very gently together. Make the mixture thoroughly hot and serve garnished with thin slices of lemon.

FISH OMELETTE

1 Cup Cooked Fish (Tinned Fish will do)
1 tablespoon butter
chopped parsley
1 teaspoon pepper, salt
3 eggs

Put the yolks of eggs into a basin, add salt, pepper and parsley and work with a wooden spoon till creamy, then add the boned fish. Beat the whites of the eggs to a stiff froth and fold lightly into the mixture. Melt the butter in a frying pan, pour in the omelette mixture and stir until beginning to set. Cook until a nice brown on the under side, then fold over and serve with slices of lemon and garnish with parsley.

FISH PIE (No. 1)

Remains of any Cold Fish
chopped parsley
little white sauce
mashed potatoes
butter
seasoning

Flake the fish. Add to it sufficient mashed potatoes to $\frac{3}{4}$ fill your pie-dish. Mix well together. Make some white sauce (or left over sauce will do) and add to it the parsley and a little butter. Mix all well together, and add seasoning to taste. Cover with breadcrumbs, place in a moderate oven and bake for half an hour.

FISH PIE (No. 2)

1 Tin Salmon or Fish Pieces
1 onion
2 teaspoons butter
3 potatoes
1 lemon
parsley
1 egg

Place fish in dish, break with fork, add lemon, grated onion and parsley, pepper and salt to taste. Cook and mash potatoes, add butter, salt and beaten egg. Put on fish with fork. Bake 40 minutes in oven.

FISH PUDDING

Fish
1 egg
salt
onions
breadcrumbs
pepper

Take 500 gr (1 lb.) fish, after boning, and put through the mincer with an onion, then add one cup breadcrumbs, pepper and salt and the well beaten egg. Mix well and steam 1½ hours.

Sauce.—Boil the bones and strain. Use the water for sauce, add some milk and cornflour to thicken and then a lump of butter and some chopped parsley. Serve nice and hot.

FRIED FLOUNDER

Flounder
2 tablespoons vinegar
breadcrumbs
1 egg
fried parsley
anchovy sauce

Sprinkle the flounder with salt and let them lie 24 hours then wash them and wipe them dry; brush over with egg and cover with breadcrumbs. Make some lard or dripping, mixed with 2 tablespoons of vinegar, boiling hot in a frying pan. Lay the fish in and fry them a nice brown colour. Drain them from the fat on a cloth and serve. Garnish with fried parsley and anchovy sauce.

ITALIAN FISH STEW

3 or 4 Onions
filleted fish
pepper and salt
pinch of pepper corns
a little chopped parsley
few slices of fat bacon
hot water
1 tablespoon vinegar
3 bay leaves
toast
flour to thicken

Slice onions and fry in saucepan with bacon. Add the fish, cover with hot water and salt, pepper and vinegar, pepper corns, bay leaves and parsley. Stew till fish is done. Thicken with flour. Make a few squares of toast and serve with the hot fish.

KEDGEREE

250 gr (½ lb.) Cooked Fish
250 gr (½ lb.) rice
60 gr (2 oz.) butter or dripping
1 egg yolk
pinch nutmeg
pepper and salt
1 teaspoon chopped parsley

Free fish from skin and bone and chop finely. Boil the rice as for curry and drain it well. Melt the butter in a saucepan and put in the fish and rice. Season with salt and pepper, add the raw yolk of an egg, mix well together and make thoroughly hot. Pile in the centre of a hot dish, making a neat pyramid and mark up the sides with a fork. Sprinkle with chopped parsley and serve very hot.

LOBSTER CUTLETS

1 Lobster, Tinned or Fresh
1 tablespoon flour
lemon juice
1 egg
breadcrumbs
2 tablespoons butter
½ cup of milk
salt and pepper

Mince the cold cooked lobster. Melt the butter in a saucepan, add the flour and blend till quite smooth. Stir in the milk and boil for a few minutes and add lemon juice and seasoning. Mix thoroughly and add the lobster. Turn the mixture out on to a meat plate to cool, and when cold divide into suitable pieces and form into the shape of a cutlet. Brush over with beaten egg, roll in breadcrumbs and fry a golden brown in deep boiling fat. Garnish with parsley.

SALMON IN JELLY

1 Tin Salmon
1 tablespoon vinegar
2 cups hot water
2 dessertspoons gelatine
2 hard boiled eggs
pepper and salt to taste

Mash salmon with a fork, and add vinegar, pepper and salt. Dissolve gelatine in the water. Mix all together. Line a wet mould with slices of the egg, pour mixture in gently and allow to set. When cold garnish with finely cut lettuce or slices of tomato.

SALMON MAYONNAISE

2 Egg Yolks
½ cup good salad oil
salmon
sugar
1 teaspoon made mustard
3 dessertspoons vinegar
salt and pepper to taste
lettuce

Place the eggs in a basin, stir with a wooden spoon and add the seasonings. Add oil, drop by drop, stirring all the time, then add vinegar very slowly, stirring well. Place shredded lettuce on individual plates, put in a small piece of salmon on centre of lettuce and cover with the dressing. *Note.*—Cream or rich milk may be used instead of oil.

SALMON PIE

1 Tin Salmon
1 cup white sauce
3 eggs
1 cup cold rice
salt and pepper

Mash up salmon, add salt and pepper, white sauce and the cooked cold rice. Beat yolks of eggs, and beat whites until stiff. Mix all together. Place in pie dish in moderate oven and bake until nicely brown.

SALMON PUFFS

Cream Puffs
30 gr (1 oz.) butter
185 ml (1½ gills) milk
lemon juice
½ crayfish or small tin salmon
30 gr (1 oz.) flour
½ teaspoon anchovy sauce
salt, and little cayenne pepper

Flake salmon, melt butter, add flour and stir till smooth. Add milk gradually and stir till boiling, then add fish, seasoning and lemon juice. Allow to cool and put in puffs.

SALMON RISSOLES

1 Small tin Salmon
a few breadcrumbs
1 egg
salt and pepper

Take a tin of salmon and remove the liquid from it. Mince the salmon and add to it a few breadcrumbs. Flavour with salt and pepper. Beat the egg and add it to the salmon. Mould into balls, roll in flour and fry. These are best fried in with sliced tomatoes and sliced apples. This is sufficient for 6 small rissoles. The liquid may be put in the pan after the rissoles are removed, and be made into a sauce by adding flour and seasoning.

SALMON SALAD

1 Tin of Salmon
1 teaspoon mustard
1 tablespoon butter
3 tablespoons vinegar
1 tablespoon flour
1 egg
¾ cup milk
1 teaspoon gelatine

Flake the salmon, blend flour with milk and stir in. Slightly melt the butter and add. Beat the egg, mix in, and add vinegar carefully. Pour the mixture into a double saucepan and cook until it thickens, stirring all the time. Soak the gelatine in a little water, remove salmon from the fire and stir in gelatine. Pour into a mould to set. Serve with shredded lettuce.

SALMON SHAPE

1 Tin Salmon
grated rind and juice of 1 lemon
a little nutmeg or mace
pepper
1 cup breadcrumbs
2 eggs
½ cup milk
salt

Mix all dry ingredients, then eggs and milk and beat together thoroughly. Place in a buttered mould and steam for ¾ of an hour. If eaten hot, make a good, rich sauce, adding hard boiled eggs and a little vinegar or capers. Pour over shape.

SAVOURY FISH ROLL

1 Tomato	seasoning
90 gr (3 oz.) cooked fish (tinned salmon is very good)	1 egg
1 teaspoon chopped parsley	15 gr (½ oz.) butter
1 tablespoon cooked rice	a little milk
	pastry

Free the fish from skin and bone and mix with the cooked rice and parsley. Slice the tomato and cook in the butter until soft. Season and add to fish mixture. Boil the egg hard, chop finely and add to fish. Moisten just enough to hold the mixture together. Make some nice pastry, cut into oblong shapes, about 13 mm (½ an inch) in thickness. Form the fish into small, long rolls, lay on the pastry, and fold over and press together, like sausage rolls. Brush over with milk and cook in a quick oven for about 20 minutes. Serve cold.

SCALLOPED SALMON

1 Small can Steak Salmon	½ teaspoon salt
1 tablespoon butter	⅛ teaspoon pepper
1 cup breadcrumbs	2 eggs
1 cup hot milk	

Remove skin and bones from salmon, and rub fine with potato masher. Melt butter in milk and add breadcrumbs and seasonings, and combine with fish. Lastly add the well beaten eggs. Put into a deep, buttered baking dish and steam one hour. When fish is done, turn on to platter and pour the following sauce around it and serve hot.

Sauce

1 Tablespoon Butter	liquid from salmon
1½ tablespoons flour	½ teaspoon salt
1 cup milk	few grains cayenne

Melt butter, add flour and slowly pour on hot milk, then add salmon liquid and seasonings.

WHITING, BOILED

Whiting	parsley
lemon	

Place the prepared fish into warm salted water and simmer for 10 minutes. Serve with slices of lemon and parsley.

STEAMED FISH

Wash fish, dry and cut into suitable pieces. Have ready a saucepan of boiling water, place the fish, seasoned, on a buttered plate, and stand on the pan. Cover with the lid of the saucepan and steam for 15 to 20 minutes, according to size of pieces. A large fish requires 15 minutes to the 500 gr (1 lb) and 15 minutes over. Serve with parsley sauce.

ENTREE

ANGELS ON HORSEBACK

½ Dozen Oysters
6 pieces bread
anchovy paste
60 gr (2 oz.) fat bacon or ham
lemon juice
cayenne
chopped parsley

Cut bread into rounds 38 mm (1½ in.) across and stamp out the bacon. Fry the bread and bacon, beard the oysters on a plate, sprinkle with lemon juice and cayenne, cover with another plate and put into a moderate oven to heat. Spread anchovy paste on each crouton. Place on each a piece of bacon and an oyster, garnished with chopped parsley. Serve hot.

BOBOLE (South African Dish)

Bread
1 onion
juice of a lemon
2 eggs
milk
cold meat
1 teaspoon curry powder
a little sour milk
pepper and salt to taste

Soak a slice of bread in milk, fry and mince an onion. Mix bread and onion with minced cold meat (either beef or mutton, or mixed), add lemon juice, curry powder and seasoning. Place in a greased pie dish. Beat up eggs with a little sour milk, pour over mixture and bake.

BRAIN PATTIES

2 Sets Brains
breadcrumbs
2 eggs
butter
lemon juice
parsley
seasonings

Soak the brains in salted water for ½ an hour, then boil lightly and mash. Boil 1 egg hard, chop it finely and add parsley and seasoning of salt and pepper to taste, with a little lemon juice. Mix well together, melt a little butter sufficient to bind the patties, and make into small flat cakes. Roll in raw egg and breadcrumbs and fry a light brown.

STUFFED CABBAGE

1 Cabbage
1 egg
butter or dripping
500 gr (1 lb.) mincemeat
1 slice of bread
pepper and salt
nutmeg

Take the best leaves of cabbage, remove part of rib, scald and drain. Mix mincemeat with egg, salt and pepper and soaked bread. Put some mincemeat on two leaves of cabbage, roll and tie with cotton. Put the rolls into a saucepan with some butter or suet and braise gently until nicely brown. Make gravy and flavour with nutmeg. Put the cabbage rolls back into the gravy and let simmer for a while. Serve with potatoes and vegetables.

STUFFED CAPSICUM

500 gr (1lb.) Mince Meat
6 capsicums
1 medium sized onion
salt and pepper

Scrape out capsicums, making sure all seeds are out. Cook the mince with seasoning; cool, and stuff the fruit with it. Bake half an hour in a medium oven, using just a little fat. Tomatoes may be done in the same way.

CAULIFLOWER WITH CHEESE

1 Cauliflower
pepper and salt
butter
cheese
white sauce
breadcrumbs

Clean and boil the cauliflower till cooked, but not broken. Drain. Break off small pieces and put into a buttered pie dish, sprinkle with pepper and salt, and grate over with cheese. Repeat until all the cauliflower is used. Pour over a little white sauce, cover with breadcrumbs and small bits of butter, and put into the oven to brown.

GENOESE CAULIFLOWER

Cooked Cauliflower
60 gr (2 oz.) butter
60 gr (2 oz.) grated cheese
salt and pepper

Break up the cauliflower into small pieces and place in a fire-proof dish. Sprinkle over grated cheese, then a layer of cauliflower, another of cheese, pepper and salt, and lastly cover with breadcrumbs and small pieces of butter. Bake in a hot oven till brown.

CELERY AND PEANUTS

1 Cupful Chopped Celery
breadcrumbs
salt and pepper
1 cup hot milk
1 cup chopped peanuts
a little onion
thyme
2 tablespoons butter

Mix the celery, peanuts, breadcrumbs, onion and seasoning together. Melt the butter in the hot milk, pour over the other ingredients, and form into a loaf. Bake in a tin in a moderate oven, basting frequently with butter and hot water in equal parts.

BAKED CHEESE

A Little Cheese
3 eggs
brown breadcrumbs
butter
salt and pepper

Cut cheese into slices about 6 mm ($\frac{1}{4}$ in.) thick, and arrange these round the sides of a buttered pie dish. Cover the bottom with the breadcrumbs, place thin pieces of cheese over, then the eggs without breaking the yolks. Dust with salt and pepper, add another layer of cheese, more breadcrumbs and a little butter. Place the dish in an oven, and bake until the eggs are quite firm. Serve hot.

CHEESE CROQUETTES

6 Medium-sized Potatoes
1 teaspoon chopped parsley
pepper and salt
dash of celery salt
yolk of one egg
180 gr (6 oz.) cheese
breadcrumbs (browned)
grating of nutmeg
fat for frying
a little butter

Boil and mash potatoes with butter. Add cheese, grated, seasonings and bind with egg yolk. Form into croquettes, roll in breadcrumbs and fry in a little fat.

CHEESE FONDU

1 Cup Grated Cheese
60 gr (2 oz.) butter
a small piece of onion
1 cup breadcrumbs
2 eggs
salt and cayenne

Boil the milk and pour it over the breadcrumbs; add the butter, cheese, finely minced onion and seasoning, also the beaten yolks of the eggs. Stir in the stiffly-beaten egg whites very lightly last thing before baking the mixture in a pie-dish for about half-an-hour.

CHEESE PASTRY

250 gr (½ lb.) Household Pastry
125 gr (¼ lb.) grated cheese
1 medium-sized onion
seasoning

Roll out the pastry evenly. Chop the onion, lay it on pastry, add grated cheese and season well. Close up and bake in a quick oven 20 minutes to half-an-hour.

CHEESE PUFF

250 ml (½ Pint) Milk
125 gr (4 oz.) grated cheese
2 eggs
60 gr (2 oz.) fresh white breadcrumbs
30 gr (1 oz.) butter
pepper and salt

Melt butter in saucepan, add milk and breadcrumbs. When just on boiling point add the cheese, and when slightly cooled, the yolks of the eggs beaten up with two tablespoonsful milk. Next add the seasoning, and lastly the stiffly whipped whites of eggs. Pour the mixture into a greased pie-dish and bake in a quick oven for 15 minutes or until well puffed up and a golden brown. Test with a skewer. If this comes out clean and dry the puff is cooked. Serve very hot.

CHEESE SAUSAGES

250 gr (½ lb.) Grated Cheese
125 gr (¼ lb.) brown breadcrumbs
1 teaspoon mixed herbs
30 gr (1 oz.) butter
1 egg
250 gr (½ lb.) cold cooked mashed potatoes
1 large onion
1 teaspoon Worcester sauce
1 cupful hot water

Dissolve butter in hot water and add sauce. Mix both thoroughly into the dry ingredients, with onion grated or chopped finely. Divide into suitably sized portions, shape as sausages, roll in egg and breadcrumbs and fry gently in hot fat until well browned.

CHEESE WITH TOMATO SAUCE

250 gr (½ lb.) Cheese
cayenne pepper
salt
30 gr (1 oz.) butter
2 tablespoons tomato sauce
buttered toast

Melt cheese in a pan with butter and add tomato sauce. Season and serve very hot on buttered toast.

COLD MEAT IN BATTER

Cold Meat (Corned Beef is particularly good)
1 egg
a little milk or water
½ cup self-raising flour
a pinch of salt
fat for frying

Make a batter with the egg, flour and milk or water. Cut the meat up finely to make one cupful and mix thoroughly into the batter. Fry in deep, smoking-hot fat until nicely browned. This is a tasty dish and useful for breakfasts when eggs are scarce. A change can be made with sliced cooked sausage, minced cold meat, tripe, etc. Parsley, finely shredded onion or mixed herbs, make a nice addition. Sauce may be served, according to what has been used for filling.

CURRIED RISSOLES

Mix well together equal quantities of cold left-over curry and rice. Shape into flat cakes, dip into flour and then in beaten egg and milk. Fry in boiling fat for 5 minutes, turning over at 2½ minutes. Serve with grilled bacon.

CURRY PIES

Make a short pastry and roll it out 6 mm (¼ in.) thick. Cut into 10 cm (4 in.) squares and spread thickly except at edges with cold, dry curry. Fold over and pinch edges together. Make a small hole in centre, brush with beaten egg or milk, and bake in a brisk oven for 15 minutes. Serve with boiled rice and hot tomato sauce.

EGG PIE

6 Hard Boiled Eggs
butter
cooked potatoes
1 onion, sliced and fried
white sauce

Put ingredients in pie dish in alternate layers and bake.

EGG AND BACON TART

250 gr (½ lb.) Pastry
4 or 5 eggs
2 rashers bacon
grated cheese

Roll out 250 gr (½ lb.) pastry into two pieces to cover a 20 cm (9 in.) dish. Line dish. Cut 2 rashers of bacon into small pieces. Place on pastry, break 4 or 5 eggs in, break eggs with a fork, sprinkle with grated cheese, pepper and salt to taste and cover with other piece of pastry. Bake in hot oven.

MADRAS EGGS

2 Hard Boiled Eggs
4 stuffed olives
buttered toast
2 tomatoes
mayonnaise
pepper and salt

Halve eggs and remove yolks, mash them with a little well-seasoned mayonnaise and return to whites. Remove a small slice from the bottom of each white. Serve on rounds of buttered toast, each one covered with a slice of tomato. Plant stuffed olives in the centre of each filling, enough for 2 persons.

SCOTCH EGGS

3 Hard Boiled Eggs
250 gr (½ lb.) sausage meat
1 raw egg
breadcrumbs
frying fat

Let the eggs become cold, remove the shells and cover each egg completely with the sausage meat. Coat carefully with beaten egg, roll in breadcrumbs and fry in hot fat until brown. Serve on crisp lettuce and garnish with cut tomatoes.

LENTEN DISH

A large saucepan or boiler is required to contain all the vegetables while cooking. Place it on the fire half full of water, and whilst water is coming to the boil, prepare your vegetables. One cabbage, or sufficient for a helping for each person, 2 turnips, 3 or 4 large potatoes, 1 large onion (cut very small). When the water boils, place the cabbage in, then the potatoes, cut in pieces, turnips and onions, salt generously, place lid on pan, allow to boil gently till all are tender. Whilst vegetables are cooking take 1 cup of plain flour, add a pinch of salt, mix into it enough cold water to make a very stiff dough, which roll out 6 mm (¼ in.) thick, cut into strips 6 mm (¼ in.) wide and 15 cm (6 in.) long; lay these strips on the vegetables, then replace the lid and allow to boil till the strips are cooked, as well as the vegetables. Have ready a pan with ½ cup of good dripping, smoking hot, into which toss a clove of garlic cut fine; also have ready a cupful of grated cheese. Strain the vegetables, place heaped up on large, hot dish, sprinkle the cheese through and over, pour over the garlic and fat and your dish is ready.

LUNCHEON DISH

Ham, Cold Meat or Tongue
1 dessertspoon butter
2 eggs
toast
1 tablespoon milk
1 tablespoon gravy

Mince the meat, put butter in saucepan, add meat, milk and gravy; season with pepper and salt; beat 2 eggs and stir in until the mixture thickens, then pour on squares of toast.

MACARONI BATTER

Cooked Macaroni
2 eggs
125 gr (¼ lb.) flour
pepper and salt
250 ml (½ pint) milk
chopped parsley

Place the macaroni in a buttered pie dish, make a batter of the eggs, milk and flour, season with pepper, salt and chopped parsley, pour over macaroni and bake for 1 hour. Serve very hot with gravy.

MACARONI CHEESE

125 gr (¼ lb.) Macaroni
½ cup of white sauce
salt
cayenne
90 gr (3 oz.) grated cheese
1 tablespoon made mustard
butter
breadcrumbs

Boil the macaroni in water with a teaspoon salt till tender. Drain and put in a pie-dish with half the cheese, and the white sauce, mix in the mustard and a saltspoon of cayenne and salt. Mix well, then spread the remainder of the cheese on top, then a layer of breadcrumbs with pieces of butter. Bake about 1 hour.

MARROW RINGS

Vegetable Marrow
cheese
eggs

Cook thick rings of vegetable marrow till tender, place each ring on a round of buttered toast, and coat the marrow thickly with grated cheese. In the centre of each ring place a poached egg and serve.

MINCE COLLOPS WITH POACHED EGGS

500 gr (1 lb.) Cold Meat
1 small onion
1 tablespoon flour
a little chopped parsley
toast
45 gr (1½ oz.) butter
1 tablespoon ketchup
250 ml (½ pint) stock
pepper and salt
eggs

Mince the meat finely by hand. Heat the butter in a frying pan, fry the onion until nicely browned, then add the flour and fry a little longer. Next put in the meat and stir over the fire for a few minutes, then add the stock, finely-chopped parsley, ketchup, and salt and pepper to taste. Cook very slowly for 15 minutes, then serve on a hot dish with a poached egg for each person on top, and garnish with sippets of toasted bread.

MOCK BRAINS

1 Cup Left-over Porridge
1 tablespoon self-raising flour
salt and pepper
1 small onion
1 egg
pinch of thyme

Chop the onion very fine, mix into the porridge, add the flour and flavouring, bind together with the beaten egg, form into rissoles, roll in flour, and fry brown in hot fat.

MOCK SCHNAPPER

3 Large Potatoes (grated)
1 tablespoon flour
2 eggs
$\frac{1}{2}$ teaspoon carb. soda
$\frac{1}{2}$ teaspoon cream of tartar

Break in eggs on the grated potatoes, and beat up. Add the flour with cream of tartar and soda; mix well. Fry in plenty of boiling fat. Serve with lemon.

MOCK TRIPE AND EGGS

2 Large Onions
1 tablespoon butter
6 hard boiled eggs
500 ml (1 pint) milk
pepper and salt to taste
flour

Boil the onions in the milk, with the butter, pepper and salt, when the onions are cooked thicken with flour. Cut the hard boiled eggs in quarters, put in saucepan with onions. Heat well and serve hot.

MOCK TRIPE AND MUTTON

1 Breast Mutton
pepper and salt to taste
2 large onions
milk

Cut up one breast of mutton, add onions, stew in milk till meat is cooked, with pepper and salt to taste. Thicken with plain flour, and serve hot.

POTATO SAUSAGES

125 gr ($\frac{1}{4}$ lb.) Cold or Tinned Meat
125 gr ($\frac{1}{4}$ lb.) mashed potatoes
pepper and salt
2 slices cooked bacon
1 onion
seasoning

Mince the meat, mix with potatoes and onion, add seasoning, pepper and salt, bind with $\frac{1}{2}$ an egg. Form into sausages, dip into the remainder of the egg, cover with brown breadcrumbs, fry in hot fat.

POTATOES STUFFED WITH CHEESE

8 Equal Sized Potatoes
cheese
salt and pepper
1 egg

Bake potatoes whole, cut a slice off each, scoop out as much of inside as possible, mash, season with salt and pepper and a little nutmeg, and add a third of its quantity in grated cheese, moistened with beaten egg. Fill potato cases, and return to oven to brown.

SMOTHERED POTATOES

6 Medium Potatoes
2 tablespoons butter
3 tablespoons flour
1½ cups milk
1 onion or more
½ teaspoon salt and pepper

Slice potatoes 6 mm (¼ in.) thick. Place layer in baking dish, sprinkle with flour and bits of butter, chopped onion, pepper and salt. Fill dish with layers ending with potatoes. Cover with milk; bake 1½ hours. Chopped parsley and cheese may be added.

STOVED POTATOES (SCOTTISH)

Potatoes and Onions
salt and pepper
dripping
water

Cut up potatoes and onion into pieces, put into saucepan with plenty of dripping and a very little water. Add salt and pepper to taste and cook slowly. Stir occasionally to prevent burning. If desired, slices of cold meat may be added.

SWEET POTATO PUFF

3 Cups of Mashed Sweet Potato
½ cup milk or cream
1 egg
3 tablespoons butter

Boil or bake the potatoes, peel and mash, then add the melted butter, milk and seasonings. Beat the egg separately, add the yolks and stir thoroughly, then fold in the whites. Bake in hot oven for twenty minutes or until puffy and brown.

PUMPKIN FRITTERS

2 Cups Stewed Sweet Pumpkin
1 slice bread
a little salt
sugar
1 cup flour
milk
a little ground cinnamon
¼ teaspoon carbonate soda
2 eggs

PUMPKIN FRITTERS—*continued*

Stew part of a sweet pumpkin until soft. Take 2 cupsful of it, well drained, and add about 1 cup flour to thicken it. Soak the bread in milk, and when soft squeeze as dry as possible. Mix with pumpkin and flour, and add a little salt and ground cinnamon, carbonate of soda and eggs. Make it the consistency of fritters by adding more flour if necessary. Cook on well-greased frying pan in spoonfuls, sprinkle with sugar and cinnamon, and serve very hot.

RICE PATTIES

500 gr (1 lb.) Rice
2 hard boiled eggs
4 onions
salt, pepper and sage

Boil rice until soft, add onions, sage, salt, pepper and eggs; make into round, flat patties, and bake in a moderate oven for ½ an hour, basting well with dripping. Serve with brown gravy.

SAVOURY RICE

155 gr (5 oz.) Rice
1 large onion
1 egg
butter
2 large carrots
90 gr (3 oz.) grated cheese
salt and pepper
little milk

Cook rice, carrots and onions until tender, drain, mash carrots and onion well; then mix together with rice and grated cheese. Add egg, salt and pepper to taste, and little milk if necessary. Put into a pie-dish, sprinkle with grated cheese, dot with butter. Lemon juice may be added. Bake in moderate oven for 40 minutes.

SARDINES ON HORSEBACK

Sardines
bacon
butter
toast
cayenne, pepper, salt

Take some skinned and boned sardines, make a smooth paste of them, mix with butter, pepper, cayenne and salt. Spread them on tiny slices of bacon, roll round and tie with fine string or cotton. Fry or boil them, and serve on fingers of buttered toast.

SARDINE SAVOURY

Toast
2 hard boiled eggs
parsley
30 gr (1 oz.) butter
1 tin sardines (boned)
1 tablespoon cream
lemon

Work very smoothly the sardines, eggs, butter and cream. Put on toast, sprinkle a little cayenne and parsley over, and serve very hot with slices of lemon.

SARDINE TOAST

1 Small Tin Sardines
1 teaspoon flour
1 teaspoon of anchovy sauce
2 eggs
30 gr (1 oz.) butter
pepper

Heat the butter and mashed sardines, beaten eggs, anchovy and pepper, dredge with flour. Stir over fire till very hot. Serve on hot buttered toast.

BAKED SAUSAGE APPLES

6 Apples
1 cup sausage meat
seasonings

Scoop out the centre of 6 good sized tart apples, leaving a thick shell. Cut all the pulp possible from the core and chop it with minced cooked sausage meat. Refill the apples with the mixture, heaping the filling, and bake in a moderate oven till the apples are tender. Serve on a hot dish with chip potatoes all round.

SAVOURY SAUSAGES

250 gr (½ lb.) Small Sausages
3 rashers of streaky bacon
5 oblongs of bread
5 mushrooms
seasoning
butter

Peel and stalk the mushrooms, wash them in cold water with a little salt added, then drain and chop them up. Remove the rind from bacon and put it through a mincer. Fry mushrooms and bacon in a little butter, at the same time fry sausages in another pan. Cut bread, toast it on one side, butter untoasted side, put a little mushroom and bacon on each piece; season to taste, and arrange 2 small sausages on top of it. Sufficient for 5 persons.

SAVOURY CASSEROLE

500 gr (1 lb.) Meat (Chops, Steak, Rabbit, etc.)
½ cup flour
½ teaspoon nutmeg, salt, pepper
1 tablespoon tomato sauce
1 tablespoon vinegar
1 cup water
1 tablespoon Holbrook's sauce
1 onion
fresh tomatoes (when possible)

Roll meat in the seasoned flour and place in dish, with onions and tomatoes on top. Mix water, sauce and vinegar and pour over meat. Put on lid. Two pie-dishes make a good substitute for casserole dish. Bake about 2 hours.

SAVOURY TOAST

2 Large White Onions
1 small cup marmite liquid
1 tablespoon butter
1 egg

Cut up two large white onions very finely and fry in melted butter, then add marmite liquid. Let simmer until the liquid is nearly absorbed. Allow to cool, add a beaten egg and stir until the mixture thickens slightly. Serve on hot, buttered toast.

SCOTCH WOODCOCK

2 Slices of Toast
3 tablespoons milk
15 gr (½ oz.) butter
2 egg yolks
1 tablespoon cream
cayenne and salt
2 or 3 anchovies or anchovy paste

Butter toast on both sides, put into a stew pan butter, egg yolks, milk, cream, cayenne and heat, but do not boil. Pound anchovies and spread on the toast, cut into strips 5 cm (2 in.) long and 25 mm (1 in.) wide, pile on a dish, pour sauce over and sprinkle with parsley. Serve very hot.

FRENCH RUMP STEAK

1 Teaspoon Sugar
3 teaspoons vinegar
1 teaspoon flour
500 gr (1 lb.) best rump steak, with some nice selvedge fat
½ teaspoon salt and pepper

Make a paste of flour, sugar, salt, pepper and vinegar. Spread this on the steak and put it uncut into a casserole, and cook in moderate oven for 1½ hours. Turn it over twice while cooking.

STEAK AND VEGETABLE MARROW

500 gr (1 lb.) Stewing Steak
1 small marrow or ½ large one
1 onion
tomatoes

Cut steak in small pieces and place in bottom of pie-dish; sprinkle well with flour and seasoning, slice onion and tomatoes on top and cover with water. Peel and cut marrow into medium sized pieces and place on top, covering up the whole of the other ingredients. Tie grease paper over the top and bake in moderate oven 2 hours.

STOVIES (A Favourite Dish)

Potatoes
rashers of fat bacon
onions
water
pepper and salt

Slice up potatoes and onions, enough to fill frying pan. Season lightly with salt and pepper, and put bacon on top barely cover with water and put a large plate or lid on top, and steam slowly on side of stove. Very tasty.

STUFFED ONIONS

4 Large Onions
1 tablespoon breadcrumbs
30 gr (1 oz.) butter
30 gr (1 oz.) grated cheese
salt and pepper to taste

STUFFED ONIONS—*continued*

Boil onions in their skin until tender, remove the centres with a fork, holding with another fork. Chop centres up finely and mix with half ingredients. Fill onions with mixture. Place in baking dish, place the rest of mixture over onions. Bake in a hot oven 15 minutes. Chopped kidney, previously cooked, is very nice in place of cheese.

STUFFED TRIPE WITH BANANA SAUCE

1 Large Flat Piece of Tripe
1 cup breadcrumbs
sage, salt and pepper
1 onion
little thyme
some fat bacon

Boil the tripe until tender, make a stuffing of minced onion, breadcrumbs, seasoning. Place on half the tripe, fold the other half over, and sew the edges securely together. Place a few slices of bacon on top, and bake in a pie dish in a hot oven. Serve with a sauce made as follows:—Boil ½ cup of sugar and 1 cup of water, till the mixture starts to thread, then pour it over a well beaten egg. Mash 4 ripe bananas with ½ a cup of lemon juice, and beat into the first mixture until smooth.

SUFFOLK MARYS

60 gr (2 oz.) Grated Cheese
60 gr (2 oz.) flour
½ teaspoon dry mustard
60 gr (2 oz.) mashed potatoes
1 heaped teaspoon baking powder
½ an egg
salt and pepper

Mix together all ingredients. Season liberally with salt and pepper, bind together with the beaten egg, and roll out 6 mm (¼ in.) thick, using more flour if the mixture breaks. Cut into rounds, brush with beaten egg, and bake in a quick oven. Split open, insert a large dab of butter and serve hot.

SWEDE SAVOURY

750 gr (1½ lb.) Swedes
butter
grated cheese
seasoning
pepper and salt

Boil swedes until ¾ done, slice them, place in a buttered baking dish in layers, the slices overlapping one another. Sprinkle each layer with grated cheese and a little melted butter, and add a little seasoning of spiced pepper and salt. Finish on top with grated cheese, and butter, and bake for ½ an hour in a moderate oven.

TINEHARLOW

1 Cup Boiled Rice
grated cheese
small chopped onion
1 cup minced meat
thyme or parsley
2 eggs
2 tablespoons milk

Grease a pie-dish, sprinkle with brown breadcrumbs, put in meat and other ingredients, season with pepper and salt and bake for half-an-hour. Turn on to a hot dish and pour brown gravy around, not over. Same mixture can be baked in small moulds for 20 minutes.

TOAD IN THE HOLE

750 gr (1½ lb.) Sausages (cooked)
250 gr (½ lb.) flour
pepper and salt
500 ml (1 pint) milk
2 eggs
500 gr (1 lb.) tomatoes
breadcrumbs

Sift flour and salt, then make a hole in centre, drop 1 egg in at a time and mix. Pour in ½ milk, mixing little more flour. Use all milk, after beating batter for half-an-hour. Skin sausages and cut each in halves lengthwise. Grease pie-dish, arrange sausages and pour over batter. Cut tomatoes, place on top and sprinkle with breadcrumbs. Cook in a moderate oven for 45 minutes.

TASTY SAUSAGES

500 gr (1 lb.) Sausages
500 gr (1 lb.) minced ham
pinch of mixed herbs
grated rind of ½ lemon
1 egg

Remove sausages from the skins, mix with ham and seasonings, bind with the egg (well beaten), shape into a roll, wrap in buttered paper, and tie in a cloth previously dipped in boiling water and floured. Boil for 45 minutes. Remove coverings and serve hot with plenty of good brown gravy. Garnish with fried tomatoes. Sufficient for three servings. Double the quantity requires 1 hour's boiling.

SCALLOPED TOMATOES

Tomatoes
seasoning
breadcrumbs
butter

Cover the bottom of a buttered baking dish with breadcrumbs, dot with butter. Slice tomatoes and place on top. Put another layer of breadcrumbs on top and dot with butter. Cover and bake in the oven.

TOMATO TOAST

1 Large Tomato
15 gr (½ oz.) of butter
a small piece of onion
1 egg
30 gr (1 oz.) of cooked ham
pepper and salt
buttered toast

Peel tomatoes and mince them with the ham and onions. Place the butter into a saucepan, and when it is melted add the tomatoes, onion and ham and cook for 10 minutes, stirring all the time. Draw from the fire, add the beaten egg and stir again over the fire till it thickens. Have ready hot buttered toast, spread the mixture on it, and serve at once.

TASTY TOMATOES

2 Tomatoes
4 tablespoons milk
small pinch of bi-carbonate of soda
butter
4 eggs
pinch of salt
salt and pepper

Peel and cut up tomatoes and cook in butter in a frying pan. Remove from fire and partly cool. Beat up eggs and milk, with seasoning, add to cooked tomato, stirring gently over heat until the mixture thickens. Serve on hot, buttered toast. The pinch of soda is added to the tomato to prevent the milk curdling when it is mixed with the tomato.

TOMATO CHEESE

4 Ripe Tomatoes
¼ teaspoon salt
same weight of tomatoes in cheese
buttered toast
a pinch of cayenne pepper

Pour boiling water over tomatoes, leave for a few minutes, then draw off the skins. Cut them finely and put in a pan with cheese (cut in small pieces), and the seasoning. Stir the mixture over a small fire until it dissolves. Serve on buttered toast.

TOMATO RICE PIE

Cooked Rice
1 egg
tomatoes
small cup of milk
pepper and salt

Almost fill a pie dish with alternate layers of cooked rice and sliced tomatoes. Season with salt and pepper. Beat the egg, add to it the milk. Pour over the rice and tomatoes and bake in a moderate oven till a pale brown.

VEGETABLE PIE

Cabbage, Carrots, Onions, Potatoes or any other Vegetable
short crust
pepper and salt
sago
butter
gravy salt

Cut vegetables up finely, put into a saucepan with a handful of sago and a little water, season with salt and pepper, stew till tender and thicken with gravy salt and butter. Turn into a pie-dish, put a good, short crust on top, and bake in moderate oven till nicely browned.

VEGETABLE RISSOLES (HEALTH)

1 Cup Brown Breadcrumbs
1 teaspoon chopped parsley
½ teaspoon dried herbs
salt to taste
2 large carrots
1 large onion
1 egg yolk
very little pepper
breadcrumbs

Put the carrots and onions through a fine mincer. Add the dried herbs, parsley, and seasonings. Bind with the beaten egg yolk, shape into balls, dip in egg and breadcrumbs and fry in deep boiling fat until brown.

WELSH RAREBIT (No. 1)

250 gr (½ lb.) Cheese
1 or 2 eggs
½ teaspoon cornflour
pepper and salt
breadcrumbs
milk

Grate the cheese, and place in a saucepan with the pepper and salt to taste. Add eggs, unbeaten, and a little milk. Place on the fire, keep stirring all the time and cook until the cheese is melted. Thicken with breadcrumbs and the cornflour dissolved in a little milk. This makes a nice filling for sandwiches, or browned in the oven can be served for lunch.

WELSH RAREBIT (No. 2)

90 gr (3 oz.) Cheese
2 tablespoons cream
½ teaspoon made mustard
30 gr (1 oz.) butter
1 egg
a little salt

Slice the cheese and put into a small saucepan with the butter, cream and seasoning. Stir over the fire until smooth and well melted, beat in a well-whisked egg and pour over neat pieces of hot buttered toast. Serve at once on a hot dish.

WHITE SWEET PUDDING (SCOTTISH)

1 kg (2 lb.) Plain Flour
500 gr (1 lb.) sugar
60 gr (2 oz.) mixed spice
1 teaspoon salt
1 kg (2 lb.) currants
625 gr ($1\frac{1}{4}$ lb.) good beef suet
$\frac{1}{2}$ teaspoon cinnamon
brawn skin

Procure from the butcher, or save when killing on the farm, 1 large brawn skin. Wash thoroughly, and blow up, using a brown paper funnel; tie, and leave until dry. This is to make sure the skins are perfect, and that there are no holes or weak places. If there are any sew them. Cut your skins in suitable lengths for handling and sew one end. Mince suet very fine, clean currants carefully, mix all dry ingredients very thoroughly together, fill the skins with the ingredients, leaving room for swelling; about a little more than half full is sufficient; sew up securely, and shake the contents equally along the skin. Prick well with a large darning needle. Put the puddings into a boiler of boiling water. It is advisable to put a plate in the bottom of saucepan when the water is put on. Boil $2\frac{1}{2}$ to 3 hours. Leave in water till it cools a little, then lift the puddings very carefully out of the water, as they break easily. Allow to get cold. The pudding is then ready for use. When required cut in slices about 6 mm ($\frac{1}{4}$ in.) to 13 mm ($\frac{1}{2}$ in.) thick, place on plates in oven until thoroughly heated through, and serve on toast. These puddings will keep good for quite a long time.

MEAT, POULTRY AND GAME

Always put roasts in a fairly hot oven and brown both sides quickly. Cook quickly for the first $\frac{1}{2}$ hour, then reduce the heat and cook slowly. Cooking meat this way keeps in the juices and makes the meat very tender.

When roasting meat, always put a layer of suet or dripping in the pan first, and then the meat. Sprinkle meat with $\frac{1}{2}$ teaspoon sugar, 1 teaspoon lemon juice or vinegar, a little salt, and dust all over with plain flour. Pour 2 tablespoons boiling water in pan. Put in quick oven, and gradually cool oven down to normal heat. Allow 20 minutes to each 500 gr (1 lb.) of meat. If at any time meat cooks too quickly, cover with a piece of buttered paper.

When boiling a ham, allow it to simmer 20 minutes for every 500 gr (1 lb.) it weighs after the water has boiled up. Leave it in the water till it is quite cold. This ensures it being juicy and tender.

Mix in a flour sifter 4 tablespoons plain flour and 1 tablespoon of ground ginger, and shake well over both sides of a joint which has been previously seasoned with salt and pepper. This will help to retain the juices of a small roast, and make the gravy brown and very tasty.

To keep meat fresh rub over with vinegar. Vinegar will also freshen up meat.

After carving from a joint of boiled salt beef or boiled gammon, put the remains of the joint back into the liquid in which it was boiled and leave it until quite cold.

Rub tough meat with lemon juice or vinegar.

When frying sausages roll in cornflour instead of flour and they will not split.

Freshly-killed meat requires longer cooking than meat which has been well hung.

When making white sauce for meat or vegetables, use celery leaves chopped fine, instead of the usual parsley.

When making rissoles, if eggs are scarce, white sauce serves the purpose very well.

If a few cloves are put in when cooking a rabbit and a little ground mace added to the thickening, quite a different flavour is given to rabbit.

For thickening stews, drop sufficient oatmeal into stew–allow it to cook.

Don't imagine that the costly cuts of meat are the best. The cheaper cuts are equal in nourishment value. Anyone can grill an undercut steak or lamb chop. It takes a good cook to prepare an appetising meal from shin beef or neck of mutton.

The flavour of a boiled fowl is improved by adding to the water a few pepper corns, whole pimento, a little celery, onion and sage. Cook gently until fowl is tender.

To cook a fowl to perfection, roast it with the breast down first, and turn when a little more than half cooked.

When singeing a fowl, do so by lighting a spoonful of methylated spirits in a saucer and holding the bird over the flame. This is much cleaner than using a piece of paper.

To make a fowl more tender add a spoonful of vinegar to the water in which it is boiled.

If a small quantity of salt, pepper and ground ginger is rubbed into the flesh of a fowl before baking, the flavour will be greatly improved.

If you want to stuff poultry or a joint and are short of breadcrumbs, oatmeal makes a very good substitute. A handful of dry oatmeal to every handful of crumbs.

BREADCRUMBS (To Prepare)

Collect all pieces of bread, white or brown, and place on a dish in the oven. Allow to become hard and brown, crush with a rolling pin, and store in closed bottles for use when required for stuffing, etc.

MEAT

BOILING MEAT

Wash and wipe the joint and tie up with string if necessary. Put fresh meat in slightly salted boiling water, and simmer until cooked. Put salted meat into cold water. Bring to boil quickly, and then simmer slowly. Time: For a piece of meat under 1½ kg (3 lb.), allow 1½ hours. Over 1½ kg (3 lb.) allow 20 minutes to 500 gr (1 lb.), and an additional 20 minutes (for fresh meat). 30 minutes to 500 gr (1 lb.) and an additional 30 minutes (for salt meat).

LAMB CHOPS (STEAMED)

Chops
flour
seasoning
chopped parsley
a little milk

Place the required number of chops in a buttered basin, first removing all fat. Season with pepper and salt, tie greased paper over the basin and steam for 3 hours. Do not put any water in the basin. When the chops are done, remove paper, strain the liquid off into a saucepan, add a little milk and chopped parsley and thicken with a little flour. Serve with green peas and mashed potatoes.

LAMB CHOPS AND BREADCRUMBS

Chops
breadcrumbs
1 egg
seasoning

Take the chops one by one and put them into the beaten egg. Then sprinkle thickly with the dry breadcrumbs with a little seasoning. Put in a baking tin in oven with a little fat and cook till a nice brown.

RAGOUT OF LAMB WITH GREEN PEAS

1 kg (2 lb.) Breast or Neck of Lamb
60 gr (2 oz.) butter
500 ml (1 pint) shelled peas
1 lump sugar
seasoning
1 tablespoon flour
some light stock
a sprig of mint
a small bunch herbs

Cut the meat into neat pieces and sprinkle it with the flour. Melt the butter in a stewpan, put in the meat and brown it slightly. Add the seasonings, peas, and enough light stock or meat boilings to cover. Stew slowly for 1¼ hours or until the lamb is quite tender. Lift out the mint and herbs before serving. One or two tablespoons of cream added to it at the last will be an improvement.

BRAISED LAMB CHOPS BUDERIM

750 gr (1½ lb.) Lamb or Mutton Chops
1 tablespoon shortening
2 level tablespoons honey
2 tablespoons seasoned plain flour
2 tablespoons Worcestershire sauce
2 tablespoons dry sherry or table wine

Trim chops and toss in flour. Fry lightly in melted shortening, 3 minutes each side. Put all other ingredients in a casserole, add chops, cover and cook in slow oven till tender, approximately 1½ to 2 hours.

MUTTON

CHOPS WITH GREEN PEAS

1 kg (2 lb.) Neck or Rib Chops
1 or 2 thinly sliced onions
a little flour
a sprig of mint
2 large cups green peas
seasoning
½ teaspoon sugar
cold water

Trim and remove surplus fat from chops. Roll them in flour, lay in greased casserole and sprinkle with salt and pepper. Cover with the onion, and then add the peas. Sprinkle the peas with pepper and salt and sugar, add the mint, and then fill casserole with water to come about half-way up sides. Cover closely and cook in a very slow oven for 2½ to 3 hours, or even longer if there is time. Thicken gravy with a little flour before serving if necessary, and then add a tiny sprinkling of chopped mint. If you use dried "blue" peas, soak 1 cupful overnight in warm water with a pinch of soda. Next morning drain and add the peas as above.

FLAP AND KIDNEY, EN CASSEROLE

1 Flap
a little flour
seasoning
1 or 2 kidneys
salt water
2 or 3 large onions
water

Remove surplus fat from the flap and cut it in about 52 mm (2 in.) squares. Cut the kidneys in half, and after soaking in salt water for ½ hour, cut into small pieces, and roll together with the flap in flour. Place in greased casserole, add pepper and salt and onion cut in quarters, and water to fill to two-thirds. Cover closely, and cook in slow oven for at least 3 hours, thickening the gravy at the end if necessary. These humble ingredients, cooked in this manner for hours until brown and savoury, make a dish fit for an epicure.

HARICOT CHOPS WITH SAVOURY BALLS

750 kg (1½ lb.) Best Neck Chops
1 carrot
a stick celery if available
1 tablespoon dripping
2 or 3 cloves
a bacon bone
1 onion
1 turnip
3 cups water
1 tablespoon flour
a pinch mace or nutmeg

HARICOT CHOPS WITH SAVOURY BALLS—*continued*

Heat dripping in frying pan and brown chops. Drain and place in saucepan. Then brown sliced onion and cut-up vegetables, drain and add to the chops. Add all the other ingredients except the flour. Cover closely, and simmer for 2 to 3 hours. About ½ hour before serving thicken the stew with the flour mixed with a little cold water, and then drop in the savoury dumplings and cook slowly for about ½ hour. Serve in a deep dish with a border of dumplings.

The Savoury Balls

250 gr (½ lb.) Self-Raising Flour
1 teaspoon chopped parsley
¼ teaspoon salt and pepper
60-90 gr (2-3 oz.) finely chopped suet
a pinch thyme and sage
water to mix

Mix all the dry ingredients and make into a light dough with cold water. Divide into small balls, roll each in flour, and drop into the boiling stew. The same balls may be cooked with a boiled leg or shoulder of mutton. For a change add a small minced onion to the above ingredients.

KNUCKLE PIE

4 Knuckles Mutton
1 onion
1 or 2 carrots
short pastry
500 gr (1 lb.) neck chops
a few cloves
1 dessertspoon chopped parsley
mashed potatoes

Where 4 knuckles are available at once, this delicious pie can be recommended. Put knuckles into saucepan or casserole with chops (more than 500 gr (1 lb.) if the family is large), add the onion stuck with cloves, carrots, salt and pepper, and barely enough water to cover it all. Cover closely, and cook very slowly on the back of the stove or in a slow oven for 5 to 6 hours, until the knuckle gristle is gelatinous and the meat parts from the bones. If it is boiled, the meat will be "rags" and a delicious dinner is spoiled. Keep it just simmering all the time, then take out the bones and the onion and mash the carrots. Thicken gravy if necessary with a little flour, add parsley and cover with a crust of short pastry or mashed potatoes. Bake in a hot oven about ½ hour. The pie can be very ordinary if the long, slow cooking of the meat is not carried out.

LAMB SHANKS WITH SAUCE

3 or 4 Lamb or Hogget Shanks
2 rashers bacon chopped
2 level tablespoons flour
1½ cups water
1 tablespoon Worcestershire sauce
1 level teaspoon dry mustard
1 tin tomato puree
1 level tablespoon brown sugar
½ cup vinegar
1 sliced onion
1 level teaspoon salt

Fry chopped bacon and shanks rolled in flour. Drain and place in casserole. Combine puree, water, sauce, vinegar, mustard, sliced onion and remaining flour and pour over shanks. Cover and cook in moderate oven till tender, approximately 2 hours.

LANCASHIRE HOT POT

1 kg (2 lb.) Best End Neck Mutton
6 good sized potatoes
a little flour
2 good sized onions
2 teaspoons chopped parsley and mint
salt and pepper
short crust

Peel and cut into neat slices the onions and potatoes. Place a layer of onions in an earthenware, fireproof dish or casserole (a deep dish is best) then a layer of chops which have been dipped in the flour, salt and pepper. Sprinkle these with parsley and mint. Fill up the dish with similar layers, placing potatoes on top. Cover all with cold water, cover with grease-proof paper and bake in a moderate oven for 3 hours. Half an hour before ready take off the paper and put on lid of short crust, made of 185 gr (6 oz.) flour 90 gr (3 oz.) lard or dripping, pinch salt and ½ teaspoon baking powder, with water to mix. Roll out to fit top of dish. Replace in oven to cook crust. Send to table with a serviette round the dish in which it was cooked.

LEG OR SHOULDER OF MUTTON (BRAISED)

The cheaper cuts also may be braised to perfection, but the process is very useful when a joint has to be cooked, and there is perhaps no oven room for it, that is, on a big baking day. Heat 2 tablespoons good dripping in a large saucepan (iron for preference) and put in the joint to brown. Turn carefully so that it browns on all sides. Care must be taken not to burn the dripping at this stage. When well browned, add a cupful of water, and if you like, a few pieces of root vegetables for flavour. Add salt and pepper, cover closely and simmer for about 2 hours on back of stove. A little more water may be added from time to time as it boils away. During the last hour, potatoes, parsnips, etc., may be browned around the joint. Dish meat and vegetables, and then drain off surplus fat. Add about 2 cups water or stock, thicken with a tablespoon flour, boil a few minutes, and serve in a gravy boat.

MARROW (STUFFED)

Marrow or Small Pumpkin
2 Flaps
1 egg
seasoning
1 shank
breadcrumbs
onion

Mince the flaps and shank meat of a sheep. Mix with seasoning, breadcrumbs, onion and moisten with egg, or a very little milk. Stuff a small pumpkin or vegetable marrow with the mixture and bake with plenty of good dripping. This is a delicious dish.

MINCED ROLL (BAKED)

A Leg of Mutton
2 well-beaten eggs
2 cups fine breadcrumbs
1 dessertspoon chopped parsley
seasoning

Mince all the meat from the leg, and add to it the breadcrumbs and egg. Add parsley and season well. Most people like it without onion, but it may be added if liked particularly. Mix all together thoroughly, and form into one large or two smaller rolls. Wrap and tie in clean greased brown paper or a paper bag, and bake in a moderate oven as you would a joint, with plenty of good dripping. Baste frequently, and turn once. It should cook in 1½ to 2 hours according to size and heat of oven. When the paper is removed you will find that it looks and tastes as unlike roast joint as can be. It is crisp and delicious served with the usual brown gravy and vegetables, but it is equally good served cold with salads, or for sandwiches. Use the bones that are left for soup.

PIQUANT CHOPS

6 Neck Chops
½ clove garlic (chopped)
1 level dessertspoon brown sugar
2 tablespoons Worcestershire sauce
1 level teaspoon mustard
¼ cup stock or water
1 small onion
1 level dessertspoon chopped green pepper
1 level teaspoon curry powder
2 tablespoons vinegar
250 gr (8 oz.) tin tomato soup

Trim chops, put into casserole and cover with rest of ingredients. Stand 3 hours. Cook in moderate oven 1½ to 2 hours. If necessary thicken gravy.

SAVOURY CHOPS (No. 1)

4 Thick Mutton Chops trimmed of fat
bay leaf
1 cup rice
1 sliced onion
1 level tablespoon chutney
½ cup milk
1 medium sized tomato
¼ cup peanuts
3 cups stock or water
2 or 3 peppercorns
1 stick chopped celery
2 level teaspoons salt
1 egg
2 cups shredded cheese
dash pepper
1 level tablespoon shortening

Place chops in saucepan with stock, bay leaf and peppercorns. Wash rice and add to saucepan with celery, onion and salt. Simmer until rice has absorbed liquid and chops are cooked. Cut meat from bones and remove bay leaf and peppercorns. Add chutney, beaten egg, milk, and one cup of cheese. Grease a casserole, put a layer of cheese in the bottom, spread with rice and meat mixture, and sprinkle with remaining cheese. Garnish with tomato slices dusted with pepper. Bake in moderate oven 30 minutes until brown. Fry nuts in shortening, spread over casserole.

SAVOURY CHOPS (No. 2)

6 or 8 Chops
salt to taste
1/3 cup vinegar
1/3 cup Holbrook's sauce
2 tablespoons flour
2 dessertspoons sugar
1/3 cup tomato sauce
2 cups water

Trim the fat from chops, and place in baking or casserole dish. Sprinkle with flour, sugar and salt. Mix together vinegar, tomato and Holbrook's sauce, and pour on the chops, then add the two cups of water. Cover dish closely and cook in a moderate oven for 1½ to 2 hours. This makes its own sauce and the chops will be very tender.

SAVOURY MUTTON PUDDING

2 Cups Self-raising Flour
a pinch of salt
750 gr (1½ lb.) mutton
1 kidney
¾ cup chopped suet
cold water
2 carrots
a little flour
seasoning

This is an excellent cold weather dish in which rather scraggy pieces of mutton may be used.

Make some pastry with flour, suet, salt and enough water to mix. Roll out and line a pudding basin with two-thirds of

SAVOURY MUTTON PUDDING—*continued*

it. Mince or cut up the mutton, carrots and a kidney if you have it. Use neck of mutton, with or without the bones or flap, or if you prefer it, a better cut such as shoulder or knuckle end of the leg. The odd pieces are just as nice though. Season the mixture well, adding herbs and an onion, if liked—though mutton alone gives a pudding a delicious flavour. Place in the lined basin, sprinkle and mix in a little flour, and then half fill with water. Cover with top crust of pastry, tie down with greased paper, and steam for 2 to 3 hours—longer if meat is in large pieces.

SHOULDER OF MUTTON (STUFFED)

1 Shoulder of Mutton
yolk of 1 egg
parsley
breadcrumbs
a little lean ham
a little milk
onions
pepper and salt

Bone the shoulder and remove the fat. Make a stuffing of chopped onion, breadcrumbs, seasoning, parsley and sufficient of the fat you removed from the meat. Bind with egg and milk. Place stuffing in the meat, roll up and tie securely, and bake in the oven. Baste well. Serve with a nice brown sauce.

SHEEP'S BRAINS

500 gr (1 lb.) Sheep's Brains
flour
frying fat
lemon

Wash the brains in cold salted water and allow to soak for 20 minutes. Boil for $\frac{1}{4}$ of an hour. Roll each piece in flour and fry in dripping. Serve with slices of lemon.

SWEET AND SOUR CHOPS

6 Neck Chops
salt and pepper to taste
1 carrot
1 level tablespoon sugar
1 cup water or stock
3 level tablespoons plain flour
1 sliced onion
1 level tablespoon chopped mint
2 tablespoons vinegar

Prepare chops, toss in seasoned flour, place in greased casserole and sprinkle with remainder of flour. Brown onion, slice carrot and add to chops. Add mint, sugar, vinegar and stock. Cover and cook in moderate oven $1\frac{1}{2}$ to $1\frac{3}{4}$ hours.

VEAL

CALF'S HEAD (BONED AND STUFFED)

½ a Calf's Head
1 tablespoon chopped parsley
60 gr (2 oz.) suet (shredded)
nutmeg
90 gr (3 oz.) breadcrumbs
1 egg
½ teaspoon mixed herbs
lemon rind
salt and pepper

After boning calf's head, stuff with above mixture. Roll up, tie in cloth and simmer for 2 hours. When cooked serve with parsley sauce.

KNUCKLE OF VEAL (STEWED)

2½-3 kg (5 or 6 lb.) Knuckle Veal
1 onion
1 leaf of celery
thyme
a few slices of bacon
1 carrot
parsley
pepper and salt
2 tablespoons rice

Put the meat into a saucepan and cover with boiling water and bring to the boil. Add the vegetables and seasoning. Simmer the veal for 3 hours. At the end of 2 hours add the rice and bacon. Make a little parsley sauce and pour over the meat.

LOIN OF VEAL (ROAST)

A Loin of Veal, about 2 kg (4 lb.)
some forcemeat
dripping
a few slices of bacon
1 cup brown sauce
lemon

Bone the veal and season with salt and pepper. Fill with forcemeat. Put a skewer through or roll up and tie. Cover with plenty of dripping and bake from 2 to 2½ hours, basting frequently. Serve with fried bacon and brown sauce.

VEAL AND HAM PIES

250 gr (½ lb.) Veal
60 gr (2 oz.) ham or bacon
1 lemon
1 teaspoon chopped parsley
salt and pepper

Cut veal into very small pieces, mince ham and add with seasoning, and a very little water. Bake in raised pastry cases for 1 hour in a moderate oven. See Hot Water Pastry.

VEAL CUTLETS

Cutlets
1 egg
some good brown gravy
seasoning
breadcrumbs
parsley

Egg and breadcrumb the cutlets, and fry them in smoking hot fat, turning them until well done. Time, 4 to 6 minutes. Then take up and pour over them a good brown gravy. Serve hot, garnished with parsley.

BEEF

AUNT ABBY'S MEAT ROLL

500 gr (1 lb.) Minced Steak
155 gr (5 oz.) breadcrumbs
½ grated nutmeg
500 gr (1 lb.) minced ham
2 eggs
pepper and salt

Mix well together, shape like a roly-poly, tie up firmly in a cloth, and boil for 3 hours. This can be eaten hot or cold.

BANANA STEAK (BAKED)

250-375 gr (½ to ¾ lb.) Beefsteak
2 bananas
seasoning
1 teaspoonful sugar
2 or 3 slices bacon
a little water

Choose a tender piece of steak one inch in thickness. Wipe it and split it open, leaving one end uncut like a book. Season with pepper, salt and a little grated nutmeg. Cut bananas in pieces, lay them on one side of the steak, sprinkle with sugar and cover with the other side. Place thin slices of bacon on top and fasten together with small skewer. Place in baking-dish with a little water and bake in oven for about ½ hour, basting occasionally. Serve garnished with parsley or watercress.

BEEF A LA MODE

2 kg (4 lb.) Beef (Shoulder)
1 onion (sliced)
8 cloves
2 tablespoons fat
vinegar
1 tablespoon sugar
½ cup celery (diced)
2 bay leaves
3 gingersnaps
salt

Place meat, onion, bay leaves and cloves in an earthen dish; half cover meat with vinegar and cover dish closely. Let stand 12 hours. Turn on the other side and let stand 12 hours longer. Heat the fat in the casserole, add the celery and meat and brown nicely on all sides; add some of the spiced vinegar or simply boiling water; cover closely, set in the oven, and let simmer and bake several hours until tender. Add salt and cook a little longer. Take out meat, strain gravy and skim off the fat. Add the gingersnaps and sugar to taste. If the gravy is desired more tart, add lemon, sliced. Return meat and gravy to the casserole, heat and serve with meat hot in the gravy.

CORNISH PASTY

500 gr (1 lb.) Mutton or Beef
2 medium onions
2 large potatoes
pepper and salt
short pastry

Make short pastry from 2 cups flour, ½ teaspoonful baking powder and dripping. Divide into 3 parts, roll out to rather less than 6 mm (¼ in.), place ingredients in centre and crimp edges. Bake in a moderate oven for 1 hour. Turnip may be used in place of potatoes.

DUTCH CUTLET

500 gr (1 lb.) Beef Steak
2 minced onions
1 tablespoon sauce
1 egg
tomato
1 cup breadcrumbs
2 cups water
some slices of bacon
salt and pepper
parsley

Put steak through mincing machine and mix with salt and pepper, breadcrumbs and 1 minced onion. Bind together with well-beaten egg. Form into a flat cake, put into a greased baking tin with water, sauce, minced onion, and slices of bacon on top, cover with buttered paper and bake about 1 hour (may take a little longer) in a moderate oven. Garnish with slices of tomato and parsley.

FRENCH CORNED BEEF

Corned Beef
½ teaspoon turmeric or other spice
½ teaspoon cayenne
1 onion

Rub the beef with the cayenne, turmeric or other spice, and put into boiling water with an onion cut in quarters. Boil a few minutes to seal the pores, then cook gently till done. A bunch of herbs can be added if liked. This is a very tasty way of cooking corned beef.

HUNGARIAN GOULASH

500 gr (1 lb.) Lean Beef
500 gr (1 lb.) lean veal
1 tablespoon fat
1 large onion, diced
1 teaspoon paprika
1 cup strained tomatoes

Cut the meat into 26 mm (1 in.) squares and brown in hot fat with the onion, salt and paprika. When the meat is brown, add the tomatoes, and ½ hour before serving add some small potatoes. Let cook slowly, closely covered.

MINCE ROLLS AND CELERY SAUCE

500 gr (1 lb.) Minced Beef
1 parsnip
1 small head celery
1 tablespoon chopped parsley
1 tablespoon wheatmeal
1 carrot
1 egg
½ teaspoonful pepper
2 tablespoons butter
½ teaspoon salt
1 tablespoon plain flour

Wash the celery, cut into small pieces and boil in 4 cups of water. Boil and mash carrots and parsnips and put them in a basin with the mixed beef. Add salt, pepper, parsley, wheatmeal and beaten egg. Mix well. When celery is almost cooked shape meat mixture into balls and drop into the boiling celery. Cook ½ hour, and then remove the meat on to a hot dish. Mix the plain flour into a smooth paste with a little cold water and stir into the celery to thicken. Boil 5 minutes, add butter, pour over the meat rolls and serve very hot.

MOCK DUCK

500 gr (1 lb.) Rump or Blade Bone Steak
1 teaspoon chopped thyme
1 chopped onion
1 cup breadcrumbs
1 teaspoon chopped parsley
1 tablespoon melted butter
salt and pepper

Spread the meat and pound it a little. Rub with lemon. Mix crumbs and seasonings, and add melted butter. Spread the crumbs over the meat, roll up, and tie into shape. Place in a covered pie dish with some good dripping and a cup of hot water. Cook about 2 hours in a moderate oven. Take cover from pie dish and allow the meat 20 minutes to brown. Serve with good gravy.

ROUND OF BEEF (BRAISED)

1½ kg (3 lb.) Round of Beef
1 onion
trimmings of ham or bacon
1 carrot
60 gr (2 oz.) good dripping
a bunch of herbs
500 ml (1 pint) stock
seasoning

Put the dripping and some trimmings of ham and bacon into a stewpan, and when melted, put in the vegetables cut into pieces, and the seasonings. Tie the meat into a neat shape with a piece of tape, and when the contents of the saucepan are hot, place it on the top with some bones or scraps round the sides. Put on the lid and cook slowly for 20 minutes until the meat has taken colour. Add the stock, and if liked, a glass of white wine. Cook slowly from 3 to 4 hours, until the meat is thoroughly tender. Lift it on to a hot dish, remove the tape and keep it warm while the gravy is prepared. If the liquid in the saucepan has reduced very much add a little stock, and strain into another saucepan. Boil for a few minutes, remove any grease from the top, pour some of this gravy round the meat and serve the remainder separately. A puree of potato is a good accompaniment with this dish.

SAVOURY STEAK (No. 1)

500 gr (1 lb.) Steak
1 teaspoon mustard
2 tablespoons Worcester sauce
2 tablespoons flour (plain)
1 teaspoon sugar
2 tablespoons vinegar
pepper and salt

Put all the ingredients into a casserole, cover with water and bake for 2 or 3 hours.

SAVOURY STEAK (No. 2)

500 gr (1 lb.) Rump Steak, Cut Thinly
1 cup milk
2 potatoes
2 onions
1 tablespoon cornflour

Lay the steak cut in pieces in a shallow baking dish and season to taste. Peel potatoes and onions and slice and lay alternately over meat. Add a little more seasoning, mix cornflour with milk, pour all over, and bake in oven for 1 hour.

SAVOURY STEAK (No. 3)

1 kg (2 lb.) Steak
1 tablespoon sugar
1 dessertspoon tomato sauce
2 tablespoons flour
1 dessertspoon Worcester sauce
1 teaspoon vinegar
salt and pepper to taste

Mix the flour and sugar, cut steak in pieces and roll each piece in the flour. Place in a casserole. Take the flour and sugar left over and mix with the sauces, vinegar, etc. Add 1½ cups water and pour over the steak. Cook in a slow oven for 2 hours. Chops may be cooked in the same way. Two pie-dishes may be used instead of a casserole.

STEAK A LA FRANÇAISE

About 1 kg (2 lb.) Topside Steak
30 gr (1 oz.) breadcrumbs
4 sour apples
juice of ½ a lemon
30 gr (1 oz.) butter

Peel, core and slice the apples thickly, then with a sharp knife make little slits in the steak and fill up each slit with a piece of apple. Sprinkle with pepper and salt, and fix up so that the apple cannot drop out. Brush all over with melted butter, roll in breadcrumbs and sprinkle with lemon juice. Wrap in greased paper and bake for 1½ hours. Serve with thick gravy and baked potatoes.

ROAST TOPSIDE STEAK

1 Thick Piece Topside
2 or 3 onions
dripping
water

Heat a little fat in a saucepan and brown the meat quickly all over. Turn with two forks so that each side may be browned. Cut up the onions and place round the meat, cover with tight fitting lid and cook gently for 3 or 4 hours. Every ½ hour add 2 tablespoons boiling water. Serve with its own gravy.

STEAK AND KIDNEY PUDDING

500 gr (1 lb.) Stewing Steak
1 cup wheatmeal
onion
2 sheep's kidneys
60 gr (2 oz.) beef suet
salt and pepper

Cut up the steak and kidneys and add chopped onion and seasoning. Mix the wholemeal flour with the suet and enough water to make a stiff paste. Put the prepared meat into a basin and cover with the pastry. Steam or boil for 3 hours.

SWEETBREAD CUTLETS

1 or 2 Sweetbreads
egg
breadcrumbs
vegetables
sauce

Soak the sweetbreads in warm, salted water for 2 hours. Parboil them and simmer for 10 minutes. Put between two plates and press until cold. Cut in 13 mm (½ in.) slices, rub in flour, egg and breadcrumb them, and fry in deep fat. Serve with a nice brown gravy and green peas.

SWISS STEAK

750 gr (1½ lb.) Round Steak
¾ cup flour
1 sliced onion
1 tablespoon fat
seasoning

Place the steak on a floured board and with the edge of a saucer pound in flour to which seasoning has been added. Do both sides. Brown the onion in fat, put the whole steak into the pan with the onion, and place in hot oven for 15 minutes. Reduce heat, cover and cook for 2½ hours.

STEWED TRIPE

500 gr (1 lb.) Tripe
1 onion
1 teaspoon cornflour
½ cup milk and water mixed
pepper and salt
some chopped parsley

Cut the tripe into small pieces, cover with cold water and boil for 15 minutes. Pour off the water, add milk and water, onion and seasoning. Bring to the boil, then reduce heat and simmer gently for about 3 hours. Thicken with cornflour and garnish with chopped parsley.

PORK

BACON ROLY POLY

250 gr ($\frac{1}{2}$ lb.) Flour
2 tablespoons baking powder
bacon
250 gr ($\frac{1}{2}$ lb.) suet
a pinch salt
onions

Make a suet paste with flour, suet, salt, baking powder and water. Make a soft dough, roll out to 6 mm ($\frac{1}{4}$ in.) thick and spread on paste, a layer of minced bacon and onion. Roll up securely in a floured pudding cloth and boil for $2\frac{1}{2}$ hours.

LOIN OF PORK (ROAST)

Pork
a little flour
salt and pepper
dripping

Score the pork all over by cutting the rind in narrow bands with a sharp knife. Rub on salt, pepper and flour well. Place in a baking tin with plenty of fat. Bake in a moderate oven, basting frequently. Allow 30 minutes to each 500 gr (1 lb.). Pork requires long and thorough cooking. Serve with baked sour apples, onions and potatoes. Pork should be a rich brown on the outside when cooked. Although very nice hot, it is best eaten cold.

PORK PIES

375 gr ($\frac{3}{4}$ lb.) Fresh Pork
1 chopped onion
pepper
$\frac{1}{2}$ teaspoon powdered sage
some good stock
salt
raised pastry

Chop the pork into small pieces, add the sage and seasoning and the chopped onion, with a little stock. Put in raised pastry cases, with slits in the top. Bake in a moderate oven for 1 hour. See Hot Water Pastry.

PORK SAUSAGES AND APPLES

750 gr ($1\frac{1}{2}$ lb.) Pork Sausages
1 chopped onion
2 cooking apples sliced
pepper and salt to taste
1 cup brown gravy
1 tablespoon brown sugar
1 level teaspoon ground ginger

Fry onion and sausages. Drain and put into casserole, cover with apples, sugar, seasoning and gravy. Bake one hour in moderate oven.

SUCKING PIG (ROAST)

A Sucking Pig
onions
apple sauce
breadcrumbs
chopped suet
herbs
garnishing

Make a seasoning by mixing breadcrumbs, suet, sage and onions, enough to stuff the entire body. Tie the upper parts of the hind legs to the body. Pull the fore feet out under the head and skewer. Brush all over with melted lard and roast from 2 to 2½ hours, basting frequently. When the animal is a rich brown remove from the oven, make a nice brown gravy and pour over. Serve with slices of lemon, parsley and apple sauce.

HAM BAKED (No. 1)

Wipe ham, wrap loosely in brown paper or aluminium foil and place fat side up in a shallow pan. Do not cover pan or add water. Bake in moderately slow oven allowing 15 minutes per 500 gr (1 lb.) for hams 6 kg (12 lb.) or over and 12 minutes per 500 gr (1 lb.) for under 6 kg (12 lb.). When within 45 minutes of baking time, remove paper or foil and remove rind. Cut across fat to make diamonds, insert a clove in each square and cover with 1 cup brown sugar dissolved in juice of 1 orange and grated rind. Bake the remaining 45 minutes uncovered in slow oven.

HAM BAKED (No. 2)

Soak ham 6 to 8 hours and wipe well. Enclose in 13 mm (½ in.) thick paste (flour and water) and seal well. Place in a greased baking dish and bake 4 hours in moderate oven, till pastry is crisp and brown. Remove pastry and skin and glaze or sprinkle with breadcrumbs.

BAKED VIRGINIA HAM

1 Ham
½ cup brown sugar
2 tablespoons breadcrumbs
1 teaspoon mustard
1 tablespoon whole cloves

Wash ham thoroughly. Put in deep pot, cover with cold water and bring to boil quickly. Reduce heat and simmer 2½ hours. Remove from pot and take off skin. Mix sugar, crumbs and mustard and spread over ham. Stick cloves in ham. Put in a roasting dish with 1 cup of water or pineapple juice or grape juice and bake for about 30 minutes, basting every five minutes.

HAM (TO BOIL)

Ham
a few cloves
a sprig of thyme

Soak the ham for 12 hours in cold water, drain and put into a large saucepan of cold water. Bring to the boil slowly—after 5 minutes remove scum, and add a few cloves and a sprig of thyme. Simmer slowly for 25 minutes to the 500 gr (1 lb.) and 25 minutes over. Cool in water in which it was cooked, lift out of pan, skin gently with fingers and dust with grated nutmeg. Decorate with cloves, or, if preferred, sprinkle with a mixture of ½ tablespoon brown sugar and fine breadcrumbs.

HAM (in the copper)

Place ham in copper, resting it on an enamel plate. Cover with cold water and add 6 cloves, 1 cup brown sugar, and 1 teaspoon mixed spice. Bring to the boil; allow to simmer for 30 minutes. Remove all fire or turn off heat. Cover copper closely with old blankets or bags, completely sealing in steam. Leave at least 12 hours or until water is cool. Lift out ham and skin and glaze, or sprinkle with crumbs.

SAVOURY DUMPLINGS FOR STEWS

250 gr (½ lb.) Flour
1 teaspoon baking powder
a little pepper
3 tablespoons good beef dripping
½ teaspoon salt
cold water
a little parsley or herbs if the flavour is liked

Mix the baking powder, salt, pepper and herbs through the flour, rub in the dripping and mix to a very stiff paste with cold water. Divide into pieces about the size of an egg and roll in flour. Place them on top of braised chops or steak or any kind of stew after it has been cooking for about 1½ hours. The dumplings will require ¾ hour longer.

YORKSHIRE PUDDING

250 gr ($\frac{1}{2}$ lb.) Flour — **500 ml (1 pint) milk**
2 eggs — **a pinch salt**

Sift the flour and add salt. Make a hole in the middle of flour, break in the eggs, and stir into them very gradually as much flour as they will take up. When they begin to get stiff add the milk, a little at a time, and mix well. When half the milk is used, all the flour should be stirred in, and the batter should be well beaten till bubbles rise. Add the remainder of the milk and allow to stand for at least $\frac{1}{2}$ an hour before cooking. Pour round the roast of beef $\frac{1}{2}$ an hour before it is to be served.

POULTRY

TO PLUCK AND DRAW A FOWL

Place the fowl in a tub and pour over it sufficient boiling water to cover. Work it well about in the water, then lift out and roll up in a towel for a few minutes. Then pluck at once, beginning with the stiff wing feathers. Next work from the breast downwards, plucking the feathers from the legs. Turn over and pluck the back. Singe. Cut off feet.

Cut round outside of leg at knee joint and draw away as many sinews as possible. Turn the fowl on its breast and cut a slit an inch long in the skin at the back of the neck. Loosen the skin and cut off neck close to body. Cut the skin still further, leaving a flap to fold over back. Remove the crop with the fingers (it should come away whole). Turn fowl on its back with the neck towards you, insert the fingers, and loosen the skin surrounding the organs. Turn the opposite way and make a slit crossways beneath the tail, being careful not to cut the intestines. Insert the fingers and loosen the membrane still further, separating the organs from the body. Grasp the gizzard and draw everything out, being very careful not to break the gall bladder. Remove the lungs from the bones, and wash the inside well with water. Wipe dry.

TO TRUSS A FOWL

Cut round the leg joints above the feet and pull off the feet. Pour boiling water over the scaly part of the legs and scrape away the scales. If the fowl is to be stuffed, insert the stuffing. Tie or sew up the end to close the opening. Then fold over the skin of the neck, fold the legs back, push a skewer through them from side to side and tie up securely with string.

GIBLETS (TO PREPARE)

The giblets are the gizzard, liver, heart and feet of poultry, the top of the wings may be included.

Make a cut in the gizzard with a sharp knife, or better still, cut with a pair of scissors. Take out the hard inner lining with contents (taking care that it comes away without breaking). Cut the gall sack (green) away from the liver and be careful not to break it. Remove the enveloping membranes from the heart, and throw all into a basin of cold water and wash thoroughly. Scald the feet by pouring over them boiling water. Allow to remain in water for a few minutes, then scrape off the outer covering. The giblets may be stewed, or used for a pie or soup, or they may be cooked, chopped and served as a sauce with the bird from which they were removed.

To test poultry to see if cooked, press flesh with blade of a knife. If well done the flesh will yield to the pressure. On no account pierce with a fork. Cover breast of duck, turkey or fowl with strips of fat bacon, or sprinkle with salt, brush over with melted butter and sprinkle with flour, or make a paste of 3 tablespoons butter and 2 tablespoons of flour, and spread over breast and legs. Baste bird every 15 minutes.

BASTING MIXTURE

⅔ cup Boiling Water | **⅓ cup butter (dripping will do)**

Put the butter in pieces over the fowl, and pour over the boiling water. Basting browns and gives a lovely flavour.

TO COOK OLD POULTRY

1 Dressed Bird | **seasoning**
vinegar

Sponge the poultry all over with vinegar, especially the legs. Put into hot water, to which a little salt has been added, and bring to the boil quickly. Boil hard for ten minutes, then set to back of stove and let boil gently for 2½ to 3 hours. Serve with white sauce. The water in which the poultry has been boiled makes good stock for soup next day.

CHICKEN PIE

Cold Chicken | **1 onion**
butter | **seasonings**
tomato sauce | **1 cup cooked rice or vermicelli**
flaky pastry | **yolk of egg**

CHICKEN PIE—*continued*

Cut the remains of a cold fowl or chicken into small pieces and place in a pan with the chopped onion and butter. Season with salt and a dash of cayenne pepper. Brown nicely, then add the rice, mix well, moisten with tomato sauce and put the mixture into a buttered pie-dish. Cover with flaky pastry, brush over with yolk of egg, and bake for 30 to 35 minutes in a brisk oven. Serve with mashed potatoes.

CHICKEN (ROAST)

1 Chicken
dripping
rashers of bacon
seasoning

Place 2 or 3 rashers of bacon on the breast of the bird after it is dressed, smear with dripping, and tie a sheet of greased paper round the chicken. Place in a brisk oven and cook for ¾ to 1 hour. When ½ cooked sprinkle with salt and pepper, take the paper from the bird and allow it to brown.

CHICKEN IN CASSEROLE

1 Roasting Chicken
flour for coating
1 cup diced celery
1 level tablespoon plain flour
¼ cup thin cream or top milk
salt and pepper to taste
½ cup oil or shortening
2 level tablespoons minced onion
¼ cup sherry

Cut up chicken, flour lightly, and fry golden brown in oil. Arrange pieces in casserole. Add celery, onion and flour to pan and stir over low heat for 2 minutes. Season lightly and add to chicken. Add wine and cream, cover and bake in moderate oven 30-40 minutes until tender.

DUCK (BRAISED)

1 Duck
1 onion
herbs
2 slices fat bacon
1 carrot
apple sauce
salt and pepper

Put the bacon in a saucepan and place the duck on it. Arrange the onion and carrot, cut in small pieces, round it. Add herbs and seasoning. Place the pan on the fire and allow to brown. Cover with 500 ml (1 pint) of good stock or water, put on the lid, and stew slowly for about 1½ hours. Serve with apple sauce.

DUCKLING (BRAISED)

1 Young Duckling
1 teaspoon cinnamon
3 dessertspoons oil or lard
1 tablespoon soya sauce
1 tablespoon brandy or dry sherry

Salt the duckling, mix the soya, brandy, or sherry and cinnamon together. Rub thoroughly into the skin of the duck. Put oil in frying pan and when smoking hot fry duckling till brown all over. Add 3 cups of water and bring to simmer. Put into saucepan and simmer for 1 hour. Thicken gravy with little cornflour. Serve with grilled slices of pineapple.

DUCK (ROAST)

1 Duck
1 cup boiling water
dripping
some strips bacon
1 teaspoon salt
apple sauce

Weigh, dress, stuff and truss the duck. Place on rack in roasting pan, with strips of bacon on the breast, and add the boiling water and salt. Roast in a hot oven 20 minutes to 500 gr (1 lb.) and 20 minutes over. Baste frequently during cooking. Serve with giblet gravy or apple sauce.

FOWL, EN CASSEROLE

1 Old Fowl
2 cups stock
parsley
peppercorns
60 gr (2 oz.) dripping
lemon juice
a bunch of herbs
salt and pepper
a few onions

Choose an old fowl and truss as for boiling, putting the liver, a piece of butter, a little minced parsley and lemon juice inside. Place the dripping in a casserole with some onions, parsley and peppercorns. Lay the fowl in and cook all together, turning and basting well till brown all over. Pour off the fat, add the stock (hot), bring to the boil, then draw to the side of stove and let simmer gently for 2 hours. Thicken the sauce round the fowl and serve.

GOOSE (ROAST)

1 Goose
seasoning

After the bird has been prepared in the usual way, trim off as much of the inside fat as possible. Season with sage and onions and bake for 2 hours. Serve with a rich, brown gravy and apple sauce.

TURKEY (ROAST)

1 Young Cock Turkey
forcemeat
flour
pepper and salt
butter
sausages

Singe, pick and rub the turkey well with a dry cloth; cut the head over by the shoulder, leaving the skin long in the front of the neck; cut through the skin only, all round, below the first joint of the legs, break the bones, draw the feet away to pull the tendons from the bird, and then draw it, taking care not to break the gall nor the gut; if properly done it will not require to be washed; break the backbone and dislocate the thigh joints; put a little salt and pepper into the inside, and put the vent over the rump. Have the forcemeat ready, and put it where the crop was taken out; sew it up and put a large skewer through the wing, the under side of the thigh, and the body, to the thigh and wing of the other side; press down the legs and put another skewer through them, down the side of the vent; have a piece of tape, put it firmly round the turkey, and fasten it on to the point of each of the skewers to keep the skin of the bird from giving way; put a piece of buttered paper over the breast of the turkey and put it to roast for 1½ to 2 hours. Dredge with flour, baste with butter, dish it, garnish with sausages, and pour the gravy over it.

GAME

KANGAROO STEAMER

500 gr (1 lb.) Kangaroo Steak
1 cup breadcrumbs
250 gr (½ lb.) bacon
1 teaspoon mixed herbs

Mince steak and bacon together. Mix well with other ingredients, moisten slightly with water, and mix again. Tie up tightly in cloth and boil quietly for 3 hours. A couple of beaten eggs may be added with advantage. Veal in the place of kangaroo is just as delicious.

KANGAROO STEAK

Leg Steaks from Kangaroo
1 teaspoon curry powder
1 egg
pepper and salt
breadcrumbs

Take nice flat steaks, roll in beaten egg, to which has been added and beaten in the curry powder, pepper and salt, and then roll in breadcrumbs and fry in hot fat. Serve with mashed potatoes.

PIGEON PIE

2 or 3 Pigeons
breadcrumbs
3 eggs (hard boiled)
seasoning
250 gr (½ lb.) rump steak
parsley
30 gr (1 oz.) butter
puff paste

Fill the pigeons with a seasoning made with butter, parsley, breadcrumbs, pepper and salt. Place half the steak in a pie-dish, lay the birds on it, and lay the remaining half of the steak on top. Around them arrange the hard boiled eggs cut in thick slices. Pour in a cup of good stock or water. Season with pepper and salt, and cover with a good puff paste. Cook for about 2 hours.

PIGEON (STEWED)

1 Pigeon
1 onion
juice of ½ a lemon
1 cup good mutton or chicken stock
1 or 2 slices of lean ham or bacon
butter
flour

Put stock, onion, bacon and lemon into a saucepan. Lay in the dressed pigeon, cover closely, and cook slowly for 2 hours. Take out the bird, add a piece of butter to gravy and thicken with flour.

RABBIT, BRAISED

1 Rabbit
30 gr (1 oz.) flour
90 gr (3 oz.) dripping
parsley
30 gr (1 oz.) butter
fat bacon
stock
thyme
lemon

Wash the rabbit and dry thoroughly. Cut it into neat pieces, and rub over with a cut lemon. Place the dripping in a pan, arrange rabbit with slices of bacon and fry quickly until nicely browned. Drain off any surplus fat, cover with some nice white stock, add salt, pepper and herbs tied in muslin, cover with a tight fitting lid and cook slowly from 1½ to 2 hours. Knead the butter and flour together and add to the contents of the saucepan about 15 minutes before serving.

RABBIT EN CASSEROLE

1 Rabbit
parsley
thyme
pepper
bacon
1½ cups milk, milk and water, or all water
breadcrumbs
nutmeg

RABBIT EN CASSEROLE—*continued*

Rub the casserole well with butter and line with breadcrumbs. Place on these some slices of fat bacon, and sprinkle with thyme and parsley (chopped). Wash the rabbit well (after having soaked in salt and water for several hours) and cut into small joints. Lay these in the casserole and sprinkle with breadcrumbs and seasonings. Cover with milk and cook slowly for about 2 hours. About 15 minutes before removing from the oven, take off the lid and allow the rabbit to brown.

RABBIT PIE

1 Rabbit
30 gr (1 oz.) breadcrumbs
1 tablespoon chopped parsley
1 onion
salt
stock or water
125 gr ($\frac{1}{4}$ lb.) fat bacon
a little grated lemon rind
1 egg
pepper
nutmeg
pastry

Wash the rabbit and dry thoroughly. Cut it into neat joints. Cook the bacon, keeping back about 30 gr (1 oz.) of the fat. Parboil the liver and heart, and chop up finely with the bacon fat. Add the parsley, seasoning and beaten egg, and make into small balls. Place the rabbit joints, the slices of bacon, and the forcemeat balls alternately in a pie-dish till all is used. Pepper and salt each layer, fill up with good stock or water in which the onion (cut finely) has been cooked, cover with a nice short crust, brush over with beaten egg, and bake for 1 hour in a moderate oven.

RABBIT, ROAST

1 Rabbit
bacon
forcemeat
dripping
salt and pepper

Wash and dry the rabbit, fill with a nice forcemeat (as for poultry), truss and tie into shape. Place in a baking dish with pieces of fat bacon on top, and plenty of good dripping. Season with salt and pepper, and bake in a moderate oven for 1½ to 2 hours, basting frequently. When rather more than three parts cooked remove the bacon to allow the rabbit to brown nicely. Dredge with flour, add a tablespoon butter, and continue basting till cooking is completed. Serve with its own gravy and apple or any tart jelly.

RABBIT WITH LENTIL PUREE

1 Rabbit
stock (2 cups)
herbs
salt and pepper
small cup lentils
butter

Cut the rabbit into joints, and stew gently in the stock with herbs, salt and pepper, adding more stock or water if required. Cook the lentils (previously soaked in warm water) in some of the stock from the rabbit, and when tender, pass through a sieve. Lift the rabbit from the saucepan, and add the lentil puree to the gravy. Return the rabbit, reheat and serve with croutons of fried bread arranged round the dish.

COLD MEATS

ABERDEEN SAUSAGE

500 gr (1 lb.) Lean Steak (or equal parts steak and shin meat)
250 gr (½ lb.) bacon or ham
1 egg
1 teaspoon sugar
grated rind of one lemon
1 large cup fresh breadcrumbs
1 tablespoon Worcester sauce
1 small teaspoon salt
plain flour

Mince the steak and bacon, add sauce, breadcrumbs and other ingredients, and bind together with egg. Shape mixture into a large sausage and sprinkle it heavily with plain flour. Place on a floured pudding cloth. Roll up and tie the ends securely. Place in boiling water and boil for 1½ hours. Leave in water until water becomes cold. Remove from cloth, sprinkle with dry breadcrumbs and garnish with parsley.

BRAWN (No. 1)

1 Sheep's Head
1 dessertspoon gelatine
salt
mixed spice
cayenne pepper
500 ml (1 pint) water

Simmer sheep's head in about 500 ml (1 pint) water for 2 hours, or until the meat leaves the bone. Then cut into small pieces and season to taste with spice, cayenne and salt. Put into a pie-dish or basin, add the liquid, and stand in a cool place to set. In hot weather it is advisable to add the gelatine and leave overnight.

BRAWN (No. 2), ECONOMICAL

½ Pig's Head
500 gr (1 lb.) shin of beef
salt
2 pig's feet
allspice
pepper

Remove eye from head and chop the head and feet well. Put head, feet and beef all together in a saucepan and just cover with water. Bring to the boil and continue boiling slowly until meat will fall from bones. Then take out and remove all bone and gristle. Put in a basin and season well. Boil liquid down to about half the quantity and pour it over the meat. Leave until quite cold and set. Scrape off any fat that may have risen to the top, then turn out.

BRAWN (OX CHEEK)

2 Ox Cheeks
1 teaspoon pepper
a little grated nutmeg
1 tablespoon salt
½ teaspoon mace
allspice

Soak the cheeks in salt and water for an hour or more, wash well, and put on to stew gently until quite tender. Add salt and other seasonings. Take the meat out when well-cooked and break up with a fork. Put back into the liquid and mix well. Pour into a basin previously rinsed with cold water and put aside until set. Turn out and garnish with parsley.

BRAWN (RABBIT)

1 Rabbit
6 allspice
1 dozen peppercorns
rind of ½ lemon
2 tspns. gelatine
1 onion
1 blade mace
185 gr (6 oz.) bacon
6 cloves
2 hard boiled eggs
a little parsley
salt

Scald bacon. Put rabbit in a saucepan, cover with cold water and bring to the boil. Add salt and skim well. Then add the bacon, onion, spice, parsley and lemon rind, and let it boil gently till the meat will come easily off the bone. Cut meat up. Cut eggs into slices and decorate the mould in which the brawn is to be set. Put in the rabbit and bacon, the rest of the egg, and a little chopped parsley. Soak gelatine in water and when soft, add to some of the rabbit stock, with a little lemon juice to flavour. Fill the moulds and set aside to set. This should make 2 moulds of 500 ml (1 pint) each.

BRAWN (KANGAROO TAIL AND PIG'S HEAD)
Original

1 Kangaroo Tail
1 blade mace
½ small pig's head
mixed herbs
pepper and salt

Cut up or joint the kangaroo tail and put it, with the pig's head and other ingredients, on to boil. Boil until the meat falls off the bones. Then take out all the bones and pour the mixture into shallow dishes and let stand until set. It needs cool weather or an ice-chest. Failing pig's head, I use belly pieces, or bacon, half fat, half lean.

CHICKEN SHAPE

1 Chicken
½ cup minced ham
1 hard boiled egg
sprig each of parsley, thyme
2 tablespoons cooked peas
2 dessertspoons gelatine
water
salt and pepper

Cut chicken into neat joints and put into double saucepan over boiling water. Add herbs, sprinkling of salt and ½ cup water. Cook until meat leaves the bones. Leave till cool and then cut into small pieces. Remove fat from liquid and add gelatine dissolved in ½ cup water. Measure liquid and if necessary make up to 500 ml (1 pint). Fill mould with pieces of chicken, minced ham, peas and slices of egg. Pour in jelly when it is just thickening. Chill and serve with green salads.

COLD MEAT MOULD

Hard Boiled Eggs
pickles
gravy
beetroot or tomatoes
beef, mutton and bacon
gelatine
parsley
pepper and salt

Butter a pie-dish, cut up hard boiled eggs in thin slices and place round the dish and at the bottom. Cut thin slices of cooked beef, mutton and bacon and lay in the dish. Spread some chopped pickles over them, and season with pepper and salt. Pour over some rich gravy in which sufficient gelatine (to set) has been dissolved. Let stand until cold. Turn out on to a dish, garnish with beetroot or tomatoes and a little parsley.

EGG AND RABBIT MOULD

1 Rabbit
2 dessertspoons powdered gelatine
½ teaspoon sugar
3 hard boiled eggs
1 onion
½ teaspoon lemon juice
pepper and salt to taste

Take a young rabbit, cut up, and place in salted water for ½ an hour. Rinse thoroughly and place in a saucepan with 2 cups water, pepper, onion and other ingredients. Bring slowly to the boil and allow to cook slowly till tender. Line a wet mould with sliced boiled eggs. Remove rabbit meat from the bones and cut into thin slices and arrange with the eggs in the mould. Dissolve the gelatine in the hot stock and strain into the mould. Freeze. Turn out on a dish and garnish with shredded lettuce, thin slices of tomato and hard boiled egg.

GARLIC SAUSAGE

500 gr (1 lb.) Topside Steak
1 egg
a small piece chopped garlic
1 large cup breadcrumbs
3 cloves
pepper and salt

Mince steak finely, add breadcrumbs, cloves and garlic, with pepper and salt to taste, and bind with beaten egg. Place in floured cloth and boil for 1½ hours. To be eaten cold.

MEAT MOULD

2 Dessertspoons Gelatine
2 cups cold meat
2 cups good stock
1 teaspoon curry powder
any seasoning desired

Soak gelatine in stock and heat over the fire. Stir until dissolved, and leave to cool. When beginning to thicken add seasoned meat. Put aside to set in a mould.

MEAT ROLL

500 gr (1 lb.) Beef Steak or Mutton
125 gr (¼ lb.) breadcrumbs
1 tablespoon milk or cream
125 gr (¼ lb.) ham
2 hard boiled eggs
1 egg to bind
salt and pepper

Mince meat and add other ingredients. Make a roll. Dip a cloth in boiling water, then sprinkle cloth with flour. Put the roll into the cloth and boil for 4 hours. Press under weights till cold.

MIDDLESEX PIE

500 gr (1 lb.) Steak or Kangaroo Steak
2 cups breadcrumbs
1 tablespoon Worcester sauce
250 gr (½ lb.) bacon or pickled cheeks, etc.
2 eggs
herbs pepper and salt

Mince meat, mix well with the other ingredients and press into a basin with greased paper in bottom. Tie down and steam for 3 or 4 hours. Turn out when cold and serve with salad.

PRESSED BEEF

About 1 kg (2 lb.) Beef (pieces will do)
salt and pepper
2 tablespoons gelatine
nutmeg
ground mace

Put the beef in a saucepan and just cover with cold water. Add salt, pepper and spices to taste. Let all simmer gently for about 4 hours. Put the meat into a basin. Dissolve the gelatine in just enough of the liquid the meat was boiled in to cover the meat. Pour over and leave till set. This is very nice served with salads.

PRESSED SHOULDER OF MUTTON

1 Shoulder of Mutton (corned by the butcher)
1 teaspoon whole allspice
1 egg cup vinegar
1 teaspoon whole pepper
hard boiled eggs

Put the mutton into boiling water with the vinegar and spices added (the spices tied in muslin), and boil till the meat leaves the bone (about 3½ hours). Scrape the meat off the bone into a basin already decorated with slices of hard boiled egg. Pour a little of the liquid on and press. Serve cold with salad. Flap is very nice prepared as above, but boned and rolled.

PRESSED TONGUE

1 Flap of Mutton
some gherkins
6 sheep's tongues
1 blade mace

Boil the mutton till tender enough for the bones to slip out. It will be one long strip. Prepare the tongues in the usual way and sprinkle with chopped gherkins or onions. Roll together in the mutton and press.

SAUSAGE JELLIED

500 gr (1 lb.) Cold Cooked Sausages
¾ cup stock
1 cup whipped cream or rich milk
1 dessertspoon gelatine
¼ cup cold water
lettuce salad

Remove the skins from the sausages and cut the meat into inch pieces. Soak the gelatine in cold water, add the stock, boiling, and when nearly cold add the cream or milk and lastly the prepared sausage meat. Set in a basin, and when cold turn out on to lettuce leaves. Serve with a lettuce salad.

VEAL LOAF

2 kg (4 lb.) Knuckle of Veal
1 small onion
4 hard boiled eggs
1 teaspoon chopped celery
salt and pepper to taste

Put meat in saucepan with onion and cover with boiling water. Cook gently until tender. Remove from liquid, cool, and put it through the mincer. Garnish bottom of mould with slices of hard boiled egg and parsley. Put in ½ of meat, cover with slices of egg and sprinkle with parsley. Cover with remaining meat. Reduce liquid to 1 cupful and pour over meat. Press and chill, turn on to a dish, garnish with parsley, and serve.

ASPIC JELLY

2 Cups Clear Stock or Water
3 slices of carrot
a few cloves
3 tablespoons vinegar
1 small onion
1 sprig of parsley
2 tablespoons gelatine
salt to taste

Soak the gelatine in a little of the stock or water. Boil the remaining ingredients for 5 minutes, add the gelatine, and strain. Put away to set. This jelly can be coloured with vegetable colourings, and cut into various shapes for use in garnishing cold meats, or it can be used as a foundation for salad by adding, when nearly cold, sliced beetroot, cold, cooked green peas, tomatoes, or any cooked vegetables, taking care to blend colours nicely. Set in glass mould, and when firm turn out on to lettuce leaves.

NOTE.—Meat, poultry or fish can also be set in aspic. For a specially clear aspic jelly, add when boiling the crushed shell and white of an egg. Care must be taken when straining; two strainings through a jelly bag may be found necessary.

CHICKEN (JELLIED)

This is an appetising method of serving a fowl that requires long cooking to reduce it to a tender condition. It is especially suitable for invalids.

1 Fowl
2 carrots
a little salt
mint leaves
2 onions
2 or 3 sticks celery
egg
about 2-3 litres (2-3 quarts) boiling water

Place the fowl with the vegetables in a saucepan, with enough boiling water to cover, and simmer until tender. A fowl weighing $1\frac{1}{2}$-2 kg (3-4 lb.) will take two to three hours. Remove the fowl, strain the stock and flavour with salt. Leave overnight to cool. Remove the flesh from the bones of the fowl, dice and place it in small moulds that have been decorated with slices of egg and mint leaves. Add jellied stock, from which fat has been removed, and which has been softened by slightly warming, to the chicken, and put in a cold place to set. Serve on lettuce leaves with salad dressing and tomato to garnish. If the stock is not sufficiently stiff, boil it in a saucepan without a lid to reduce the quantity of water and thus render it more gelatinous.

REHEATED MEATS

AUSTRALIAN PIE

500 gr (1 lb.) Cold Roast Mutton
4 Oxo cubes
2 tablespoons flour
250 ml (½ pint) milk
slices bread
30 gr (1 oz.) dripping
1 large onion
½ teaspoon baking powder
1 egg
pepper and salt

Put a few slices of mutton at the bottom of a dish. Sprinkle with minced onions, pepper and salt, and cover with the bread. Repeat until the dish is full. Spread the top slices of each layer thickly with dripping and moisten with ½ an Oxo cube, mixed with hot water. Make a batter with the flour, milk, egg and baking powder. Pour into the pie-dish and bake in a moderate oven for ¾ hour.

A DEVIL (very hot)

Some Thin Slices of Cold Meat, Fowl or Kidneys
1 teaspoon mustard
2 teaspoons Worcester sauce
½ teaspoon cayenne pepper
1 teaspoon lemon juice or a wine glass of claret or Burgundy
1 teaspoon white wine or vinegar
2 teaspoons mushroom ketchup
1 teaspoon salad oil or butter, if no fat on meat

Cut up thin slices of meat and lay on a shallow dish. Pour over the mixture made from the above ingredients. Set dish in oven and let meat stew slowly for about ¼ hour.

FRICASSEE OF SHEEP'S TONGUES

1 Tin Sheep's Tongues
1 dessertspoon flour
1 onion
1 egg
a pinch mace
1 dessertspoon butter
2 tablespoons milk
1 cup gravy made from gravy salt
a little parsley
a pinch nutmeg
seasoning

Empty tin of tongues into a stewpan and add gravy. Place on fire and allow to heat thoroughly (the tongues can be cut in halves), with the seasonings and parsley added. Put the butter and the flour blended with the milk, into a small pan and cook for a few minutes after it boils. Lift the tongues on to a dish and add butter mixture to the gravy. Draw aside from fire and add well-beaten egg. Return the tongues to saucepan and heat but do not boil. Serve with mashed potatoes.

MEAT SHAPE (A Nice Hot Dinner)

Meat
30 gr (1 oz.) butter
pinch ground mace
parsley
1 small teacup breadcrumbs
2 eggs
1 small onion (if liked)
pepper and salt

Carefully remove all skin and gristle from cold meat. Mince or chop finely. Season with pepper and salt, mace and a little chopped parsley, onion and breadcrumbs. Add the well-beaten eggs and melted butter. Mix well together, pour into a buttered basin, cover with a sheet of buttered paper, and steam for 2 hours. Turn out on hot dish, cover with a rich brown gravy, and serve with mashed potatoes.

MEAT TIMBALE

250 gr ($\frac{1}{2}$ lb.) Cold Meat
125 gr ($\frac{1}{4}$ lb.) cooked mushrooms
rind of $\frac{1}{2}$ lemon
2 eggs
60 gr (2 oz.) breadcrumbs
125 ml ($\frac{1}{4}$ pint) stock
$\frac{1}{2}$ teaspoon chopped parsley
pepper and salt

Mince meat finely, chop mushrooms and soak crumbs in stock. Put them all together in a bowl with the parsley, seasoning and beaten eggs and mix well. Turn into a greased bowl and steam for 30 minutes, then dish up and decorate with mashed potatoes or green peas.

MINCE LOAF

500 gr (1 lb.) Steak (or any cold meat)
2 onions
1 potato
$\frac{1}{2}$ cup plain flour
125 gr ($\frac{1}{4}$ lb.) fat ham or bacon
1 tomato
a few herbs
1 egg
pepper and salt

Mince together the steak, ham, onions, tomato, potato and herbs, then add pepper and salt to taste. Then mix together the flour and egg. Mix well together and roll in a ball. Place in a saucepan with 1 cup water and a little dripping and place round some potatoes and onions. This makes a nice lunch for 4 or 5 persons.

MUTTON (SCRAMBLED)

1 Tin Boiled Mutton
2 tablespoons gravy
3 eggs
125 gr (4 oz.) butter
seasoning
buttered toast

Place butter and gravy with seasoning into a saucepan, add mutton cut into small pieces, and when the meat is thoroughly hot, add the eggs slightly beaten. Stir, and when the mixture stiffens, put on pieces of hot buttered toast and serve.

RISSOLES FROM TINNED MEAT

1 Cup Minced Tinned Mutton or Beef	**2 cups mashed potatoes**
1 onion, minced	**1 tablespoon cornflour**
1 egg	**pepper and salt**
	a little nutmeg to taste

Mix all ingredients well together and mould together with egg (if small two eggs may be required). Roll in breadcrumbs. Drop into smoking hot fat, and cook till a nice brown. Serve with tomato sauce made hot.

ROAST MUTTON

2 Cups Tinned Roast Mutton	**1 egg**
1 onion	**a little stock**
some chopped parsley	**salt and pepper**
1 cup breadcrumbs	

Put the meat and onion through the mincer (or chop finely), add breadcrumbs and seasoning to taste, beat the egg and add to stock, and mix all together thoroughly. Well grease a pie-dish, sprinkle over with breadcrumbs, put in the mixture, and press well down. Bake in a moderate oven until nicely browned. Serve with tomato sauce made hot.

SHEEP'S TONGUES

1 Tin Tongues	**breadcrumbs**
melted butter	**seasoning**

Remove the tongues from the tin, cut into pieces, dip in melted butter, and coat with breadcrumbs. Season to taste, and fry in bacon fat till nicely browned.

SHEPHERD PIE

250 gr ($\frac{1}{2}$ lb.) Cold Mutton	**500 gr (1 lb.) mashed potatoes**
30 gr (1 oz.) dripping	**250 ml ($\frac{1}{2}$ pint) stock**
1 small onion	**salt and pepper**

Cut the meat into small, thin slices. Melt the dripping in a stewpan, put in the potato, salt and pepper, and stir over the fire until well mixed and brown. Grease a pie-dish, line the bottom thinly with potato and sprinkle with the parboiled and chopped onion. Lay in the meat, sprinkle with the rest of the onion, season with salt and pepper, and pour in the stock. Cover with a lid of potato. Roughen the top with a fork, dot with dripping and bake in a moderate oven for 40 minutes.

STEAK ROLY POLY

250 gr (½ lb.) Cooked Steak
2 dessertspoons chopped parsley
1 dessertspoon ketchup
suet crust
1 dessertspoon chopped onion
½ teaspoon powdered herbs
2 tablespoons gravy
salt and pepper

Mince the meat finely and add to it the finely chopped onion, parsley and powdered herbs. Mix well, season with salt and pepper and moisten with the ketchup and the gravy. Roll out the suet crust into oblong shape about 19 mm (¾ in.) thick. Wet round the edges with water and spread with the meat mixture, keeping it an inch from the edge all round. Roll up, pressing the edges well together, tie up in a floured cloth, plunge in boiling water, and boil for 2 hours.

RICE AND MEAT (A Tasty Dish)

2 Cups of Cold Cooked Meat
1 egg
1 cup of stock (hot)
2 tablespoons breadcrumbs
1 cup of rice
1 small onion (minced)
1 teaspoon celery salt
pinch of herbs
pepper to taste
1 teaspoon salt
3 cups boiling water

Steam the rice in the boiling water with salt for 25 minutes. Chop the meat finely, add all seasonings, then the beaten egg, stock and breadcrumbs. Line the bottom and sides of a greased basin with half an inch thick of cooked rice, pack in the meat, cover closely with rice. Cover with greased paper and steam for 45 minutes. Loosen the edge, turn on to a hot plate and serve with hot tomato sauce poured over. Garnish the top with chopped parsley.

CURRY DISHES

CURRIED EGGS

1 Onion	1 apple
pepper and salt	curry powder
a little chutney	butter
1 hard boiled egg for each person	stock

Melt some butter in a frying pan (about 1 tablespoon), chop the apple and onion and fry them in butter. Add about 1 dessertspoon curry powder. Fry for about 10 minutes and then stir in a cup of good stock, and add seasoning, chutney and the hard boiled eggs. Cook for about 20 minutes and serve with boiled rice.

CURRIED FRESH MEAT

250 gr ($\frac{1}{2}$ lb.) Fresh Meat	3 onions
1 tablespoon curry powder	$\frac{1}{2}$ cup of cream
$\frac{1}{2}$ sliced apple	stock
salt to taste	lemon juice
90 gr (3 oz.) butter	

Put the butter into a saucepan with sliced onions, and cook till brown. Add the meat cut in small pieces, with the curry powder sprinkled over it; allow it to colour, and then add the stock and apples. Stew for an hour or more, and add salt and lemon juice. Add cream just before serving.

CURRIED KIDNEYS AND EGG SURPRISE

2 Sheep's Kidneys	1 small onion
30 gr (1 oz.) butter	30 gr (1 oz.) flour
2 eggs	$\frac{3}{4}$ cup stock or water
$\frac{1}{2}$ teaspoon chopped parsley	2 slices of bread
pinch of salt	1 teaspoon curry powder

Parboil the kidneys and chop into small pieces, melt butter and fry onion a golden brown. Remove onion and fry kidneys. Stir in the flour, stock and curry powder, parsley and salt. Simmer for $\frac{1}{2}$ an hour. Toast the bread, cut into rounds and serve the kidneys on these with a lightly poached egg on top of each.

CURRIED LENTILS

1 Breakfast Cup Lentils
1 teaspoon vinegar
1 teaspoon curry powder
90 gr (3 oz.) butter
1 small saltspoon of salt
boiled rice
1 small chopped onion

Soak the lentils overnight in cold water. Next morning boil in just sufficient water to cover them, adding the vinegar, butter and salt. Stir constantly as they burn readily. When all the moisture is absorbed, and the lentils form a smooth paste, add the curry powder and onion. The onion should first be fried a good brown in butter. Make all very hot, and serve with boiled rice.

CURRIED MEAT

500 gr (1 lb.) Finely Minced Cold Meat, Beef or Mutton or any other cold meat available
2 onions
1 tablespoon cooking butter
pepper, pinch of salt
1 tablespoon curry powder, or less if liked mild
1 large cooking apple
1 dessertspoon flour
a few sultanas
1 cup of stock or water

Cut the apple and onions very fine and fry in the butter. Mix the curry powder and flour and add the salt, pepper and stock. Stir in the meat and sultanas, and simmer gently for 20 minutes, stirring frequently. Serve very hot with rice. Coconut is an improvement in all curries.

CURRIED RABBIT

1 Rabbit
2 tablespoons good dripping
1 tablespoon curry powder
2 cups good mutton stock
1 teaspoon each flour and salt
2 medium sized onions
1 tablespoon coconut
juice of 1 lemon
½ cup milk
rice
a little cinnamon and nutmeg

Cut up the rabbit and soak overnight in milk and water Next morning cut the rabbit meat into small pieces, slice the onions very thin, dredge them with flour and curry powder and fry in the dripping till tender. Add the meat and stir till slightly browned. Add hot stock, salt, nutmeg, cinnamon, coconut, and simmer slowly for about 2 hours. Add the lemon juice, and lastly the milk. Serve very hot with dry rice prepared as for other curries.

CURRIED RISSOLES

500 gr (1 lb.) Lean Meat
1 dessertspoon vinegar
1 egg
1 large onion
1 tablespoon curry powder
water
a pinch herbs
1 dessertspoon sugar
salt and pepper
1 tablespoon flour
a little Worcester sauce
a little desiccated coconut

Mince the meat, add the herbs, salt, pepper, vinegar, sugar and sauce. Beat the egg well and add to the mixture. Form into small round cakes. Fry the onion in a little dripping till brown, mix in the flour and curry powder, and add enough water to make a nice rich gravy. Drop in the rissoles and simmer for ¾ of an hour if raw meat is used. If cooked meat is used 20 minutes will be sufficient. Before dishing sprinkle in a little coconut.

CURRY, WITH SALAD

Make a dry curry (the onions must be fried in butter, or it will be greasy). When the curry is quite cold (it may be placed on ice) place portions on crisp lettuce leaves. Serve each portion with salad and a good dressing and decorate with slices of tomatoes. This curry is very good in using up scraps, left over tongues or sausages.

DRY CURRY

1 Sliced Onion
curry powder
1 tablespoon marmalade
1 dessertspoon Worcestershire sauce
1 dessertspoon butter
1 sliced apple
salt and pepper
½ cup milk
cold meat

Fry the onion until it is quite brown. Have ready a clean frying pan, into which put your curry powder; well brown the powder and add butter, fried onion, apple, sauce, marmalade, seasonings and milk. Have your meat cut into very small pieces and add, stirring all together. Cook for about 35 minutes or until the gravy has dried up. Garnish with boiled rice.

TOMATO CURRY

125 gr (4 oz.) Rice
1 tablespoon milk
1 teaspoon curry powder
2 tomatoes
1 teacup stock (or meat essence and water)
seasoning
45 gr (1½ oz.) butter
2 shallots, or half a small onion

TOMATO CURRY—*continued*

Dripping may be used instead of butter. Melt the butter, add the shallots, peeled and cut up. When golden brown, stir in curry powder, cook for another five minutes. Add rice, which has been thoroughly washed and drained, the stock, thickened with a little flour if necessary, and the milk. Blend all carefully together. Add more liquid if necessary.

Stir in tomato, peeled and diced, with salt, pepper and grated nutmeg to taste. Stir gently and often, and let it simmer till the rice is quite tender. Serve piled up on a hot dish, with slices of tomato placed around it, and if liked a few sprigs of cress or parsley.

VEGETABLE CURRY

30 gr (1 oz.) Butter
1 small apple
juice 1 lemon
1 cup water
sugar
1 teaspoon curry powder
1 teaspoon chutney
1 onion
salt and pepper
cold vegetables

Peel the apple and onion and slice very thinly. Fry in the butter for a few minutes, add flour, curry powder and the chutney, then the water, and stir until it boils. Season to taste and add the lemon juice. Have ready any cooked vegetables, place these in the curried sauce, and allow to simmer for a few minutes. Serve with boiled rice.

RICE FOR CURRY

Put your rice into boiling water with a little salt. Boil very fast for 15 to 20 minutes. Pour rice into sieve, wash it well under a tap of cold water, then put near fire to dry. Turn it about with a wooden spoon, so as to dry and separate the grain. Drop a few drops of lemon juice into the rice while boiling. It whitens it.

Add raisins to any curry recipe, and you will find they will improve it a great deal.

To give a delicious flavour to a curry add one tablespoon raspberry jam just before serving.

LIVER DISHES

When cooking lamb's fry boil the liver for a few minutes in boiling water. This will keep it from becoming hard when frying. Lift out of the water and dry. Roll in flour and drop in boiling fat.

BAKED LIVER AND BACON

1 Fry
1 medium sized onion
1 tablespoon of flour
250 gr (½ lb.) bacon
pepper to taste

Place a layer of liver, dredged in flour, in a casserole, then some onion, then bacon, till the casserole is full. Cover with water and bake in a moderate oven for 1½ to 2 hours.

BAKED LIVER

750 gr (1½ lb.) Calf Liver
1 egg
3 tablespoons butter
2 onions (medium size)
1 cup of tomato soup
1½ cups browned breadcrumbs
2 large tablespoons minced parsley
1 tablespoon minced celery leaves
1 large cup good soup stock
pepper, salt and nutmeg to taste

Place the liver in a basin and pour over it enough boiling water to completely cover. Allow to stand for 5 minutes. Drain and dry the liver, and put it through the mincer. Add the breadcrumbs, herbs, seasonings and onion, minced finely; bind with the well-beaten egg. Mix well and mould with the hands into a shape to fit a cake or bread tin and keep the hands well floured while moulding. Bake in a moderate oven for 1 hour. Mix together the stock and tomato soup, and heat. If on the thin side thicken with a little cornflour blended with milk, but do not allow to boil more than 1 minute after thickening is added. Pour over the baked loaf and return to the oven for about 15 minutes.

BRAISED CALF'S LIVER

1 Liver
a few slices of bacon
parsley
1 turnip
pepper and salt
celery
2 carrots
2 onions
3 cloves
butter
boiling water
6 allspice

BRAISED CALF'S LIVER—*continued*

Tie the liver in a roll. Fry the onion and carrot (sliced) in butter. Put the bacon in a saucepan and cook a few minutes; then lay in the liver, keep turning and allow to heat on all sides. Add the fried vegetables, other vegetables and seasonings, and enough boiling water to half cover the liver. Lay a slice of bacon on top, cover and bring to a rapid boil, then draw aside and simmer gently for 2 hours or more. When the liver is perfectly cooked and firm to the touch place on a hot dish and put the vegetables around it. Bring the gravy to a quick boil, add to it a thickening made of a teaspoon of butter and a large teaspoon of flour, stirred over the fire till brown and blended with a little of the gravy. Stir and boil briskly for a few minutes. Serve with the liver.

CURRIED LAMB'S FRY

1 Lamb's Fry	**bacon**
onions	**pepper and salt**
1 dessertspoon curry powder	**1 dessertspoon flour**

Slice the fry and roll slices in flour. Place a layer in a casserole or pie-dish, then a layer of bacon, and so on until the dish is nearly full. Place a layer of sliced onions on top, season with salt and pepper, cover with water and cook in a slow oven for 2½ hours. About ½ an hour before it is cooked mix together the curry powder and flour with water and stir in.

CURRIED LIVER

250 gr (8 oz.) Liver or Lamb's Fry	**1 teaspoon flour**
1 teaspoon good chutney	**1 teaspoon curry powder**
2 teacups of stock	**½ teaspoon of lemon juice**
slice of apple or ½ stick of rhubarb	**seasoning to taste**
	1 onion

Make the sauce first. Peel, scald and chop the onion and chop the apple or rhubarb. Blend the flour and curry powder in a little of the stock (stock must be free from fat).

Put the rest of stock on to boil, add onion, apple, chutney and cook till the onion is tender. Stir in flour, etc., and simmer 2 minutes longer. Meanwhile cut the liver in small pieces as for any other curry. Add to the curry sauce, and simmer for 15 minutes, or till the liver is tender. Add the lemon juice. Serve with a little plain boiled rice.

Liver lightly grilled and served with cooked tomato makes quite a pleasant dish.

FAGGOTS

1 Sheep's Fry
1 dessertspoon dried sage
pepper and salt to taste
125 gr (¼ lb.) bacon
2 cups oatmeal
flour

Cut the fry into thick slices, fry in hot fat for 2 minutes on each side, then put through a mincer with the bacon. Add sage, oatmeal, pepper and salt. Mix all together in a basin and roll into balls. Rub some fat on a roasting tin, place faggots on this and cover with a greased paper. Bake in a hot oven for ½ an hour. Put a heaped tablespoon of flour into dripping in the frying pan in which the liver was cooked, stir with a wooden spoon till a pale brown colour and add boiling water or stock to make a thick gravy. Season and serve with faggots and mashed potatoes.

LIVER AND BACON

1 Sheep's Fry
250 gr (½ lb.) bacon
1 tablespoon dripping
4 onions

Wash the fry and cut into slices 52 mm (2 in.) thick. Melt a tablespoon of dripping in a frying pan and cook the slices on both sides till brown. Roll bacon rashers on skewers, and place on a tin in oven shelf to cook. Slice and fry 4 onions and make a gravy and serve very hot with mashed potatoes. Make the gravy the same as for faggots.

LIVER AND VEGETABLES, EN CASSEROLE

250 gr (8 oz.) Liver
1 onion
pinch of powdered herbs
1 tablespoon mushroom ketchup
1 teacup of stock
1 heaped teaspoon parsley
pepper and salt
2 tomatoes

Peel and slice the onion, slice the tomato, cut the liver in slices and chop the parsley. Place the vegetables in the casserole, sprinkling the parsley between. Add the stock. Place in a hot oven and cook till the vegetables are nearly ready. Add the sliced liver, piling the vegetables on top of it. Put on the lid, return to the oven, and cook till the liver is tender (about 30 minutes longer). This dish may be varied, by varying the vegetables. Mushrooms are nice when procurable.

LIVER PASTE

1 Liver
¼ teaspoon mace
1 tablespoon vinegar
1 teaspoon cloves
1 teaspoon of salt
¼ teaspoon cayenne pepper
cold water
30 gr (1 oz.) of butter
1 teaspoon whole pepper

Cut the liver into finger lengths and put into a jar or double saucepan. Add salt, cayenne pepper, vinegar, mace and water, (cloves and whole pepper tied in a muslin bag). Cover closely and simmer slowly for 3 or 4 hours. When cooked, lift out the liver and pass through a mincer. Mix with the gravy, add the butter, and pour into jars when cold.

MOCK GOOSE

Liver
sage, onions
flour
potatoes
cup of water
pepper and salt

Place a layer of thin slices of fry in a baking dish, then a layer of sliced potatoes and sprinkle generously with chopped sage and onions. Add alternate layers of fry and potatoes until the dish is full. Dredge with flour, season with pepper and salt. Add a cup of cold water and cook 2 hours in a slow oven.

STEAMED LAMB'S FRY

1 Lamb's Fry
1 dessertspoon butter
1 cup water
salt and pepper

Wash the fry and wipe it dry with a cloth. Butter a small casserole dish, the lid as well. Put in the fry, add cold water, put butter in small dabs on top of fry. Put on lid and bake in a moderate oven for 1 hour, basting and turning fry every 15 minutes. After it has been cooking for ½ an hour, both sides for an equal period, season with salt and pepper. Serve with its own gravy. Very suitable for anaemic people.

FORCEMEATS

CELERY AND APPLE STUFFING FOR GOOSE

1 Tablespoon Minced Onion
1 cup minced celery
1 cup minced apples
2 tablespoons butter
1 cup soft breadcrumbs
salt and pepper

Put the onion and the butter in a frying pan and brown, then add celery and apple. Cook for 5 minutes, then put in the breadcrumbs and seasoning.

FORCEMEAT

1 Cup Breadcrumbs
1 onion
seasoning
60 gr (2 oz.) butter
1 egg
1 teaspoon dried herbs
milk

Mix all the dry ingredients together. Put the butter into a frying pan, add the onion chopped fine, and fry to a golden brown. Add to the remaining ingredients and add sufficient milk to bind the mixture. This is suitable for stuffing any kind of game or meat.

FORCEMEAT (VEAL)

250 gr (½ lb.) Breadcrumbs
2 teaspoons herbs
⅛ teaspoon cayenne
salt
2 tablespoons chopped parsley
60 gr (2 oz.) suet or butter
1 grated lemon rind
egg
milk

Grate suet, add other dry ingredients and add sufficient egg and milk to make a crumbly mixture.

SEASONING FOR XMAS TURKEY

2 Pork Sausages
90 gr (3 oz.) chopped suet
½ teaspoon mixed herbs
½ lemon rind and juice
185 gr (6 oz.) breadcrumbs
3 tablespoons chopped parsley
1 egg
milk
salt and pepper

Mix together dry ingredients with lemon rind and juice and blend with egg and milk to a crumbly mixture.

PLAIN DRESSING FOR FOWL OR FISH

½ Loaf Bread
1 egg
seasoning
1 small ½ cup butter and add a little milk
1 teaspoon powdered sage

Cut the bread in slices, dip in cold water to soften, chop the butter into small pieces and add with seasonings to the bread. Stir in the well-beaten egg. Fill the cavity in fowl, fish or meat with the dressing. Allow for swelling. A great variety of dressings may be made by adding chopped onions, dates, celery, parsley, raisins or chopped giblets.

SAUCES

APPLE SAUCE (No. 1)

500 gr (1 lb.) Soft Apples
salt
1 tablespoon vinegar
pepper
sugar

Grate the apples, add seasonings and vinegar and simmer till tender. Serve with poultry or roast pork.

APPLE SAUCE (No. 2)

6 Cooking Apples
⅓ cup water
2 tablespoons sugar
juice of ½ lemon

Wipe, quarter, peel and core apples, add water and cook until tender. Add sugar and lemon if desired, but sauce should be fairly dry.

CELERY SAUCE

1 Head Celery
1 tablespoon butter
1 tablespoon flour
1 cup milk
seasonings

Break the celery into small pieces, and cover with cold water. Bring to boil, boil 2 or 3 minutes and drain off the water. Add the milk and simmer until the celery is tender. Rub through a sieve. Melt the butter, work in the flour, and add with seasoning to the celery. Heat up again and serve.

CREAM SAUCE

250 ml (½ Pint) Milk
2 egg yolks
1 tablespoon butter
seasonings

Warm the milk, add the butter, and then the egg yolks, with salt and pepper to taste. Beat all together, and just bring to boiling point. Serve with boiled fish or fowl.

DUTCH SAUCE

60 gr (2 oz.) Butter
2 tablespoons vinegar
yolks of 2 eggs
1 small teaspoon flour
2 tablespoons water
juice of half a lemon

Blend the flour and butter, add the vinegar and water, and stir over the fire for a minute, then add the yolks of the eggs, well beaten, and continue to stir till it thickens. It must not boil. When ready for serving, add the lemon juice. Great care is required in preparing, as it is likely to curdle, when it will require straining.

MINT SAUCE (An Easy Way)

Sugar
mint leaves
vinegar

Take a jar (one with a glass lid), put a layer of sugar in the bottom, then a layer of mint leaves (use only the leaves), then a layer of sugar, then more leaves, and so on alternately until the bottle is full. Press down tightly as each layer is added. Fill the bottle to the top with vinegar (the best), then close. Keep in a dry place. You have mint sauce ever ready. It can be added to if required from time to time, as it is used, by adding more leaves and sugar.

SAUCE FOR COLD MEAT (No. 1)

3 or 4 Tablespoons Red Currant or Grape Jelly
1 tablespoon mustard
a little water
juice of 1 lemon
minced peel of ½ an orange

Mix well together.

SAUCE FOR COLD MEAT (No. 2)

1 Tablespoon Mixed Mustard
1 tablespoon castor sugar
2 tablespoons vinegar
4 tablespoons thick cream
yolk 1 hard boiled egg
1 tablespoon salad oil
2 tablespoons Worcester sauce
a little salt

Mix well together. This sauce may be used for fish.

NUT SAUCE (for Poultry)

1 Small Cup Almonds or Walnuts
½ cup clear stock
1 dessertspoon milk
1 tablespoon butter
1 egg yolk
1 teaspoon flour
salt and pepper

NUT SAUCE—*continued*

Blanch and dry the nuts and chop into small pieces. Fry to a pale golden colour in the butter, and add salt and pepper to taste. Pound until smooth, and add with the stock to 1 teaspoon of butter and the flour, which have been mixed over the fire until smooth. Add gradually and alternately until all the nuts and stock are used, and the mixture is of a nice consistency. Add to the boiling mixture the milk in which the egg yolk has been beaten, and serve.

TARTARE SAUCE (for Meat or Fish)

1 Yolk of Egg
1 teaspoon dry mustard
4 teaspoons vinegar
salt and pepper
4 tablespoons salad oil
2 small onions
2 gherkins
pinch of cayenne
teaspoon of capers or mixed pickles

Beat the egg with the pepper, salt and mustard. Stir into this—first in drops and then in teaspoons—the salad oil, adding in the same manner 1 teaspoon of vinegar after every two teaspoons of oil. Beat well for a minute or two between each addition so that it is smooth and creamy. Mince the onions, gherkins and capers, and stir these into the sauce with a pinch of cayenne.

WHITE SAUCE (for Vegetables, etc.)

1 Tablespoon Butter
1 cup of hot milk
1 tablespoon flour
salt
pepper

Heat the butter in a saucepan and stir in the flour; pour on gradually the hot milk, season to taste, bring to the boil and simmer gently for about 10 minutes.

For Fish

Instead of using all milk, use half milk and half liquid in which the fish has been boiled, and just before removing from the fire add 1 tablespoon of chopped parsley.

For Meat

Use half stock and half milk and add parsley as above directed. Do not allow sauce to boil after the addition of the parsley. Boiling destroys the green colour of this herb.

GRAVIES

BROWN GRAVY

2 Tablespoons Flour **1 cup water or stock**

After roasting meat drain off excess fat. Sift flour into dish and cook until lightly brown. Gradually stir in cold liquid and cook five minutes stirring until smooth and thickened. Season to taste with salt and pepper. Strain if desired.

CARAMEL

250 gr ($\frac{1}{2}$ lb.) Brown or White Sugar **boiling water**

Place sugar and 1 tablespoon water in an old iron saucepan (keep one for the purpose), stir over a slow fire until it turns a deep, rich brown colour; add 250 ml ($\frac{1}{2}$ pint) of boiling water and simmer gently 20 minutes. Cool, bottle and cork. Be careful not to burn. If burnt it is useless. Excellent for darkening cakes, puddings, soups, etc.

VEGETABLES

Vegetables are essential to perfect health, and should always be eaten as fresh as possible. Fresh vegetables will cook in just about half the time required for those that have been kept for a long time.

Serve vegetables as soon as they are cooked, and cook till they are just tender. Over-boiling vegetables spoils them.

Root vegetables should be cooked in salted boiling water, with the lid on.

Old potatoes should be covered with cold water and brought to the boil. Serve either plain or mashed with a little milk, butter and pepper.

Cook greens in fast boiling soft water, until tender, keeping the lid off saucepan.

Cabbage and cauliflower should be steeped in cold, salted water for ½ hour before boiling.

Charcoal placed in a bag of potatoes will prevent them from sprouting.

Wash parsley in hot water. It has a better flavour and chops more easily.

A few drops of lemon juice in the water in which the old potatoes are boiling will keep them white.

When boiling potatoes in the jacket put in water (unbroken skins) boil for 3 minutes, then put to one side and allow to simmer until cooked. The potatoes will be mealy when turned out.

STEAMING VEGETABLES

Most green vegetables can be steamed, and this method is far ahead of boiling—none of the valuable food in the vegetables is wasted. To steam cabbage, cauliflower, turnips, carrots, etc., place the vegetable to be steamed in a saucepan with about 1 cup of boiling water and a piece of butter or dripping the size of an egg. Put on the lid and steam slowly over a clear fire for 25 to 30 minutes, or until the liquid is exhausted. A little seasoning of salt may be added.

HEALTH HINT

Vegetables should not be peeled, just scrubbed clean. A small hard nail brush is useful for this purpose. Try your carrots, turnips, potatoes, pumpkins this way, and you will be delighted with the results. All kind of vegetables (unpeeled) may be steamed together.

Vegetables should be served in the skins. You will never serve pumpkin otherwise, once you have tried it the health way. If any liquid remains after the vegetables are tender, use it for vegetable soup, etc.

ARTICHOKES (BOILED)

Artichokes
melted butter
a few drops vinegar
white sauce
pepper and salt

Wash the roots thoroughly, scrape off the skin and boil until tender in slightly salted water with a few drops of vinegar. Take out of water immediately they are soft and put over them a little melted butter and some pepper. Serve with a white sauce. Artichokes are easily grown and very prolific.

ASPARAGUS (STEAMED)

Asparagus
butter
boiling water
seasoning

Cut the asparagus in equal lengths and stand on end in a deep saucepan of boiling water. The heads should be about 52 mm (2 in.) out of the water. Boil ½ an hour or longer. Part of the stalk will be quite soft and delicious and the heads will be cooked by the steam. Lift carefully on to a vegetable dish, season, and place pieces of butter on the vegetable. Put in the oven just a minute to melt the butter. Serve.

AUBERGINE

Wash aubergine (egg-plant), cut in slices, sprinkle with salt, cover and let stand ½ hour. Wash well and pat dry with paper towel. Cook in pan with melted butter, season to taste, serve with grilled or roast meat. Aubergines can be sliced in half lengthways and centre scooped out and stuffed with filling of onion, parsley, cheese, and baked in a little oil.

BEANS (BROAD)

Beans
butter
salt and pepper

Shell and boil for 30 to 45 minutes in salted boiling water. Strain and add pepper and butter.

BEANS (FRENCH)

Beans
butter
salt and pepper

String the beans and cut off the ends. Shred finely, put in boiling salted water and boil for 20 minutes. Strain, and serve with butter and pepper. Runner and Tongan beans are treated in a similar manner. Tongan beans require longer boiling and take a little more salt. If possible, always boil greens in soft rain water.

BEANS (FRENCH) WITH TOMATOES

Beans
butter or good dripping
tomatoes
salt and pepper

Boil the beans, drain and allow to cool. Skin and slice the tomatoes. Put the fat into a frying pan, add tomatoes and cook for 5 to 6 minutes. Then add the beans, mix together and let get thoroughly hot. Season with salt and pepper.

CABBAGE

Cabbage
1 tablespoon butter, lard or dripping

Cut up roughly as if for salad. Place in saucepan with the butter and cook without water. Young cabbage will do in 5 minutes. Old cabbage takes 10 minutes. In this way, all the good of the vegetable is saved and there is no objectionable odour from the water.

CABBAGE (BOILED)

Cabbage
butter
salt and pepper

Wash the cabbage well and cut into small pieces. Put into boiling salted water and cook quickly without a lid until tender (about 5 minutes). Drain well through a colander, press all the water out with a plate, mash and add butter and pepper to taste.

CARROTS

Carrots
milk or cream
butter
pepper and salt

Use whole, small, young carrots, or cut carrots into thin slices. Boil till tender, drain and add butter, pepper and salt and a little milk or cream. Simmer for a few minutes and serve.

Turnips may be served in the same way.

CARROTS, EN CASSEROLE

Carrots
90 gr (3 oz.) butter
1 onion
pepper and salt
parsley

Take about a dozen young carrots and cut them in pieces. Lay them in a casserole, cover with finely chopped onion, sprinkle with salt and pepper and some chopped parsley, dot them over with small pieces of butter, place the lid on, and place in a medium oven till soft.

CAULIFLOWER (BOILED)

1 Cauliflower
white sauce
seasonings

Cut off the large outside leaves and remove the stump. Stand the cauliflower in salted water for a short time, drain and place in boiling salted water, and cook gently until tender. Remove from pan, drain well, and serve with a white sauce or melted butter.

CELERY (BOILED)

Celery
cream or butter sauce
salt and pepper

Break the celery into short pieces and take off all the stringy outside. Place in a saucepan, cover with boiling salted water and boil for 10 minutes. Make a cream or butter sauce, pour over the celery and serve.

CUCUMBER (BOILED)

Cucumber
white sauce
60 gr (2 oz.) butter
parsley
pepper and salt

Peel the cucumber, cut in two or three pieces, and boil for 10 minutes. Drain and cut into thick slices. Melt the butter in a saucepan, add the cucumber, salt and pepper and then add the sauce and chopped parsley. Make all thoroughly hot and serve.

LEEKS (BOILED)

Leeks
white sauce
chopped parsley
salt

Use the white part only. Wash well and cut in equal lengths. Put into salted boiling water and cook until tender. Drain, pour over a white sauce and sprinkle with chopped parsley.

MAIZE (INDIAN CORN)

Young Corn Cobs | **pepper and salt**
butter

Cut off the stalks and remove the outer leaves and fibres from each cob. Put the cobs in boiling salted water and cook gently until tender. Drain, season, pour melted butter over the cobs and serve.

MUSHROOMS (STEWED)

Mushrooms | **60 gr (2 oz.) butter**
1 tablespoon flour | **1 tablespoon lemon juice**
milk | **pepper and salt**

Peel the mushrooms and cut off the stalk ends. Melt the butter in a saucepan, add the mushrooms and lemon juice, season and cook gently, stirring frequently for about $\frac{1}{2}$ an hour. Mix the flour with some milk, stir it into the mushrooms and boil gently for 5 minutes. Serve very hot.

ONIONS (BAKED)

Onions | **breadcrumbs**
30 gr (1 oz.) sugar | **salt and pepper**
30 gr (1 oz.) butter

Boil the onions in salted water. Drain them well. Put a layer in a baking dish with some of the butter and seasoning, then make a layer of breadcrumbs and continue in this manner until the dish is filled. Cover with buttered paper and bake until browned.

PARSNIPS (BROWNED)

Parsnips | **sugar**

Boil parsnips, cut in slices 13 mm ($\frac{1}{2}$ in.) thick and brown in a hot, greased pan or in the oven with roasting meat. A little sugar may be added, if baked in a separate dish. It must be remembered that although these are delicious their caloric value is very high, and therefore they are not suitable for those who are trying to slim.

PEAS, BLUE (BAKED WITH EGGS)

Boiled Blue Peas | **milk**
eggs

Spread the peas in a pie-dish, pour over the eggs whipped with milk. Place in the oven and bake till slightly browned.

PEAS, BLUE (BOILED)

Peas
vinegar
1 teaspoon soda per 500 gr (1 lb.) of peas

Soak the quantity of peas required overnight in water, to which the soda has been added. Boil for ½ an hour, then pour off the water and add fresh water with salt to taste. Boil until soft. A little vinegar added when nearly cooked is sometimes an improvement. Properly cooked blue peas can hardly be distinguished from fresh green peas, and are a very cheap dish.

PEAS AND CARROTS

Peas
butter
carrots
flour
pepper and salt

Cook peas and carrots, chop carrots into dice, and add to peas, leaving a little of the water. To this add a little butter, pepper and salt, and then thicken with flour to the consistency of sauce.

PEAS, GREEN (BOILED)

Peas
mint
butter
pepper and salt

Shell the peas, put in boiling salted water with a sprig of mint, and boil gently for 20 minutes, or until tender. Drain and stir in a little butter. A little sugar added when peas are tender is an improvement.

POTATOES (BAKED IN SKINS)

Choose large equal sized potatoes. Wash in cold water and scrub with brush. Put into a fairly hot oven, not crowded together. Bake at 175° C (350° F) for 40 to 60 minutes, according to size, turning occasionally. Directly after baking turn on to a cloth. Potatoes yield easily if cooked thoroughly. Make a deep cross cut in top of each with a knife, and allow steam to escape, protecting fingers from heat with a cloth. In order that the steam shall break through and the potatoes become mealy, press each one with both hands until it bursts open. Shake in salt and pepper. Paprika adds attractive colour, but must be used sparingly. Top with butter and serve on a hot dish lined with a napkin or paper mat.

POTATOES (CHIPPED)

Peel potatoes and let them soak for 30 minutes in cold water. Cut them in thin slices, then into thin strips, and allow to dry. Have ready a pan of hot fat. Put the chips in a frying basket, dip them in the fat, leave a moment, then lift out, dip in again and lift out, and then put in the fat and fry until they become a golden brown. Sprinkle with salt and serve.

POTATOES, SWEET (MASHED)

Sweet Potatoes **pepper and salt**
butter

Wash potatoes thoroughly, boil in their skins till tender, then peel and mash. Season with pepper, salt and butter and bake in a pie-dish until brown.

POTATOES, SWEET (STEAMED)

Sweet Potatoes **salt and pepper**
butter, or good dripping

Peel the potatoes, cut in thick slices and place in a frying pan with a little water and plenty of butter or dripping. Cover with a lid and steam for 30 to 45 minutes. Season with salt and pepper. The sweet potato can be boiled or baked. They take longer to cook than ordinary potatoes.

PUMPKIN

Pumpkin **pepper and salt**
butter

Peel, cut and remove the seeds from the pumpkin. Cook for 20 to 30 minutes in boiling water. Strain, mash and add pepper and butter. Pumpkin can be baked—time about 45 minutes.

PUMPKIN (BAKED)

Pumpkin **water**
butter **salt and pepper**

Peel and seed the pumpkin and cut into convenient sizes. Place in a dish, sprinkle with salt and pepper, and add just a little water. Cover and bake in a moderate oven until soft. Add a little butter and serve.

SILVERBEET

Beet **pepper and salt**
butter

Wash thoroughly and chop into small pieces. Boil for 20 minutes (or better still, steam), strain and serve with pepper and butter. Turnip tops, rape, spinach and tops from broad bean plants may be cooked in the same way.

SPINACH

Spinach
chopped parsley
tablespoon butter
little nutmeg
pepper and salt

The stalks take ten minutes, the leaves from 3 to 5 minutes. If time permits it is worth cutting off the stalks and putting them on 5 minutes earlier than the leaves. Place about a table-spoon butter in a saucepan, then the spinach, but no water. Add chopped parsley and, when cooked, sprinkle with pepper, salt and a little nutmeg. Silverbeet can be cooked in the same manner.

TOMATOES

Tomatoes washed and dried and cut in halves and put into a greased dish, cut part uppermost, and baked till tender, can be served with any hot dinner. Sprinkle with salt before serving.

TOMATO SAVOURY

500 gr (1 lb.) Tomatoes
1 large white onion
breadcrumbs
salt and pepper to taste
1 dessertspoon butter
cheese

Slice tomatoes and onions, place in alternate layers in buttered dish, and add salt and pepper to taste. Cover with breadcrumbs and grated cheese (optional) and nobs of butter on top. Bake in moderate oven till tender.

TOMATOES (STEWED)

500 gr (1 lb.) Tomatoes
½ cup sugar
vinegar
salt and pepper
1 good sized onion
1 tablespoon sago
water
spices

Cut up the tomatoes and onions, and boil in a little water, to which a little vinegar has been added. Add sugar and sago, salt, pepper and spices. Boil all together until the onions are well cooked. These are very nice with hot or cold meat and specially good to serve with sausages.

STUFFED VEGETABLE MARROW

1 Small Marrow
onions
seasonings
boiled rice
tomatoes
tomato sauce
butter

Scrub the marrow, scoop out the centre and fill with the following. Enough cooked rice steamed with an equal quantity of onions and tomatoes and a little butter. Put in a pie-dish and bake in the oven until marrow is tender—about 45 minutes. Serve with tomato sauce.

VEGETABLE DISH

1 Vegetable Marrow **pepper and salt**
butter

Cut the marrow into fair sized cubes and put in a casserole (or pie-dish) with a tablespoon water, a tablespoon butter, pepper and salt. Cook for 1½ hours in a moderate oven and serve, if possible, in the baking dish. No sauce is needed.

ZUCCHINI

Cut in half and remove seeds, stuff with mince and onion, season to taste, hold together with skewer and bake in moderate oven about ¾ hour.

TO DRY MUSHROOMS

Place mushrooms on a shallow tin, place in the oven, and leave the door open. When mushrooms are dry and brittle, crush and bottle. These are useful for flavouring.

TO DRY VEGETABLES

1 Small Carrot **1 small turnip**
1 small swede **1 small parsnip**
3 or 4 sticks celery (centre) **a small bunch parsley and mint**

Wash and peel all vegetables. Dry, and cut into small pieces, then sprinkle with salt, spread on greaseproof paper and dry in oven. It may take 2 or 3 days to dry. Store in jars, ready for use.

PASTRIES, PIES AND PUDDINGS

Wet fruit will make your pudding heavy, so have it thoroughly dry before adding it to your pudding.

A pinch of salt is an improvement to all puddings, but don't overdo it.

Most puddings are improved by standing a little while after mixing. Batter puddings are better to stand at least 30 minutes before cooking.

A bread pudding or a pudding containing a quantity of bread, should be tied rather loosely to allow for swelling. Tie batter puddings fairly loosely, and fruit puddings tightly.

When a boiled pudding is finished cooking, lift out carefully, and dip in cold water. This will keep your puddings from breaking and the cloth will come away readily.

You cannot overboil a pudding. 2 to 4 hours is about the right time.

If a few drops of lemon juice are put in the mincing machine before grinding fruits such as figs, raisins and dates, the mincer will be easier to clean, and the fruit will not stick to the machine.

To prevent suet sticking to the knife when chopping, sprinkle with a little ground rice.

Suet will keep fresh if rubbed with flour.

In making custard for milk pudding, warm the milk first. The custard will set quicker and firmer.

When boiling rice, add a little lemon juice to the water. This makes the rice white and grainy when cooked.

When making any kind of fruit pie, a few dabs of butter among the fruit will prevent juice boiling over and spoiling the pastry, and it improves the flavour of the fruit.

When making pastry, if you melt the butter or lard, and whip to a cream before mixing with the flour, half the quantity of shortening is required.

Pastry makers in hot weather should use a bottle filled with cold water for rolling the paste. This keeps the pastry cool while being made.

Unless your pastry is to be eaten as soon as it comes out of the oven, stand it on the plate rack to cool slowly, or in some other warmish spot in the kitchen. Never put it into the cold larder while it is still hot or you may spoil all the careful work of making and baking it.

A squeeze of lemon juice and $\frac{1}{4}$ teaspoon olive oil added to water with which pastry is mixed will make it light.

When pastry is a little dry and stale, it can be freshened so that it eats like new again, if it is brushed over with milk and put into a moderately heated oven for a few minutes. Pastry that has only gone soft but is not stale can also be made crisp again by reheating in the oven, but in this case it does not need brushing with milk.

When boiling a pudding in a cloth, put in a few pieces of orange peel. The peel collects the fat and makes the pudding cloth easier to wash.

When peeling apples or pears, have at hand a pan of cold water to which a squeeze of lemon juice has been added. As the apples are prepared drop them into the water, and they will not discolour.

Left over coffee thickened with cornflour makes a delicious coffee mould or pudding.

When making milk puddings, allow 1 tablespoon of rice, sago, ground rice or tapioca to 1 cup of milk (or half milk and half water) with an egg added. When using cornflour or arrowroot allow 1 heaped dessertspoon to one cup of milk.

In frying fritters, use a saucepan. Have depth enough of fat to quite cover them, and have it boiling hot, which will be after it ceases to bubble, and when a blue steam rises. It is much easier to cook fritters to perfection if you have a frying basket.

All baked puddings of the consistency of custard require a gentle oven, and are spoiled by fast cooking. Those containing butter, on the contrary, should be put into one sufficiently brisk to raise them quickly.

FRUIT TO STEW

Apples: Peel and core apples, slice and put in saucepan with small amount of water, sugar to taste, cloves or cinnamon to flavour. *Apricots:* Wash and cook apricots, cover with water and sugar to taste. *Pears:* Peel and core pears, cover with water, 2 or 3 cloves and sugar to taste. *Plums:* Wash and cook whole, cover with water and sugar to taste. *Peaches:* Peel and cut in halves, remove stones if wished, cover with water and sugar to taste. *Rhubarb:* Wash stalks well and rub dry, remove ends, cut in pieces, place in saucepan with a little water, and sugar to taste. A sliced lemon added to the rhubarb whilst cooking makes a nice flavour.

Sugar: A general rule—2 oz. (60 gr) per kg (2.2 lb.).

PASTRY

BISCUIT PASTRY

2 Tablespoons Sugar
1½ cups self-raising flour
1 egg
125 gr (4 oz.) butter
a pinch salt
a few drops water or milk

Rub the sugar and butter into the flour, adding a pinch of salt, then mix with slightly beaten egg, and a few drops milk or water to make a fairly stiff dough. This pastry can be used for tarts, turnovers, etc.

FLAKY PASTRY (No. 1)

250 gr (½ lb.) Flour
1 teaspoon lemon juice
250 gr (½ lb.) butter
a little salt

Mix the flour with very cold water with lemon juice added. Roll out, place butter in centre, fold and leave for 10 minutes. Roll out and fold again. Repeat this rolling every 10 minutes for 7 times, when it is ready for baking. Keep it as cold as possible. Use for tartlets, sausage rolls or any other small fancy goods.

FLAKY PASTRY (No. 2)

250 gr (½ lb.) Flour
185 gr (6 oz.) butter or 90 gr (3 oz.) butter, 90 gr (3 oz.) lard)
½ teaspoon baking powder
1 egg yolk
pinch salt
water

Rub the shortening lightly into the flour with the finger tips, add salt and baking powder, and make into a thick paste with the egg yolk and a very little water. Turn on to a baking board and roll out twice. Use for meat pies, etc.

HOT WATER PASTRY—FOR RAISED PIES

250 gr (½ lb.) Flour
¼ teaspoon salt
60 gr (2 oz.) lard
½ cup water or milk

Place lard and water in a saucepan and bring to the boil. Sift flour with salt in a basin, make a well in the centre, and pour in the hot liquid, mixing with a knife; then complete with the hands, mixing quickly until all is formed into a ball. Turn on to a lightly floured baking board and knead until free from cracks. Mould into shape while warm. Divide into pieces according to size you wish to make the pies, knead each piece well and quickly (it must not get cold), and form into balls. With

HOT WATER PASTRY—FOR RAISED PIES—*continued*

the thumb and finger work up until small cases are formed, keeping an even thickness all round. Make lids to fit each case, and after filling, lay on top and press edges of pie and lid well together. Trim neatly and dent all round with the back of a knife. Brush over with egg and milk. Make a slit in the top of each pie. Cut double strips of stout paper sufficient to go round the pies. Brush one side of paper with dripping, and when the pies are in place on a cold oven slide, fasten these bands round the pies to support them when cooking. Bake in a moderate oven from 1 to $1\frac{1}{4}$ hours, according to size. Do not put much moisture in with the filling. Fill stock or fruit juice through the slit in lid after the pie is cooked. Raised pies are very suitable for pork or veal and ham pies, recipes for which may be found in meat section.

PASTRY WITH OIL

500 gr (1 lb.) Flour
salt
water
1 teaspoon baking powder
wineglass of salad or olive oil

Sift the dry ingredients and mix with the oil added to the water, about three parts water and one part oil, but keep the dough stiff.

PUFF PASTRY

500 gr (1 lb.) Plain Flour
juice of $\frac{1}{2}$ a lemon
500 gr (1 lb.) butter
yolk of 1 egg
$\frac{1}{2}$ breakfast cup water

Have the flour dry and well sifted, free from lumps, and the butter free from moisture. Place the flour on a cold baking board (a marble baking slab is best) rub into it 60 gr (2 oz.) of the butter and a pinch of salt. Make a hole in the centre of the flour, put in the yolk of egg, the lemon juice and the water, and mix lightly with a knife to a smooth paste, adding a little more water, if required, but avoid using too much. Well flour the board, roll out paste, and also roll out the butter to about the same size. Place the butter on the paste, fold up and roll out once, then fold and let it stand in a good draught, or on a plate of ice, if convenient, for 1 hour. Then roll out twice more, and it is ready for use. Bake in a brisk oven. It should be rolled out to 6 mm ($\frac{1}{4}$ in.) in thickness, as it will rise to 5 cm (2 in.) in baking. It is good for small jam tarts, cheese cakes, or sausage rolls. This paste will keep uncooked for several days. It is an improvement to allow the paste to stand for 10 or 15 minutes after second and third rollings—in an ice chest or on ice if possible; if not, in a very cold place.

QUICK PUFF PASTRY

250 gr (8 oz.) Self-raising Flour
185 gr (6 oz.) butter or substitute
1 egg yolk
½ teaspoon salt
¼ cup milk

Sift dry ingredients, cut shortening into small pieces and cut into flour with a sharp knife. Mix to a pliable dough with egg yolk and milk. Turn on to floured board and knead lightly. Roll out thinly, cut to desired shape and bake in hot oven.

SHORT PASTRY

60 gr (2 oz.) Self-raising Flour
½ teaspoon salt
squeeze lemon
185 gr (6 oz.) plain flour
125 gr (4 oz.) good shortening
4 tablespoons water

Sift dry ingredients, rub in shortening. Mix to a dry dough with lemon juice and water. Turn on to floured board and knead lightly. Roll out to shape required and bake in hot oven.

THREE MINUTE PASTRY

2 Cups Flour
1 teaspoon cream tartar
½ teaspoon salt
¾ cup dripping
½ teaspoon carbonate soda
boiling water

Melt dripping in boiling water until it forms a cream. Mix in other ingredients. Roll out and bake.

APPLE CAKE (No. 1)

2 Tablespoons Butter
2 tablespoons sugar
1 egg
4 tablespoons self-raising flour
2 teaspoons cinnamon
500 gr (1 lb.) cooked apples

Boil or bake the apples and mash to a pulp. Cream the butter and sugar and add beaten egg. Sift in the flour and mix lightly. Turn on a floured board. Cut into two. Roll each piece out to shape of sandwich tin, place one piece in tin and cover with a layer of apple, well drained. Cover with second piece and cook in moderately hot oven until brown on top. Test with skewer. While still hot, spread lightly with butter, sprinkled with cinnamon and sugar.

APPLE CAKE (No. 2)

6 Tablespoons Plain Flour
3 tablespoons sugar
2 teaspoons baking powder
4 tablespoons cornflour
3 teaspoons cinnamon
125 gr (¼ lb.) melted butter
a little milk

Put dry ingredients into a basin, pour melted butter in and mix with enough milk to make a stiff paste. Roll out and use portion of pastry to cover a shallow tin. Put a layer of cold stewed apples on the pastry, then place the remainder of paste on top. Bake for 35 minutes in a moderate oven. Serve with cream.

APPLE CUSTARD TART

3 Apples
2 eggs
butter
1 cup milk
sugar
nutmeg
pinch of salt
grated rind of ½ a lemon
flaky pastry

Stew the apples in a very little water, and to each cup of pulp add about 1 teaspoon sugar, a pinch of salt, flavouring of nutmeg, and a dessertspoon of butter. Mix well. Beat the eggs until light, add the milk and grated lemon rind. Mix well with the apple mixture, and pour into a dish lined with flaky pastry. Place strips of pastry lattice-wise across the top, and bake in a moderate oven till done. When cold, sift castor sugar on top.

APPLE DUMPLINGS (BAKED)

Short Pastry
½ cup golden syrup
apples
½ cup butter
1 cup boiling water
cloves
sugar

Peel, core and cut apples into quarters. Wrap each piece of apple in a piece of pastry, adding a clove and a sprinkling of sugar. Place as many as required, quite close together, in a pie-dish. Pour over them the mixture made from the syrup, butter and boiling water. Stir mixture well before adding. Bake in a moderate oven until apples are cooked (about ½ to ¾ of an hour).

APPLE DUMPLINGS (STEAMED)

375 gr (¾ lb.) Flour
1 teaspoon baking powder
a pinch of salt
155 gr (5 oz.) suet, finely chopped
water
sugar
apples

Mix flour, suet, baking powder and salt to a nice consistency with cold water. Roll out 13 mm (½ in.) in thickness and line a buttered basin with it. Put in the apples and sugar and cover with pastry. Pinch round, dip a cloth in boiling water, dredge with flour, tie over basin and steam for 3 hours.

APPLE PIE (No. 1)

4 Large Apples
½ cup self-raising flour
½ cup coconut
1 tablespoon melted butter
1 cup sugar
½ cup dates
1 egg
juice of 1 lemon

Peel, core and dice apples. Mix all dry ingredients. Add apple, egg, butter and lemon juice. Stir well. Bake in a pie-dish for ¾-1 hour in a fairly hot oven.

APPLE PIE (No. 2)

4 Cups Apples (pared and sliced)
1 teaspoon cinnamon
¾ cup flour
1 cup sugar
½ cup warm water
½ cup butter

Place the sliced apples in a baking dish, sprinkle on the sugar, then the cinnamon and the warm water. Mix together with finger tips the butter and the flour. Place this crumbly mass on top of fruit and bake until apples are tender, and the top is a golden brown.

APPLE PIE (No. 3)

½ Cup Sugar
1 cup stale cake crumbs
1½ cups milk
1 teaspoon butter
6 apples
1 egg
cinnamon or nutmeg

Rub sugar and butter together and line a pie-dish with it; then alternate layers of apples (cut very fine) and cake crumbs, with cinnamon or nutmeg to taste. Beat the yolk of egg with milk, add 1 tablespoon of sugar, pour over mixture, then bake slowly. When cooked, beat white of egg, add 1 tablespoon sugar and beat well. Cover top and brown. Serve with sauce or cream. This pie will serve six persons.

APPLE PUDDING (No. 1)

185 gr (6 oz.) Breadcrumbs
1 teaspoon baking powder
185 gr (6 oz.) apples
30 gr (1 oz.) peel
125 gr (4 oz.) sugar
½ nutmeg, grated
90 gr (3 oz.) suet
2 eggs

Cut up the apples, chop the suet finely and mix both with the sugar, nutmeg, breadcrumbs and peel, cut finely. Mix in the beaten eggs and baking powder. Turn into a well-buttered basin, cover with buttered paper and steam for 2 hours.

APPLE PUDDING (No. 2)

750 gr (1½ lb.) Apples
1 large tablespoon butter
1½ cups milk
½ teaspoon essence lemon or vanilla
¾ cup water
2 tablespoons plain flour
2 eggs
sugar

APPLE PUDDING (No. 2)—*continued*

Peel the apples and cut into slices, then cook them in the water, adding sugar to taste. Put into a pie-dish to cool while you prepare the crust. Melt the butter in a saucepan, blend in the flour and stir until smooth; then gradually add the milk. Boil for three minutes, stirring all the time; then beat the eggs well with 2 tablespoons sugar and add to the mixture with the lemon essence. Pour this over the apples and bake 20 to 30 minutes.

Rhubarb may be used instead of apples.

APPLE PUDDING (No. 3)

4 Cooking Apples (large)
1 cup cold water
1 tablespoon butter
¾ cup sugar
2 tablespoons self-raising flour
pinch salt

Peel, core and cut apples in halves. Put in ovenproof dish. Rub butter into flour, add sugar and salt and water. Pour over apples and bake about 30 minutes in hot oven. Serve hot or cold with custard or cream.

APPLE ROLL (CANADIAN)

2 Cups Self-Raising Flour
¾ cup milk
½ cup water
a little salt
3 tablespoons butter
1 cup sugar
2 teaspoons cinnamon
apples

Sift together the flour and a little salt. Rub in 2 tablespoons butter or good dripping, add the milk and mix into a firm dough. Roll out about 13 mm (½ in.) thick and cover with finely sliced apples and some sugar. Roll up and place in a greased baking dish. Boil together the sugar, water and cinnamon. Pour this over the apple roll and add 1 tablespoon butter. Bake for 1 hour in a moderate oven, baste occasionally. Serve with cream or custard.

APPLE SANDWICH

250 gr (½ lb.) Butter
2 teaspoons baking powder
1 cup cleaned currants
1 teaspoon cinnamon
1 egg
2 breakfast cups flour (sifted)
2 or 3 apples
1 piece of peel
1 lemon
2 tablespoons sugar

Rub butter into flour, add baking powder and make into a firm dough with water. Mince all other ingredients, add cinnamon and mix with egg. Roll out paste, place mince between, sandwich-like, and bake.

APPLE SHORTBREAD

3 Medium Sized Apples
1 tablespoon cold water
85 gr (6 oz.) self-raising flour (spare)
2 large tablespoons plain flour
1 tablespoon milk
2 or 3 drops lemon essence
2 tablespoons sugar
3 cloves or a little grated lemon rind
60 gr (2 oz.) sugar
125 gr (¼ lb.) butter
1 egg
a pinch of salt

Peel and cut apples small. Add to them the cloves, water and 2 tablespoons sugar. Put all on together and stew gently (place a mat under saucepan when fruit simmers). Cook gently till soft. Prepare pastry while apples cool. Drain off the juice. Sieve the flour and salt, and add 60 gr (2 oz.) sugar, butter or butter and fat or lard mixed. Then add egg beaten with milk or water and lemon essence. Line a tin with 2-3rds of the pastry. Let it stand well up round the edge, and spread with stewed apples. Damp the edges, put rest of pastry on top, brush over with milk or beaten egg, sprinkle over with coarse sugar, prick well and bake for 8 to 10 minutes in a hot oven. Reduce the heat and cook for ½ an hour in all. Let cool for 5 minutes, remove from the tin, cut into squares and dust with icing or castor sugar. If eaten as a dessert, it may be accompanied by a lemon sauce. The same recipe is good for small jam tarts.

APPLE SLICE

1 kg (2 lb.) Cooking Apples
125 gr (¼ lb.) good dripping or lard
1½ cups self-raising flour
¼ cup sugar
1 tablespoon cinnamon

Cook apples with sugar and allow to cool. Add ½ teaspoon cinnamon. Put in a basin, flour, sugar, fat and cinnamon, rub all together and mix with a little water, not too stiff. Roll out in a long sheet, put apple over half, turn other half over. Bake on oven shelf in a moderate oven for ½ an hour.

APPLE TARTS

Pastry
cooked apple
castor or icing sugar

Make the pastry from the recipe for Biscuit Pastry. Roll out, cut into shapes to line patty tins. Put a spoonful of cooked apple in each, then put strips of pastry across. Bake till a biscuit colour. Sift castor or icing sugar over. Use hot or cold.

APPLE TARTS (SMALL)

125 gr (4 oz.) Sugar	185 gr (6 oz.) butter
4 tablespoons milk	500 gr (1 lb.) self-raising flour
2 eggs	cinnamon
stewed apples	a pinch of salt

Beat butter and sugar to a cream, add well-beaten eggs and salt, then milk. Sift in the flour, mix well and roll out very thin. Line patty tins with the pastry, fill with apple flavoured with cinnamon and bake for 15 to 20 minutes in a moderate oven.

BAKED BANANA ROLL

1 Cup Flour	4 bananas
1 tablespoon butter	2 tablespoons sugar
1 egg	extra sugar
1 cup milk	lemon juice

Rub fat into flour, add sugar and beaten egg to make stiff dough and roll out. Mash bananas, sprinkle in a little sugar and a squeeze of lemon juice. Spread over pastry. Roll up and put into pie-dish with a cup of boiling milk. Bake in a quick oven about 20 minutes by which time the milk should be absorbed and the pudding light and brown.

BANANA PLUM PUDDING

2 cups Bread or Cake Crumbs	2 cups mixed fruits
1 cup milk	1 cup mashed bananas
1 tablespoon jam	1 teaspoon carb. soda

Mash bananas, add jam, crumbs and fruit. Dissolve soda in milk and add. Pour into greased basin and steam 2½ hours.

BAKEWELL TARTS

Short Pastry	60 gr (2 oz.) butter
2 tablespoons apricot jam	125 gr (4 oz.) coconut
125 gr (4 oz.) sugar	1 egg
4 tablespoons currants	

Line patty tins with short pastry, fill with apricot jam and currants mixed together, then mix together the butter and sugar, add coconut and beaten egg, and put this mixture on top of jam filling. Bake in a moderate oven till a golden brown—about 20 minutes.

BLACK AND WHITE PUDDING

½ Cup Sugar
a small ½ cup milk
1½ teaspoons baking powder
1 tablespoon cocoa
1 egg
1 dessertspoon butter
1 cup flour
½ teaspoon vanilla
1 saltspoon cinnamon
salt

Cream butter and sugar and add egg, milk and vanilla. Divide batter and add cocoa and cinnamon to one half. Place alternately in a buttered mould and steam for 1 hour. Serve with chocolate sauce or cream.

BREAD PUDDING (STEAMED)

250 gr (½ lb.) Stale Bread
60 gr (2 oz.) shredded suet
1 egg
60 gr (2 oz.) sugar
90 gr (3 oz.) currants
a little milk
a little nutmeg or other flavouring

Soak bread in cold water, then strain and squeeze. Beat up well and add suet, currants and sugar. Beat up egg with flavouring and stir in with a little milk, if necessary, but do not make very wet. Put into greased basin and steam from 1½ to 2 hours.

BROKEN HILL PUDDING (BOILED)

2 Cups Plain Flour
½ teaspoon salt
2 tablespoons shortening
½ cup sultanas
1 teaspoon spice
1 cup sugar
1 cup currants
mixed peel if desired

Boil 2 cups milk in saucepan, then add 1 dessertspoon carb. soda. Add this to dry ingredients. This mixture is very wet. Put in cloth that has been dipped in hot water and sprinkled with flour and boil 2-2½ hours.

BROWN PUDDING (No. 1)

Weight of 2 eggs in Butter (or Good Dripping and a Squeeze of Lemon)
weight of 2 eggs in flour
weight of 1 egg in sugar
2 tablespoons jam
1 teaspoon carbonate soda
2 eggs

Beat the butter to a cream, add gradually the flour, then the eggs, soda and jam. Steam in a buttered mould for 1½ hours.

BROWN PUDDING (No. 2)

2 Tablespoons Currants
2 tablespoons chopped dates
2 tablespoons breadcrumbs
2 tablespoons flour
3 large tablespoons minced beef suet
1 piece lemon peel cut finely
2 tablespoons raisins
2 tablespoons sugar
2 tablespoons ground rice
½ teaspoon mixed spice
½ teaspoon soda
a pinch of salt
a little milk

Mix well together. Make into a medium light batter with milk, and boil in a buttered basin for 2 or 2½ hours.

CARAMEL FRUIT PUDDING

Pastry

125 gr (4 oz.) Butter or Dripping
250 gr (8 oz.) flour
½ teaspoon baking powder
a pinch salt
cold water

Caramel

45 gr (1½ oz.) Sugar
45 gr (1½ oz.) butter

Filling

stewed apples or rhubarb, sweetened

Mix the sugar and butter together with a spoon until smooth, and spread thickly over the inside of the basin. Prepare the pastry, roll and cut out a round to fit the top of the basin. Roll out the rest and line the inside of basin with it, pressing well to the sides. Fill with the sweetened fruit, wet the edge of pastry lining and put on the pastry cover, pressing the edges well together. Cover with greased paper and bake for 1 hour in a fairly quick oven.

CHANDOS PUDDING

2 Tablespoons Breadcrumbs
2 tablespoons sugar
2 tablespoons sultanas
1 teaspoon carbonate soda
2 tablespoons hot water
2 tablespoons flour
2 tablespoons currants
a piece of peel
1 egg
2 teaspoons vinegar

Dissolve the carbonate soda in the water and add vinegar. Mix all the other ingredients together, and add the soda. Steam in a greased pudding basin for 3 hours.

CARROT PUDDING

60 gr (2 oz.) Butter
1 egg (2 if small)
1 eggspoon carbonate soda
½ grated carrot (large carrot)
60 gr (2 oz.) sugar
¾ cup self-raising flour
½ cup breadcrumbs
4 tablespoons milk

Beat the butter and sugar to a cream. Add egg, well beaten, then the breadcrumbs soaked in the milk. Add carrot, then sift in flour with soda. Grease a pudding basin, pour in the mixture, and steam for two hours or longer. Serve with a sweet sauce flavoured with lemon.

CHOCOLATE PUDDING (STEAMED)

60 gr (2 oz.) Butter
60 gr (2 oz.) sugar
2 tablespoons milk
1 tablespoon cocoa
125 gr (4 oz.) self-raising flour
1 egg
vanilla

Cream butter and sugar till as white as possible, add the beaten egg, then milk in which the cocoa has been blended, and lastly the sifted flour and the vanilla. Pour into a greased mould or basin, cover with greased paper, and steam for 1½ to 1¾ hours. Remove paper, turn on to a hot dish and serve with chocolate sauce.

CHOCOLATE SAUCE

½ Tablespoon Cornflour
½ tablespoon cocoa
½ tablespoon sugar
250 ml (½ pint) milk
1 teaspoon butter

Blend cornflour and cocoa with a little milk. Put remainder on to boil with sugar, and when almost boiling, add the cornflour, etc. Cook for 1 minute after it comes to the boil, add the butter, and serve at once in a hot sauce bowl.

CHOCOLATE SAUCE PUDDING

60 gr (2 oz.)Butter
½ cup sugar
1 egg
1 cup self-raising flour
½ cup milk
vanilla
2 dessertspoons cocoa
½ cup sugar

Cream butter and sugar, add unbeaten egg and vanilla and mix. Fold in flour alternately with milk. Place in greased oven proof dish and sprinkle with topping of mixed cocoa and sugar. Finally pour over 1¼ cups of hot water and bake in moderate oven for 35-40 minutes.

CHRISTMAS PUDDING

500 gr (1 lb.) Butter
500 gr (1 lb.) seeded raisins
500 gr (1 lb.) currants
250 gr (½ lb.) peel
375 gr (¾ lb.) flour
1 teaspoon baking powder
1 teaspoon mixed spice
½ teaspoon nutmeg
½ cup brandy or fruit juice
500 gr (1 lb.) light brown sugar
500 gr (1 lb.) sultanas
125 gr (¼ lb.) almonds
250 gr (½ lb.) breadcrumbs
¼ teaspoon salt
1 grated carrot
1 teaspoon cinnamon
9 eggs
125 gr (¼ lb.) dates
125 gr (¼ lb.) figs

Have ready a saucepan 2-3rds full of boiling water and place plate on bottom. Sift flour, salt, baking powder and spices together. Cream butter and sugar until light and frothy, add well-beaten eggs, and beat for 5 minutes. If it curdles add a little flour and continue beating. Add fruit and flour in handfuls alternately, and add fruit juice last. A little caramel will darken the pudding. Boil 5 hours.

CHESTER PUDDING

185 gr (6 oz.) Flour
90 gr (3 oz.) sugar
125 ml (1 gill) milk
a pinch salt
90 gr (3 oz.) butter
125 gr (4 oz.) currants, raisins or dates
1 egg
a little nutmeg
1 teaspoon baking powder

Cream butter and sugar, add beaten egg, and then other ingredients. Mix well and bake in a buttered pie-dish. Dust over with sugar before serving. A sauce of boiled custard is an improvement.

COTTAGE PUDDING

1 Cup Butter or Dripping
1 large cup sugar
½ teaspoon cream of tartar
3 eggs
500 gr (1 lb.) flour
1 teaspoon baking powder
1 small ½ teaspoon baking soda
milk to mix
a pinch of salt

Rub shortening into the flour, add the sugar, salt and risings, then the eggs, well beaten. Mix with milk to a stiff batter, put into a greased pie-dish, and bake in a moderate oven for 1 hour until a golden brown. Serve with syrup or jam.

CREAM TART

Short Pastry
2 tablespoons sugar
cream
2 tablespoons coconut

Line a plate with pastry, pour in enough cream to fill, add the sugar and the coconut. Bake in a moderate oven. This is nice served with preserved fruit, especially pineapple or peaches.

CUP PUDDING

1 Cup Flour
1 cup shredded suet
1 cup sultanas and currants mixed
1 cup breadcrumbs
1 cup sugar
1 cup milk
1 teaspoon carbonate soda

Mix all the dry ingredients together and add the milk to which the carbonate of soda has been added. Steam for 3 hours or longer.

CUSTARD TART

Custard

375 ml (¾ Pint) Milk
2 eggs
1 tablespoon sugar
flavouring

Crust

125 gr (¼ lb.) Flour
30 gr (1 oz.) sugar
60 gr (2 oz.) butter
½ teaspoon baking powder
1 egg

Make the custard by beating the eggs, then add the sugar and milk (cold), and stir well. Add flavouring. To make the pastry, sift the flour and baking powder, rub in butter, mix in sugar and mix to a stiff paste with sufficient beaten egg. Roll out, line a tin, strain in the custard, grate nutmeg on top and bake in a hot oven for about 10 minutes.

CUSTARD–BOILED

2 Cups New Milk
1 tablespoon sugar
1 teaspoon cornflour
2 eggs
lemon rind, or other flavouring

Mix the cornflour with a little milk, simmer the remaining milk with the lemon rind, and half of the sugar, bring to the boil and pour on to the blended cornflour and return to saucepan to thicken. Beat the egg and sugar until light, and pour onto it the heated milk and cornflour. Return to saucepan and just bring to boiling point. Pour into a jug and allow to cool.

CUSTARD–STEAMED OR BAKED

1 Cup Milk
1 dessertspoon sugar
2 eggs
lemon or vanilla flavouring

Beat the eggs, add the sugar, milk and essence. Stir until the sugar is dissolved, then pour the mixture into a greased basin, and stand over a saucepan of gently boiling water. Allow to steam slowly until set, about ½ an hour. This custard can be baked in a pie-dish in a slow oven. A little grated nutmeg sprinkled on top of custard before baking is an improvement.

DARK STEAMED PUDDING

½ Cup Butter
½ cup milk
1 small teaspoon carbonate soda
½ cup jam (fig for preference)
1 cup plain flour
white sauce

Beat together the butter and jam, and then add the milk, flour and soda. Steam for 2½ hours. Serve with white sauce.

DATE PUDDING (No. 1)

1½ Tablespoons Dripping or Butter
2 tablespoons sugar
½ teaspoon carbonate soda
1 cup cold tea
1 cup stoned dates
flour

Dissolve the soda in the tea, cream the fat and sugar together, add tea and soda, and then enough plain or self-raising flour sifted in to make a fairly stiff mixture. Add the dates stoned and halved and steam in a greased pudding basin for 1½ hours. Serve hot with sweet sauce.

DATE PUDDING (No. 2)

125 gr (¼ lb.) Breadcrumbs
125 gr (¼ lb.) sugar
125 gr (¼ lb.) suet, well chopped
125 gr (¼ lb.) dates
2 or 3 eggs

Mix all together and boil for 2 or 3 hours in a buttered basin. Serve with sweet sauce.

DATE PUDDING (No. 3)

3 Tablespoons Sago
625 ml (1¼ pints) milk
½ teaspoon carbonate soda
375 gr (¾ lb.) dates
butter the size of a walnut

Let sago stand all night in milk. Next day add dates, stoned, soda and butter. Cover basin with greaseproof paper, stand in a saucepan of water, and boil for 3 or 4 hours. Put a tablespoon of cream on each serving.

DRIED FRUIT PUDDING

125 gr (¼ lb.) Cooking Figs
125 gr (¼ lb.) prunes
1½ tablespoons sugar
155 gr (5 oz.) chopped suet
125 gr (¼ lb.) dried apricots
500 ml (1 pint) cold water
310 gr (10 oz.) self-raising flour
pinch of salt

If plain flour is used, add 1 level teaspoon baking powder. Wash the figs, apricots and prunes well and remove the stalks from the figs. Put them into a basin with the cold water and let them soak for 24 hours. Turn the fruit into a strainer and let it drain, saving the water. Sift the flour into a basin with a pinch of salt, add the shredded suet and mix together thoroughly.

DRIED FRUIT PUDDING—*continued*

Add sufficient water to make a pliable paste. This paste should not be too dry, but should be soft and easy to roll. Cut off 1-3rd of the paste and put it aside for the top covering of the pudding, and roll out the large piece to a round about 1½ times the size of the top of the pudding basin. Grease the basin and line with the suet crust, pressing it evenly to the sides of the basin. Add the prepared fruit, adding the sugar when the basin is about ½ full of fruit. There should be sufficient fruit to fill the basin. Add also some of the water in which the fruit was soaked. Roll out the remainder of crust to a round the same size as the basin top, damp the edge of the crust round the basin, and place the lid on, pressing the edges of the crust together securely. Cover with greased paper and a floured cloth, knotting the ends on the top. Stand the pudding in a saucepan of boiling water and boil it for about 2 hours. Any water in which the fruit was soaked which is left over can be boiled with a little extra sugar for a few minutes to make a little hot syrup to serve with the pudding, together with cream or custard.

DRIED FRUIT (STEAMED)

All dried fruits may be used. Pour boiling water over the required quantity. Shake well. Pour off the liquid and just cover with cold water, and allow to soak overnight. To each 250 gr (½ lb.) of dried fruit add a teaspoon of honey and steam for ten minutes. Serve with cream, or use plain.

DUMPLINGS (BAKED), WITH SYRUP

Short Pastry
sugar
golden syrup
apples
butter
lemon juice
water

Make some short pastry and roll out. Cut into about 76 mm (3 in.) squares, put some apples, sliced finely, on each, sprinkle with sugar and lemon juice, wet the edges and fold over the corners. Turn upside down in your baking dish. If liked, raisins, sultanas, dates or any other fruit may be used instead of apples.

The Syrup

1 Tablespoon Butter
2 heaped tablespoons golden syrup
½ breakfast cup sugar
juice of 1 lemon
1 cup water

Put all together in a saucepan and bring to the boil. Boil for about 5 minutes and pour over the pastry. Bake about 20 minutes in a medium oven.

DUMPLINGS (BOILED)

2 Tablespoons Golden Syrup
2 cups water
½ cup chopped suet
1 tablespoon butter
2 cups self-raising flour
1 dessertspoon sugar
a pinch of salt

Put golden syrup, butter and water into a saucepan and bring to the boil. Take the flour, suet, salt, sugar and mix all into a stiff dough with water. Break off pieces and mould round. Drop all into the syrup and simmer gently for 20 minutes. When serving put syrup they were cooked in over them.

GOLDEN DUMPLINGS

1 Cup Self-raising Flour
1 egg
1 tablespoon butter
a little milk

Rub butter into flour and add beaten egg and milk. Roll into small balls and drop into boiling syrup.

Syrup

1 Cup Water
1 cup sugar
1 tablespoon butter
1 tablespoon golden syrup

These may be put into a greased pie-dish, syrup poured over and cooked in moderate oven for 20 minutes, instead of boiling 20 minutes.

ECONOMICAL PUDDING

1½ Cups Flour
½ cup sugar
1 teaspoon carbonate soda
½ cup good dripping
2 tablespoons raspberry jam
½ cup milk

Sift flour, rub in fat and add sugar. Add milk, in which soda has been dissolved, and, lastly, stir in the jam. Pour into well-greased basin, cover with greased paper and steam for 1½ to 2 hours.

EGGLESS PUDDING

1 Cup Flour
1 teaspoon carbonate soda
2 tablespoons jam
3 tablespoons sugar
2 tablespoons dripping
1 large cup milk
a pinch of salt

Cream the dripping and sugar, add jam, then portion of the flour and milk. Beat well, add rest of flour with soda added and salt, and make into a soft batter with the balance of the milk. Pour into a well buttered basin. Cover with a pudding cloth, and steam for 2 hours. This is a very soft mixture. Raspberry, black-currant jam, or golden syrup can be used.

FIVE MINUTE PUDDING

3 Teaspoons Baking Powder	68 gr ($2\frac{1}{4}$ oz.) flour
60 gr (2 oz.) sugar	2 eggs
jam	a pinch salt

Mix well together the sugar and sifted flour, into which a pinch of salt and the baking powder have been sifted. Add eggs, unbeaten, mix all together and spread the mixture thinly over a very shallow baking tin. The paste does not want beating, but must be smooth. Bake 5 minutes, turn out of the tin, pour some heated jam over, roll up, and dust thickly with sugar. Serve with sauce or cream.

FLUFF PIE

1 Cup Sugar	3 eggs
juice of 3 lemons	grated rind of 1 lemon
3 tablespoons hot water	$\frac{1}{4}$ teaspoon salt

Beat yolks of eggs very lightly, add lemon juice and grated rind, hot water and salt, add $\frac{1}{2}$ cup sugar. Cook in a double boiler until thick. Add the remainder of the sugar to the stiffly beaten egg whites and fold into the cooked mixture. Fill a pie-dish with the mixture and brown in a moderate oven.

FRENCH PANCAKES

60 gr (2 oz.) Butter	2 eggs
60 gr (2 oz.) flour	1 cup milk
60 gr (2 oz.) sifted sugar	

Beat butter and sugar to a cream, beat in the eggs, then milk and flour. Stir well, put on buttered plates, and bake in fairly hot oven for 20 minutes. Serve with lemon and sugar, or preserves.

FRUIT PUFF

1 Tablespoon Butter	1 tablespoon sugar
1 cup flour	1 egg
$\frac{1}{4}$ teaspoon carbonate soda	$\frac{1}{2}$ teaspoon cream tartar
a pinch salt	milk

Mix until like a cake batter, using milk. Spread over stewed fruit and bake for 15 to 25 minutes in a hot oven.

FRUIT PASTRY

Pastry
1 level cup sultanas
2 small apples, peeled and cored
½ cup sugar
1 level cup currants
2 tablespoons lemon peel
a little suet
juice of 1 lemon
a little spice

Make the pastry from the recipe for biscuit pastry. Put the sultanas, currants, lemon peel (fresh or candied), apples and suet through the mincer, then add the sugar, lemon juice and a little spice to taste. Mix well and bake between two layers of pastry.

HONEY SPONGE (STEAMED)

1 Tablespoon Butter
2 tablespoons honey
1 teaspoon cinnamon
1 cup self-raising flour
2 tablespoons sugar
4 tablespoons milk
½ teaspoon carbonate soda
1 egg
a pinch of salt

Beat the butter and sugar to a cream and add the well-beaten egg. Mix the honey in the milk and add to the mixture. Sift together with flour, cinnamon, soda and salt and stir lightly into other ingredients. Steam in a buttered basin for 1½ hours. Serve with sweet white sauce.

INDIAN FRITTERS

3 Tablespoons Flour
boiling water
2 eggs
a pinch of salt

Mix dry flour with sufficient boiling water to make a stiff paste, break eggs into paste and beat well till thoroughly mixed. Drop in spoonsful into hot lard or dripping and fry a golden brown. Drain and serve with maple syrup, honey or jam.

JAM TARTS

Puff Pastry
raspberry jam

Make the puff pastry from the 1st puff pastry recipe given. In making jam tarts, cut out with round, plain or fluted cutter, then use a small cutter (a large thimble will do in an emergency) and mark a round in the centre of tart, place jam on this, raspberry for preference, as it does not melt and run over pastry. The paste will rise above the jam, leaving the jam in a hollow.

JAM TURNOVERS

125 gr (4 oz.) Flour
60 gr (2 oz.) butter
60 gr (2 oz.) sugar
250 ml (½ pint) milk
1 egg

Rub butter in flour, add sugar and lastly egg and milk. Beat well and pour a little of the mixture on to well-greased saucers and bake in a hot oven for 20 minutes. Then spread raspberry jam on each, turn them over and serve hot.

JUBILEE TART

4 Heaped Tablespoons Cornflour
1 tablespoon sugar (medium)
1 egg
4 heaped tablespoons plain flour
4 tablespoons butter (medium)
1 teaspoon baking powder
125 ml (¼ pint) milk

Sift the baking powder with the flour, add sugar, and rub in butter. Add yolk of egg and then milk. Roll out to size of plate and bake about 15 minutes until a golden brown. Fill centre with jam or stewed fruit, whip white of egg and put evenly on top Put in oven till set. A little sugar can be sprinkled on if liked. This mixture is very short, and if difficult to handle, use 3 tablespoons cornflour and 5 tablespoons plain flour.

KITTY PUDDING

1½ Cups Flour
1 cup fruit
1 cup milk
2 tablespoons treacle
ginger
2 tablespoons dripping
1 teaspoon carbonate soda
2 tablespoons sugar
2 tablespoons breadcrumbs
spice

Dissolve the soda in the milk and mix all ingredients together. Steam for 3 hours.

LEMON MERINGUE

500 ml (1 Pint) Milk
2 eggs
½ cup sugar
1 cup breadcrumbs
30 gr (1 oz.) butter
juice of 1 small lemon
½ grated rind of lemon

Warm the milk and pour it on the breadcrumbs. Cream butter and sugar, add yolks of eggs, beat well and add to breadcrumbs. Then add the lemon and bake in buttered dish till firm and slightly brown. Make a meringue of the whites of eggs, beaten to a stiff froth with 3 tablespoons sugar and a little lemon juice. Pour over and brown slightly. Serve hot or cold with cream.

LEMON PIE

1 Cup Breadcrumbs
30 gr (1 oz.) butter
sugar
flavouring
1 cup water
3 eggs
juice and grated rind of 2 lemons
pastry

Beat together the butter and 1 cup sugar and add the well-beaten egg yolks. Mix well and add the water and the bread-crumbs alternately, then add the lemon juice and grated rind. Line a pie-dish with some pastry, put mixture in and bake. Beat up the whites of eggs until stiff, with about 3 tablespoons of sugar and flavouring, place on top of pie when cooked and return to oven for a few minutes until brown.

LEMON PUDDING (No. 1)

250 gr (½ lb.) Flour
105 gr (3½ oz.) suet or dripping
1 lemon (rind and juice)
60 gr (2 oz.) sugar
1 teaspoon baking powder
milk to moisten

Shred or chop finely suet or dripping, grate rind of lemon and squeeze juice and put these ingredients with the dry ingredients. Moisten all with a little milk and place in a greased basin. Tie with a cloth and steam for 1½ hours.

LEMON PUDDING (No. 2)

1 Cup Sugar
2 eggs
500 ml (1 pint) water
2 lemons
2 heaped tablespoons cornflour
30 gr (1 oz.) butter
salt

Grate the peel and place it with the sugar and water in a saucepan to boil. Mix smoothly the cornflour with yolks of eggs and lemon juice, and pour the boiling water on to mixture, stirring all the time. Pour back into saucepan and stir over fire till cooked. Add butter and pour into a buttered pie-dish. Beat the whites of eggs to a stiff froth, add 2 tablespoons sugar and bake till a pale brown. Serve hot or cold. The beaten whites must be piled high on the top of the pudding.

LEMON AND HONEY TARTS

1 Lemon
1 egg
1 tablespoon honey
45 gr (1½ oz.) butter
60 gr (2 oz.) sugar
1 heaped teaspoon cornflour
250 gr (½ lb.) short pastry

Melt butter in a saucepan, stir in the cornflour, add strained juice and grated rind of lemon, honey and sugar and stir over a moderate heat for 4 minutes. Remove from fire and add well-beaten egg. Stir over gentle heat in a double saucepan until it thickens. Leave till cold, then fill pastry-lined patty pans with the mixture and bake in a hot oven.

LEMON AND APPLE TART

Short Pastry
½ cup sugar
1 egg
1 apple, chopped finely
piece butter, size of a walnut
grated rind and juice of lemon

Make a short pastry and put on plate. Mix all ingredients together with the beaten egg and beat well. Spread on pastry and bake until a nice brown.

LEMON MERINGUE PIE

Make crust as desired, either short or biscuit pastry and bake.

Filling

1 Cup Water
¼ cup water
1 teaspoon lemon rind
juice 1½ lemons
1 heaped tablespoon cornflour
½ cup sugar
2 tablespoons sugar
2 eggs

Boil 1 cup water, ½ cup sugar, lemon rind and juice. Place in bowl cornflour and 2 tablespoons sugar, mix in egg yolks and ¼ cup water. Stir into boiling mixture and return to gentle heat until thickened, stirring all the time. Pour into pastry case and top with meringue made from egg whites beaten with 2 tablespoons sugar. Brown lightly.

LEMON SAGO

1 Cup Sago
1 tablespoon treacle or golden syrup
1 cup sugar
4 cups water
juice of 2 lemons

Put all the ingredients into a saucepan and bring to the boil, stirring occasionally to keep free from lumps. Keep boiling till it is clear and thick. Pour into wetted mould to cool.

LEMON TART

Line plate with short pastry. Beat 2 eggs with 1 cup sugar thoroughly. Add grated rind of 1 lemon and the juice of 2 lemons. Pour into pastry and bake in moderate oven till set.

LINDISFARNE PUDDING

1 Cup Flour
1 cup jam
1 teaspoon carbonate soda
1 cup suet
1 cup milk
a pinch salt

Mix well together and steam for 2½ hours.

MACARONI PUDDING

60 gr (2 oz.) Macaroni
60 gr (2 oz.) sugar
500 ml (1 pint) milk
2 eggs
orange rind and juice of 1 orange

Boil the macaroni in salted boiling water until tender. Drain and wash in cold water. Put into a pie-dish, add the milk, the well-beaten eggs, the orange juice and the rind. Bake for about ½ an hour in a slow oven. Some orange marmalade, if liked, may be placed in the pie-dish before pouring in the custard.

MARGUERITE PUDDING

125 gr (¼ lb.) Butter
250 gr (½ lb.) self-raising flour
125 gr (¼ lb.) sugar
2 eggs
a little milk to make thin

Beat butter and sugar to a cream, add eggs, then milk and lastly the flour. Grease well a basin, spread it with jam, pour in the mixture and steam 1 hour. This makes a large pudding.

MANCHESTER PUDDING

500 gr (1 lb.) Breadcrumbs
1 large cup sugar
rind of 1 lemon
3 eggs
500 ml (1 pint) milk
juice of 2 lemons
piece of butter, size of an egg
jam

Boil the milk and pour over the breadcrumbs, sugar, lemon juice, grated rind and butter. Add the beaten yolks of egg and mix all together well. Put in a greased pie-dish, spread the top with jam and place in a moderate oven until set. Beat the whites of the eggs until stiff and pile on top of the cooked pudding. Return to the oven to brown.

FRUIT MINCEMEAT (No. 1)

250 gr (½ lb.) Currants
375 gr (¾ lb.) seeded raisins
250 gr (½ lb.) mixed peel
rind of 2 lemons
a little ground nutmeg
a little ground cloves
250 gr (½ lb.) apples
250 gr (½ lb.) good beef suet
250 gr (½ lb.) sugar
juice of 2 lemons
a little ground cinnamon
mixed spice to taste

Peel the apples and chop finely. Mince the suet. Cut up peel and raisins. Mix all ingredients together and put into a glass or stone jar. Cover closely. Will be ready for use in about 1 month. A wineglass of brandy is an improvement. Butter 185 gr (6 oz.) may be used instead of suet. Line patty pans with short pastry, fill with mince, put on lids, glaze with beaten egg. Dust with icing sugar when cooked.

FRUIT MINCEMEAT (No. 2)

90 gr (3 oz.) Butter
125 gr ($\frac{1}{4}$ lb.) beef suet
375 gr ($\frac{3}{4}$ lb.) sugar
90 gr (3 oz.) grated apple
60 gr (2 oz.) lemon peel
small wineglass brandy
60 gr (2 oz.) orange peel
250 gr ($\frac{1}{2}$ lb.) sultanas
250 gr ($\frac{1}{2}$ lb.) currants
1 large nutmeg
rind and juice of 1 lemon

Mince suet, peel, sultanas, and apple. Mix all ingredients together and store in glass jars.

MOUNTAIN FRUIT CAKES

500 ml (1 Pint) Sour Milk or Buttermilk
2 tablespoons butter
1 tablespoon water
saltspoon salt
2 cups flour
1 teaspoon baking soda
2 eggs
fruit

Add the flour gradually to the milk, beating it until quite smooth. Cover this mixture and let it remain for 10 hours (a good plan to mix overnight) in a place where it cannot become chilled. Then add the salt, melted butter, soda dissolved in cold water and the well-beaten eggs. Have ready 3 cups of small fruit or very ripe peaches or pears, thoroughly crushed and sweetened to taste. Bake or fry the batter in 8 large pancakes of equal size, butter each as it comes from the pan and spread with the prepared fruit. Stewed apples can be used. Serve with lightly whipped sweetened cream. If cream is not to be had, white of egg beaten to a stiff froth and sweetened, is recommended.

NIENICH TARTS

60 gr (2 oz.) Butter
155 gr (5 oz.) self-raising flour
pinch of salt
1 tablespoon sugar
1 egg
custard
icing

Cream butter and sugar, rub in flour and salt and mix to a stiff paste with the egg. Knead well. Roll on a well-floured board till very thin, line patty tins with the paste and fill with a good thick custard. Glaze the tops with thin icing. Use chocolate and white alternately.

OLNEY PUDDING (No. 1)

60 gr (2 oz.) (or Medium Tablespoons) Butter
125 gr (4 oz.) (or heaped tablespoons) flour
1 teaspoon essence lemon
2 eggs
$\frac{1}{4}$ teaspoon carbonate soda
2 large tablespoons jam
60 gr (2 oz.) sugar

OLNEY PUDDING (No. 1)—*continued*

Beat butter to a cream, add sugar and mix well. Stir in the flour and well-beaten eggs. Dissolve soda in a teaspoon cold water, stir into jam and add quickly to the mixture. Steam for 2 hours. Serve with sweet sauce and add 1 tablespoon of the same jam. A piece of greased paper in the bottom of the pudding basin prevents sticking.

OLNEY PUDDING (No. 2)

2 Eggs
weight of 2 eggs in butter
2 tablespoons raspberry jam
weight of 2 eggs in flour
weight of 1 egg in sugar
½ teaspoon soda

Beat butter and sugar, add well-beaten eggs, flour and jam. When all are well beaten, add the soda dissolved in a spoonful of water. Have a mould ready greased and sprinkled with sugar. Put in quickly, cover with paper and steam for 2½ hours.

ONE EGG PUDDING

250 gr (½ lb.) Flour
125 gr (¼ lb.) sugar
1 egg
125 gr (¼ lb.) suet
250 gr (½ lb.) currants
½ teaspoon carbonate soda
a little milk

Mix dry ingredients, add egg and soda melted in the milk, and mix lightly. Steam for 4 hours in a buttered mould.

ORANGE CUSTARD PIE

60 gr (2 oz.) Flour
125 gr (4 oz.) sugar
125 ml (¼ pint) orange juice
60 gr (2 oz.) butter
250 ml (½ pint) milk
2 eggs
grated rind of ½ an orange

Line a deep plate or sandwich tin with short pastry. Melt butter in a saucepan, stir in the flour, then the milk, and stir until boiling and boil for 3 minutes. Remove from the fire, stir in the sugar mixed with the orange juice, and the beaten yolks of eggs. Beat the mixture well. Whisk the whites of the eggs to a stiff froth and fold into the mixture. Pour into the pastry lined plate, and bake until pastry is nicely browned, and the custard is set. Time from 25 to 35 minutes.

ORANGE PUDDING (STEAMED)

125 gr (¼ lb.) Dripping or Butter
2 eggs
185 gr (6 oz.) self-raising flour
125 gr (¼ lb.) sugar
1 orange
2 tablespoons milk

Put dripping and sugar in a bowl and beat to a cream. Add the eggs separately, beating continuously, then add orange juice and milk, then the flour and grated orange rind. Place in a well buttered basin. Steam 2 hours.

ORANGE PUDDING (STEAMED)—*continued*

Orange Sauce

1 Cup Water
1 tablespoon sugar
1 teaspoon cornflour
juice and grated rind orange

Mix the cornflour with some water. Put the cup of water, sugar and orange juice and rind on the stove, add the cornflour when hot and stir till boiling. Pour over the pudding and serve.

PEAR CROQUETTES

6 Large Pears
3 eggs
60 gr (2 oz.) butter
breadcrumbs
sugar

Peel, core and grate the pears. Mix with them the butter, (melted) and sugar to taste. Beat the eggs until light, add to the fruit, mix in as large a quantity of breadcrumbs as will make the mixture stiff. From this mixture mould the croquettes egg-shape, with two tablespoons, drop into boiling water, and merely simmer for about 20 minutes till done. Drain, roll in pounded sugar, lay on hot napkin and place a little ground cinnamon on top of each. Serve very hot with or without sauce.

PINEAPPLE PUDDING

1 Tin Pineapple
125 gr (4 oz.) flour
60 gr (2 oz.) butter
125 gr (4 oz.) sugar
3 eggs

Butter a pudding dish and put in it the pineapple, chopped finely. Melt the butter in a saucepan and add flour. Cook for 5 minutes, stirring all the time. Then add the pineapple juice and stir till thick. Add sugar, then take off the fire and allow to cool a little. Then beat in the yolks of the eggs, one at a time and bake in oven till set. Make a meringue with the whites of eggs and a little sugar, and brown lightly in a cool oven. To be eaten cold.

PLUM PUDDING (CHRISTMAS)

250 gr ($\frac{1}{2}$ lb.) Flour
375 gr ($\frac{3}{4}$ lb.) breadcrumbs
500 gr (1 lb.) raisins
250 gr ($\frac{1}{2}$ lb.) sultanas
125 gr ($\frac{1}{4}$ lb.) figs
2 tablespoons brandy
$\frac{1}{2}$ teaspoon carbonate soda
8 eggs
500 gr (1 lb.) sugar
500 gr (1 lb.) beef suet
500 gr (1 lb.) currants
125 gr ($\frac{1}{4}$ lb.) dates
250 gr ($\frac{1}{2}$ lb.) lemon peel
30 gr (1 oz.) mixed spice
$\frac{1}{4}$ teaspoon cream of tartar
a little salt
a few drops essence lemon

PLUM PUDDING (CHRISTMAS)—*continued*

Rub carbonate soda through the flour, then mix in the suet, salt, breadcrumbs and cream of tartar. Beat eggs with sugar and add fruit, then brandy and essence lemon. Then add to the dry ingredients. Put into a floured cloth or a greased pudding mould and boil for 8 hours. This mixture can be made into a number of small puddings. An hour will be required to re-boil before using. This pudding will keep for months. If required for immediate use, omit the brandy and add instead another egg or a little milk.

PLUM PUDDING

2 cups Self-raising Flour
½ cup strong cold tea
185 gr (6 oz.) sugar
1 egg
1 teaspoon each spice, ground ginger and carb. soda
125 gr (4 oz.) butter
500 gr (1 lb.) mixed fruits
¼ cup rum or sherry

Boil tea, butter, sugar and fruits for 2 minutes. Cool. Add beaten egg and rum or sherry. Stir in sifted flour with spices, soda, and pinch of salt. Steam in greased basin 3 hours.

PLUM PUDDING (ECONOMICAL)

2 Breakfast Cups Self-raising Flour
1 breakfast cup sugar
1 breakfast cup currants
1 egg
1 tablespoon butter
1 breakfast cup raisins
1 tablespoon dripping
1 teaspoon carbonate soda
boiling water

Put dry ingredients, including butter and dripping, in a basin. Then add the beaten egg and enough boiling water to form into a stiff dough. Mix well and let stand overnight. Next morning cover with greased paper and steam for 5 hours. Serve with custard.

POTATO PUDDING

1 Cup Mashed Potatoes
2 cups milk
1 cup flour
2 eggs
flavouring if desired

Mix well the mashed potatoes with the flour, boil the milk and pour over. Mix well and beat the eggs into the mixture. Pour into a large pie-dish and bake for ½ an hour. If a sweet pudding is preferred, serve with sugar and milk. This is sufficient for 6 servings.

PUFF BALLS

1 Cup Boiling Water
3 eggs
1 cup flour
a pinch of salt

Mix flour and salt in boiling water, beat till smooth and then add eggs and stir well. Drop by spoonsful into boiling fat and fry a golden brown. Serve with lemon and sugar.

PUMPKIN PIE

2 Cups Well-Drained Cooked Pumpkin
½ cup brown sugar
1 teaspoon salt
½ teaspoon nutmeg
½ teaspoon ginger
1 cup sweet milk
2 tablespoons flour
1½ teaspoons cinnamon
½ teaspoon allspice
2 eggs
puff pastry

Stir milk into the pumpkin, add beaten eggs, flour, sugar, salt and spices and beat well for about 5 minutes. Line a pie-dish with puff pastry and brush over with white of egg. Pour in the pumpkin mixture. Bake for about 5 minutes on top shelf of hot oven. Remove to bottom shelf, reduce heat and bake till pastry is cooked and custard is set and brown. The pastry can be cooked first if desired. The time to cook custard is 30 minutes.

QUEEN PUDDING

60 gr (2 oz.) Breadcrumbs or Cake Crumbs
2 eggs
3 tablespoons jam
2 cups milk
2 tablespoons sugar
grated lemon rind
a few drops lemon essence

Boil milk and pour over crumbs and grated lemon rind. Separate the whites of eggs from the yolks and beat the sugar and egg yolks well, then add to the milk and crumbs. Flavour to taste, and pour into a buttered pie-dish. Stand the pie-dish in a baking tin containing a little cold water, and cook in a moderate oven till set. Take out and spread with jam. Whip the whites of the eggs to a stiff froth, stir in 60 gr (2 oz.) castor sugar lightly, spread over the top of the pudding and put back in the oven till set and a pale brown colour.

RAISIN PIE

1 Cup Raisins
2 tablespoons sago
1 egg
3 tablespoons lemon juice
1 tablespoon butter
2 cups water
¼ teaspoon salt
½ cup sugar
grated rind of ½ a lemon
pastry

RAISIN PIE—*continued*

Soak raisins for several hours. Add the sago and salt and cook in a double boiler until the sago is clear, stirring frequently. Add small quantity of hot sago to the slightly beaten egg, return to boiler and cook for 3 minutes, stirring constantly. Add sugar and stir until dissolved. Remove from heat and add lemon juice, rind and butter. Line a pie plate with pastry and moisten edges with water. Fill the pie shell with the raisin mixture, cover with a top crust and bake in a hot oven for 15 to 20 minutes, reduce the heat and bake for another 15 to 20 minutes.

ROLY POLY PUDDING (BAKED)

1 Cup Self-Raising Flour
sugar
2 tablespoons good dripping
1 cup cold water
golden syrup or jam

Rub fat into the flour and mix to a stiff paste with a little water. Roll out as for a roly poly and spread with golden syrup. Roll up paste, enclosing syrup, taking care not to seal the ends. Place in a greased pie-dish. Just before putting in the oven, sprinkle sugar over the pastry and pour the cup of cold water over the whole. Bake in a moderate oven from 30 to 40 minutes.

ROLY POLY PUDDING (BOILED)

Suet Crust
jam

Make a suet crust and roll it out to an oblong shape. Spread it with jam (not quite to the edges) and roll up, damping edge to make it adhere. Roll the pudding in a floured pudding cloth and tie it securely at each end. Boil the roly poly for 1½ hours. Golden syrup may be substituted for jam, but it should first be mixed with a few breadcrumbs to make it a better consistency. If a spice flavour is liked, add a level teaspoon of either ground cinnamon or ginger to the syrup and crumbs.

SAGO PLUM PUDDING

4 Tablespoons Sago
1 cup mixed fruit
½ teaspoon carbonate soda
1 tablespoon butter
1 cup breadcrumbs
1 teaspoon spice
½ cup sugar
½ cup milk
self-raising flour

Soak the sago overnight in enough water to cover well. Mix butter and sugar, stir in sago, then breadcrumbs and fruit. Then add milk and soda dissolved in a little milk, and lastly add enough self-raising flour to bind. Boil in a floured pudding cloth for 3 hours.

SNOWBALL PUDDING

250 gr (½ lb.) Rice
60 gr (2 oz.) butter
500 gr (1 lb.) cooking apples
125 gr (4 oz.) sugar

Wash the rice and place in a pudding cloth, allowing plenty of room for swelling. Boil for 15 minutes, take out of saucepan and place in a colander. Open the cloth and spread the rice out. Have the apples peeled, cored and cut small and place them in the centre of the rice. Bring the rice over the apples to form a crust. Re-tie the cloth and boil for 1½ hours. Turn on to a dish, when the snowball will burst. When serving, place a small piece of butter on each portion, and sprinkle liberally with sugar.

SPONGE PUDDING (No. 1)

1 Tablespoon Butter
1 cup flour
1 teaspoon baking powder
½ cup sugar
2 eggs
milk

Beat well together the butter, sugar and eggs, then add the flour, baking powder and enough milk to make the mixture the consistency of batter. Put in well-buttered basin and steam for 1 hour, without once raising the lid. Serve with sweet sauce or cream.

SPONGE PUDDING (No. 2)

2 Tablespoons Sugar
1 cup self-raising flour
2 eggs
2 tablespoons butter
4 tablespoons milk
salt
vanilla essence

Cream the sugar and butter and beat in the eggs. Add the salt, flavouring, flour and milk. Mix well. Line a basin with jam and then pour in the mixture. Steam for 1 hour and serve with boiled custard.

STANLEY PUDDING

1 litre (1 Quart) of Milk
3 eggs
vanilla
4 tablespoons flour
sugar
jam

Separate the whites from the yolks. Mix the yolks with the flour, add to milk and boil till it gets thick, adding a little sugar and vanilla to taste. Pour into a pie-dish, put jam on top, and make meringue with white of egg. Bake about ½ an hour.

STEAMED PUDDING (No. 1)

1 Tablespoon Butter
1 small cup self-raising flour
2 eggs
a little milk
½ small cup sugar
1 tablespoon boiling water
a pinch of salt
golden syrup or jam

Beat together the butter and sugar, add the eggs and beat again. Then add the flour, salt, milk and boiling water. Place in a greased basin that has golden syrup or jam at the bottom and steam for 1 hour.

STEAMED PUDDING (No. 2)

2 to 3 Cups Honey
½ teaspoon soda
2 eggs
¼ teaspoon cloves
2 teaspoons baking powder
1 cup milk
1 cup chopped raisins
½ teaspoon salt
½ teaspoon cinnamon
½ teaspoon allspice
2 tablespoons ground chocolate
1¼ cups flour (more if needed)

Mix all well and steam in a buttered basin for 3 hours.

STRAWBERRY SHORTBREAD (AMERICAN)

250 gr (½ lb.) Flour
½ cup milk
1 egg
2 tablespoons butter
1 tablespoon sugar
a pinch of salt

Add the salt to the flour, rub in butter and sugar and mix into a scone dough with beaten egg and milk. Divide into two equal parts, roll out and lay one sheet smoothly on the other. Bake on a buttered tin plate. While warm separate the sheets, lay on a coating of strawberries and sifted sugar and cover with upper crust. Cut into triangles and serve with cream over each slice.

SUET PUDDING

2 Cups Self-raising Flour
sliced apples
1 cup sugar
1 cup shredded suet
2 cups water
1 tablespoon butter
milk

Mix together the flour and the suet and make into a very stiff dough with some water or milk. Roll out into a narrow strip, place on it sliced apples, roll up, wetting edges to make it hold, and place in a buttered pie-dish. Make a syrup by boiling together for a few minutes the sugar, butter and water. Pour over the paste and then bake for 30 or 40 minutes.

SWEET CHEESE CAKE

60 gr (2 oz.) Cream Cheese
1 teaspoon vanilla essence
4 eggs
short pastry
125 gr (4 oz.) castor sugar
125 gr (4 oz.) butter
60 gr (2 oz.) sultanas
pinch of salt
milk

Line a large pie plate with short crust, ornament the edges. Prick the bottom all over with a fork. Beat the butter and sugar to a cream. Stir in the crumbled cheese, 4 beaten egg yolks (reserving enough to glaze the top), vanilla, salt and sultanas. Beat egg whites to a stiff froth and fold into the mixture. Pour into the pastry. Brush over with egg yolk and a little milk. Put into a hot oven at first, reduce the heat and bake till custard is set and pastry a pale brown.

TAPIOCA AND APPLES

¾ Cup Tapioca
½ cup sugar
4 medium sized apples
a pinch of salt
milk

Soak tapioca in warm water for a few hours, then pour off any surplus water and add apples, pared and sliced, sugar and salt. Cover with milk and bake in a moderate oven for about 1 hour.

TAPIOCA CUSTARD

2 Tablespoons Tapioca
2⅓ cups milk
3 eggs
2 tablespoons desiccated coconut
½ cup sugar
flavouring

Soak tapioca overnight in a cup of cold water. Next day boil in the milk till soft. Beat the sugar and yolks of eggs together and add to the tapioca after it has cooled a little. Add coconut and mix well. Then put back on the fire and cook a little, but do not boil. Turn into a pie-dish, whip the whites of eggs (with any flavouring desired) till stiff, and pile roughly on top of pudding. Bake till a pale brown. When half cooked sprinkle with coconut.

TEA PUDDING (AMERICAN)

2 Cups Self-raising Flour
1 cup sultanas or raisins
1 large tablespoon butter
1 cup currants
½ cup sugar
1 cup strong tea
2 teaspoons carbonate soda

Rub butter into the flour, add fruit and sugar, put soda into the tea and mix with dry ingredients. Boil in a pudding cloth for 2 hours.

TREACLE PUDDING

1 Cup Flour
1 teaspoon salt
1 large teaspoon ground ginger
2 tablespoons dripping
2 tablespoons sugar
1 teaspoon carbonate soda
2 tablespoons treacle
1 cup milk

Mix all dry ingredients, rub in the dripping, add treacle and lastly milk. Steam in a buttered mould for 2 hours. Serve with sauce or custard. This mixture also makes a nice cake if baked in a moderate oven about an hour.

TWENTY MINUTE PUDDING

1 Egg
1 cup flour
1 teaspoon baking powder
30 gr (1 oz.) butter
1 cup sugar
flavouring

Cream butter and sugar, add beaten egg, flour, baking powder and enough water to moisten the whole. Fill 4 buttered cups $\frac{3}{4}$ full. Bake for 20 minutes and serve with flavoured cornflour sauce.

VERMICELLI PUDDING

60 gr (2 oz.) Vermicelli
2 eggs
grated rind of $\frac{1}{2}$ a lemon or orange
500 ml (1 pint) milk
2 tablespoons sugar
pinch of salt

Put milk, salt and rind into a wet saucepan. Bring to the boil, stir in the broken vermicelli and simmer for $\frac{1}{2}$ an hour, or until vermicelli is tender, then add the sugar. Cool a little and add well-beaten eggs. Pour into a greased pie-dish, set in a pan of hot water and place in a moderate oven. Bake till custard is set, about 20 minutes.

PUDDING SAUCES

If a few drops of lemon juice are required for flavouring, puncture the lemon in two or three places with a knitting needle or small skewer. Squeeze out the juice required. This does not injure the lemon for keeping, and is therefore much better than cutting, as the fruit is often wasted by so doing.

A lemon will give twice the quantity of juice if placed in boiling water for a few minutes before squeezing.

BRANDY SAUCE

125 gr (4 oz.) Butter
3 tablespoons brandy
250 gr (8 oz.) icing sugar
1 egg white

Cream butter and sugar and add stiffly beaten egg and brandy, whipping all the time. Before serving heat over boiling water, stirring occasionally.

GINGER SAUCE

1 Small Piece Whole Ginger
½ cup water
juice of 1 lemon
2 tablespoons sugar
1 piece lemon rind
1 glass white wine or 1 tablespoon brandy

Grate the ginger and mix it with sugar (pounded and sifted), water and lemon rind, and simmer gently for 10 minutes. Add the lemon juice and wine; strain and serve.

LEMON SAUCE

1 Cup Sugar
juice and rind 1 lemon
2 cups water
1 tablespoon cornflour

Boil sugar, water, lemon juice and grated rind and thicken with the cornflour, blended with a little water. Boil about 7 minutes.

MOCK MAPLE SYRUP

Honey
boiling water
golden syrup
a pinch cinnamon
a few drops essence lemon

Take equal parts of honey, golden syrup and boiling water and add a few drops essence lemon and a pinch of cinnamon.

ORANGE SAUCE

2 Oranges
125 gr ($\frac{1}{4}$ lb.) butter
60 gr (2 oz.) sugar
1 teaspoon ground almonds

Wash the oranges and grate the rind. Put the butter in a basin, add the sugar and beat to a soft cream. Add the grated orange rind and the juice of 1 orange. Stir in the almonds. Pile on a dish and serve a little with each helping of pudding. Allow the sauce to become quite set before serving.

PLUM OR DARK PUDDING SAUCE

60 gr (2 oz.) Butter
1 dessertspoon brandy
75 gr ($2\frac{1}{2}$ oz.) fine sugar
1 tablespoon light wine
a little nutmeg

Beat the butter and sugar together until light and white, add the wines and nutmeg by degrees and beat till thoroughly mixed.

SAUCE FOR BOILED PUDDING

1 Small Glass Sherry Wine
15 gr ($\frac{1}{2}$ oz.) castor sugar
$\frac{1}{2}$ cup water
1 tablespoon apricot jam
1 teaspoon lemon juice

Put all into a saucepan and let simmer for 10 minutes. Strain and serve.

TREACLE SAUCE FOR PLAIN BOILED PUDDING

$\frac{1}{2}$ Cup Treacle
1 tablespoon butter

Melt over fire and stir well. Boil for 2 minutes and serve.

WHITE SAUCE

2 Cups Milk
1 tablespoon sugar
1 tablespoon cornflour
1 dessertspoon butter
vanilla essence or flavouring to taste

Put milk on to heat. Mix cornflour with additional milk and add to milk when almost boiling. Boil for 3 minutes, then add butter and flavouring.

COLD SWEETS

If difficulty is found in making jellies set in hot weather, beat them well and add a stiffly beaten egg white to each pint of jelly.

Fruit juices can be easily converted into jellies by adding 30 gr (1 oz.) gelatine to 500 ml (1 pint) juice that has been sweetened to taste.

Gelatine dissolves more easily if soaked in a little cold water before hot water is added.

If a jelly is wanted quickly, the gelatine may be soaked in one or two teaspoons cold water, dissolved by standing the basin in boiling water for a few minutes, and the remainder of the liquid added cold.

Jellies cannot be made from fresh pineapple juice unless it has previously been boiled for two minutes. This destroys the enzyme present in fresh pineapple which breaks down the gelatine so that it will not set.

Milk should be absolutely fresh and only lukewarm when added to either packet or home-made jellies, otherwise it will curdle.

Before putting dessert oranges on the table on a cold day, roll them for a few minutes in the palms of the hands before the fire. Or place lemons on the stove for a few minutes. They will be much juicier.

To make a quick dessert for unexpected visitors, peel and grate a couple of nice apples, sprinkle with sugar and pile on a little cream. This is very nice, but should be served immediately.

To make lemon jelly that can be used as a basis for fruit mould, take 30 gr (1 oz.) gelatine, 4 tablespoonsful cold water, 1 cup (1½ gills) hot water, 185 gr (6 oz.) sugar and 1 cup (1½ gills) lemon juice. Soften the gelatine in cold water, dissolve the sugar in the hot water and, when cool, add the lemon juice. Strain into a wetted mould and put in a cold place until set. A more carefully prepared and clarified lemon jelly may be made as follows. Put the above ingredients with the thinly peeled rind of a lemon, and the white and crushed shell of one egg in a saucepan. Bring to the boil, cool slightly and strain through a scalded cloth or jelly bag.

ALMOND JAPONAISE TORTE

4 Egg Whites
125 gr (4 oz.) castor sugar
125 gr (4 oz.) ground almonds mixed with 125 gr (4 oz.) castor sugar
small pinch of cream of tartar
extra chocolate filling
toasted coconut

Place egg whites with cream of tartar into a scalded dry bowl, and whip until stiff but not dry. Gradually beat in 125 gr (4 oz.) of castor sugar until meringue will hold its shape. Mix the ground almonds with the remaining 125 gr (4 oz.) of sugar. Blend gently but thoroughly into meringue mixture. Draw three 20 cm (8 in.) circles, using a 20 cm (8 in.) cake pan as a guide, on greaseproof paper. Pipe mixture through a large plain tube and cover each circle to a depth of 13 mm (½ in.). Smooth over, using the back of a spoon. Bake in a slow oven 35 minutes.

Cool and carefully remove from paper. Sandwich layers together with chocolate filling, then coat all over sides and top with the same filling cream. Roll in toasted coconut, pressing on firmly and leaving a 52 mm (2 in.) circle without coconut in centre top. This is then filled with a thin circle of melted chocolate. Allow to ripen for several hours, then chill before serving.

Note: If nuts are preferred to coconut, roast either almonds (blanched) or hazelnuts until golden colour; cool, then grind in almond grinder and use on torte.

Chocolate Filling

2 Eggs
90 gr (3 oz.) butter
90 gr (3 oz.) sugar
60 gr (2 oz.) chocolate

Grate and slowly soften chocolate over a "water-bath". Whisk egg and sugar in a basin over a saucepan of hot water until as thick as custard. Remove from heat and continue whisking until cool. Cream butter until soft, mix with melted chocolate, then gradually beat in the egg mixture. Use one or two quantities of this filling as desired.

Round the 52 mm (2 in.) circle of melted chocolate place blanched almonds close together.

ANGEL FOOD (No. 1)

2 Level Tablespoons Powdered Gelatine
1 cup of hot water
½ cup sugar
grated rind of 1 lemon and 1 orange
4 eggs
juice 2 lemons, 2 oranges

Dissolve the gelatine in a cup of hot water, add the sugar, juice and grated rind of oranges and lemons. Beat the egg yolks well and add to the mixture. Give it a stir now and then until it begins to set. Beat the whites to a very stiff froth and fold into the mixture, allow to set. May be served with cream or custard.

ANGEL FOOD (No. 2)

1 litre (1 Quart) Milk
4 eggs
30 gr (1 oz.) gelatine
60 gr (2 oz.) sugar
$\frac{1}{2}$ cup hot water
essence lemon to taste

Beat together the yolks of eggs and the sugar, add to the milk, place on the fire and stir until the custard comes to the boil. Remove from the fire. Allow to cool. Add flavouring and gelatine which has been dissolved in hot water. When almost cold, stir in the stiffly beaten whites of the eggs. Pour into a wet mould to set. Serve with custard, cream or stewed fruit.

APPLE SNOW

3 Large Cooking Apples
2 eggs
90 gr (3 oz.) castor sugar

Cut up the apples and stew them with skins on with very little water, about 1 tablespoon, then put the pulp through a sieve. Beat the whites of the eggs to a stiff froth and gently add the sugar, then the apple and beat till light and soft like snow. Pile roughly on a glass dish and serve with custard.

BANANA AND PINEAPPLE FLUFF

30 gr (1 oz.) Gelatine
4 tablespoons hot water
2 whites of eggs
a small tin of shredded pineapple
4 tablespoons cold water
60 gr (2 oz.) sugar
2 bananas
cherries and angelica
125 ml (1 gill) pineapple juice

Soak the gelatine in the cold water. Dissolve the sugar in the hot water, add to the gelatine and pineapple juice. Allow to cool until nearly set, then add the bananas, mashed, chopped pineapple and stiffly beaten egg whites. Prepare a souffle case or round glass dish by tying a band of strong paper round and removing when jelly is set. By this means the level of fluff is raised above that of the dish, suggesting that the pudding has raised and is very light. Decorate with glazed cherries and angelica.

BANANA MOULD

Sponge Cakes
raspberry jelly
bananas

Line a mould with bananas, cut in strips and rings, then a layer of sponge cakes, then bananas and cake till mould is full; pour over raspberry jelly made from packet. Serve with cream.

CARAMEL CUSTARD

60 gr (2 oz.) Sugar
3 eggs
2 tablespoons sugar
2 tablespoons water
3 cups milk
vanilla to taste

Put sugar and water on the fire. Boil until brown and pour into a basin and coat all the inside by turning round until all is covered. Beat up eggs, add milk, sugar and vanilla, pour into the basin and bake until set. Turn out when cold.

CHARLOTTE RUSSE

15 gr ($\frac{1}{2}$ oz.) Gelatine
500 ml (1 pint) milk
1 cup water
1 cup sugar
4 eggs

Beat yolks of eggs and sugar together, soak the gelatine in a cup of cold water. Put milk on to boil, and while boiling stir in the yolks and sugar. Let this cool until nearly as thick as custard, then add the soaked gelatine. When nearly cold add the whites of eggs whipped to a stiff froth, flavour with vanilla essence and pour into a mould lined with sponge cakes.

CHARLOTTE ORANGE

30 gr (1 oz.) Gelatine
1 teacup sugar
juice 1 lemon
whites of 3 eggs
$\frac{1}{3}$ cup cold water
$\frac{1}{3}$ cup boiling water
3 oranges
sponge fingers

Soak powdered gelatine in cold water, add boiling water, lemon juice, sugar and all the pulp and juice of the oranges. Bring all to the boil. When quite cold and beginning to set, whip to a froth, whipping in the beaten whites of eggs. Pile on a glass dish, decorate with sponge fingers and serve with custard made from egg yolks.

CHOCOLATE AND ORANGE CUSTARD

$\frac{3}{4}$ litre ($1\frac{1}{2}$ Pints) Milk
2 tablespoons cornflour
60 gr (2 oz.) chocolate
2 tablespoons sugar
2 eggs
2 or 3 oranges

Put milk on to boil, keeping back sufficient to blend cornflour and cocoa and add this to milk when boiling and stir for 10 minutes. Remove from fire and add yolks of eggs, sugar and vanilla flavouring. Let the mixture cool. Skin the oranges and slice them thinly and put in glass dish; if sour sprinkle with sugar and pour the chocolate mixture over them. Whip the whites of the eggs to a stiff froth, add a little sugar and pile on top. The eggs can be omitted and whipped cream put on top.

CHOCOLATE PEACHES

1 Tin Peaches
1 dessertspoon powdered chocolate or cocoa
1 dessertspoon cornflour
1 dessertspoon water

Draw the syrup from the tin of fruit. Mix the cornflour, cocoa and water together and add to syrup. Boil mixture for a few minutes until thick. Place fruit in dish, pour syrup over and top off with cream.

CHOCOLATE RAISIN PIE

1 Tablespoon Cornflour
1 cup seeded raisins
$\frac{1}{2}$ tablespoon cocoa
2 cups milk
2 tablespoons sugar
vanilla to flavour
2 eggs
short pastry

Mix cornflour, sugar and cocoa and blend with a little milk. Boil remainder of milk and stir in cornflour mixture. When cool, add beaten egg yolks, raisins and vanilla. Line a dish with pastry, pour in mixture and bake in moderate oven for 20 minutes. Whisk whites of eggs, when stiff fold in a tablespoon sugar. Pile on tart and brown in the oven. Serve cold.

COFFEE CREAM

250 ml ($\frac{1}{2}$ Pint) Milk
2 eggs
15 gr ($\frac{1}{2}$ oz.) gelatine
60 gr (2 oz.) sugar
2 tablespoons strong coffee
cream

Make a custard from the milk, sugar and eggs and add the coffee. Allow the custard to cool, then add the gelatine dissolved in a little water and about 1 tablespoon of cream. Pour into a mould and allow to set.

CHOCOLATE JELLY

1 Dessertspoon Cocoa
1 cup hot water
3 teaspoons castor sugar
500 ml (1 pint) packet vanilla jelly
1 cup milk
1 egg
coconut

Mix cocoa to paste with a spoonful of milk. Bring remainder of milk to the boil, stir in the cocoa and boil one minute. Allow to cool a little and add well-beaten egg, then stand the pan containing the mixture in a pan of boiling water, add sugar and stir constantly until custard thickens. When cooked, pour into a basin to cool. Dissolve the jelly according to the directions on the packet, and when cold stir by degrees into custard. Pour into small fancy moulds. When set turn on to a glass dish and sprinkle each with coconut.

CHRISTMAS PUDDING (WESTERN AUSTRALIAN)

- 500 gr (1 lb.) Lady Fingers
- 250 gr (½ lb.) shelled almonds
- 250 gr (½ lb.) crystallised cherries
- 500 ml (1 pint) hot milk
- ½ cup sugar
- 500 gr (1 lb.) macaroons
- 500 ml (1 pint) sherry wine
- 2 tablespoons flour
- 1 litre (1 quart) cream, whipped stiff
- 1 egg

Soak the macaroons in the wine. Blanch and chop the almonds, not too finely. Make a custard by mixing sugar and flour with the egg until very light, add gradually to the hot milk, and let cook in double boiler until very thick, stirring constantly. Cool, add almonds, cherries and the cream whipped very stiff. Line glass bowl with lady fingers, cut in half. Add the custard, macaroons, cream, putting cherries all through the bowl. Pile the cream on the top and decorate with the cherries.

CHRISTMAS PUDDING (CHILLED)

- 250 gr (8 oz.) Pkt. Sweet Biscuits (arrowroot, ginger nuts, coffee, nice, etc.)
- 1 pkt. 375 gr (12 oz.) seeded raisins
- 60 gr (2 oz.) almonds
- ¼ cup orange juice
- 1 cup sugar
- 1 level tablespoon gelatine
- 1 pkt. 125 gr (4 oz.) cherries
- 185 gr (6 oz.) butter
- ¼ cup sherry
- ½ cup water

Roll biscuits finely and add to chopped fruits, cherries and nuts, and moisten with orange juice and sherry. Melt butter and add. Boil sugar and water and gelatine for 5 minutes. Cool. Beat till white and thick. Add to first mixture. Spices may be added if desired. Pour into well-greased basin and refrigerate for at least 12 hours. Serve sliced with ice cream.

COLD SWEET

- 30 gr (1 oz.) Gelatine
- lemon juice
- pineapple juice or sherry
- walnuts
- ¾ cup castor sugar
- orange juice
- ⅓ cup cold water
- ⅓ cup boiling water

Melt gelatine in cold water, add castor sugar and dissolve in 1-3rd cup of boiling water, stir in 3 tablespoons of lemon juice and ½ cup of orange juice, ½ cup of pineapple juice or sherry. Rinse a shallow dish with cold water, and pour into it half the jelly mixture, when it is nearly set cover the top with halved walnuts, placing them 26 mm (1 in.) apart. Leave until set and then slowly pour over it the remaining half of the jelly. Serve cut into squares, with sweetened whipped cream.

DELICIOUS PUDDING

1 Tablespoon Butter
1 tablespoon self-raising flour
juice and rind of 1 lemon
$\frac{1}{2}$ cup sugar
$1\frac{1}{4}$ cups milk
2 eggs

Cream butter and sugar, add flour, rind and juice of lemon and milk. Beat yolks and add, and, lastly, mix in the stiffly beaten whites. Pour into pie-dish, bake until set in moderate oven. Serve cold with cream.

FLUMMERY

1 Tablespoon Gelatine
1 tablespoon plain flour
6 passionfruit
1 cup sugar
juice 2 oranges
juice 2 lemons
2 cups water

Put gelatine, sugar and 1 cup of water in a saucepan and bring to the boil, stirring all the time. Add flour mixed smooth in a cup of cold water and boil for several minutes, stirring all the time. Put aside to cool; when cool add orange and lemon juice. Beat mixture for 25 minutes or until thick, then add passionfruit and put aside to set.

GOLDEN LEMON PUDDING

1 Cup Sugar
1 heaped dessertspoon gelatine dissolved in 1 cup hot water
rind and juice 1 large lemon
2 eggs

Beat egg yolks and sugar. Add rind and juice of lemon. Stir in gelatine and hot water and add stiffly beaten egg whites. Pour into glass dish and set in refrigerator.

JELLY FLUFF

1 Pkt. Jelly Crystals (any desired flavour)
1 small tin evaporated milk
$\frac{1}{4}$ cup sugar
$\frac{3}{4}$ cup hot water
1 tablespoon lemon juice

Melt jelly crystals in hot water and stir till dissolved. Allow to cool and begin to set. Whip milk with sugar and lemon juice and whip in jelly. Serve in glass dish garnished with fruit, whipped cream, or chopped jelly.

LEMON MOUSSE

3 eggs
2 tablespoons sugar
1 or 2 lemons
15 gr (½ oz.) gelatine
a little water
cream

Divide yolks from whites of eggs, putting them into separate basins. Add sugar and grated rind of ½ lemon to yolks and beat with wooden spoon until light and creamy. Then add strained juice of 1 or 2 lemons according to size and taste. Dissolve gelatine in small quantity of water and strain into egg mixture. Continue beating until mixture begins to set. Then stir in very lightly whites of eggs beaten to a stiff froth. Put the mousse into a glass bowl and keep in a cool place until required. Serve with a little whipped and sweetened cream on top.

LEMON SNOW

625 ml (1¼ Pints) Milk
3 tablespoons cornflour
2 lemons
½ cup sugar
4 eggs

Boil milk, add cornflour and sugar mixed with a little cold milk. Stir till thick. When cool add lemon juice and the stiffly beaten whites of eggs. Set in a mould and serve cold with boiled custard.

LEMON SWISS (BAKED)

60 gr (2 oz.) Butter
½ cup sugar
2 tablespoons plain flour
1 large lemon
1 cup milk
2 eggs
grated rind of lemon

Cream butter and sugar, add flour, then lemon juice and grated rind. Next add egg yolks, then milk and lastly fold in the stiffly beaten whites. The ingredients must be mixed in this order. Pour into a greased pudding dish and bake in a moderate oven slowly for 1 hour. As soon as pudding starts to brown, stand in a dish of cold water on the bottom shelf of oven.

When cooked this pudding will be a cake mixture on top with a lemon sauce underneath. May be eaten hot or cold, with or without cream.

MOCK SPONGE

750 ml (1½ Pints) Water
4 tablespoons arrowroot
2 lemons
½ cup sugar
whites of 3 eggs

Boil water with rinds of lemon, strain and bring to boil again. Mix arrowroot and sugar with a little water and lemon juice, add to boiling water and stir over fire till smooth. When cool beat in the stiffly beaten whites of eggs, decorate mould with fancy slices of lemon. Pour mixture in and serve when set and cold, with cold boiled custard poured around.

ORANGE FOAM

2 Cups Hot Water
2 tablespoons cornflour
½ lemon
¾ cup sugar
juice 2 oranges
3 eggs

Boil water in saucepan, add sugar when boiling and add cornflour, already mixed with cold water; stir. Let cook for 5 minutes, then add juices. Whip whites of eggs, pour over cornflour mixture. When cold beat very light. Make a soft custard of 500 ml (1 pint) milk, 2 tablespoons sugar, ½ teaspoon vanilla and yolks of 3 eggs. Pour over orange foam.

ORANGE SNOW

6 Oranges
3 tablespoons sugar
1½ cups water
3 Eggs
1 lemon
1 tablespoon gelatine

Place gelatine and water on fire. Stir until dissolved, add sugar, juice of oranges and lemon. Allow to cool; beat in stiffly beaten egg whites. Pour into a wetted mould and leave to set. Serve with boiled custard.

ORANGE SOUFFLE

250 ml (½ Pint) Cream
3 eggs
rind and juice of 2 oranges
1 lemon
3 sheets gelatine
90 gr (3 oz.) sugar

Place rind, yolks and sugar over pan of boiling water and stir until thick. Remove from fire and stir until cool. Then add lemon and orange juice and melted gelatine and lastly the whipped cream and stiffly beaten whites of eggs. Put into a souffle dish and leave until firm.

PAVLOVA

4 egg whites
1 cup sugar
1 dessertspoon cornflour
1 teaspoon vanilla
1 teaspoon vinegar

Beat egg whites till stiff, add sugar gradually and beat till sugar is completely dissolved. Add vinegar and vanilla, lastly fold in cornflour. Bake in cool oven 225°F or 100°C for 1½-2 hours.

PEACH BOATS

Peel and halve ripe peaches, arrange in a dish, hollow side up. Fill each peach with jelly and sweetened whipped cream.

PINEAPPLE MARSHMALLOW TART

1 Small Tin Crushed Pineapple (or pineapple pieces)
hot water
1 pkt. lemon jelly
1 cooked, cooled 20 cm (8 inch) pastry case
1 tablespoon gelatine
1 dessertspoon lemon juice

Drain syrup from pineapple and make up to 375 ml (¾ pint) with hot water. Mix gelatine with jelly crystals and pour on hot pineapple syrup. Stir until dissolved. When cold and thickening, beat till thick and creamy. Fold in pineapple and lemon juice. Pour into cooked pastry shell and chill. Serve with cream, ice cream or custard.

PLUM PUDDING (CHILLED, No. 1)

125 gr (4 oz.) Sultanas
125 gr (4 oz.) drained cherries
60 gr (2 oz.) prunes or figs
30 gr (1 oz.) crystallised ginger
2 bananas
30 gr (1 oz.) currants
60 gr (2 oz.) seeded raisins
60 gr (2 oz.) shredded peel
30 gr (1 oz.) blanched almonds
3 tablespoons gelatine dissolved in 3 tablespoons cold water
125 ml (¼ pint) sherry
2 tablespoons lemon juice
4 tablespoons sugar
½ teaspoon grated rind of lemon

Cook sultanas, raisins and prunes in a little hot water till plump. Strain. Shred almonds, chop ginger, prunes or figs and slice bananas and cherries. Pour over half the sherry and cover closely. Put ½ cup hot water in saucepan with sugar, lemon juice, and rind, and bring to boiling point. Strain and add dissolved gelatine and cold water to make up to 250 ml (½ pint). Add balance of sherry and pour over the fruit. Chill and serve with ice cream, cream or cold custard.

PLUM PUDDING (CHILLED, No. 2)

1 Cup Cake or Biscuit Crumbs
30 gr (1 oz.) gelatine soaked in ½ cup cold water
3 cups milk
1 cup sugar
½ cup rum, brandy or sherry
3 eggs
½ teaspoon each nutmeg and cinnamon
2 tablespoons cocoa
60 gr (2 oz.) each chopped walnuts, almonds, cherries, raisins
125 ml (¼ pint) whipped cream (opt.)
pinch salt

Soak fruits in wine. Make an unsweetened custard with milk, cocoa and egg yolks. Add dissolved gelatine. Add cake or biscuit crumbs and beat well. Put aside till mixture starts to thicken. Whip cream till stiff. Beat egg whites with sugar until very stiff and glossy. Fold both cream and meringue into mixture. Turn into a large mould or basin. Chill thoroughly. Serve with cold boiled custard or ice cream.

RASPBERRY JELLY WHIP

½ Pkt. Raspberry Jelly Crystals
cold water
1 banana
125 ml (¼ pint) boiling water
1 cup prepared fruit salad
whipped cream

Dissolve jelly in hot water, add enough cold water to make up to 250 ml (½ pint). When quite cold and beginning to thicken beat until thick and fluffy. Fold in the fruit salad and chopped banana. Chill and serve with whipped cream or ice cream.

ROMAN CANDLES

Pineapple
whites of eggs
cherries
bananas

Allow one round of pineapple to each person. Place on pudding plate. Into the centre stand a banana, place a cherry on the top to represent the light of a candle. Whip whites of eggs stiffly and place a little round the bottom of the candles. Chill before serving.

SAGO SNOW

½ Cup Sago
1 cup sugar
3 cups cold water
whites of 2 or 3 eggs
3 lemons (rind of 2, juice of 3)

Wash sago and boil in water, adding sugar and grated rind of 2 lemons. When boiled add juice of 3 lemons; stir well. When nearly cold add stiffly beaten whites of eggs. Serve cold with custard made from yolks of eggs.

SAGO AND CURRANT MOULD

75 gr (2½ oz.) Sago
60 gr (2 oz.) sugar
60 gr. (2 oz.) currants
625 ml (1¼ pints) milk
30 gr (1 oz.) butter
lemon flavouring

Boil milk, sprinkle in sago, simmer 10 minutes, then add currants. Cook about 15 minutes, then add butter, sugar and flavouring, turn into a wetted mould.

SNOW FLAKE BLANC-MANGE

1 Cup Milk
2 tablespoons cornflour
1 cup water
2 tablespoons sugar
2 eggs

Mix the milk and water, bring to the boil, then add cornflour mixed smooth with a little cold water. Add the sugar and boil a few minutes. Beat the whites of the eggs to a stiff froth with a little flavouring, fold in carefully. Set aside in mould to get cold. The yolks of eggs can be used for custard to serve with the sweet along with jelly.

SPANISH CREAM

750 ml ($1\frac{1}{2}$ Pints) Milk
23 gr ($\frac{3}{4}$ oz.) gelatine
3 eggs
$\frac{1}{2}$ cup sugar
flavouring, lemon, etc.

Put the milk on to boil. When boiling stir in the sugar and the well beaten egg yolks. Remove from the fire. Add flavouring to taste. Dissolve the gelatine in a little hot water, and add to the mixture. Pour on to the stiffly beaten whites of the eggs. Place in a wet mould and when firm turn out. The custard *must boil,* or it will not separate. The top of the pudding should be clear amber and the custard below, forming 2 distinct layers. It should only just boil. Do not keep it cooking.

TIPSY CAKE

1 Large Sponge Cake
6 tablespoons brandy
500 ml (1 pint) good custard
sherry wine or fruit juice
90 gr (3 oz.) blanched almonds
whipped cream
jelly to garnish

Take a stale cake, sponge savoy or rice cake will do. Cut to fit the dish it is to stand in. Make a hole in the underside of cake and pour in and over the cake the wine and brandy, mixed with sufficient syrup to well soak the cake. When the cake is well soaked cut the almonds into strips and stick them all over the cake and pour round it a rich custard made with 4 or 5 eggs to 500 ml (1 pint) of milk and well flavoured. Whip some cream and put in heaps on the custard, and decorate with coloured jelly.

TRIFLE

$\frac{1}{2}$ of 18 cm (7 inch) Sponge, approx.
12 ratafias
500 ml (1 pint) rich custard
125 ml (1 gill) cream
6 macaroons
30 gr (1 oz.) blanched almonds
125 ml (1 gill) of sherry
raspberry jam
cherries and angelica

Spread the sliced sponges with jam and arrange in a glass bowl with the macaroons and ratafias. Pour over the sherry gradually and allow to stand 15 minutes. Add the custard. Just before serving decorate with the whipped cream, sliced almonds, cherries and angelica.

ICE CREAM (No. 1)

$\frac{1}{2}$ Tin Condensed Milk
4 tablespoons powdered milk
1 teaspoon vanilla
500 gr (1 pint) fresh milk
2 level teaspoons gelatine

Soak gelatine in $\frac{1}{4}$ cup hot water. Warm milk, add other ingredients and beat. Freeze till starting to set. Rebeat and return to freezing compartment of refrigerator.

ICE CREAM (No. 2)

1 Teaspoon Gelatine
4 heaped tablespoons full cream powdered milk
3 tablespoons sugar
1½ teaspoons vanilla essence
½ cup hot water
1½ cups water or milk

Dissolve gelatine in 1 tablespoon cold water, then mix with the ½ cup hot water. Beat together powdered milk, sugar, 1½ cups hot water, add gelatine mixture and vanilla. Beat well, turn into freezing trays. When frozen to consistency of thick cream remove, beat until doubled in bulk. Freeze firm.

ICE CREAM (No. 3)

500 ml (1 Pint) Milk
½ cup hot water
6 tablespoons powdered milk
1 teaspoon vanilla essence
½ cup sugar
1 dessertspoon gelatine
pinch of salt

Whisk powdered milk with fresh milk (all powdered milk may be used). Add sugar, salt and vanilla and beat well. Dissolve gelatine in hot water, and beat into other ingredients. Chill until set, then beat for 10 minutes. Freeze.

ICE CREAM (VANILLA)

500 ml (1 Pint) Milk
yolks 6 eggs
185 gr (6 oz.) sugar
500 ml (1 pint) separated cream
1 tablespoon vanilla essence

Scald the milk, beat yolks and sugar together until very light, then add them to the milk. Cook until the mixture thickens, stirring constantly. Take from the fire, add the cream and, when cool, add flavouring and freeze.

BANANAS (FROZEN)

1 Dozen Bananas
juice 2 oranges
500 gr (1 lb.) sugar
500 ml (1 pint) water
500 ml (1 pint) cream

Peel and cut bananas in slices and then mash very fine. Boil the sugar and water together for 5 minutes. Strain, and when cool, add orange juice and bananas. Freeze. When frozen, stir in very carefully the whipped cream. Return to freezer and leave for 1 hour to ripen.

BOMBE ALASKA

3 Egg Whites
½ teaspoon vanilla
1 tray hard frozen ice cream
¼ cup sugar
1 block sponge cake 25 mm (1 in.) thick
coarsely chopped almonds or walnuts

Beat egg whites stiffly, gradually adding sugar and vanilla. Beat till mixture will hold its shape. Cover a board with aluminium foil or double greaseproof paper. Put cake on it. Cake must be large enough to extend 25 mm (1 in.) all around the ice cream block. Sprinkle cake with sherry and put ice cream on it. Cover quickly with meringue making sure it goes right down to the paper all around the cake. Sprinkle with nuts and bake in *hot* oven for 3-4 minutes to tint the meringue. Slide off the board on to a chilled serving dish, garnish with glace fruits if desired, and serve at once.

COFFEE CUSTARD (FROZEN)

250 gr (½ lb.) Sugar
500 ml (1 pint) milk
4 eggs
250 ml (½ pint) cream
1 cup strong coffee

Put the milk in a double saucepan to scald. Beat the eggs and sugar together until very light, add them to the hot milk and cook for about 1 minute. Remove from the fire and add the cream and coffee gradually. Allow to become cold and then freeze.

ORANGE SOUFFLE (FROZEN)

500 ml (1 Pint) Orange Juice
yolks 6 eggs
1 litre (1 quart) cream
500 gr (1 lb.) sugar
15 gr (½ oz.) gelatine

Soak the gelatine in ½ cup of cold water for 1 hour, then add ½ cup boiling water. Mix the orange juice and sugar together. Whip the cream. Beat the egg yolks until light and then add to the orange and sugar; add gelatine and freeze. When frozen, stir in the cream and allow to stand for about 2 hours to ripen.

SALADS AND SALAD DRESSINGS

Daintiness in serving a salad is essential, as nothing is more tempting than a cool crisp salad served with care.

Vegetables for salads should be well washed and drained.

Salads may be prepared from fruit, vegetables, meats or fish. Cooked vegetables are really good and constitute an excellent way to use up left-overs.

The dressing of the salad is very important. Only the very best oil and vinegar should be used. Some people substitute cream or milk for oil and lemon juice for vinegar. Do not be afraid to use plenty of oil or cream, but be sparing on the vinegar or lemon juice. Use just enough to form a nice light cream.

To peel apples easily, pour boiling water over them, cover and leave for 10 minutes and then the skins will come off easily. This is much more economical and easier than peeling with a knife.

A little lemon juice sprinkled over apples that have been chopped for salad will prevent them discolouring and add to the flavour of the dish.

If vinegar is added to the water in which greens or salads are washed, the insects will die and drop off, whereas when salt is used the insects cling to the leaves.

A squeeze of lemon juice will freshen lettuce in 5 minutes, or place anything steel in the water with the lettuce.

Strong vinegar should not be used on beetroot, salads, etc. Always use equal quantities of vinegar and water.

When cutting hard-boiled eggs, dip the knife in water. When boiling eggs, dip first in cold water. This prevents the shells cracking.

APPLE AND NUT SALAD

Apples
lettuce
nuts
celery
salad dressing

Chop up equal quantities of apples and celery, cover with salad dressing and blend well together. Sprinkle chopped nuts on top and serve with lettuce. Bananas may be used in place of apples.

BEETROOT MOULD

2 Dessertspoons Gelatine
$1\frac{1}{4}$ cups hot water
2 average size beets (cooked)
$\frac{1}{2}$ cup vinegar
pepper, salt and sugar to taste

Peel and slice beetroot and line a mould with slices. Fill the centre with small pieces of beetroot. Dissolve gelatine in hot water, add sugar, salt, pepper and vinegar. Leave to thicken slightly, then pour over beetroot and allow to set. If liked more vinegar and less water may be used, also other vegetables may replace some of the beetroot. Serve garnished with lettuce leaves and slices of tomato and mayonnaise dressing. Sufficient for six servings.

COOKING BEETROOT AS A SALAD

A quicker method with the same results as the old one may be obtained by first peeling and cutting the beetroot into slices ready for the table. Then cover with half water and half vinegar and a little sugar, and simmer till tender. When cool the beetroot is ready to serve.

CUCUMBER SALAD

1 Cucumber
white onion

Slice cucumber thinly, add salt and drain. Slice onions and mix together and cover with vinegar, salt and pepper to taste. Add small teaspoon of salad oil.

FIGS (STUFFED)

Figs
nuts
salt
cream cheese
cayenne
cream
lettuce

Wash and dry whole fresh figs, remove stalks and make an incision in each. Then work up some cream cheese with finely chopped nuts, cayenne and salt, adding a little cream, if necessary, to soften it. Stuff figs with this mixture and arrange them on individual dishes with a few curly lettuce leaves. Extra salad with French dressing may be served separately.

LETTUCE SALAD

Lettuce
eggs
tomatoes

Separate the leaves and put them in cold water and leave until nice and crisp. Wash well, dry by shaking in a clean tea cloth, roll several leaves tightly together and shred very finely with a stainless knife. Pile in a glass salad bowl and decorate with slices of hard boiled eggs and tomato, or cucumber and tomato, or diced eggs and sliced beetroot. Squeeze over the juice of a lemon and sugar, or use a prepared dressing.

MACARONI SALAD

1 Small Onion
90 gr (3 oz.) macaroni
1 small bunch of cress or parsley
½ small cucumber
1 tomato
4 tablespoons mayonnaise dressing

Cook the macaroni in plenty of salted boiling water. Drain and allow to get cold. Chop the onion finely, cut the cucumber into dice and mix the macaroni lightly with the onion and cucumber. Add the dressing. Place in a salad bowl, piling up in the centre. Decorate with the greens and garnish with sliced tomato.

MIXED FRUIT AND VEGETABLE SALAD

1 Lettuce
some pineapple cubes
2 oranges
a few nuts
salad dressing

Wash and trim the lettuce, place in cold water to crisp it and drain well. Place lettuce in a bowl, nicely arranged, with pieces of orange and pineapple between the leaves. Chop a few nuts and scatter over roughly. Serve with a French salad dressing. The trimmings from the lettuce can be shredded and used to decorate.

POTATO SALAD

1 kg (2 lb.) Potatoes
1 white onion
celery
parsley or mint
salad dressing
cooked peas

Boil potatoes and when cold dice. Chop celery and onion and parsley finely, and mix with potatoes. Shortly before serving pour over salad dressing and garnish with peas.

TOMATO SALAD

Tomatoes
sugar
a little salt
vinegar

To prepare tomatoes, put them into boiling water and then drop into cold water to loosen skins. Remove the skin and slice thinly. Put in a glass dish and sprinkle with salt, sugar and vinegar. Sliced onion may be mixed with the tomato if liked. A prepared salad dressing may be used in place of salt, sugar and vinegar.

VEGETABLE SALAD

1 Crisp Lettuce
3 tomatoes
a little watercress
1 carrot
the centre of a firm, white cabbage
2 spring onions
a sprig of mint
mayonnaise dressing

Wash and shred the lettuce finely. Wash the cabbage and chop as finely as possible. Slice the tomatoes and chop the onions very finely. Mix all together in a glass dish with the watercress and mint and garnish with a grated carrot. Serve with mayonnaise dressing.

WATERMELON SALAD

Use a not very ripe melon. Slice melon thinly. Sprinkle with chopped onions or chives. Serve with your favourite mayonnaise.

WINTER VEGETABLE SALAD

1 Cup Raw, Shredded Carrots
1 cup shredded turnip
lettuce
1 cup shredded cabbage
4 sweet gherkins, chopped
salt and pepper

Mix together the raw carrots, cabbage and turnip and season with salt and pepper. Add the gherkins and moisten with ½ cup of liquid from a bottle of sweet gherkins. Serve in nests of crisp lettuce.

DRESSINGS

FRENCH SALAD DRESSING

(Will keep 6 months.)

250 ml (½ Pint) Milk
1½ Cups Vinegar
2 teaspoons mustard
1 teaspoon salt
3 eggs
1 cup sugar

Put milk on stove, beat eggs and sugar together well, add the vinegar, salt and mustard (blended with vinegar). When milk is just on the boil, pour in mixture and stir all the time till as thick as honey. Do not let it boil. When cool, bottle.

HONEY DRESSING

2 Tablespoons Lemon Juice
2 tablespoons honey
olive oil or cream

Mix together the lemon juice and honey and carefully add a tablespoon of rich cream or a teaspoon of olive oil.

MAYONNAISE DRESSING

Yolks of 2 Raw Eggs
about 2 tablespoons vinegar
1 saltspoon mustard
oil
1 teaspoon salt
a little cayenne pepper

Place the yolks in a basin and beat until smooth with a stainless or silver fork, and add oil (the very best), a few drops at a time, until it begins to thicken, when it can be increased in quantities, but it must be stirred constantly and very rapidly. When it becomes thick, add a few drops of vinegar or lemon juice. Beat quickly and repeat until about 2 tablespoons of vinegar have been added, then add the salt, mustard and a little cayenne pepper. The usual proportion of oil to vinegar is 3 times as much oil as vinegar. Some cooks use 6 times as much oil—it is just a matter of taste. The mayonnaise can be coloured with vegetable colouring if desired.

MUSTARD DRESSING

1 Teaspoon Mixed Mustard
1 tablespoon vinegar
salt and pepper
1 small ½ cup cream
sugar if liked

Mix together the mustard, pepper, salt and vinegar. Beat in the cream gradually. Orange juice may be substituted for vinegar.

SALAD DRESSING (No. 1)

1 Tablespoon Best Salad Oil
½ teaspoon sugar
1 small teaspoon salt
1 teaspoon lemon juice
1 egg
cayenne pepper
1 teaspoon best vinegar
2 tablespoons cream

Whip all together, with enough cayenne pepper to taste, and pour over the prepared salad just before serving. The vinegar and oil must be added very gradually in drops.

SALAD DRESSING (No. 2)

1 Tin Condensed Milk	**8 tablespoons vinegar**
1 eggspoon mustard	**salt and pepper**

Mix all together well, and put in a Mason's jar with a lid. This will keep for weeks. When going to use, take a tablespoon of mixture and mix with a little fresh milk and vinegar.

SALAD DRESSING (No. 3)

2 Hard Boiled Eggs	**pepper and salt**
2 tablespoons vinegar	**mustard**
3 tablespoons cream	

Cut the eggs up when cold and mash whites as well. Add pepper, salt and mustard to taste, the cream or 1 tablespoon of condensed milk and the vinegar.

SALAD DRESSING (COOKED)

8 Teaspoons Sugar	**4 teaspoons flour**
2 teaspoons salt	**½ teaspoon mustard**
1 cup vinegar	**2 eggs**
butter size of two walnuts	**cayenne pepper**

Mix all the dry ingredients together and add the vinegar slowly. Heat in a double saucepan. Beat eggs very lightly, then pour the seasoned vinegar on to the eggs with the butter. Set back over the hot water and cook until it thickens, stirring constantly. When cold put in a jar, or bottle and cork. When required for use take a spoonful (or more) and thin with sweet cream or milk, beat well, and put on salad. This will keep well.

HORS D'OEUVRE

Hors d'œuvre are small side dishes, served cold, generally before the soup—merely to create an appetite. These little dishes make an attractive addition to the dinner table, if daintily served. Those most in favour are sardines, olives, oysters, sausage, fancy savouries, fruits, etc.

The making of these dishes is purely a matter of taste and skill on the part of the cook. The garnishing allows for original ideas. White and yolk of hard boiled egg, celery, parsley, watercress, beet, capers, gherkins and aspic jelly are all useful.

In these days when diet is so very important, the serving of fruit is becoming popular, and certainly should be equal, if not preferable to highly seasoned savouries.

ANCHOVY PASTRY

Make some tiny pastry cases with puff or short crust, and prick all over with a fork. Place a piece of greased paper over each and fill with rice (to prevent pastry rising). Bake in a hot oven till lightly browned and crisp. Remove the paper and rice and fill with anchovy cream. Sprinkle with paprika and garnish with capers.

ANCHOVY CREAM

3 or 4 Anchovies
1 dessertspoon butter
1 hard boiled egg
3 tablespoons cream
cayenne pepper

Wash and bone the anchovies, pound them with the egg yolk, cream and butter until smooth, and season with cayenne.

CHEESE SOUFFLES

3 Heaped Tablespoons Grated Cheese
1 cup cream
cayenne
1 tablespoon gelatine
1 cup milk
salt

Soak the gelatine in the milk for about ½ an hour, then stir it over the fire until dissolved. Allow to cool, add the cheese, cream, stiffly whipped, and the seasoning. Turn into small moulds, and leave to set. Turn out on to lettuce leaves and serve garnished with aspic jelly.

CHICKEN SAVOURY

90 gr (3 oz.) Cold Chicken
3 or 4 slices cooked beetroot
1 hard boiled egg
2 fillets smoked herring
1 large cold, boiled potato
mayonnaise sauce

Cut the chicken, potato, beet and herring into small pieces, and season with the sauce. Mix well, and place on six boat shaped pastry cases. Decorate with finely chopped yolk of egg.

GRAPEFRUIT

Select nice ripe fruit, wipe, and cut them in halves, take out the white core and pips, and loosen the fruit from the skin. Cut the fruit into small pieces, but leave in skin as if uncut. Drain off the escaped juice, sweeten, and flavour, and pour over the fruit. Decorate with angelica.

Rock and water melon, iced, and various fancy savoury biscuits are suitable to serve as hors d'œuvre.

TOMATO AND SHRIMP OR SARDINES

Tomatoes
cucumber
salad dressing
fish
parsley
cayenne
salt and pepper

Skin the tomatoes, cut in halves and remove the pulp. Fill with a salad made from half the pulp, blended with an equal quantity of fish, and seasoned with salt, pepper, cayenne and a good salad dressing. Place a thin slice of cucumber on each, garnish with parsley and serve.

SAVOURIES, SANDWICHES AND FILLINGS

APPLE SANDWICHES

Apples	castor sugar
lemon juice	bread and butter

Peel the required quantity of apples, cut into very thin slices and lay evenly on slices of buttered bread. Sprinkle with castor sugar and a few drops of lemon juice, then press a slice of buttered bread on top. Raisins or dates may be added. Pears may be substituted for apples.

BISCUIT SAVOURIES (No. 1)

1 Cup Milk	2 tablespoons cornflour
1 tablespoon butter	4 tablespoons grated cheese
1 teaspoon tomato sauce	pepper and cayenne to taste
a little salt	curry powder if liked
2 small beaten eggs	

Make a thick cream of the above ingredients by heating milk and stirring in eggs and cornflour (blended with a little milk). Add other ingredients and heat until thickened. Place small portions of this mixture on tiny dry biscuits and decorate with olives, scraps of pickled gherkins, finely grated yolk of egg, fragments of white of egg, small cubes of beetroot, finely chopped parsley and chopped capers. Arrange neatly.

BISCUIT SAVOURIES (No. 2)

125 gr ($\frac{1}{4}$ lb.) Grated Cheese	1 egg
butter size of walnut	1 teaspoon mixed mustard
$\frac{1}{4}$ cup milk	devilled almonds

Beat all together, except the almonds, and bring to the boil. Stir till it thickens and let stand until nearly cold. Have plain biscuits ready, spread 1 teaspoonful of mixture on each biscuit, and put 1 devilled almond on top.

CHEESE AND TOMATO SAVOURY

1 Egg
2 large skinned tomatoes
125 gr (¼ lb.) cheese
1 dessertspoon butter
cayenne and salt to taste

Cut up tomatoes and cheese into a saucepan and add butter and seasoning. Boil for 5 minutes and add well-beaten egg. Stir a minute or two and then leave to cool. Spread on bread and butter or toast.

CHEESE BISCUITS

250 gr (8 oz.) Self-raising Flour
185 gr (6 oz.) grated cheese
90 gr (3 oz.) butter
cayenne pepper and salt

Rub butter into flour. Add cheese, cayenne and salt. Mix with cold water to scone consistency. Roll 6 mm (¼ in.) thick and cut into rounds. Bake in medium oven. Remove and split down centre. Return to oven and brown.

CHEESE BISCUITS (RICH)

60 gr (2 oz.) Butter
90 gr (3 oz.) grated cheese
90 gr (3 oz.) self-raising flour
cayenne pepper and salt

Rub butter and cheese into flour with cayenne pepper and salt. Roll into little balls; roll in coconut. Bake in slow oven.

CHEESE BUTTONS

500 gr (1 lb.) Butter
500 gr (1 lb.) grated cheese
coconut
500 gr (1 lb.) plain flour
1 teaspoon cayenne pepper

Soften butter, mix flour with butter and add cheese and cayenne pepper. Knead mixture well. Take teaspoonful of mixture, roll and pat flat; toss in coconut. Cook in moderate oven. Makes 12 dozen.

CHEESE RUSKS

90 gr (3 oz.) Self-raising Flour
90 gr (3 oz.) grated cheese
lemon juice
small quantity water
60 gr (2 oz.) butter
1 egg yolk
pinch salt

Mix to a nice dough and roll out 13 mm (½ in.) thick. Cut in fingers and bake in fairly hot oven. Split while hot and return to oven till crisp and brown. Nice buttered with savouries.

CHEESE SAVOURY

Slices of Bread
cheese

The following is a change from serving biscuits or plain bread with cheese. Cut the slices of bread about 6 mm ($\frac{1}{4}$ in.) thick. Take a pastry cutter or small pepper tin and stamp out rounds. Toast until crisp and serve with cheese.

CHEESE STRAWS (No. 1)

60 gr (2 oz.) Flour
30 gr (1 oz.) butter
yolk of 1 egg
60 gr (2 oz.) grated cheese
a pinch of salt
cayenne
a few drops of lemon juice

Rub butter into flour, add other ingredients and mix. Roll out thin and cut in strips about 10 cm (4 in.) long and 6 mm ($\frac{1}{4}$ in.) wide. Bake for a few minutes, till a light brown, in a moderate oven.

Note.–Cheese straws should be well kneaded. The above is an excellent recipe. After mixing, take the ball and knead it with the fingers as you would knead a lump of plasticine. When fine enough roll out. If it gets a little dry, add a few more drops of lemon juice.

CHEESE STRAWS (No. 2)

155 gr (5 oz.) Cheese
155 gr (5 oz.) flour
lemon juice
125 gr (4 oz.) butter
2 egg whites
a little cayenne pepper

Grate the cheese finely, mix through the flour, rub in butter and pepper and blend well together. Make into a paste with the whites of egg and the lemon juice, roll out thin, cut into strips and bake a light brown in a hot oven.

CHEESE STRAWS (No. 3)

90 gr (3 oz.) Cheese
60 gr (2 oz.) butter
1 teaspoon boiling water
60 gr (2 oz.) flour
yolk of 1 egg
cayenne pepper
salt to taste

Sift flour and salt, rub butter in with the finger tips and then add grated cheese, cayenne pepper and beaten egg yolk. Mix to a stiff paste with boiling water, turn on to a floured board and knead lightly. Roll out, cut in strips about 10 cm (4 in.) long and 6 mm ($\frac{1}{4}$ in.) thick and cook to a pale brown in a moderate oven.

CREAM PUFF SAVOURIES

Cream Puffs
ham
mayonnaise dressing
lettuce

Make some cream puffs. Chop the lettuce as for a salad. Make some very thick mayonnaise dressing. Chop the ham very finely, pour dressing over ham and lettuce and put in cream puff shells at the last moment.

CRISP TWISTS

125 gr (4 oz.) Plain Flour
1 level teaspoon salt
meat extract
15 gr (½ oz.) lard
65 ml (½ gill) water (cold)
table salt

Sift flour with salt, rub the lard into it, mix to a dough with water. Using plenty of flour on rolling pin and board roll mixture into a rectangle. Pat entire surface with a wooden spoon. Fold into three and seal open edges. Repeat the rolling out and sealing twice more. Roll very thinly. Mix 2 teaspoons meat extract with a little water and brush over dough and sprinkle with table salt. Cut in thin strips as for cheese straws and curl slightly when placing on greased tray, keeping side with meat extract uppermost. Bake in hot oven for four or five minutes. They will twist more during baking.

MONTPELLIER BUTTER

Watercress
fresh butter
salt and pepper

Pull the leaves, which must be green and fresh, from the stalks and chop them very fine. Dry thoroughly in a cloth, then mince again and knead up with the butter till it is a bright green colour, seasoning with salt and pepper. Serve in tiny round balls. They are excellent served with cold fish. Parsley may be used in place of watercress if preferred.

OYSTER PATTIES

Pastry
60 gr (2 oz.) butter
125 ml (1 gill) milk
cayenne pepper
squeeze lemon juice
fresh or tinned oysters
30 gr (1 oz.) flour
65 ml (½ gill) oyster liquor
salt
2 tablespoons cream—or instead of cream, use yolks of 2 eggs

The Cases

Take 250 gr (½ lb.) of puff pastry (recipe in pastry section). Roll out to 6 mm (¼ in.) in thickness. Allow to rest for 5 minutes before cutting, then take a small cutter and stamp out as many rounds as you require. Dip cutter in hot water before cutting.

OYSTER PATTIES—*continued*

Cut quickly and evenly. Mark the middle of these rounds to about half their depth, with a smaller cutter, a border being left outside the centre. The pastry should be icy cold when cut. Lay the rounds on a cold baking tin, and brush over the tops with beaten egg, being very careful not to put any egg on the edges. Bake for 20 minutes in a hot oven. Lift off the inner circle of pastry, and remove the paste from the interior, to make room for the filling. If lids are wanted, roll out remaining pastry and cut rounds with the smaller of the two cutters used and bake on a separate tin for 10 minutes.

The Filling

Cut the oysters into small pieces. Melt half the butter in a saucepan, mix in the flour and cook for two minutes. Pour in the milk and oyster liquor. Stir until boiling, and allow to cook for about two minutes, then add cream, oysters and seasoning. Make all thoroughly hot and stir in the remainder of the butter broken into small pieces. It should be of the consistency of cream. When required, warm the patty cases and fill them with the mixture piling it high in the centre. Put on the lids of pastry and garnish each with a sprig of parsley. Patty cases can be filled with minced ham, vegetables, mince meat, sardines, etc. or with sweet fillings and cream.

OLIVES AND ANCHOVIES

1 Dozen Anchovies
thin slices of fried bread
1 dozen olives
butter

Wash and wipe the anchovies, fillet them and use half for pounding with pieces of butter (anchovy butter). Stone the olives, keeping them as whole as possible. Stuff them with the anchovy mixture and shape them nicely. Cut neat rounds from the fried bread, spread with anchovy butter and place a stuffed olive in the centre of each; then place a fillet of anchovy round each olive.

PARSLEY BUTTER

2 Tablespoons Parsley
2 tablespoons butter
lemon juice

Chop the parsley very finely (removing all stems). Blend it with the butter and add a few drops of lemon juice. Spread on white or brown bread and sandwich. Bananas, raisins, dates or walnuts are an additional improvement.

SALTED ALMONDS

1 Cup Shelled Almonds	**1 teaspoon salt**
1 teaspoon olive oil or butter	

Blanch the almonds, drop into cold water as you skin them to keep them crisp. Wipe and dry. Then coat each almond with oil and salt and bake on a tin dish in a moderate oven till a golden brown. Shake the plate occasionally so that the almonds are browned equally all over. Pick out the almonds, throwing away any loose salt that remains. The oil may be omitted and salt alone used.

SAUSAGE ROLLS

Pastry (Short or Puff)	**salt and pepper**
sausage meat	

Make pastry, roll out thinly and cut into long strips wide enough to roll. Place meat on strips of pastry, damp edges, fold over and cut into even sections. Glaze. Bake in hot oven 15-20 minutes.

SAVOURY (No. 1)

Chopped Walnuts	**pepper and salt**
chopped apple	**whipped cream**
chopped celery	

Mix together some chopped walnuts, celery and apple. Add a little pepper and salt and some whipped cream. Place in small quantities on cheese biscuits and garnish with parsley or chillies.

SAVOURY (No. 2)

6 Fingers of Bread	**cayenne pepper**
cheese	**salt and pepper**
6 sardines	

Fry the bread. Free the sardines from oil and place on a well-buttered baking dish, sprinkle with salt and pepper and heat in the oven. Lay a sardine on each piece of toast and add grated cheese and a little cayenne pepper. Make very hot and serve.

SAVOURY (No. 3)

6 Sliced Tomatoes	**2 sliced onions**
2 tablespoons sugar	**$\frac{1}{2}$ teaspoon pepper**
$\frac{1}{2}$ cup vinegar	**1 small teaspoon salt**
2 sliced apples	

Mix all ingredients together and cook for $\frac{1}{2}$ an hour.

SAVOURY BREAD

Slices of Buttered Bread
bacon
tomato
onion

Butter slices of bread about 6 mm ($\frac{1}{4}$ in.) thick. Cut into small squares or fancy shapes. Place on top small pieces of tomato, onion and bacon, and bake in oven till crisp and golden. Serve hot.

Grated cheese sprinkled with cayenne or cheese and bacon are tasty alternatives.

SAVOURY CREAM

3 eggs
3 tablespoons grated cheese
1 tablespoon finely chopped mint
2 cups milk
1 dessertspoon gelatine
1 tablespoon chopped parsley
pepper and salt

Soak the gelatine in 1 tablespoon cold milk and bring the balance of the milk to boiling point. Add well-beaten eggs and return to the fire and stir till mixture coats the spoon, then add dissolved gelatine, cheese, mint and parsley. Stand aside to cool, stirring occasionally. It is best made overnight and used the next day.

SAVOURY EGGS

6 Eggs
1 dessertspoon chopped parsley
1 saltspoon mixed mustard
few drops of vinegar
90 gr (3 oz.) butter
squeeze of lemon and little rind
salt and cayenne to taste

Halve hard boiled eggs. Mix yolks with other ingredients, fill whites and garnish.

SCHOOL LUNCHES

It is important in preparing a school lunch to see that it is not only nutritious, but also designed to prevent dental decay. The following are recommended:—1. One or two sandwiches with a savoury filling of meat or fish, egg, grated or thinly sliced cheese, celery and nuts, or sliced apple. 2. A similar sandwich with butter alone or very thinly spread honey, jam, raisins, marmalade, tomato, dates or figs. 3. Wheaten scones, bran scones or nutbread with butter. 4. An apple or orange. Other fruit in season. Celery and carrot.

In packing lunches:—1. Every precaution should be taken to keep foods in lunch box or basket in a good condition. 2. In hot weather the use of soft, moist food should be avoided. 3.

SCHOOL LUNCHES—*continued*

Lunch wraps are useful. 4. Each kind of food should be wrapped in a separate parcel. 5. In packing, the foods less likely to crush should be placed at the bottom.

When cutting bread for children's lunches remember the bread is only there to hold the filling.

CHEESE AND TOMATO SANDWICH PASTE

3 Large Tomatoes
30 gr (1 oz.) butter
60 gr (2 oz.) grated cheese
1 onion
1 egg
125 gr (4 oz.) dry breadcrumbs
pepper and salt to taste

Place the tomatoes in boiling water, then remove the skins and cut finely. Mince the onion, add the butter and tomatoes and simmer over the fire till tender. Mash to a pulp, add seasoning and well-beaten egg and cook a little, but do not boil. Take off the fire, add the grated cheese and breadcrumbs and mix till very fine. Put away in jars. This paste will keep fairly well in summer and very well in winter. It is advisable to make half quantity in hot weather.

EGG AND CELERY SANDWICHES

2 Cups Finely Chopped Celery
lettuce
4 hard-boiled eggs
mayonnaise
salt and pepper

Chop eggs and mix with celery. Spread on brown bread and butter with lettuce and mayonnaise.

FRUIT PASTE

60 gr (2 oz.) Currants
60 gr (2 oz.) raisins or dates
juice of ½ a lemon
60 gr (2 oz.) sultanas
1 sour apple
15 gr (½ oz.) castor sugar

Put the currants, sultanas and raisins and the peeled and cored apple through the mincer. Squeeze in the lemon juice and sift in the castor sugar. Mash well with a fork and pack into jars. If liked, minced or chopped nuts may be added.

WALNUT SANDWICHES

Spread bread and butter with chopped walnuts and honey; chopped walnuts and brains; chopped walnuts and vegemite.

MOCK CRAB

60 gr (2 oz.) Grated Cheese
1 dessertspoon Worcester sauce
60 gr (2 oz.) butter
1 tablespoon tomato sauce
½ teaspoon mustard

Mix together all the ingredients and use as a paste for sandwiches.

POTTED CHEESE

125 gr (4 oz.) Butter
2 eggs
1 cup grated cheese
pepper and salt to taste

Put the butter into a saucepan, and when melted, add the cheese and seasoning. Allow to get thoroughly hot, but do not boil. Remove from the fire and add the well-beaten eggs. Stir well together and place in air-tight jars when cold. Matured cheese is best to use for this.

PREPARED MUSTARD (MILD)

250 ml (½ Pint) Vinegar
2 heaped tablespoons cornflour
a pinch of cayenne pepper
3 heaped tablespoons mustard
1 teaspoon turmeric or curry powder
1 teaspoon salt
nutmeg

Boil the vinegar. Mix the dry ingredients till perfectly smooth with cold vinegar, and add to the boiling vinegar, stirring all the time. Boil for 10 minutes. If too thick more vinegar may be added. Fill small, open-mouthed jars with mixture. Vaseline pots or marmite jars are suitable. Screw on covers. It is ready for use as soon as cold, and is nice for salads, sandwiches, on bread and butter and meats. If liked slightly sweet, a teaspoon of sugar may be added to the mixture.

RABBIT PASTE

1 Rabbit
2 tablespoons water
pepper and salt
1 blade of mace
2 rashers bacon
a little grated nutmeg

Cut the rabbit into joints, put it in a saucepan with the mace and 2 tablespoons water, and simmer gently for 1 hour. Cut the bacon in dice and add, then, after 10 minutes, put in ½ a cup of water and simmer another hour. Pour the gravy into a cup. Shred the meat off the bones and put through a mincer, add pepper and salt to taste, then add the gravy and a little grated nutmeg. Mix well and put into small jars with melted butter on top.

SANDWICH FILLING (No. 1)

125 gr (4 oz.) Beef Steak
mixed herbs
125 gr (4 oz.) fat bacon
60 gr (2 oz.) butter
pepper and salt

Put the meat through a mincer, season with mixed herbs and pepper and salt and put into a buttered basin. Steam (not boil) for 2 hours. Let it get nearly cold and then beat in the butter. This is nourishing and good.

SANDWICH FILLING (No. 2)

1 Teaspoon Butter
1 dessertspoon tomato sauce
1 egg
1 dessertspoon milk
½ teaspoon Worcester sauce
cayenne pepper
pepper and salt

Put into a saucepan the butter, milk, tomato sauce, Worcester sauce, pepper and salt and a dash of cayenne pepper. Add the egg, unbeaten, stir well and hold over the fire till the mixture thickens. Do not let it boil.

SAVOURY SANDWICHES

1 Cup Sultanas
185 gr (6 oz.) cold minced ham
cream or salad dressing
a few drops lemon juice
3 pickled gherkins
pepper and salt to taste

Mix all ingredients together with enough cream or salad dressing to bind, and place between thin slices of brown bread and butter.

SEFTON SANDWICHES

1 Tin Sardines
lemon juice or vinegar
white or brown bread
cheese
pepper and salt
creamed butter
cream or milk

Skin and bone the sardines and pound them with an equal amount of cheese in a mortar until smooth, adding seasoning and lemon juice to taste, and as much cream or milk as is needed to moisten the whole. Then rub through a fine sieve. Put a layer of this preparation between thin slices of bread and butter; press well, trim and cut into desired shapes.

TASTY PASTE

1 Small Tin Smoked Herrings
2 eggs
a little Worcester sauce
250 gr (½ lb.) butter
pepper to taste
cayenne pepper

Put the herrings through the mincer, then put with the butter, eggs, pepper and a dash of cayenne pepper into a pan, and simmer for 10 minutes. Add a little Worcester sauce. Keep stirring while cooking. Place in pots with some melted butter on top. It keeps very well.

CAKES

The success of a cake depends very much on the baking; constant attention is necessary. Test the heat of your oven—different cake mixtures require different temperatures—learn by experience.

If a cake browns before it rises, your oven is too hot. A large loaf cake should rise first at the edge, then the middle should come up, crack just a very little, settle back, and the cracks close. If a cake cracks and remains open, your mixture has been too stiff—too much flour has been used.

A good plan with rich fruit cakes, rich plain, or madeira cakes, is to leave the centre just a trifle lower than the edges—just hollow out, smoothing the mixture towards the edges with the back of a spoon.

After taking cakes out of the oven, let them stand in their baking tin for two or three minutes—no longer—and they will turn out easily without breaking away at the bottom.

It is never wise to mix a new bag of flour with the remains of an old one. The texture will be almost certainly a little different, the older flour probably being slightly the heavier. Save this for making gravies and sauces and keep the new flour for cakes and pastry.

When recipe requires cream of tartar or baking powder to be added to flour, the flour is plain unless otherwise directed.

If a plain cake is at all heavy and close textured, it has probably not been cooked in a hot enough oven. Plain cakes, because they contain more flour in proportion to the amount of fat, and because the mixture is not so dense as in a fruit cake, need to be cooked in a rather hot oven.

If using dripping for cakes, etc., a lemon or two squeezed in will take away the fatty taste.

Good lard or dripping can be partly or wholly substituted for butter, but don't expect the same results.

When currants are required quickly, and there is not sufficient time to wash and dry them, place them in a colander, sprinkle well with flour and rub them hard, placing the colander on a piece of paper or a plate. The stalks and damaged fruit pass through with the flour.

In cold weather, when trying to cream butter and sugar, try adding a tablespoon of boiling water. It does not harm any mixture and produces a very nice smooth cream.

When you wish to soften butter, instead of putting it in the oven or on the rack, which makes it oily, heat a basin with boiling water and invert the basin over the butter. A lid taken off a kettle or saucepan will do quite well for the purpose.

To Clarify Dripping as a Substitute for Butter.—Save all skimmings from soup stock, roasts, etc. Treat your dripping in the following way:—Put all pieces and scraps and skimmings into a saucepan with sufficient cold water to cover it. Bring to the boil and boil for three minutes. Pour into a basin and add to every 1 kg (2 lb.) of dripping ¼ of an eggspoon of carbonate soda. Stir round well. Let stand till firm, then lift the cake of fat off the water, and remove any impurities by scraping the under part of the cake. Dripping from marrow bones and beef stock is excellent for mixing with mutton dripping. The addition of lard is of further benefit—a nice soft dripping results.

BOILED CAKES

Cake Tin Size in Relation to Quantity of Ingredients Used: ¼ lb. (125 gr) butter—6 inch (15 cm) cake tin; ½ lb. (250 gr) butter—8 inch (20 cm); 1 lb. (500 gr) butter—12 inch (30 cm).

Sponge Cakes: 4 eggs—8 inch (20 cm) cake tin; 3 eggs—7 inch (16 cm) cake tin.

BOILED CAKE

- 1 Cup Water
- 1 cup sugar
- ½ cup butter
- 2¼ cups self-raising flour
- 2 teaspoons cinnamon
- 1 cup currants
- 1 cup sultanas
- ¼ cup boiling water
- 2 eggs
- 2 teaspoons mixed spice
- 1 small teaspoon carbonate soda

Put the cup of water, currants, sugar, sultanas, butter and spice into a saucepan and boil for 3 minutes. When cold add the carbonate of soda dissolved in the boiling water, then the flour and, lastly, the eggs, well-beaten. Put into a greased cake tin and bake for 1¼ hours in a moderate oven.

BOILED FRUIT CAKE

- 2 Tablespoons Butter
- 1 cup sultanas
- 1 cup cold water
- 1 teaspoon mixed spice
- 1 cup plain flour
- 1 cup currants
- 1 cup sugar
- ½ cup lemon peel
- 1 teaspoon carbonate soda
- 1 cup self-raising flour
- 1 egg

Boil together for 3 minutes the sugar, butter, fruit and water, then add the spice, soda and flour, last of all the egg, well-beaten. Mix well together and bake in a greased cake tin in a moderate oven for 2 hours.

COLD TEA CAKE

1 Cup Strong Cold Tea
125 gr (¼ lb.) butter
250 gr (½ lb.) plain flour
125 gr (¼ lb.) sugar
250 gr (½ lb.) mixed fruit
1 teaspoon spice
1 teaspoon carb. soda

Put tea, butter, sugar, fruit and spice in saucepan and boil for three minutes. Allow to cool. Sift in flour and soda. Mix well and bake in lined tin in moderate oven for 1¼ hours.

EASY FRUIT CAKE

2¾ Cups Plain Flour
½ teaspoon each allspice, ground cloves, ginger, cinnamon
½ cup walnuts or almonds
½ cup cherries
½ cup drained crushed pineapple
½ cup sultanas
1 tablespoon chopped peel
2½ cups raisins
125 gr (4 oz.) butter
2 tablespoons sherry
1½ cups water
1 teaspoon carb. soda
1 teaspoon baking powder
½ teaspoon salt
2 eggs
1½ cups sugar

Sift flour, soda, salt and spices together. Take out 1 cup flour mixture. Mix water, sugar, sultanas and raisins together, and boil for 5 minutes, stirring occasionally. Add butter and stir till melted. Allow to cool. Add beaten eggs and add gradually to dry ingredients. Mix nuts, cherries, pineapple and peel with remaining cup flour and stir into cake batter. Add sherry. Grease and line a tin and spoon mixture in, hollowing slightly. Bake in slow oven 2-2½ hours.

EGGLESS SPICE CAKE

1½ Cups Sugar
2 cups water
1 teaspoon cinnamon
1 teaspoon ground cloves
1 teaspoon baking soda
2 tablespoons butter
2 cups chopped raisins and sultanas
½ teaspoon salt
¼ teaspoon nutmeg
¼ teaspoon spice
3 cups plain flour

Boil sugar and water and spice for 5 minutes; remove from fire, add butter and fruit and allow to cool. Sift flour, salt and soda together and add to other cooled ingredients. Mix well, pour into a greased cake tin, lined with paper, and bake in a moderate oven for 45 to 60 minutes. This cake will keep fresh a long time.

HONEY CAKE

250 gr ($\frac{1}{2}$ lb.) Sultanas
125 gr ($\frac{1}{4}$ lb.) currants
125 gr ($\frac{1}{4}$ lb.) raisins
60 gr (2 oz.) lemon peel
60 gr (2 oz.) cherries
60 gr (2 oz.) almonds
1 cup honey
125 gr ($\frac{1}{4}$ lb.) butter
1 cup water
2 teaspoons mixed spice
1 teaspoon carb. soda

Boil all together for 5 minutes. Allow to cool. Add 2 well-beaten eggs. Stir in 2 cups plain flour sifted with 1 teaspoon baking powder. Bake in a moderate oven in a well-lined tin for 2 hours. Makes a good Christmas cake.

NAIRN CAKE

2 Breakfast Cups Plain Flour
2 breakfast cups fruit (sultanas and currants)
1 breakfast cup white or light brown sugar
1 breakfast cup cold tea
125 gr ($\frac{1}{4}$ lb.) butter
a pinch of salt
1 small teaspoonful carbonate of soda

Put fruit, sugar, tea, butter and salt into a saucepan, bring to the boil and boil for 3 minutes. Turn into a basin and, when tepid, stir in flour sifted with soda. Put into a greased tin and bake in a moderate oven for about two hours.

ONE EGG FRUIT CAKE

1 Egg
1 cup self-raising flour
1 cup plain flour
500 gr (1 lb.) pkt. mixed fruit
155 gr (5 oz.) butter
1 cup sugar
1 cup water
2 teaspoons spice
$\frac{1}{2}$ teaspoon carb. soda

Boil fruit, butter, sugar, spice and water for 3 minutes. Allow to cool. Beat egg and add. Sift flours and soda and add. Line tin with paper, hollow out mixture slightly and bake in moderate oven $1\frac{1}{4}$-$1\frac{1}{2}$ hours.

RICH FRUIT CAKES

AUNT MARY'S CHRISTMAS CAKE

500 gr (1 lb.) Butter
500 gr (1 lb.) currants
250 gr ($\frac{1}{2}$ lb.) raisins
125 gr ($\frac{1}{4}$ lb.) sweet almonds
60 gr (2 oz.) ground rice
rind of 1 orange (grated)
1 teaspoon almond essence
500 gr (1 lb.) castor sugar
500 gr (1 lb.) sultanas
250 gr ($\frac{1}{2}$ lb.) glazed cherries
500 gr (1 lb.) flour
500 gr (1 lb.) mixed peel
rind of 1 lemon (grated)
1 teaspoon vanilla
1 teaspoon mixed spice
8 eggs (or 6 eggs and 1 cup milk)

AUNT MARY'S CHRISTMAS CAKE—*continued*

Clean the currants and raisins, blanch and chop the almonds, shred the peel and cut the cherries into halves. Cream the butter and sugar, add the eggs one at a time, and beat well with the hand. Add the prepared fruit, grated orange and lemon rind, and the essence. Mix well, add flour, ground rice and spice. Put into well-greased tins lined with paper. Cook very slowly for about 5 hours. This quantity makes two large cakes. It is best to make this cake one month before Christmas. Wrap the cakes in a cloth and put in a tin. A fortnight before use, put on a layer of almond paste and ice.

Almond Paste for above.—Beat the yolks of 4 eggs with essence of almond, vanilla, ratafia, maraschino, florida water and juice of 1 lemon. Add 500 gr (1 lb.) ground sweet almonds, 250 gr (½ lb.) icing sugar 250 gr (½ lb.) castor sugar, and mix well. Put on to a sugared board and roll out. Brush top of cake with white of egg and cover with almond paste. Make ordinary icing, adding all above flavourings. Ice and decorate.

BRANDY SYRUP FRUIT CAKE

1 kg (2 lb.) Mixed Fruit
250 gr (½ lb.) butter
1½ cups brown sugar
5 eggs
2½ cups plain flour
1 cup cornflour
½ cup golden syrup
½ cup brandy
¼ teaspoon salt
125 gr (¼ lb.) each blanched almonds, cherries, and shredded peel

To make the golden syrup/brandy, melt 1 tablespoon butter and add golden syrup and brandy. Bring to boil, simmer 2 minutes and use immediately.

Cream butter and sugar, add eggs singly with sprinkle of flour, beating well. Mix in golden syrup/brandy. Add sifted flours and salt and fruit. Grease and line a 20 cm (8 in.) tin and fill with mixture. Bake in slow oven 4 hours. Cool in tin.

CANADIAN CHRISTMAS CAKE

First Mixture

125 gr (4 oz.) Crystallised Pineapple
125 gr (4 oz.) cherries
3 tablespoons orange juice
125 gr (4 oz.) peel
125 gr (4 oz.) blanched chopped almonds

Remove sugar from pineapple. Mix all ingredients and cover and leave overnight.

CANADIAN CHRISTMAS CAKE—*continued*

Second Mixture

250 gr (8 oz.) Butter
$1\frac{1}{2}$ cups sugar
250 gr (8 oz.) coconut
250 gr (8 oz.) sultanas
250 gr (8 oz.) raisins
6 eggs
3 cups self-raising flour
$\frac{1}{4}$ cup brandy
$\frac{1}{2}$ cup orange juice

Soak coconut in brandy for $\frac{1}{2}$ hour. Cream butter and sugar. Add egg yolks, then soaked coconut. Fold in sifted flour alternately with orange juice. Add prepared first mixture, raisins and sultanas.

Beat egg whites till stiff and fold in. Line a tin with several thicknesses of paper and turn in mixture, hollowing slightly. Bake in moderate oven 3 hours. Cool in tin.

CHRISTMAS CAKE (No. 1)

750 gr ($1\frac{1}{2}$ lb.) Plain Flour
500 gr (1 lb.) seeded raisins
500 gr (1 lb.) currants
12 eggs
2 good teaspoons cream of tartar
1 good teaspoon of carbonate of soda
1 teaspoon essence almond
250 gr ($\frac{1}{2}$ lb.) blanched, shredded almonds
500 gr (1 lb.) sugar
500 gr (1 lb.) sultanas
500 gr (1 lb.) butter
1 grated nutmeg
1 teaspoon mixed spice
1 teaspoon ground ginger
1 teaspoon cinnamon
1 teaspoon essence lemon
1 teaspoon essence vanilla
250 gr ($\frac{1}{2}$ lb.) mixed peel
1 teaspoon salt

Beat butter and sugar together and add eggs one at a time, beating all the time; add prepared fruits, spices, peel and almonds. Beat for about 15 minutes, or until mixture curdles. Have the flour, salt and rising thoroughly sifted together and add to mixture. Lastly add essence and, if too stiff, add a small quantity of milk. Beat until smooth (about 10 minutes). Bake in well-papered tins in a moderate oven for 3 to $4\frac{1}{2}$ hours, according to size of tins. This mixture makes two fairly large cakes.

CHRISTMAS CAKE (No. 2)

750 gr ($1\frac{1}{2}$ lb.) Flour (plain)
750 gr ($1\frac{1}{2}$ lb.) dates
750 gr ($1\frac{1}{2}$ lb.) raisins
125 gr ($\frac{1}{4}$ lb.) chopped almonds
625 gr ($1\frac{1}{4}$ lb.) brown sugar
1 teaspoon spice
750 gr ($1\frac{1}{2}$ lb.) butter
750 gr ($1\frac{1}{2}$ lb.) currants
750 gr ($1\frac{1}{2}$ lb.) sultanas
125 gr ($\frac{1}{4}$ lb.) mixed peel
1 dozen eggs
$\frac{1}{2}$ teaspoon grated nutmeg
1 teaspoon carbonate soda dissolved in wineglass of brandy

Cream butter and sugar, add eggs, two at a time, and beat well. Stir in fruit, almonds, peel and spices. Then sift in flour and, lastly, add brandy and carbonate soda. Beat well. Bake in well papered cake tins for 6 or 7 hours if in one loaf, reduce baking time, if mixture is divided. Makes 5 kg (10 lb.) leaving out 750 gr ($1\frac{1}{2}$ lb.) fruit.

CHRISTMAS CAKE (No. 3)

750 gr (1½ lb.) Butter
875 gr (1¾ lb.) flour (plain)
750 gr (1½ lb.) currants
250 gr (½ lb.) lemon peel
14 eggs
¾ teaspoon carbonate soda
750 gr (1½ lb.) sugar
500 gr (1 lb.) sultanas
250 gr (½ lb.) almonds
1 nutmeg
½ glass brandy
15 gr (½ oz.) packet mixed spice

Beat butter and sugar to a cream, add eggs, well-beaten, then soda in a little boiling water and two teaspoons burnt sugar in ½ glass brandy. Add flour with spice and, lastly, fruit. Bake about 3 hours.

CHRISTMAS CAKE (No. 4)

500 gr (1 lb.) Self-raising Flour
500 gr (1 lb.) sugar
1 teaspoon cinnamon
¾ teaspoon mace
1 kg (2 lb.) sultanas
500 gr (1 lb.) lemon peel
250 gr (½ lb.) shredded figs
½ cup grape juice or wine
500 gr (1 lb.) butter
12 eggs
¾ teaspoon allspice
½ teaspoon ground ginger
500 gr (1 lb.) currants
250 gr (½ lb.) chopped almonds
2 tablespoons lemon juice

Cream together butter and sugar, then add the yolks of eggs and beat again. Then add the flour with mace, cinnamon, allspice and ginger. Now add lemon juice and grape juice (or wine); next fold in the stiffly beaten whites of the eggs. Then add the floured fruit. Turn into well-greased and papered dishes and allow ½ an hour for each 500 gr (1 lb.) of cake. Bake in a moderate oven 5 hours. This will make a 4½ kg (9 lb.) cake.

C.W.A. BIRTHDAY CAKE

1 kg (2 lb.) Butter
16 eggs
2 teaspoons baking powder
1 kg (2 lb.) sultanas
2 teaspoons mixed spice
250 gr (½ lb.) shelled almonds
500 gr (1 lb.) sugar
1⅛ kg (2¼ lb.) flour
500 gr (1 lb.) currants
500 gr (1 lb.) mixed peel
salt
¼ cup caramel
flavouring

Beat butter and sugar to a cream, add eggs separately and beat well. Then add fruits (well dried) and flour previously sifted with baking powder, spice and salt. Mix thoroughly and, lastly, add caramel and flavouring. Bake 5 hours in hot oven to start with and gradually decrease heat. Always prepare ingredients beforehand; weigh the quantities, have fruits cleaned and dried, and tins lined with paper. This quantity makes two large cakes or three smaller. When ready, cover with almond paste and, finally, royal icing and decorate. Keeps indefinitely in air-tight tin.

CHRISTMAS CAKE (ECONOMICAL)

- 750 gr-1 kg (1½-2 lb.) Mixed Fruit
- 2 tablespoons chopped peel
- ¼ cup sherry
- 250 gr (8 oz.) butter
- 250 gr (8 oz.) brown sugar
- 2¾ cups plain flour
- ½ teaspoon carb. soda
- ½ teaspoon vanilla
- ½ teaspoon almond essence
- ½ cup mashed banana
- 4 eggs
- 3 tablespoons orange juice
- 1 teaspoon spice
- pinch salt

Place prepared fruit and peel in basin and pour sherry over. Cover and leave overnight. Cream butter and sugar, banana and essences till soft and light. Add eggs one at a time with sprinkle of flour; beat well. Fold in fruit and sifted flour, spice, soda and salt. Stir in orange juice. Line a 20 cm (8 inch) square or round tin with 3 thicknesses of paper, fill with mixture, hollow slightly. Bake in slow oven 3½-4 hours.

FRESH FRUIT CHRISTMAS CAKE

- 250 gr (½ lb.) Butter
- ¾ cup brown sugar
- 1 teaspoon vanilla
- 4 eggs
- 2 dessertspoons treacle
- ¼ cup each chopped figs, dates, prunes, nuts, cherries
- 1 tablespoon chopped ginger
- 1 teaspoon each nutmeg, spice, ground cloves, carb. soda
- 500 gr (1 lb.) mixed fruit
- ¼ teaspoon salt
- ½ cup grated carrot
- ½ cup chopped pineapple
- ¾ cup grated apple
- 1 mashed banana
- 2 tablespoons orange juice
- 1 tablespoon lemon juice
- 310 gr (10 oz.) flour
- 1 tablespoon brandy or sherry

Cream butter, sugar and vanilla. Add eggs one at a time and mix well. Add treacle, pineapple, carrot and apple. Mix orange and lemon juice with banana and add. Fold in flour sifted with salt, spices and soda. Add fruits. Lastly add brandy or sherry.

Line tin with 3 thicknesses of paper. Bake in very moderate oven for approximately 4 hours. Allow to cool in tin.

FRUIT CAKE

- 500 gr (1 lb.) Butter
- 2 cups sugar
- 10 eggs
- 1 lemon jelly
- ½ packet mixed spice
- ½ teaspoon nutmeg
- ¼ teaspoon ground cloves
- 625 gr (1¼ lb.) flour (½ plain, ½ S.R.)
- 500 gr (1 lb.) raisins
- 500 gr (1 lb) sultanas
- 500 gr (1 lb.) currants
- 1 packet lemon peel
- 500 gr (1 lb.) mixed fruit
- 1 packet cherries
- almonds
- vanilla and lemon essence
- brandy and sherry

FRUIT CAKE—*continued*

Prepare the fruit the day before, sprinkle with brandy and sherry and leave.

Cream butter and sugar and add lemon jelly, mixed spice, nutmeg, cloves, essence vanilla and lemon and beat. Add eggs one at a time; beat well. Sift flour and add flour and fruit alternately, mix well and place in papered tins.

Cook in hot oven at first, cake should be just starting to colour in an hour, keep even low fire for 5 to 6 hours. Cover cake mixture with paper when placing in oven. A mug of water placed in oven will help cake from burning and drying.

WEDDING CAKE

500 gr (1 lb.) Butter
750 gr (1½ lb.) flour
500 gr (1 lb.) currants
250 gr (½ lb.) blanched almonds
185 gr (6 oz.) crystallised cherries
½ teaspoon ground cloves
½ teaspoon ground mace
½ teaspoon salt
½ teaspoon essence lemon
500 gr (1 lb.) sugar
500 gr (1 lb.) sultanas
500 gr (1 lb.) seeded raisins
310 gr (10 oz.) mixed peel
12 eggs
½ teaspoon cinnamon
½ teaspoon allspice
1 teaspoon baking powder
½ teaspoon essence almond
6 tablespoons brandy or grape juice

Cream butter and sugar, add the eggs one at a time (unbeaten) and beat well with the hands, then add the flour to which has been added the baking powder and salt. Beat well, add fruit and spices and mix thoroughly, then add essence and brandy. Put mixture into a greased baking tin, lined with three thicknesses of paper, cover the top of cake (after it begins to colour) with a sheet of buttered paper. Bake 3½ to 4 hours in a moderate oven. Do not open the oven door for at least 15 minutes after the cake has been baking. Allow heat to decrease a little after the first hour.

WHITE CHRISTMAS CAKE

375 gr (¾ lb.) Butter
375 gr (¾ lb.) sugar
375 gr (¾ lb.) plain flour
125 gr (¼ lb.) self-raising flour
¼ cup sherry, brandy or milk
6 eggs
250 gr (½ lb.) crystallised pineapple
250 gr (½ lb.) cherries
250 gr (½ lb.) finely chopped walnuts
125 gr (¼ lb.) lemon peel

Beat butter and sugar, add eggs one at a time with a sprinkle of flour. Add sifted flour. Add fruit and liquid. Bake in slow oven for 2 hours in well-greased and lined tin.

AMERICAN BEAUTY CAKE

125 gr (¼ lb.) Butter
2 eggs
250 gr (½ lb.) self-raising flour
1 teaspoon cinnamon
½ cup milk
1 level teaspoon carb. soda
125 gr (¼ lb.) sugar
1 tablespoon dark jam (plum, raspberry, etc.)
1 tablespoon cocoa
½ teaspoon nutmeg
½ teaspoon vanilla
1 tablespoon boiling water

Cream butter and sugar, add eggs singly and jam. Sift in flour with cocoa, cinnamon, nutmeg, add milk and vanilla. Dissolve carb. soda in boiling water and add. Bake in a moderate oven 30-40 minutes.

APPLE NUT CAKE (NO EGGS)

2 Cups Flour
½ cup butter
2 dessertspoons cocoa
½ teaspoon grated nutmeg
1 teaspoon cream tartar
½ cup chopped nuts
1 cup sugar
1½ cups warm stewed apples
2 teaspoons carb. soda
½ teaspoon cinnamon
½ cup raisins

Cream butter and sugar. Dissolve soda into 1½ cups apple. Add to creamed butter. Add other ingredients. Lastly mix in flour with level teaspoon cream of tartar and ½ teaspoon soda. Bake in moderate oven ¾ hour. If self-raising flour is used only 1 teaspoon soda is needed in apple and only two small teaspoons cocoa.

APRICOT CAKE

250 gr (½ lb.) Flour
155 gr (5 oz.) sugar
1 teaspoon baking powder
155 gr (5 oz.) butter
3 eggs
3 tablespoons apricot jam
some chopped almonds browned in the oven

Cream butter and sugar, beat in the eggs, sift flour and baking powder and mix all well together, adding a little milk if necessary, then the jam. Bake in a moderate oven for 1½ hours. Cover the whole cake with apricot icing, then cover the sides with browned almonds. Decorate the top of cake with strips of dried apricots and preserved cherries.

CHERRY CAKE

375 gr (12 oz.) Self-raising Flour
250 gr (8 oz.) butter
155 gr (5 oz.) castor sugar
185 gr (6 oz.) chopped cherries
4 large eggs

Cream the butter and sugar. Add the eggs one at a time and beat well. Rub the cherries through the flour and add gradually to the mixture. Bake in moderate oven 1 hour.

CHOCOLATE CAKE (No. 1)

90 gr (3 oz.) Butter
2 tablespoons milk
3 teaspoons cocoa
1 teaspoon carbonate soda
1 small cup sugar about 180 gr (6 oz.)
1 cup flour
2 eggs
2 small teaspoons cream tartar

Beat the eggs and add to the creamed butter and sugar. Sift the cream of tartar and the cocoa through the flour and add to the above mixture. Dissolve the soda in the milk and add. Bake 18 to 20 minutes in fairly quick oven. Allow to cool and ice with Lamington icing and decorate with nuts.

Lamington Icing

1 Cup Icing Sugar
1 dessertspoon butter
1 dessertspoon cocoa
2 tablespoons boiling water

Melt in pan over fire, but do not allow to boil.

CHOCOLATE CAKE (No. 2)

125 gr (4 oz.) Butter
1½ cups self-raising flour
½ cup hot water
½ cup cocoa
1 cup sugar
1 egg
½ teaspoon carb. soda
½ cup sour milk (to sour add 1 teaspoon vinegar)
vanilla to taste

Dissolve butter in hot water. Add vanilla. Sift flour, soda and cocoa. Add sugar, water and butter, milk and beaten egg. Beat well for 3 minutes with mixer or egg beater. Bake in a moderate oven 30-35 minutes.

CHOCOLATE AND ALMOND CAKE

185 gr (6 oz.) Flour
125 gr (4 oz.) butter
60 gr (2 oz.) currants
2 eggs
almond flavouring
38 gr (1¼ oz.) cocoa
140 gr (4½ oz.) castor sugar
60 gr (2 oz.) sultanas
1 teaspoon baking powder
a little milk

Clean the fruit. Sieve the flour, cocoa and baking powder together. Beat the sugar and butter to a cream and add the eggs separately, stirring in each quickly. When well-beaten, stir in the flour and fruit alternately with milk, as required. Add a few drops almond flavouring and mix well. Grease a cake tin and line with paper, allowing it to come above the sides. Put in the prepared cake mixture and bake in a moderate oven for ¾ hour.

CHOCOLATE MACAROON CAKE

125 gr (4 oz.) Butter
¾ cup sugar
2 egg yolks
2 tablespoons coconut
2 cups self-raising flour
1 cup milk
½ cup chopped dates
2 tablespoons chopped walnuts
2 dessertspoons cocoa
pinch salt

Beat butter and sugar, add egg yolks and coconut and mix. Sift flour, salt and cocoa together, and fold in alternately with milk.

Topping

2 Egg Whites
salt
½ cup sugar
almond essence

Beat until stiff then fold in carefully ½ cup coconut. Spread on top of cake and bake in a very moderate oven 1 hour. If top gets too brown place a piece of paper over it until cooked. Leave in tin a little while before turning out.

CHOCOLATE NUT CAKE

2 or 3 Eggs
3 tablespoons butter
1 cup self-raising flour
½ teaspoon spice
½ cup sugar
little milk
3 teaspoons cocoa
125 gr (¼ lb.) chopped walnuts
vanilla essence

Beat the butter and sugar to a cream, add eggs, then milk, cocoa, vanilla, spice, flour and walnuts. Cook in a moderate oven 20 to 25 minutes, for preference in 20 cm (8 in.) square tins.

Icing

1 Tablespoon Butter
3 teaspoons cocoa
4 tablespoons icing sugar
vanilla flavouring

Blend all together and spread on cake.

CINNAMON FRUIT CAKE

250 gr (½ lb.) Butter
3 cups flour
1 small cup milk
2 pieces lemon peel
1¼ cups sugar
3 eggs
1 cup chopped sultanas
1 small teaspoon carbonate soda
2 large teaspoons ground cinnamon

Cream butter and sugar, add the beaten eggs and then the milk with the soda dissolved in it; lastly the fruit and flour Bake about 1½ hours.

CINNAMON NUT CAKE

185 gr (6 oz.) Butter
90 gr (3 oz.) brown sugar
2 eggs
2 large tablespoons ground cinnamon
250 gr (8 oz.) self-raising flour
90 gr (3 oz.) white sugar
½ cup milk
a little nutmeg
a small teacup of chopped nuts or, if preferred, sultanas

Cream butter and sugar and add the well-beaten eggs. Lightly mix in the flour, into which the cinnamon and nutmeg have been previously sifted. Moisten with the milk as you add the flour so that the mixture does not get too stiff, and then add the nuts or fruit. Bake in a moderate oven for 1 hour.

CINNAMON COFFEE CAKE

3 Cups Flour
500 gr (1 lb.) seeded raisins
1 tablespoon cinnamon
4 level teaspoons cream of tartar
250 gr (½ lb.) butter
1½ cups sugar
1 egg
1½ cups strong coffee
2 level teaspoons carbonate soda

Dissolve the soda in the coffee. Cream butter with the sugar and add the egg and coffee, then the flour, sifted with the cream of tartar, cinnamon and a pinch of salt. Bake in a moderate oven in a shallow tin, lined with paper, for 1½ to 2 hours.

COFFEE CAKE

3 Cups Flour
125 gr (¼ lb.) butter
4 eggs
1 large teaspoon carbonate soda
2 cups sugar
375 ml (¾ pint) milk
flavouring to taste
2 teaspoons cream of tartar

Beat butter to a cream, add sugar, then eggs and milk in which carbonate soda has been dissolved. Beat thoroughly for a few minutes and then add flour and cream of tartar. Beat well and bake in a shallow tin for almost an hour. Ice or spread while hot with butter and then sprinkle over with about half a saucer of sugar, to which has been added enough ground cinnamon to make rich brown.

CORNFLAKE COFFEE CAKE

2 Tablespoons Butter
½ cup sugar
1 egg
1½ cups self-raising flour
⅔ cup milk
½ teaspoon nutmeg
pinch salt

CORNFLAKE COFFEE CAKE—*continued*

Cream butter and sugar. Add egg and beat until light. Mix flour, nutmeg and salt and add alternately with milk.

Topping

Melt 1 tablespoon butter, add $\frac{1}{4}$ cup sugar, 2 teaspoons cinnamon, 3 tablespoons cornflakes, slightly crushed. Sprinkle over mixture. Bake $\frac{1}{2}$ hour in moderate oven.

CRUMB CAKE (EGGLESS)

$1\frac{3}{4}$ Cups Flour
4 level tablespoons butter
$\frac{1}{2}$ teaspoon ground cloves
1 teaspoon carbonate soda
1 cup brown sugar
1 cup raisins
1 teaspoon cinnamon
1 cup sour milk or buttermilk
a pinch of salt

Crumb together the flour, brown sugar and butter (keeping out a heaped tablespoon of crumbs to sprinkle on the cake). Add the raisins, ground cloves, cinnamon, salt and carbonate of soda. Mix well with the milk. Put into a greased tin, sprinkle crumbs on top and bake in a moderate oven for about 1 hour.

DATE CAKE (No. 1)

185 gr (6 oz.) Butter
$\frac{3}{4}$ cup sugar
2 eggs
250 gr ($\frac{1}{2}$ lb.) dates
$1\frac{1}{2}$ cups self-raising flour
1 teaspoon carbonate soda
1 cup boiling water

Chop dates, sprinkle soda on, and pour boiling water over. Allow to stand for 1 hour. Cream butter and sugar together, add eggs one at a time, add date mixture, then flour, and beat well. Bake in a shallow tin in a moderate oven. Ice with chocolate icing and chopped walnuts.

DATE CAKE (No. 2)

500 gr (1 lb.) Dates
185 gr (6 oz.) butter
$\frac{1}{2}$ cup desiccated coconut
2 eggs
1 cup water
1 small cup sugar
2 cups plain flour
a few walnuts
1 teaspoon carbonate soda

Pour water over the stoned and cut dates and add the soda. In another basin cream the butter and sugar, add the eggs and beat well. Then add the date mixture; add flour, coconut and nuts. Bake in a moderate oven for $1\frac{1}{4}$ to $1\frac{1}{2}$ hours and ice with chocolate icing.

DELICIOUS CAKE

Pastry

125 gr ($\frac{1}{4}$ lb.) Self-raising Flour
60 gr (2 oz.) butter
a little milk

Sponge

1 Cup Sugar
1 cup self-raising flour
60 gr (2 oz.) butter
2 eggs
a little milk

To make the pastry mix the butter through the flour and add enough milk to make a nice paste. Roll out and place on a flat baking tin. Spread with jam and scatter 250 gr ($\frac{1}{2}$ lb.) currants on the jam. Now make a sponge with the ingredients given and pour it over currants. Bake in hot oven and, when cool, ice with lemon icing.

DUTCH CAKE

Pastry

$\frac{1}{2}$ Cup Butter
$1\frac{1}{2}$ cups flour
$\frac{1}{4}$ cup sugar
1 egg
1 level teaspoon baking powder

Sponge

2 Tablespoons Butter
4 tablespoons milk
2 eggs
1 teaspoon cinnamon
a little vanilla
4 tablespoons sugar
8 tablespoons flour
1 level teaspoon baking powder
1 teaspoon cocoa
some chopped walnuts

For the pastry, cream the butter and sugar, add egg, then flour and baking powder. Roll out and line sandwich tins. Then cream the butter and sugar for the sponge. Add milk, vanilla, eggs, flour (sifted with baking powder, cinnamon and cocoa) and nuts. Beat for a few minutes, then pour mixture over pastry, first having spread pastry with raspberry jam. Put a few strips of the pastry crossways on cake and bake in a fair oven about $\frac{1}{2}$ an hour. Nuts are not essential.

EASTER CAKE

250 gr ($\frac{1}{2}$ lb.) Flour
125 gr ($\frac{1}{4}$ lb.) sultanas
185 gr (6 oz.) butter
$\frac{1}{2}$ teaspoon ground cloves
1 teaspoon mixed spice
125 gr ($\frac{1}{4}$ lb.) peel
125 gr ($\frac{1}{4}$ lb.) sugar
375 gr ($\frac{3}{4}$ lb.) currants
3 eggs
$\frac{1}{2}$ teaspoon carbonate soda
1 teaspoon cinnamon
60 gr (2 oz.) golden syrup
milk

EASTER CAKE—*continued*

Prepare the fruit and shred the candied peel. Whisk the eggs, warm the syrup and add to the eggs. Beat well together. Sift the flour with the soda and spices. Beat butter and sugar to a cream, add gradually the flour and fruit, alternately with egg mixture and add a little milk if too stiff. The texture depends on size of the eggs, and the weather also affects the dough. Turn the mixture into a lined greased cake tin and bake about 2 hours.

Or put half the mixture into tin, then put on the dough a layer of almond icing, then the rest of cake mixture on top. When cooked and cold, put a layer of almond icing on top and then a layer of plain icing. The cake may be decorated. Use almond icing No. 1 (p. 249) for this cake.

FEATHER CAKE

125 gr (¼ lb.) Butter
3 cups self-raising flour
250 gr (½ lb.) sultanas
1 cup sugar
1 cup milk
4 eggs

Beat butter and sugar to a cream and then add eggs, one at a time, beating well between each egg. Add flour, then milk and, lastly, sultanas. Cook in a buttered shallow tin for about 1 hour in a moderate oven.

FRENCH TEA CAKE

1 Egg
½ cup milk
1 cup self-raising flour
1 tablespoon butter
½ cup sugar
salt
vanilla

Beat egg white and sugar. Add egg yolk and milk, essence and flour, then melted butter. Sprinkle well with cinnamon and sugar, and bake in hot oven about 20 minutes.

FRUIT AND BUTTERMILK CAKE (NO EGGS)

375 gr (¾ lb.) Flour
250 gr (½ lb.) sugar
1½ teacups buttermilk
375 gr (¾ lb.) currants or sultanas, or mixed
60 gr (2 oz.) butter
1 teaspoon carbonate soda

Rub butter into flour, add sugar and soda sifted together, then fruits and mix well with buttermilk. Bake in slow oven for about 2 hours. This is a nice cake and most useful on a farm.

FRUIT CAKE (No. 1)

375 gr (¾ lb.) Flour (Half Plain and Half Self-raising)
250 gr (½ lb.) butter
375 gr (¾ lb.) mixed fruit
1 teaspoon cinnamon
5 eggs
250 gr (½ lb.) sugar
125 gr (4 oz.) almonds
60 gr (2 oz.) mixed peel
½ teaspoon spice
1 wineglass of brandy

Clean and dry the fruit some days before using. Six eggs should be used if brandy is omitted. Beat eggs well, then add them to the creamed butter and sugar and beat all together until light and creamy. Add the spices, then the flour and fruit alternately, and mix with eggs to a nice consistency. (Cake batter should never be too stiff.) Put in tins with two layers of paper high at sides, and put in a fairly hot oven, reducing the heat gradually. Bake for 2½ hours.

FRUIT CAKE (No. 2)

500 gr (1 lb.) Plain Flour
250 gr (½ lb.) butter
1 teaspoon mixed spice
1 teaspoon cinnamon
3 eggs
250 gr (½ lb.) sugar
625 gr (1¼ lb.) mixed fruit (sultanas, currants, dates or cherries and lemon peel)
½ cup milk
1 teaspoon carbonate soda

Rub butter into flour and add sugar, pinch salt, fruit and spices. Beat eggs and add to dry ingredients. Mix soda in warm milk, add to batter and beat well. Put mixture into greased cake tins and let stand for 1 hour. Bake in a moderate oven for 2 hours.

FRUIT CAKE (No. 3)

2 Cups Sugar
4 cups flour
1 cup sultanas
1 teaspoon mixed spices
1 cup melted butter
1 cup currants
1 cup raisins
1 teaspoon cocoa
1½ teaspoons carbonate soda

Mix with sour milk and bake in a moderate oven for 1½ hours.

FRUIT CAKE (No. 4)

185 gr (6 oz.) Butter
185 gr (6 oz.) sugar
250 gr (½ lb.) plain flour
pinch salt
½ teaspoon baking powder
3 eggs
750 gr (1½ lb.) mixed fruits
¼ teaspoon spice
1 teaspoon cinnamon
1 tablespoon golden syrup
1 tablespoon apricot jam
2 tablespoons brandy, sherry or fruit juice

FRUIT CAKE (No. 4)—*continued*

Mix fruit in basin. Add brandy, golden syrup and jam. Cover and leave 24 hours. Cream butter and sugar, add eggs singly, beating well. Sift in flour, baking powder, spices, salt. Add prepared fruit, mixing well. Put into greased lined tin and bake 2-2½ hours in slow oven.

FRUIT CAKE (PINEAPPLE)

625 gr (1¼ lb.) Mixed Fruit
185 gr (6 oz.) butter
60 gr (2 oz.) cherries
60 gr (2 oz.) peel
1 teaspoon grated orange rind
3 eggs
250 gr (½ lb.) plain flour
1 cup pineapple syrup
½ cup crushed or shredded pineapple
155 gr (5 oz.) brown sugar
2 tablespoons chopped walnuts or almonds
¼ teaspoon baking powder
pinch salt

Prepare fruit, add cherries and peel and cover with pineapple syrup, and leave overnight.

Cream butter and sugar, add eggs singly, beating well. Add sifted flour, baking powder and salt alternately with fruit, pineapple and nuts. Turn into paper-lined tin and bake in slow oven 3½-4 hours.

FRUITY CARROT CAKE

2 eggs
¾ cup raw sugar
Grated rind one medium lemon
¾ cup safflower oil
1 ripe mashed banana
1 cup grated carrot
1½ cups self-raising flour
¾ cup well drained crushed pineapple
½ cup chopped walnuts

Beat eggs, sugar and lemon rind until thick, gradually add oil, beating constantly. Beat in sifted flour, then stir in banana, carrot, pineapple and walnuts. Mix thoroughly, turn into 20 cm deep tin and bake 50 to 60 minutes in moderate oven. Leave in tin 10 minutes, and turn out. Keeps moist, freezes well.

GENOA CAKE

500 gr (1 lb.) Flour
375 gr (¾ lb.) sugar
375 gr (¾ lb.) butter
125 gr (¼ lb.) blanched almonds
375 gr (¾ lb.) sultanas and currants mixed
250 gr (½ lb.) mixed peel
8 or 9 eggs
2 teaspoons baking powder

Cream the butter and sugar. Break each egg separately and add one at a time to mixture, beating well between each. Add the fruit and mix very thoroughly. When thoroughly mixed, add the flour with the baking powder. Bake for about 2 hours in a moderate oven.

GINGERBREAD (No. 1)

1 Cup Sugar
1 cup butter
2 eggs
3 cups plain flour
1 cup treacle
1 cup milk
4 teaspoons ground ginger
2 teaspoons (small) carbonate soda
1 tablespoon hot water

Cream the butter, add sugar and cream again. Then add the eggs (beaten) and the treacle dissolved in the milk. Add the flour and the spices and, lastly, the soda dissolved in the hot water. Put into square, shallow, greased baking dish and bake in a slow oven for 1 hour.

GINGERBREAD (AMERICAN) No. 2

1 Cup Treacle
1 teaspoon carbonate soda (level)
2 teaspoons ground ginger
¼ teaspoon allspice
1 teaspoon lard
1½ cups plain flour
1 egg
1 tablespoon brown sugar
½ teaspoon salt
¼ teaspoon cinnamon
1 tablespoon butter
½ teaspoon cream of tartar
¾ cup milk
a little mixed peel

Stir all ingredients together after melting treacle, butter, lard and sugar. Beat vigorously and when batter is smooth and free from lumps stir in well-beaten egg. Bake in a shallow buttered tin in a moderate oven for 40 minutes. When cold this gingerbread can be iced.

GINGERBREAD (No. 3)

2 Breakfast Cups Flour
1 dessertspoon cinnamon
1 saltspoon salt
8 level tablespoons butter
3 eggs
½ cup milk
1 teaspoon carbonate soda
2 dessertspoons ground ginger
1 teaspoon mixed spice
1 scant cup sugar
½ cup golden syrup
½ teaspoon essence lemon
¼ cup boiling water

Beat the butter to a cream, add sugar and beat again; then add eggs one at a time and then the golden syrup dissolved in the milk. Now add the essence of lemon. Sift all the dry ingredients together and add. Dissolve the soda in the boiling water and stir in. Beat well. Butter a shallow baking tin and put in the mixture. Bake ¾ of an hour in a moderately cool oven. Watch carefully as it burns readily. Good dripping may be used instead of butter.

GINGERBREAD (CHOCOLATE)

2 Cups Flour
1 cup treacle
1 teaspoon carbonate soda
1 teaspoon ginger
3 tablespoons butter
½ cup sour milk
1 teaspoon cinnamon
60 gr (2 oz.) chocolate

Mix treacle with milk and dissolve soda in a little warm water and add. Melt chocolate and butter and stir into the mixture. Then add flour, well sifted, with the ginger and cinnamon. Grease a cake tin well, pour in the mixture and bake 1½ hours in a moderate oven.

GINGER CAKE (No. 1)

¼ Cup Butter
½ cup new milk
3 eggs
1 teaspoon ground ginger
1 small cup sugar
½ cup golden syrup
½ teaspoon cinnamon
½ teaspoon carbonate soda
1½ cups plain flour

Beat butter and sugar, then add eggs. Warm the golden syrup and add, then add the milk. Sift spices with flour and add. Put carbonate soda in a little hot water and add. Beat well together. Put in a shallow tin and bake for 1 hour in a slow oven.

GINGER CAKE (No. 2)

2½ Cups Flour
½ cup sour cream or milk
½ cup brown sugar
½ tablespoon ground ginger
½ teaspoon cloves
½ cup butter
½ cup treacle
1 heaped teaspoon carbonate soda
½ teaspoon cinnamon
currants, or raisins, if preferred

Sift flour and spices, add sugar. Melt butter and treacle together and add. Stir 1 heaped teaspoon carbonate soda with sour milk and add. Bake in moderate oven 35-45 minutes.

FRUIT GINGERBREAD

1 kg (2 lb.) Self-raising Flour
250 gr (½ lb.) butter
60 gr (2 oz.) ground ginger
125 gr (4 oz.) sultanas
125 gr (4 oz.) mixed peel
1 cup milk
375 gr (¾ lb.) castor sugar
2 eggs
60 gr (2 oz.) mixed spice
125 gr (4 oz.) currants
500 gr (1 lb.) treacle
a pinch of salt

Mix all dry ingredients (except salt) well together. Melt the treacle with milk and butter and add beaten eggs and salt. Add dry ingredients and stir the mixture till it makes a thick batter. Pour into a large greased baking tin and bake for 2½ hours in a moderate oven.

GOLD AND SILVER CAKE

Golden Half

125 gr (4 oz.) Butter
yolks of 4 eggs
2 level teaspoons baking powder
125 gr (4 oz.) sugar
185 gr (6 oz.) flour
125 ml (1 gill) milk
vanilla essence

Beat the butter and sugar to a cream, beat in the yolks, then flour and milk by degrees, mixing baking powder with last spoonful of flour. Add the flavouring.

Silver Half

Whisk the whites of 4 eggs to a froth, use the same proportions of ingredients as above and mix in the same way. Line a deep cake tin with butter paper, and place alternate spoonsful of the yellow and white mixtures in the tin, so that when the cake is cut the colours will be nicely mixed. Bake in moderate oven for 2½ hours.

JEWISH CAKE

125 gr (¼ lb.) Butter
1½ cups self-raising flour
1 teaspoon cinnamon
a few chopped sultanas
125 gr (¼ lb.) sugar
3 eggs
a few chopped almonds
3 tablespoons milk
essence lemon to flavour

Beat butter and sugar to a cream and add the unbeaten eggs, then the milk, essence, fruit and flour. Bake in a moderate oven 20 to 30 minutes. Keep one white of egg back for icing. Beat white of egg with 4 tablespoons of icing sugar. Ice while cake is still hot.

KENTISH CAKE

125 gr (¼ lb.) Butter
½ cup chopped almonds
¾ cup sugar
1 tablespoon cocoa
2 eggs
¾ cup milk
2 tablespoons coconut
1 large cup self-raising flour

Beat the butter and sugar to a cream, add eggs, cocoa, coconut and almonds and then the milk and flour. Bake in a moderate oven for 40 minutes. Ice with 1 tablespoon butter, ¼ cup milk, chopped almonds, vanilla and enough icing sugar to thicken.

LEMON CHEESE CAKE

1 Large Breakfast Cup Plain Flour
125 gr (4 oz.) butter
lemon cheese
1 egg
125 gr (4 oz.) sugar
1 teaspoon baking powder (heaped)
essence lemon
milk

Rub the butter into the flour, add the sugar and mix well, and then add the baking powder. Make into a fairly stiff dough with the well-beaten egg and a little milk, flavoured with essence of lemon. Divide the paste into two pieces. Grease a deep sandwich tin and press one portion into the tin with the hands, covering the whole surface. Spread thickly with lemon cheese. Work the other piece into a round with the hands, and place on top of the other portion and glaze with beaten white of egg. Sprinkle with chopped almonds and bake in a moderate oven from 30 to 35 minutes.

LUNCHEON CAKE

2 Eggs
250 gr (½ lb.) butter
500 gr (1 lb.) flour (plain)
¼ teaspoon carbonate soda
a little peel
250 gr (½ lb.) sugar
½ cup milk
2 tablespoons golden syrup
500 gr (1 lb.) currants and sultanas mixed
a few almonds

Beat butter and sugar to a cream and add eggs one at a time. Beat well and then add milk with soda, golden syrup, fruit and nuts and, lastly, the flour. If the mixture is too stiff add a little more milk. Bake for 2½ hours in a moderate oven.

MACAROON CAKE

125 gr (4 oz.) Butter
1 cup sugar
1 cup coconut
3 eggs
1 large cup self-raising flour
½ cup milk

Cream butter and ½ cup sugar. Add egg yolks and beat. Add flour and milk and put into cake tin. Beat egg whites till stiff, add ½ cup sugar, and beat. Mix in coconut then spread on top of cake mixture. Bake in moderate oven ¾ hour. Leave to cool before taking from tin.

MADEIRA CAKE

125 gr (¼ lb.) Butter
¾ cup milk
2 cups self-raising flour
¾ cup sugar
3 eggs
some grated lemon rind

Cream butter and sugar, add well-beaten eggs, then the lemon rind and the milk gradually. Lastly add sifted flour and mix lightly. Place in a well-greased cake tin and cook in a moderate oven about 1¼ hours.

MARBLE CAKE

185 gr (6 oz.) Butter
250 gr (½ lb.) flour
a little milk
cocoa
185 gr (6 oz.) sugar
3 eggs
2 small teaspoons baking powder
cochineal

Beat the butter and sugar to a cream, add the well-beaten eggs and the milk, then the flour with the baking powder sifted through. Beat all well. Divide the mixture into 3 equal parts. Add a few drops of cochineal to one part, a dessertspoonful of cocoa to another and leave one plain. Place a tablespoonful of each colour into a cake tin alternately and bake in a moderate oven.

MOIST CARROT CAKE

180 gr (6 oz.) grated carrot
2 eggs
½ cup sugar
¼ cup vegetable oil
1 cup self-raising wholemeal flour
60 gr coconut
60 gr currants
1 level teaspoon mixed spice
1 level teaspoon cinnamon

Whisk eggs, sugar and oil until light and fluffy. Fold in remaining ingredients, turn into greased loaf tin or ring tin and cook in a moderate oven for 40 to 45 minutes. Cool in tin for 15 to 20 minutes before turning out.

NEW YEAR BUN (SCOTCH) or CURRANT LOAF

Pastry

1½ Cups Plain Flour
250 gr (½ lb.) butter
½ teaspoon baking powder
water

The Bun

500 gr (1 lb.) Plain Flour
1 kg (2 lb.) currants
60 gr (2 oz.) orange peel
125 gr (4 oz.) almonds (blanched and chopped)
1 dessertspoon ginger
½ teaspoon black pepper
a pinch nutmeg
1 small teaspoon cream tartar
3 eggs
250 gr (½ lb.) castor sugar
1 kg (2 lb.) seeded raisins
60 gr (2 oz.) lemon peel
1 dessertspoon cinnamon
1 dessertspoon allspice
a pinch ground cloves
a pinch mace
1 small teaspoon carbonate soda
milk to moisten

To make the Pastry.—Sift the flour with the baking powder, rub in the butter and mix to a firm dough with water. Roll out thin and line the inside of a well-greased round or square cake tin with the paste, keeping back sufficient paste for a top.

To make the Bun.—Mix together the flour (with soda and cream of tartar sifted through), sugar, fruit and spices. Beat the eggs well (reserve a little beaten egg to glaze the bun) and make up to a breakfastcupful with milk. This is just sufficient to moisten the ingredients nicely. Mix very thoroughly (using

NEW YEAR BUN (SCOTCH) or CURRANT LOAF—*continued*

the hands). Put the mixture into the lined tin and make it even on top, wet the edges and put on covering of paste, pinching edges well together. Prick all over with a fork, brush with beaten egg, place in a moderate oven and bake from 3 to 3½ hours. Cover with greased paper after the paste has become a nice pale brown. The bun is best made a month before the New Year. It improves with keeping. If well made it will keep from one New Year until the next.

Note.—Do not fill your tin too full, as the paste will be forced up and the mixture will be allowed to escape.

ORANGE CAKE

- 1 Cup Sugar
- 3 eggs
- ¼ cup butter
- 1 orange
- 1 cup self-raising flour

Cream butter and sugar, add 2 eggs, one at a time, then ½ cup flour, grated rind and juice of orange, another ½ cup of flour and, lastly, 1 more egg. Bake in a moderate oven for 40 minutes.

PEACH BLOSSOM CAKE

- ½ Cup Butter
- ½ cup milk
- 1½ teaspoons cornflour or maizena
- 1 cup sugar
- 1½ cups self-raising flour
- 3 egg whites

Cream butter and sugar, add stiffly beaten egg whites, then add flour, maizena and milk. Mix quickly and bake in shallow tin for 20 minutes. Ice with icing made by blending whipped white of 1 egg and icing sugar. Flavour as desired. Colour some coconut pink and sprinkle on top.

PLAIN CAKE (No. 1)

- 1 Cup Butter
- 2 cups self-raising flour
- 1 cup sugar
- ½ cup milk
- 4 eggs
- flavouring

Cream butter and sugar for about 10 minutes. Beat the eggs till creamy and add to sugar and butter. Add milk and then beat in flour lightly. Bake in flat tin for ¾ to 1 hour in a moderate oven, after the oven has been hot and is cooling off.

Variations of Above.—Add the grated rind of a large orange and ice with orange flavoured icing. Divide the cake into two. Flavour one half with orange rind and the other half with vanilla, and colour with 3 teaspoons cocoa mixed with a little boiling water. Ice the light one with orange icing and the dark one with chocolate icing.

PLAIN CAKE (No. 2)

625 gr ($1\frac{1}{4}$ lb.) Flour
375 gr ($\frac{3}{4}$ lb.) sugar
5 eggs
1 teaspoon carbonate soda
250 gr ($\frac{1}{2}$ lb.) butter
1 cup milk (hot or cold)
2 teaspoons cream tartar
a little salt
a few drops essence almond

Beat the sugar and butter to a cream, then add eggs one at a time, then milk and flour (with cream of tartar and salt). Add essence. Wet carbonate soda with a tablespoon boiling water and stir well. Add to mixture and bake for 1 hour in a moderate oven.

POTATO CAKE (DEVONSHIRE RECIPE)

250 gr ($\frac{1}{2}$ lb.) Mashed Potatoes
60 gr (2 oz.) suet
30 gr (1 oz.) lemon peel
90 gr (3 oz.) sultanas or currants
1 teacup flour
90 gr (3 oz.) brown sugar
$\frac{1}{2}$ teaspoon baking powder
8 drops essence lemon

Mix all dry ingredients and add mashed potatoes. Put into greased Yorkshire pudding tin, spread with knife, cut into squares and bake for $\frac{1}{2}$ an hour in fairly hot oven. This may be eaten hot or cold.

Note.—If cold potatoes are used the whole may be mixed with a little cold milk.

PRIZE CAKE

500 gr (1 lb.) Plain Flour
375 gr ($\frac{3}{4}$ lb.) butter
125 gr ($\frac{1}{4}$ lb.) mixed peel (finely chopped)
250 gr ($\frac{1}{2}$ lb.) glace cherries
1 teaspoon grated nutmeg
$\frac{1}{2}$ teaspoon carbonate soda
375 gr ($\frac{3}{4}$ lb.) sugar
2 kg (4 lb.) fruit (sultanas, raisins and currants)
90 gr (3 oz.) almonds
1 teaspoon cinnamon
1 teaspoon cream tartar
10 eggs

Sift the flour three times with soda, cream tartar and spices. Cream butter and sugar, then add eggs (not previously whipped), beating each one in well. Then add the sifted flour and then fruit, and beat all well together. Bake in round tin with three layers of buttered paper and another piece placed on top when in oven. Have the oven fairly hot at first, then let the fire die down a little, keeping it at the same heat until the cake is cooked. This cake should take between 4 and 5 hours to cook.

PUMPKIN FRUIT CAKE (No. 1)

125 gr (4 oz.) Butter or Margarine
2 eggs
1 cup hot mashed pumpkin
1 cup sugar
1 tablespoon golden syrup
2 cups self-raising flour
1 packet mixed fruit
pinch salt
lemon icing

Cream butter and sugar, add eggs beaten in one at a time. Add golden syrup, then pumpkin. Sift in flour and salt. Mix lightly, fold in fruit. Bake in moderate oven $1\frac{1}{2}$ hours. Ice when cold.

PUMPKIN FRUIT CAKE (No. 2)

2 Eggs
1 heaped tablespoon butter
1 tablespoon golden syrup
1 teaspoon mixed spice
1 tablespoon grated orange rind
1 cup sugar
1 cup lukewarm mashed pumpkin
1 packet mixed fruit
1 teaspoon cinnamon
2 cups self-raising flour
pinch salt
essence to taste

Cream butter and sugar, then add eggs and pumpkin, golden syrup, fruit, spice, cinnamon and orange rind. Add self-raising flour and salt and essence to taste. Bake 2 hours in a very moderate oven.

PUMPKIN SULTANA CAKE (EGGLESS)

3 Tablespoons Margarine
1 cup mashed pumpkin
2 cups self-raising flour
1 cup sultanas
$\frac{3}{4}$ cup sugar
$\frac{1}{2}$ cup milk
pinch salt
1 teaspoon vanilla essence

Cream margarine and sugar, then add essence and pumpkin. Mix well. Fold in sifted flour and salt alternately with milk. Add sultanas. Bake in 20 cm (8 in.) tin in moderate oven for $1\frac{1}{2}$ hours. Ice with butter icing flavoured with lemon or orange juice, and top with chopped peel.

RED INDIAN CAKE

750 gr ($1\frac{1}{2}$ lb.) Plain Flour
500 gr (1 lb.) currants
250 gr ($\frac{1}{2}$ lb.) raisins
4 eggs
500 gr (1 lb.) butter
500 gr (1 lb.) sugar
250 gr ($\frac{1}{2}$ lb.) lemon peel
2 cups milk
2 teaspoons carbonate soda

Cream butter and sugar and add well-beaten eggs, half the milk and then the flour, to which soda has been added, rest of the milk and then the fruit. Bake in a slow oven.

SEED CAKE

310 gr (10 oz.) Flour
1½ teaspoons baking powder
2 eggs
a pinch of salt
185 gr (6 oz.) sugar
125 gr (4 oz.) butter
125 ml (1 gill) milk
1 dessertspoon carraway seeds

Grease a round cake tin. Cream butter and sugar until white. Beat eggs well and add gradually to the butter and sugar. Add milk, carraway seeds and flour with baking powder. Mix lightly and pour into prepared tin. Bake in a moderately hot oven for 1½ hours.

SCOTCH SHORTBREAD (No. 1)

500 gr (1 lb.) Flour
250 gr (½ lb.) butter
60 gr (2 oz.) ground rice
125 gr (¼ lb.) castor sugar

Beat butter to a cream and dredge in flour, ground rice and sugar. Work paste until quite smooth. Divide it into three pieces and roll out to about 5 cm (2 in.) in thickness. Put each cake on a separate piece of paper and bake in a moderate oven about 30 minutes.

SCOTCH SHORTBREAD (No. 2)

250 gr (½ lb.) Butter
125 gr (¼ lb.) rice flour
30 gr (1 oz.) orange peel
375 gr (¾ lb.) plain flour
60 gr (2 oz.) almonds
155 gr (5 oz.) sugar

Mould into a dough by working together the butter, sugar, flour and ground rice. Knead well into a smooth paste. Roll out about 5 cm (2 in.) thick. Pinch round the edges, prick on top and lay on white paper on oven shelf. Decorate the cakes with blanched and sliced almonds and minced orange peel. Bake for ¾ of an hour in a slow oven.

SODA CAKE (No. 1)

250 gr (½ lb.) Flour
250 gr (½ lb.) raisins (stoned)
125 gr (¼ lb.) currants
250 gr (½ lb.) brown sugar
2 eggs
125 gr (¼ lb.) orange peel
1 teacup milk
60 gr (2 oz.) butter
1 teaspoon carbonate soda
1 teaspoon ground ginger
1 teaspoon ground cinnamon
½ grated nutmeg
125 gr (¼ lb.) dates

Put into a basin the flour, sugar, currants, raisins, orange peel, carbonate soda, spices and mix well. Warm the butter sufficiently to melt it a little and then beat the eggs and mix them with the butter. Afterwards add the milk. Now stir the milk, butter and eggs among the mixture in the basin, and mix well. Have a cake tin greased and covered with paper, into which pour the cake and bake for 1 hour at the least.

SODA CAKE (No. 2)

500 gr (1 lb.) Flour
250 gr (½ lb.) brown sugar
1 teaspoon mixed spice
1 heaped teaspoon carbonate soda
125 gr (¼ lb.) butter or lard
250 gr (½ lb.) mixed fruit
a pinch salt
250 ml (½ pint) boiling milk

Rub the butter into the flour and all other dry ingredients, except soda. Dissolve the soda in boiling milk and mix all well together. Put into well-greased tin and bake in a moderate oven. This cake is improved by putting 2 teaspoons vinegar on top when in the tin and before baking.

SPICE CAKE

3 Eggs
1 heaped breakfast cup flour
1 heaped teaspoon baking powder
½ teaspoon ground cinnamon
1 level teacup sultanas
1 level teacup raisins
essence lemon
125 gr (¼ lb.) butter
1 tablespoon treacle
1 teaspoon mixed spice
1 level teacup sugar
1 level teacup currants
2 pieces candied peel (shredded)
a little milk

Beat butter and sugar to a cream, add eggs, then the treacle, warmed, and the flour with powder and spices. Lastly add the fruit. If too stiff add a little milk. Bake in shallow baking dish for 1 hour in a slow oven.

SULTANA CAKE

185 gr (6 oz.) Butter
3 eggs
60 gr (2 oz.) mixed peel
1 teaspoon baking powder
375 gr (¾ lb.) sugar
125 gr (¼ lb.) ground rice
310 gr (10 oz.) plain flour
½ cup milk
250 gr (½ lb.) sultanas

Beat the butter and sugar to a cream and add the eggs one at a time. Then add the ground rice, sultanas and mixed peel. Lastly, add flour and baking powder mixed together, and the milk. Bake in moderate oven for 1½ hours.

VINEGAR CAKE

185 gr (6 oz.) Sugar
375 gr (12 oz.) plain flour
60 gr (2 oz.) mixed peel
3 teaspoons vinegar
185 gr (6 oz.) butter
250 gr (8 oz.) sultanas
¾ teaspoon carbonate soda
milk

Cream butter and sugar, add the flour and beat all till like thick cream. Add fruit and a little milk if required. Put the soda in a cup, add the vinegar, mix thoroughly and add to cake mixture. Place immediately in a moderate oven for 1½ hours.

WALNUT CAKE

3 Eggs
1 small cup sugar
1 large cup flour
1 cup chopped walnuts
125 gr ($\frac{1}{4}$ lb.) butter
1 dessertspoon ground cinnamon
2 teaspoons baking powder
a few drops vanilla essence

Beat butter and sugar to a cream, add eggs separately, then flour and cinnamon through sifter and, lastly, add baking powder and walnuts. Bake in a moderate oven.

WEST INDIAN CAKE

250 gr ($\frac{1}{2}$ lb.) Sugar
250 ml ($\frac{1}{2}$ pint) milk
1 level teaspoon carbonate soda
2 eggs
250 gr ($\frac{1}{2}$ lb.) butter
500 gr (1 lb.) plain flour
1 teaspoon nutmeg
500 gr (1 lb.) mixed fruit
250 gr ($\frac{1}{2}$ lb.) lemon peel

Beat butter and sugar to a cream, then beat in eggs one at a time. Add milk and stir in flour, sifted with soda and nutmeg. Lastly add fruit and lemon peel. Bake in fairly warm oven for 3 hours.

WHITE MOUNTAIN CAKE

$\frac{1}{2}$ Cup Butter
2 cups flour
2 eggs
1 teaspoon cream tartar
1$\frac{1}{2}$ cups coconut
1 cup sugar
$\frac{1}{2}$ cup warm milk
$\frac{1}{2}$ teaspoon carbonate soda
icing

Beat butter and sugar to a cream, add eggs, well-beaten, then milk and lastly, flour and rising. Bake in a moderate oven.

Icing.—Bring to the boil $\frac{3}{4}$ cup milk and 2 cups sugar. Add 1$\frac{1}{2}$ cups coconut and ice while the cake is lukewarm.

WHOLESOME APPLE FRUIT CAKE

125 gr (4 oz.) Butter
185 gr (6 oz.) sugar
2 tablespoons milk
1 cup of cold apple pulp
310 gr (10 oz.) S.R. flour
juice of one lemon
3 eggs
$\frac{1}{4}$ teaspoon carbonate of soda
375 gr ($\frac{3}{4}$ lb.) sultanas
60 gr (2 oz.) peel

Cream butter with the lemon juice, add sugar, then the eggs beaten, then the milk, mix soda with apple pulp and add, then flour and fruit. Bake 1 to 1$\frac{1}{2}$ hours, according to depth of cake tin used.

SPONGE AND SANDWICH CAKES

Sandwich or sponge cakes will come away from tins quite clean without breaking edges, if, immediately on removing from the oven, the bottom of tin is wiped over with a cloth wrung out of cold water.

When breaking eggs, always break them into a cup, emptying each one from the cup as soon as you find it is good.

Add a tiny pinch of salt when beating eggs. They froth more quickly, and are stiffer than they would otherwise be.

BLOWAWAY SPICED SPONGE

- 3 Eggs
- 1 teaspoon golden syrup
- ½ cup arrowroot
- ½ teaspoon carbonate soda
- 1 teaspoon cocoa
- 1 cup white sugar
- 1 tablespoon flour
- 1 teaspoon cream of tartar
- 2 teaspoons ginger
- 1½ teaspoons cinnamon

Beat together for 5 minutes the eggs and sugar. Then add the golden syrup and beat for 10 minutes. Sift thoroughly 3 times the flour, arrowroot, cream of tartar, soda, and spices. Stir well into the creamed mixture. Divide, and bake in greased sandwich tins for 10 minutes. Do not open the oven door until the sponge is cooked. Omit spices if a plain sponge is required.

BLOWAWAY CAKE

- ½ Cup Arrowroot
- ¾ cup sugar
- 1 teaspoon cream of tartar
- 1 teaspoon plain flour
- ½ teaspoon carbonate soda
- 4 eggs

Break eggs into a basin, beat for 10 minutes, then add sugar, and beat for another 10 minutes. Then add arrowroot, soda, cream of tartar, flour (after these have been well sifted together). Mix thoroughly, put into sandwich tins, and bake in a moderate oven—on the bottom—for 10 to 20 minutes.

BROWN SANDWICH CAKE

1 Small Cup Sugar
3 eggs
1 level teaspoon cream of tartar
2 teaspoons cocoa
½ cup cold water
1 tablespoon butter
1 large cup flour
½ teaspoon carbonate soda
1 teaspoon cinnamon
a few drops vanilla essence

Beat butter and sugar together, then add eggs well-beaten, and proceed in the usual way, adding cold water last. Bake in sandwich tins, ice with brown icing, and use cream filling. Self-raising flour may be used.

BROWN CREAM ROLL

1 Cup Sugar
2 tablespoons boiling milk
2 teaspoons cinnamon
1 teaspoon cream of tartar
3 eggs
1 cup flour
1 teaspoon spice
½ teaspoon carbonate soda

Beat eggs and sugar until creamy, add the milk, then stir in the flour and spices (sifted together) and lastly the cream of tartar and soda. Spread on a baking slide previously greased and papered, and bake in a medium oven. When done, turn on to paper sprinkled with sugar, and cover with a damp cloth for a few moments. Peel off paper and roll up. When cold unroll, fill with whipped cream, and roll up again.

CARAMEL NUT CAKE

60 gr (2 oz.) Butter
½ cup brown sugar
1 egg
1 cup self-raising flour
3 tablespoons milk
vanilla

Filling

¼ Cup Brown Sugar
2 dessertspoons melted butter
3 dessertspoons flour
¼ cup chopped walnuts
2 teaspoons cinnamon

Cream butter and sugar, add egg and mix well. Fold in sifted flour alternately with milk and essence. Place half mixture in greased 18 cm (7 in.) tin. Cover with filling prepared by adding other ingredients to melted butter. Spread evenly over cake mixture, cover with balance of cake mixture. Bake in moderate oven 35-40 minutes.

CHOCOLATE CAKE (No. 1)

2 Eggs
1 cup sugar
½ cup butter
½ cup milk
2 tablespoons cocoa
2 tablespoons boiling water
1¾ cups plain flour
1½ level teaspoons cream of tartar
¾ level teaspoon carbonate soda
salt

Beat the butter and sugar to a cream, add egg yolks and beat well, then add cocoa which has been mixed with boiling water. Stir in milk a little at a time, then beat in the dry ingredients. After all is thoroughly mixed fold in the stiffly beaten whites of the eggs. Bake in sandwich tins or make into a loaf cake. Bake 20 to 30 minutes.

CHOCOLATE CAKE (No. 2)

2 Cups Self-raising Flour
1 teaspoon carb. soda
1 teaspoon cinnamon
1 egg
½ teaspoon vanilla
2 tablespoons cocoa
1 cup sugar
¼ cup brown sugar
⅓ cup shortening
1 cup milk

Sift dry ingredients into bowl. Add sugars and softened shortening, vanilla and milk. Beat well for 2 minutes. Add egg and beat another minute. Bake in 20 cm (8 in.) tins in moderate oven 25-35 minutes.

CHOCOLATE CAKE (No. 3)

125 gr (4 oz.) Butter
1 cup sugar
1½ cups self-raising flour
2 teaspoons cocoa
1 cup milk
1 tablespoon golden syrup
2 teaspoons cinnamon
1 teaspoon carb. soda

Heat together until melted, butter, ½ cup milk, sugar and golden syrup. Add sifted flour, cinnamon and cocoa. Dissolve soda in remainder of milk and mix in lightly. Bake 20 minutes in moderate oven.

CHOCOLATE BUTTER SANDWICH

4 Eggs
1 teacup self-raising flour
½ cup boiling water
1 teacup sugar
1 tablespoon butter
small half cup of cocoa
few drops essence of vanilla

Boil butter, water and cocoa together. Beat eggs and sugar until light and fluffy, then add well-sifted flour with pinch of salt. Lastly add cocoa mixture. Bake in sandwich tins and fill with mock cream filling.

Mock Cream Filling

1 Cup Icing Sugar
1 egg white well beaten
1 tablespoon butter
1 tablespoon chopped walnuts

Melt butter, add sugar and beat to a cream, add egg white, beat until smooth, add nuts. Ice with chocolate icing to which ½ teaspoon mixed spice has been added. Decorate with ½ walnuts.

CHOCOLATE DATE CAKE

125 gr ($\frac{1}{4}$ lb.) Butter
3 eggs
250 gr ($\frac{1}{2}$ lb.) flour
$\frac{1}{2}$ teaspoon carbonate soda
250 gr ($\frac{1}{2}$ lb.) sugar
$\frac{1}{2}$ cup milk
1 teaspoon cream of tartar
2 heaped tablespoons cocoa

Beat butter and sugar to a cream. Beat in the eggs separately, add the milk, then the flour, cream of tartar, soda, and cocoa sifted together. Bake in two sandwich tins in a moderate oven for 20 to 30 minutes. *Filling*: Stone about 15 dates and put in a saucepan with 1 tablespoon butter and $\frac{1}{2}$ cup milk. Let boil, stirring occasionally. Put this mixture between cakes when cold. *Icing*: Sift together 6 dessertspoons icing sugar, and 1 dessertspoon cocoa. Add 1 teaspoon of melted butter and about 1 tablespoon of boiling water. Mix well, and pour over the top of the cake.

CINNAMON SANDWICH

2 Small Cups Self-raising Flour
$\frac{3}{4}$ cup sugar
2 teaspoons vanilla essence
a pinch of salt
125 gr ($\frac{1}{4}$ lb.) butter
3 eggs
2 teaspoons cinnamon
a little extra rising
$\frac{1}{4}$ cup milk

Beat butter and sugar to a cream, add eggs separately, then essence and cinnamon. Sift flour, salt and cream of tartar, and add. Then add milk, and soda dissolved in hot water, to the mixture. Pour into greased tins, and cook in a moderate oven for 20 minutes. *Filling*: Chop 12 dates finely, add a piece of butter the size of a walnut, vanilla essence, and $\frac{1}{4}$ cup milk, put in a saucepan and boil, stirring all the time. When cold join cakes with it, and ice with white icing and chopped almonds.

COCOA CAKE

125 gr ($\frac{1}{4}$ lb.) Butter
250 gr ($\frac{1}{2}$ lb.) self-raising flour
6 tablespoons milk
250 gr ($\frac{1}{2}$ lb.) sugar
3 eggs
4 heaped teaspoons cocoa

Beat the butter and sugar to a cream, add the well-beaten eggs, milk, and then the flour and cocoa. Cook in sandwich tins in a moderate oven for 20 minutes. *Filling*: Beat 2 tablespoons icing sugar and 1 tablespoon butter till creamy. Add 1 teaspoon cocoa and vanilla essence. *Icing*: Mix together 2 tablespoons icing sugar, 1 small teaspoon boiling water or fruit juice. 1 teaspoon cocoa, spread over cake, and decorate with chopped nuts.

COFFEE SANDWICH

1 Cup Self-raising Flour
4 eggs
125 gr (¼ lb.) walnuts
1 cup sugar
2 tablespoons butter
1 tablespoon coffee essence

Beat butter and sugar to a cream, add eggs, one at a time, and beat until it looks light. Sift in flour, walnuts, and coffee essence. Beat thoroughly, put into sandwich tins, and bake for 15 minutes. Make a filling of 1 level tablespoon cornflour, 1 tablespoon sugar, 1 tablespoon butter, ½ cup milk, and the yolk of 1 egg. Stir on fire till thick, beat till smooth, add beaten white of egg, 1 tablespoon walnuts and 1 teaspoon coffee essence.

COFFEE SPICE CAKE

2 Cups Self-raising Flour
½ teaspoon ground cloves
1½ teaspoons ground cinnamon
1 cup brown sugar
2 eggs
1 teaspoon ground ginger
½ teaspoon allspice
1 teaspoon salt
125 gr (¼ lb.) butter
2-3rds cup cold strong coffee

Cream butter and sugar together, add eggs one at a time, and beat well. Add flour, well sifted with the spice and cold coffee. Turn into two sandwich tins and bake in a moderate oven for 20 to 25 minutes. Fill and ice with a coffee flavoured icing, and decorate the top with chopped walnuts.

COCONUT ROLL

4 Eggs
1 cup self-raising flour
¾ cup sugar
jam
coconut

Beat eggs and sugar for 5 minutes, add flour, and mix well. Spread on paper on oven shelf, and bake for 10 minutes in a moderate oven. Spread with jam, roll up, smear outside with jam, and roll in coconut.

COFFEE SPONGE

4 Eggs
1 cup flour
½ teaspoon carbonate soda
¾ cup sugar
1 tablespoon coffee essence
1 teaspoon cream of tartar
½ teaspoon vanilla essence

Beat eggs and sugar for 20 minutes, add coffee essence, and mix in flour, with soda and cream of tartar. Flavour, and bake for 20 to 30 minutes. *Coffee Filling*: Beat together a piece of butter about the size of a small egg, 1 tablespoon coffee essence, ½ teaspoon vanilla essence, and enough icing sugar to make a stiff paste. Spread on one half, and sprinkle thickly with coconut.

COLD WATER SPONGE

3 Eggs
3 tablespoons cold water
¾ cup sugar
1 cup self-raising flour

Beat eggs, sugar and water until thick. Fold flour in gently and bake in moderate oven 20-25 minutes.

DEVIL'S FOOD CAKE

½ Cup Butter
2 eggs
1 tablespoon pure dark cocoa
½ teaspoon carbonate soda
1 cup sugar
1½ cups milk
2 cups self-raising flour
1 teaspoon vanilla essence

Cream together the sugar and butter till light and fluffy, add the yolks of eggs well-beaten, and the cocoa dissolved in hot water. Mix well, and add flour with carbonate of soda, in small quantities alternately with the milk. Add vanilla, and then the whites of eggs, beaten to a stiff froth. Bake in two large sandwich dishes for 30 minutes. When cool, ice with chocolate icing and spread icing between the layers.

EGGLESS CHOCOLATE SANDWICH

1½ Cups Flour
1 teaspoon carbonate soda
1 tablespoon butter
2 dessertspoons cocoa
¼ teaspoon salt
¾ cup sugar
1 cup sour milk

Sift together three times the flour, cocoa, soda, and salt. Then mix together the melted butter, sugar, and milk. Add to dry ingredients, beat for 3 minutes, and bake in sandwich tins for 15 minutes in a medium oven.

EGGLESS SPONGE

1 Tablespoon Butter
½ teaspoon carb. soda
1 large tablespoon golden syrup
1 teaspoon ground ginger
½ cup sugar
½ cup milk
1 large cup self-raising flour
1 teaspoon cinnamon

Cream butter and sugar. Dissolve carb. soda in milk and add golden syrup. Beat well. Sift in flour, ginger and cinnamon. Bake 20 minutes in moderate oven.

FRENCH BROWN COFFEE CAKE

185 gr (6 oz.) Flour
½ teaspoon carbonate soda
2 eggs
125 gr (¼ lb.) butter
1 teaspoon cream tartar
a pinch of salt
125 gr (¼ lb.) sugar
1 tablespoon coffee essence
2 dessertspoons milk

Cream butter and sugar, add well-beaten eggs, sift dry ingredients together, mix in lightly, and then stir in coffee essence, blended with milk. Put in sandwich dishes and bake slowly for 15 minutes. *Icing*: Cream well together 1 heaped dessertspoon each of butter and coffee essence and 3 well heaped tablespoons icing sugar. Spread between layers and roughly on top when cold. Sprinkle freely with chopped nuts.

GENOESE SPONGE

6 Large Eggs
250 gr (8 oz.) castor sugar
185 gr (6 oz.) butter
155 gr (5 oz.) flour
30 gr (1 oz.) cornflour

Whisk the eggs and sugar for 30 minutes. Clarify the butter and add to the eggs with the sieved flour and cornflour. Pour into a lined greaseproof papered tin, and bake in a moderate oven till firm (about 20 minutes). This sponge is good for cutting into various shapes and iced for afternoon tea.

BANANA CAKE

125 gr (¼ lb.) Butter or substitute
¾ cup sugar
1½ cups self-raising flour
2 eggs
3 medium sized bananas
¼ cup milk
½ teaspoon bicarbonate of soda

Cream butter and sugar until fluffy. Add eggs one at a time, beating well after each addition.

Mash bananas (making 1 cup of mashed banana). Add to creamed mixture, beat until just combined. Fold in flour alternately with combined milk and soda.

Bake in 1 lamington or 2 sandwich tins in moderate oven for 25 to 30 minutes or until cooked when tested. When cold, ice or fill with cream.

GINGER SPONGE (No. 1)

3 eggs
½ cup arrowroot
1 teaspoon cocoa
1 teaspoon ginger
½ teaspoon carbonate soda
½ cup sugar
2 teaspoons flour
1 teaspoon cinnamon
1 teaspoon cream of tartar
1 dessertspoon golden syrup

Beat together the eggs and sugar for 15 minutes. Roll the arrowroot well, and add to it all the dry ingredients. Fold lightly into the beaten eggs and sugar, and lastly stir in the golden syrup, previously warmed. Pour into buttered sandwich tins, and bake in a moderately hot oven for 10 minutes.

GINGER SPONGE (No. 2)

½ Cup Sugar
½ cup milk
1 egg
1 teaspoon cinnamon
1 teaspoon baking powder
1½ cups flour
½ cup golden syrup
1 teaspoon ginger
1 teaspoon carbonate soda
½ cup butter

Beat butter and sugar to a cream, add egg, and beat well, then add syrup and milk, with the soda dissolved in it, then the flour with the baking powder and spice sifted through it. Mix well, pour into sandwich tins and bake in a slow oven.

LEMON FEATHER CAKE

1 Tablespoon Butter
½ cup milk
2 eggs
1 teaspoon cream of tartar
1 teacup sugar
1½ cups flour
½ teaspoon carbonate soda
grated rind of 1 lemon
1 teaspoon lemon essence

Beat sugar and butter to a cream, add eggs well-beaten, then milk and lemon rind. Sift in flour with cream of tartar and carbonate soda. Bake in sandwich tins. When cooked (about 30 minutes), split open and spread jam or lemon cheese between.

LEMON JELLY SPONGE

1 Cup Sugar
4 eggs
cup self-raising flour
3 tablespoons boiling water

Beat sugar and eggs together for 15 minutes, then add the boiling water, and sift in the flour. Have sandwich tins ready and put into the oven quickly. Bake 10 or 12 minutes. *Filling*: Mix together the grated rind and juice of 2 lemons, 1 tablespoon butter, 1 teaspoon cornflour, ½ cup sugar, and ½ cup cold water, and boil until thick.

MARSHMALLOW SQUARES

125 gr (4 oz.) Flour
1 small teaspoon baking powder
60 gr (2 oz.) butter
125 gr (4 oz.) castor sugar
2 eggs
1 dessertspoon milk
essence vanilla

Beat butter and sugar to a cream, add well-whisked eggs, and vanilla. Add flour gradually, mixing the baking powder in the last of the flour. When quite smooth, add the milk. Turn into a shallow baking tin which has been well greased and sprinkled with castor sugar. Bake in a moderate oven for 20 minutes. *Filling*: Chop 125 gr (4 oz.) marshmallows and put into a double saucepan with 1 tablespoon milk and 1 tablespoon boiling water. Stir until marshmallows are quite soft, add icing sugar and mix. Split cake through centre, spread on this filling and press together again. Ice top and cut in squares.

MOIST SPONGE SANDWICH

4 Large Eggs
1 level cup flour
1 level teaspoon cream of tartar
1 level cup sugar
½ teaspoon carbonate soda
4 tablespoons milk
3 teaspoons butter

Separate the whites from the yolks and beat to a stiff froth. Then add the yolks and beat for 5 minutes. Add the sugar and beat for 15 minutes. Sift in the flour with the baking soda and cream of tartar. Stir until evenly mixed. While beating have the milk and butter boiling on the stove. Add this to the mixture and cook in tin measuring 23 by 30 cm (9 by 12 in.). Place in an oven which has been very hot, but with a diminishing heat. Bake for 20 minutes.

ORANGE CAKE (No. 1)

2 Eggs
1 breakfast cup self-raising flour
4 tablespoons sugar
3 tablespoons butter
3 tablespoons milk
1 orange

Grate orange rind and take 1 large tablespoon grated rind and 1½ tablespoons orange juice. Beat sugar and butter to a cream, add eggs, and beat again. Then add the sifted flour and milk, and lastly the juice and grated rind. Bake in two sandwich tins. Ice with orange icing and fill with orange filling. See Icings and Fillings.

ORANGE CAKE (No. 2)

125 gr (¼ lb.) Butter
1 cup plain flour
3 eggs
1 teaspoon cream of tartar
¾ cup sugar
1 tablespoon cornflour
juice and rind of 1 orange
½ teaspoon carbonate soda

Beat butter and sugar to a cream, add juice and grated rind of orange, then eggs one at a time, and beat well. Sift in flour, cornflour, cream of tartar, and soda. Fold in lightly, pour mixture into greased sandwich tins, and bake for 15 minutes in a fairly hot oven. *Frosting*: Add 1 teaspoon gelatine to ½ cup orange juice, stand cup in hot water till gelatine dissolves, and leave till cold. Beat egg white till stiff, add the gelatine gradually, then add icing sugar, whisking all the time till thick. Spread between the cakes, and pile on top. A sprinkling of coconut on top is a nice finish.

RAINBOW CAKE (No. 1)

500 gr (1 lb.) Sugar
6 eggs
500 gr (1 lb.) flour
1 teaspoon carbonate soda
250 gr (½ lb.) butter
1 small breakfast cup milk
2 teaspoons cream tartar
4 teaspoons cocoa
essence lemon, vanilla and cochineal

Beat the butter and sugar to a cream, add the eggs one at a time, then flour with cream of tartar and soda sifted through. Mix well together and beat for a few minutes. Then divide the mixture into three equal parts. Flavour one with essence of lemon, and colour with cochineal. Flavour another with vanilla and colour with cocoa mixed with a little water. Bake in shallow tins in a moderate oven 20 to 30 minutes. When cooked and cool put together with any cake filling or icing and ice the top.

RAINBOW CAKE (No. 2)

1 Cup Butter
3 cups flour
1 teaspoon carbonate soda
cochineal
2 cups sugar
2 teaspoons cream of tartar
5 eggs
cocoa

Beat the butter to a cream, add the sugar and well-beaten eggs. Mix cream of tartar in the flour, dissolve soda in milk, and add the flour last. Divide in three. Leave one its own colour, colour one with cochineal, and one with cocoa. When cool, place on top of each other, and put butter icing between.

SPICED SPONGE

4 Eggs
1 cup plain flour
2 teaspoons cream of tartar
2 teaspoons cocoa
1 teaspoon mixed spice
4 tablespoons milk
¾ cup sugar
1 tablespoon cornflour
1 teaspoon carbonate soda
1 teaspoon cinnamon
a pinch of salt
a lump of butter (about 1 dessertspoon)

Beat together the eggs and sugar, then sift in the flour, and other dry ingredients. Put the milk in a saucepan with the butter, and bring to the boil. Add quickly to the mixture, and bake in a moderate oven for 20 minutes. *Filling*: Mix together 1 tablespoon butter and 1 teaspoon honey, then add enough icing sugar to spread easily. Whipped cream may be used instead of this filling.

SPONGE CAKE (No. 1)

4 Eggs
1 cup sugar
1 cup self-raising flour
lemon essence

Beat eggs and sugar until light, add flour and essence, and bake in hot oven for about 10 to 15 minutes.

SPONGE CAKE (No. 2)

3 Eggs
125 gr (4 oz.) flour
1 teaspoon cream of tartar
2 tablespoons boiling water
125 gr (4 oz.) sugar
½ teaspoon carbonate soda
1 tablespoon melted butter
jam or cream

Beat eggs till thick, add sugar, and beat till creamy. Sift in the flour with soda and cream of tartar. Add boiling water to the melted butter, and stir in lightly. Cook about 20 minutes

STRAWBERRY SHORTCAKE

2 Eggs
125 gr (4 oz.) butter
60 gr (2 oz.) maizena
½ teaspoon baking powder
125 gr (4 oz.) sugar
60 gr (2 oz.) flour
½ teacup milk
grated rind of 1 lemon
a few drops of vanilla

Cream the butter and sugar, break in the eggs, and beat for 5 minutes. Sift the flour, maizena and baking powder together, and mix in lightly. Add the milk, the lemon rind, and the vanilla. Pour the mixture into a well-greased tin and bake in a moderate oven for 40 minutes. Turn out and when cold cut through the middle and put a layer of whipped cream and strawberries on the top. Lemon cheese, maizena, or jelly may be used instead of strawberries.

SWISS ROLL

3 Eggs
¾ cup sugar
¾ cup self-raising flour
jam
icing sugar

Beat together the eggs and sugar until very light. Add the flour, folding in lightly. Pour on to a piece of paper on a cold oven slide, and bake for 9 minutes in a moderate oven. Put some icing sugar on a piece of paper the same size as sponge, turn the sponge when cooked on to it, and peel off paper on which roll was cooked. Spread with jam, and roll up quickly.

THREE MINUTE SPONGE

1 Large Cup Plain Flour
¾ cup sugar
3 tablespoons melted butter
1 teaspoon cream of tartar
a pinch salt
3 eggs
3 tablespoons milk
½ teaspoon carbonate soda

Put into a basin the flour and salt, and sugar, then break the eggs in, add the melted butter, and the milk, and mix well for 3 minutes. Add the cream of tartar and soda, and cook in sandwich tins or cake tin in moderate oven for 30 minutes.

WALNUT AND DATE CAKE

250 gr (½ lb.) Butter
3 eggs
1 cup walnuts
1 cup water
1 teacup sugar
500 gr (1 lb.) dates
250 gr (½ lb.) flour
1 small teaspoon carbonate soda

Soak the dates in the water, with soda added, for 1 hour. Beat the butter and sugar together, add the eggs, then the dates and walnuts, sift in the flour lightly, and pour into prepared cake tins. Bake for ¾ of an hour in a moderate oven.

WALNUT CAKE

250 gr (½ lb.) Flour
185 gr (6 oz.) sugar
125 gr (¼ lb.) currants
90 gr (3 oz.) walnuts
1 tablespoon baking powder
185 gr (6 oz.) butter
125 gr (¼ lb.) raisins
60 gr (2 oz.) candied peel
3 eggs
a little milk

Cream butter and sugar, add well-beaten eggs, then add dry ingredients, and a little milk. Beat well for 5 minutes. Put into two cake tins, place walnuts on top, and bake in a moderate oven for 1 hour.

WALNUT CREAM CAKE

125 gr (4 oz.) Butter
3 eggs
2½ cups flour
1½ cups sugar
½ to 1 cup milk
½ cup broken walnuts
2 teaspoons baking powder
a pinch of salt

Beat butter and sugar to a cream, then add eggs, well-beaten, the walnuts, and the flour with baking powder sifted through. Add milk enough to make a nice mixture, mix thoroughly, and pour into two large sandwich tins, and bake in a moderately heated oven for 20 to 30 minutes. Join sandwich when cold with cream, butter icing, or coffee icing.

AFTERNOON TEA CAKES, SCONES AND GIRDLE CAKES

If nuts are not available for making a nut loaf, use a similar quantity of desiccated coconut.

Coloured jubes cut into strips and small rounds make an uncommon decoration for iced cakes. Ice some small patty cakes with white or coloured icing, place small pieces yellow jube on the centre of icing, then place strips to form petals, and press gently into icing to make them adhere properly. Larger cakes offer scope for artistic designs which are easily and quickly executed. Cut jubes into strips before commencing to work. Use suitable colours. One may purchase endless varieties in the softer kind of jubes.

Scones will be tough if mixed with milk that has been scalded.

Half cup of cream instead of butter is an improvement in scones.

Cook your scones and pastry on the top shelf of oven. Cook sponges and large fruit cakes on the low shelf or on the bottom of oven. Cook gingerbread on the bottom of a cool oven.

To make perfect Scotch shortbread always use plain flour and castor sugar.

When making apple cake, napoleons, or biscuits, try this way of placing on to the slide. Roll the mixture on the rolling pin, place on the slide and roll back.

ALMOND PUFFS

90 gr (3 oz.) Ground Almonds
3 tablespoons flour
½ teaspoon baking powder
3 tablespoons sugar
90 gr (3 oz.) melted butter
½ cup of milk

Beat all together. Butter some patty pans and half fill them with mixture. Bake in moderate oven 20 minutes.

APRICOT CAKE

125 gr (¼ lb.) Butter
250 gr (½ lb.) self-raising flour
a little milk
125 gr (¼ lb.) sugar
3 eggs (2 will do)
a few dried apricots

Soak the apricots and cut into small pieces. Beat butter and sugar to a cream, add the eggs one at a time, then the flour to which the apricots have been added. Put into small tins or paper cases and bake for 10 minutes in a quick oven.

BISCUIT TARTS

3 Tablespoons Butter
3 teaspoons milk
2 cups self-raising flour
3 teaspoons sugar
1 egg
jam or lemon butter

Melt the butter and sugar, then beat in the egg and milk and add flour. Make into a dough and roll out very thinly. Cut in rounds and put in deep patty tins. Add a teaspoon of jam or lemon butter and bake in a fairly quick oven.

CHERRY NUT SQUARES

125 gr (4 oz.) Butter
2 eggs
60 gr (2 oz.) chopped walnuts
½ cup milk
185 gr (6 oz.) sugar
60 gr (2 oz.) chopped cherries
250 gr (8 oz.) self-raising flour
pinch salt
vanilla

Cream butter, sugar and vanilla. Add eggs one at a time. Fold in cherries and nuts, then flour alternately with milk. Fold into greased slab tin and bake in moderate oven for about 30 minutes.

When cool, top with warm icing and decorate with whole cherries and nuts. Cut into squares.

CHINESE CHOUX

1 Cup Self-raising Flour
125 gr (¼ lb.) butter
1 cup sugar
1 egg
1 small cup chopped dates, raisins, nuts, preserved ginger

Place flour, sugar, fruit and nuts in basin, and pour over melted butter. Add beaten egg and press into shallow dish. Bake in slow oven, and cut into squares while still warm, but leave in tin to cool. Ice with lemon icing.

CHOCOLATE BISCUIT

125 gr (¼ lb.) Butter
1 cup coconut
1 cup self-raising flour
½ cup brown sugar
pinch salt

Place dry ingredients in basin and mix with melted butter. Press into tin about 18 cm (7½ inches) square. Bake 20 minutes in moderate oven. Ice with chocolate icing 5 minutes after taking from oven. Cut up 5 minutes later.

CHOCOLATE CAKELETS

250 gr (½ lb.) Flour
125 gr (4 oz.) butter
1 egg
vanilla flavouring
185 gr (6 oz.) sugar
45 gr (1½ oz.) cocoa
1 good teaspoon baking powder
milk to mix

Sieve the flour, cocoa and baking powder. Beat the sugar and butter to a cream, add the egg, and beat well for a few minutes. Stir in the dry ingredients with some milk, as required, and mix all together with a few drops of vanilla. The mixture should be fairly stiff. Put into small greased cake tins and bake in a hot oven for 20 minutes.

CHOCOLATE CRUNCH

1 Cup Self-raising Flour
3 cups weeties or other breakfast cereal
1 cup sugar
125 gr (4 oz.) butter
1 tablespoon cocoa
1 egg
pinch salt
vanilla

Mix all dry ingredients in basin. Add melted butter and beaten egg. Press into swiss roll tin. Bake in moderate oven 30 minutes. Ice while hot with chocolate icing. Cut into fingers when cold.

CHOCOLATE FINGERS

1 Egg
125 gr (¼ lb.) castor sugar
125 gr (¼ lb.) flour
½ cup milk
60 gr (2 oz.) powdered chocolate
vanilla essence

Beat the egg with the milk and flavour with vanilla. Then sift in the dry ingredients. Bake in a shallow tin for ½ an hour. When cold ice with the following icing:—30 gr (1 oz.) icing sugar and 30 gr (1 oz.) powdered chocolate worked to a proper consistency with water and vanilla essence. Spread the mixture on the cake with a wet knife, sprinkle coconut on top and cut into dainty fingers.

CHOCOLATE HONEY KISSES

90 gr (3 oz.) Sugar
90 gr (3 oz.) butter
1 cup milk
1½ teaspoons baking powder
2 tablespoons cocoa
1 dessertspoon honey
2 eggs
1½ cups flour
pinch carbonate soda
1 teaspoon vanilla essence

Beat the butter to a cream. Add the sugar and beat until very light. Add the eggs, well beaten, and blend thoroughly. Sift the dry ingredients and add with milk, honey and vanilla, to the cake batter. Mix until very smooth. Bake in hot gem irons; using a moderate oven. When cool, cover with honey icing.

Honey Icing

2 Cups Sifted Icing Sugar
1 tablespoon cocoa
vanilla flavouring
1 dessertspoon honey
1 tablespoon butter
hot water

Rub the butter into the sugar. Add essence, honey and cocoa. Use sufficient hot water to make a smooth icing. Put a coating of icing all over the cakes and roll them in crushed nuts, or nuts and coconut, or all coconut.

CONTINENTAL SQUARES

125 gr (4 oz.) Butter or Margarine
125 gr (4 oz.) self-raising flour
1 teaspoon cocoa
60 gr (2 oz.) sugar
60 gr (2 oz.) coconut
blackcurrant or apricot jam

Beat butter and sugar together until light and fluffy. With your hands knead in flour, cocoa and coconut sifted together. Press mixture into a greased swiss roll tin, making it about 6 mm (¼ in.) thick. Bake in moderately hot oven about 25 minutes. Leave in tin to cool and while still hot spread thinly with jam.

Icing

2 Teaspoons Cocoa
4 tablespoons sifted icing sugar
1 teaspoon butter
1 or 2 tablespoons milk

Blend cocoa, butter, icing sugar, and warmed milk. Beat until smooth. Spread over top of jam, smoothing with back of spoon. Cut into squares and let them get cold.

CINNAMON AND DATE CAKES

75 gr (2½ oz.) Butter
1 egg
1 cup self-raising flour
1 small cup sugar
1 teaspoon cinnamon
¾ cup chopped dates

Beat sugar and butter to a cream, add egg, then dates and cinnamon, and lastly flour. The mixture should be fairly stiff. Place small pieces on a cold oven shelf and bake about 7 minutes.

COCONUT DAINTIES

125 gr (4 oz.) Butter
250 gr (8 oz.) flour
1 teaspoon baking powder
125 gr (4 oz.) sugar
1 egg
strawberry or raspberry jam filling

Cream butter and sugar, add beaten egg, and stir in sifted flour and baking powder. Turn on to a floured board, roll out thinly, cut into rounds with a fancy cutter, and line greased patty pans with these rounds. Place a little jam in each and fill with the following mixture. Mix together 2 cups coconut and 1 cup sugar. Add a well-beaten egg and a few drops of almond essence. Bake in a very moderate oven about 15 minutes.

COCONUT TARTS

3 Tablespoons Sugar
2 eggs
raspberry jam
3 tablespoons coconut
60 gr (2 oz.) butter
rough puff pastry

Line patty ,tins with rough puff pastry. Put into each a scant $\frac{1}{4}$ teaspoonful of raspberry jam. Fill with a mixture made by mixing together the sugar, coconut, butter and eggs. Bake in a quick oven.

CREAM PUFFS

125 gr (4 oz.) Plain Flour
60 gr (2 oz.) butter
250 ml ($\frac{1}{2}$ pint) unscalded cream
3 or 4 large eggs
250 ml ($\frac{1}{2}$ pint) water
1 tablespoon icing sugar
$\frac{1}{2}$ teaspoon vanilla

Put water and butter into a saucepan and bring to the boil. Add flour and beat till smooth over the fire until the mixture leaves the side of the pan. Beat eggs well, and when the mixture is cool, add them gradually. Mix well and put in small heaps on a greased slide. Bake in a moderate oven for $\frac{1}{2}$ an hour. When cold make an opening in the side and remove the centre. Whip cream and add sugar and vanilla to taste. Fill puffs with cream and sprinkle with sugar. A little raspberry jam may be put in before the cream.

C.W.A. FLUFFS

125 gr ($\frac{1}{4}$ lb.) Butter
1 teaspoon vanilla
60 gr (2 oz.) ground rice
60 gr (2 oz.) castor sugar
1 egg
90 gr (3 oz.) self-raising flour
raspberry jam

C.W.A. FLUFFS—*continued*

Beat butter and sugar to a cream. Add the unbeaten egg and beat well together. Then add ground rice, flour, and vanilla. This mixture is rather stiff, and should be so. After having put into patty pans, make a hole in the middle of each little cake and drop in a little raspberry jam (about enough to go on a saltspoon)—too much spoils them. Bake in a quick oven for 10 minutes.

DATE MELTAWAY

2 Tablespoons Butter	**2 tablespoons sugar**
1½ cups self-raising flour	**2 tablespoons milk**
1 egg	**date mixture**

Meltaway Pastry

Melt the butter and sugar, add the milk and well-beaten egg, mix well, and add the flour. Roll out, and line a baking dish with the paste, keeping back half for a covering.

Date Mixture

1 cup of stoned dates, ½ a cup of sugar, 1 cup of water. Boil together until thick. Allow to cool, then spread over the Meltaway pastry in baking dish, and cover with another layer of the pastry. Brush over with a little milk, and bake a golden brown. Stewed apples may be used in place of the date mixture if preferred.

DATE MUFFINS

3 Cups Self-raising Flour	**2 tablespoons sugar**
3 tablespoons butter	**½ cup chopped nuts**
1 egg	**a pinch of salt**
1 cup dates	

Cream butter and sugar, add beaten egg, then chopped dates, flour, and salt. Add enough milk to mix and put into patty pans. Sprinkle with chopped nuts and bake in a hot oven for 15 minutes. Split and butter. Serve hot or cold.

DATE SQUARES

125 gr (4 oz.) Butter or Margarine	**1 cup flour**
2 tablespoons golden syrup	**½ cup chopped dates**
¼ teaspoon baking powder	**1 egg**
¼ cup walnut pieces	**few drops of vanilla**
¼ cup sugar	**pinch of salt**

DATE SQUARES—*continued*

Cream the shortening and sugar well, and add the golden syrup and unbeaten egg. Mix well, sift in flour, baking powder, and salt. Blend, then add chopped dates, walnut pieces and vanilla essence. Spread in a lightly greased swiss roll tin and bake in a slow oven for 30 minutes. Nice either uniced or spread with lemon icing. Cut into squares while still hot and leave to cool.

DOUGHNUTS

2 Eggs
1 cup sugar
flour
¼ teaspoon salt
½ cup milk
15 gr (½ oz.) butter
a little nutmeg
½ teaspoon carbonate soda

Mix all together, adding enough flour to make a pliable paste. Roll out thin. Cut in rings, using a thimble to cut middle for rings. Fry in sufficient boiling fat to allow the doughnuts to float. Brown lightly. These are best eaten hot.

DUTCH CAKE

250 gr (½ lb.) Butter
185 gr (6 oz.) sugar
30 gr (1 oz.) almonds
310 gr (10 oz.) flour
½ teaspoon cinnamon
1 yolk of egg
a pinch of salt

Beat butter and sugar to a cream, add egg yolk, then flour, in which salt and cinnamon have been mixed. Shape into a large meat tin or 2 sandwich tins. Place halves of almonds all over and brush with white of egg. Bake about half an hour in a moderate oven. Cut into pieces while hot, but leave in tin till cold.

EASTER CAKES (No. 1)

The usual Easter Cake is a short cake made very thin and cut into rounds with crimped edges. The top is sometimes decorated with pieces of peel cut into strips. They should be baked so that they are nicely brown round the edges. The following is a good recipe for same.

250 gr (8 oz.) Flour
125 gr (4 oz.) sugar
a little nutmeg or spice
155 gr (5 oz.) butter
30 gr (1 oz.) currants
1 egg

Make in the usual way as for biscuits, roll out very thin, cut into rounds about 10 cm (4 in.) across, and decorate with cut peel. Bake in a moderate oven.

EASTER CAKES (No. 2)

½ Cup Flour
90 gr (3 oz.) butter
2 eggs
90 gr (3 oz.) sugar
1 small teaspoon baking powder

Beat butter to a cream and beat in 1 egg, then add half the sugar and the other egg, then remainder of sugar, then flour and baking powder mixed (if too thick add a little milk). It should be like thick cream. Half fill greased patty pans with mixture and bake in quick oven for 10 minutes. Ice when cold.

ECLAIRS

30 gr (1 oz.) Butter
60 gr (2 oz.) flour
45 gr (1½ oz.) grated chocolate
125 ml (1 gill) milk
125 gr (¼ lb.) castor sugar
3 eggs
a pinch of salt

Boil butter in milk, stir into it the flour, take off the fire and work with a spoon for ¼ an hour. Then add yolks only of the eggs, one by one, beating each in well. Grease tin baking sheet, divide mixture into 12 pieces, and roll into shapes of fingers. Bake in a quick oven for 15 minutes. While baking make a chocolate icing as follows: Dissolve the chocolate in a very little water over the fire. Stir it with the sugar in a basin. Beat white of 1 egg, and mix with chocolate and sugar. When cool work with a spoon till quite smooth, then spread over eclairs with a brush. Return to cool oven to dry. Cut open and fill with whipped cream flavoured with vanilla.

FAIRY BUTTER CAKE

1 Cup Flour
¾ cup sugar
1 teaspoon cream of tartar
125 gr (¼ lb.) butter
3 eggs
½ teaspoon carbonate soda
vanilla essence

Cream the butter and sugar and add the well-beaten egg, flour, cream of tartar, and soda. Bake in patty tins, in a hot oven for 10 minutes. When cold, ice with Fairy Butter. *Fairy Butter*: Mix together 125 gr (¼ lb.) butter, ½ cup icing sugar, a few drops of vanilla essence, and colour half with grated chocolate. Spread icing over each cake, and press white Fairy Butter in fancy pattern on them, through an icing tube.

FAIRY CAKES

60 gr (2 oz.) Butter
60 gr (2 oz.) flour
60 gr (2 oz.) glace cherries
1 teaspoon baking powder
60 gr (2 oz.) sugar
60 gr (2 oz.) cornflour, ground rice or ground almonds
1 egg
a little milk

Cream the butter and sugar and add the well-beaten egg, then the flour and cornflour with the baking powder. Mix into a stiff dough with a little milk. Place in paper cases or patty pans and put a glace cherry on each. The cherries may be cut in halves and mixed in the dough.

FOUNDATION CAKE MIXTURE

1 Cup Sugar
3 cups self-raising flour
3 eggs
1 cup milk
¾ cup butter
flavouring

Mix in the usual manner and bake in a flat tin for a block cake or in patty cases for small cakes. This mixture can be used for many kinds of cakes by dividing up and adding dates, sultanas and peel etc.; also those made from the plain mixture may be iced with pink, white, chocolate or coffee icing.

FRUIT SLICE

185 gr (6 oz.) Rough Puff Pastry
1 finely chopped apple
1 tablespoon sugar
¾ cup sultanas and currants, mixed
1 teaspoon mixed spice
1 dessertspoon mixed peel
rind and juice ½ lemon

Make pastry and roll thinly in a long slice, then cut in two and put one piece on a baking tin. Mix together all other ingredients, and spread on the pastry. Cover with the second piece of pastry, and prick over the top with a fork. Mark into squares with the back edge of a knife, cook in a hot oven for about 15 minutes, and glaze with sugar glazing. Trim edges, cut in squares, and serve hot or cold.

JUBILEE CAKE (No. 1)

1½ Cups Self-raising Flour
2 tablespoons castor sugar
½ cup sultanas
1 egg
1 dessertspoon butter
½ cup currants
lemon peel
½ cup milk

Mix all dry ingredients, rub in butter, add well-beaten egg and milk and make into shape. Bake 30 minutes in hot oven. While still hot ice with icing sugar mixed with milk and sprinkle with coconut.

JUBILEE CAKE (No. 2)

1 Cup Sugar
1 small cup sultanas
1 small teaspoon butter
1 teaspoon cream of tartar
2 cups flour
1 cup milk
½ teaspoon carbonate soda
1 egg
a pinch salt

Rub butter into flour, add salt, sugar and sultanas. Beat the egg and milk and stir into the flour. Bake about ½ an hour in a slow oven. Pour over a water icing while cake is still hot.

JUBILEE ROLL

1½ Cups Self-raising Flour
2 tablespoons sugar
½ cup sultanas and finely chopped peel
1 tablespoon butter
½ cup milk
1 egg

Sift flour, rub in butter, add the sugar, sultanas, and peel. Beat egg into milk and mix. Knead into an oval shaped loaf and bake in a nice hot oven for 25 to 30 minutes. When cool, ice and sprinkle with coconut. When ready for use, cut in slices and spread with butter. Make an icing by mixing 2 tablespoons of icing sugar with milk, and pour over hot.

JUBILEE TWIST

1½ Cups Self-raising Flour
1 or 2 tablespoons sugar
½ cup currants
1 tablespoon butter
1 egg
½ cup milk
a little lemon peel

Rub the butter into the flour, add all dry ingredients, then the egg and milk. Roll out into two long rounds and twist one around the other. Bake 20 minutes. Boil 1 tablespoon sugar and 1 tablespoon water for 3 minutes and put on twist while hot. Sprinkle with coconut.

KISSES (No. 1)

125 gr (4 oz.) Butter
125 gr (4 oz.) self-raising flour
90 gr (3 oz.) sugar
icing sugar
125 gr (4 oz.) cornflour
2 eggs
raspberry jam
essence

Cream butter and sugar together and add well-beaten eggs. Mix flour and cornflour, and add slowly. Flavour, and drop in teaspoonsful on oven slide. Bake in moderate oven for 10 minutes. When cooked and cool, place 2 together with jam and sprinkle with icing sugar.

KISSES (No. 2)

125 gr ($\frac{1}{4}$ lb.) Butter
1 small cup self-raising flour
1 tablespoon icing sugar
1 tablespoon arrowroot

Cream butter and sugar, and add arrowroot and flour. Grease an oven slide and put in quarter teaspoonsful on to slide and press with a fork. Cook in a moderate oven until a pale brown. Join together with jam when cold.

LAMINGTONS

250 gr ($\frac{1}{2}$ lb.) Butter
1 cup milk
4 eggs
2 teaspoons cream of tartar
$1\frac{1}{2}$ cups sugar
3 cups flour
1 teaspoon carbonate soda
vanilla essence

Beat butter and sugar to a cream, add eggs, well-beaten, then milk, with soda, and flour, with cream of tartar. Bake in a small meat dish for about $\frac{1}{2}$ an hour, cut in squares, ice, and roll in coconut.

LEMON CHEESE TARTLETS (No. 1)

$1\frac{1}{2}$ Cups Self-raising Flour
125 gr ($\frac{1}{4}$ lb.) butter
$\frac{3}{4}$ cup sugar
1 egg
a little milk

Rub butter lightly into the flour, add sugar, then the eggs and sufficient milk to roll out, not too soft. Form into a ball handling lightly. Roll out fairly thin and cut into rounds, or oblong shapes. Place in patty pans, or paper cases. Put small $\frac{1}{2}$ teaspoons of lemon cheese in the centre, then cut small rounds of the pastry so as to just cover the lemon cheese. When set a delicate brown, place evenly and quickly over the tartlets some soft white icing. Return to the oven, and watch carefully until a light brown.

LEMON CHEESE TARTLETS (No. 2)

Pastry

155 gr (5 oz.) Self-raising Flour
60 gr (2 oz.) butter
60 gr (2 oz.) sugar
1 egg
a pinch of salt

Filling

250 gr ($\frac{1}{2}$ lb.) Sugar
juice of 1 or 2 lemons
60 gr (2 oz.) butter
3 eggs
rind of $\frac{1}{2}$ a lemon

LEMON CHEESE TARTLETS (No. 2)—*continued*

Beat butter and sugar to a cream, add egg, and beat in, finally add the sifted flour. This is difficult to roll out at times, and needs plenty of flour during the rolling process. This amount makes from 2 to 2½ dozen tarts. To make the filling, put the sugar, butter, and beaten-up eggs into a double saucepan, or an enamel mug or basin inside an ordinary saucepan. Add lemon rind, stir well, and then add lemon juice. Keep stirring until the mixture is the consistency of honey. Use when cold.

MACAROON TARTLETS (No. 1)

Pastry

185 gr (6 oz.) Flour
45 gr (1½ oz.) lard
water

Sponge

60 gr (2 oz.) Cornflour
30 gr (1 oz.) butter
1 egg
125 gr (4 oz.) sugar
90 gr (3 oz.) coconut
almond essence

Make the pastry, cut into rounds, and line patty pans with it. Place in each a little jam, raspberry or plum, and fill with the sponge mixture. Roll out a piece of pastry and place on top. Bake from 10 to 15 minutes in good oven.

MACAROOON TARTLETS (No. 2)

185 gr (6 oz.) Self-raising Flour
125 gr (4 oz.) butter
185 gr (6 oz.) coconut
250 gr (8 oz.) sugar
2 eggs
glace cherries

Sift flour into basin, add 125 gr (4 oz.) sugar, rub in butter and mix to a dry dough with egg yolks. Roll out on floured board, cut into rounds and press into greased patty tins. Whip egg whites stiffly, add 125 gr (4 oz.) sugar gradually, fold in coconut. Put teaspoonsful into patty cases, top with half-cherry and bake in slow oven 15 minutes.

MELTING MOMENTS (No. 1)

185 gr (6 oz.) Butter
250 gr (½ lb.) cornflour
90 gr (3 oz.) sugar
1 teaspoon baking powder
2 eggs

Cream butter and sugar, add eggs, well-beaten, then cornflour and baking powder. Beat all well together, drop about 1 teaspoonful into each patty pan and bake in a moderate oven about 20 minutes.

MELTING MOMENTS (No. 2)

125 gr (4 oz.) Butter
30 gr (1 oz.) icing sugar
90 gr (3 oz.) plain flour
30 gr (1 oz.) cornflour
a pinch of salt

Cream butter and sugar, sift flour, cornflour, and salt, and add. Drop in spoonsful on buttered tray and bake in a moderate oven till a pale brown.

NAPOLEON, No. 1 (QUICKLY MADE)

500 gr (1 lb.) Puff Paste
¾ cup sugar
2 tablespoons butter
1 cup self-raising flour
1 egg

Cream butter and sugar, add well-beaten egg, and then flour. Then take over to stove and quickly add and mix enough boiling water to make a fairly thick consistency. Have paste rolled out thinly and cut exactly in half, spreading each piece with raspberry jam. Spread mixture on to one piece of paste and put other piece on top, the jam sides to the sponge mixture. Bake in a fairly hot oven. Ice with pink icing and sprinkle with coconut.

NAPOLEON, No. 2 (ORANGE)

Sponge

6 Eggs
½ teaspoon cream of tartar
½ cup sugar
1 small cup flour
lemon flavouring
¼ teaspoon carbonate soda

Puff Pastry

125 gr (¼ lb.) Butter
lemon juice
125 gr (¼ lb.) flour
water to make a soft dough

Orange Filling

2 Tablespoons Cornflour
1 tablespoon butter
juice 1 orange
2 egg yolks
1 cup boiling water
juice ½ a lemon

Put into a saucepan the boiling water, butter, orange juice, and lemon juice, and allow to come to the boil. Have ready the cornflour, dissolved in a little cold water, and stir it into the boiling mixture. Then add the lightly beaten eggs, and simmer for a few minutes till thick. Set aside to get cold. Make a sponge with the ingredients given, and bake in a square or oblong tin. When cold split in two. Spread one piece of sponge with orange filling, and cover with baked puff paste, which has been made from the above ingredients, then spread pastry with remainder of orange filling, and place second piece of sponge on top. Ice top with orange icing made as follows: Mix together 1 tablespoon butter, 1 small cup icing sugar, and juice of 1 orange. Sprinkle chopped almonds on the icing.

NUT AND DATE CAKE

½ Cup Sugar
2 cups self-raising flour
1 cup walnuts
½ teaspoon carbonate soda
250 gr (½ lb.) butter
500 gr (1 lb.) dates
2 tablespoons boiling water
1½ teaspoons cinnamon
2 eggs

Cream butter and sugar, add eggs, beat well, add chopped fruits, etc., and lastly add soda dissolved in water. Bake in a moderate oven for 10 to 15 minutes. This recipe fills about 50 small paper patties.

ORANGE CAKES

1 Large Cup Self-raising Flour
1 tablespoon butter
rind of 1 orange
½ cup sugar
2 eggs
juice of ½ an orange
a pinch of salt

Mix butter and sugar together with salt, add eggs, rind, and juice, then add flour. Cook in cake containers for 10 minutes.

PATTY CAKES

2 Cups Self-raising Flour
½ cup milk
3 eggs
¾ cup sugar
125 gr (¼ lb.) butter
essence to taste

Mix butter and sugar, add eggs, milk, and flour, and then essence. Put in paper containers and bake in a moderate oven for 15 minutes.

QUEEN CAKES (No. 1)

250 gr (½ lb.) Flour
185 gr (6 oz.) butter
½ teaspoon baking powder
4 eggs
250 gr (½ lb.) sugar
250 gr (½ lb.) currants
1 teaspoon brandy
a little salt

Beat the butter and sugar to a light cream. Add the yolks of the eggs, sift in the flour, baking powder and salt. Add whites of eggs beaten till stiff, then currants, and lastly brandy. Put into patty pans. Bake 15 to 20 minutes in a fairly quick oven.

QUEEN CAKES (No. 2)

125 gr (¼ lb.) Butter
1 good cup flour
1 teaspoon cream of tartar
¾ cup sugar
3 Eggs
1 tablespoon milk
½ teaspoon carbonate soda

Beat butter and sugar to a cream, add eggs, then flour and cream of tartar, and lastly the soda mixed with the milk. Bake in patty pans.

RASPBERRY SHORTBREAD

125 gr (¼ lb.) Butter
1½ cups self-raising flour
1 cup coconut
1 small cup sugar
1 egg
raspberry jam

Beat butter and sugar to a cream, add egg well-beaten and then the flour. Mix and roll out. Spread lightly with raspberry jam. Beat together 1 egg, a small ½ cup sugar, and 1 large cup of coconut. Spread on top of jam. Bake 30 minutes in a moderate oven and cut into squares.

RICE BUBBLE SQUARES

90 gr (3 oz.) Butter
1 tablespoon creamed honey
125 gr (4 oz.) sugar
4 cups rice bubbles (or cornflakes)

Boil butter, sugar and honey for 6 minutes. Pour over rice bubbles. Press into flat tin and when cool cut into squares. They can also be baked in patty pans.

ROCK BUNS

2½ Cups Self-raising Flour
155 gr (5 oz.) butter
2 eggs
¾ cup sugar
1 small cup sultanas
salt
milk

Mix all together with enough milk to make the mixture the consistency of scones. Drop in spoonsful on a buttered sheet, and bake in a fairly quick oven for 5 to 7 minutes.

SHORTBREAD MERINGUE CAKE

310 gr (10 oz.) Flour
155 gr (5 oz.) butter
125 gr (4 oz.) coconut
185 gr (6 oz.) icing sugar
60 gr (2 oz.) sugar
2 eggs
1 flat teaspoon baking powder

Cream the butter and sugar, beat in the egg yolks, add flour and baking powder sifted together, make into a stiff dough, and press into buttered shallow tin. Spread with jam, beat up whites of eggs, add icing sugar and coconut, and spread on top of the jam. Bake for ½ an hour in a moderate oven.

SNOWBALLS

½ Cup Butter
2 cups self-raising flour
1 cup sugar
2 eggs
¾ cup milk

Cream butter and sugar, beat in eggs, milk, and other ingredients. Bake in gem scone irons, putting a little mixture in each. When cold cover with plain lemon icing, and roll in coconut. Make the icing in a basin, and dip the cakes in it, using 2 forks to handle cakes when dipping in icing. If wished, variety can be had by colouring some of the icing with cocoa and proceeding as for lamingtons.

SPICED GINGER CAKES

1 Heaped Cup of Flour
½ cup castor sugar
1 egg
½ teaspoon ground ginger
½ teaspoon nutmeg
½ teaspoon cinnamon
1-3rd cup treacle
1-3rd cup butter
pinch of salt
½ teaspoon ground cloves
1 teaspoon baking soda
½ cup of hot water

Sift together the flour, spices, salt, and soda. Beat butter to a cream. Stir in the castor sugar, and the beaten eggs then the treacle (warmed), then the spiced flour, and lastly stir in the hot water slowly. Fill well-greased gem tins half full. Bake in a moderate oven about 15 minutes. If a measuring cup is used, allow 1 cup and 3 tablespoons of flour.

SPONGE LILIES

3 Tablespoons Sugar
4 eggs
2 heaped tablespoons self-raising flour
flavouring

Beat eggs and sugar, then add flour, and flavouring. Place two tablespoons of mixture at intervals on tray covered with grease-proof paper, leaving space for it to spread. Cook in a hot oven, and when cooked, roll over in shape of a lily, and leave until cold. Fill with jelly and whipped cream.

SWISS TEA CAKE

½ Cup Sugar
1½ cups self-raising flour
125 gr (¼ lb.) butter
1 egg

Cream butter and sugar and add the egg, well-beaten, then the flour. Grease oven slide well, roll out paste, and spread with raspberry jam. Make a topping for this cake by mixing together a small ½ cup of flour, ½ cup of sugar, ½ cup of butter, and ¾ cup of coconut. Crumble all together and sprinkle on cake. Bake in a moderate oven, and when cooked cut into fingers.

TEA CAKES (RICH)

125 gr (4 oz.) Butter
60 gr (2 oz.) cornflour
185 gr (6 oz.) sugar
a pinch salt
185 gr (6 oz.) self-raising flour
125 gr (4 oz.) sultanas
3 eggs
milk

Beat butter and sugar together, then add well-beaten eggs, a little milk, flour, cornflour, and salt sifted together. Bake in paper cases in a fairly hot oven for 10 minutes.

TONGOES

½ Cup Sugar
250 gr (½ lb.) butter
½ cup plain flour
1 teaspoon carbonate soda
1½ cups self-raising flour
250 gr (½ lb.) finely cut dates
¾ cup chopped walnuts
1 egg
milk

Mix butter and sugar to a cream, add egg, then flour, dates, and nuts. Dissolve the soda in a little milk and add. Put a teaspoonful on a greased slide and bake in a moderate oven for 15 to 20 minutes.

VANILLA SLICES

30 gr (1 oz.) Castor Sugar
250 ml (½ pint) milk
1 teaspoon butter
puff pastry
25 gr (¾ oz.) flour
1 egg or 2 yolks
½ teaspoon vanilla essence
water icing
chopped nuts

Roll the prepared pastry to 3 mm (⅛ in.) in thickness. Cut into oblongs 44 mm x 10 cm (1¾ x 4 in.). Bake on a baking sheet in a quick oven till pastry is fully risen. Reduce the heat and finish baking. Cool on a cake rack. Melt the butter in a saucepan, stir in sugar and flour, and take pan to side of fire. Stir in the milk, a teaspoon at a time and beat the mixture till smooth. Return to the fire and cook, stirring constantly for 3 or 4 minutes, then draw again to side of fire, and stir in the well-beaten egg and vanilla. Stand over a pan of boiling water, and cook for a few minutes, then leave till cool. Put between the pastry, spread the tops with water icing (some may have coloured icing), and sprinkle with chopped nuts.

VIENNESE TARTLETS

2 Egg Whites
125 gr (4 oz.) currants
60 gr (2 oz.) icing sugar
vanilla

Make some short crust paste for small patty pans. Beat up whites to a stiff froth and add icing sugar and vanilla. Stir in carefully the currants which have previously been cooked in a little sherry or fruit juice. Fill patty pans with the mixture and bake in a moderate oven for about 20 minutes. Sprinkle with sifted sugar.

WEET-BIX MARSHMALLOW SLICE

4 Weet-Bix
1 cup coconut
125 gr (¼ lb.) butter
¾ cup brown sugar
¾ cup self-raising flour

Crush Weet-Bix and add sugar, coconut, self-raising flour and melted butter. Mix and press into dish and cook in moderate oven till set. When cold pour over marshmallow.

Marshmallow

2 Small Cups Sugar
1 cup hot water
2 dessertspoons gelatine

Boil for 8 minutes and beat until thick.

SCONES AND LOAVES

COFFEE ROLLS

2 Large Breakfast Cups of Sifted Flour
1 heaped teaspoon cream of tartar
1 heaped tablespoon of butter
2 dessertspoons of sugar
½ teaspoon salt
½ teaspoon carbonate soda
2 eggs
½ cup milk

Cream butter and sugar together, add well-beaten egg, then milk and lastly flour and dry ingredients well sifted together. Mix well, turn on to a board and knead or roll into a ball. Roll out about 13 mm (½ in.) thick, and cut into rounds, fold over half as you place them on the greased oven tray, and bake in quick oven 10 to 12 minutes.

SCONES

500 gr (1 lb.) S.R. flour (use half wholemeal S.R. flour if preferred)
1 tablespoon full-cream powdered milk
375 ml (12 oz.) water
1 level teaspoon salt
60 gr (2 oz.) soft margarine

Sift dry ingredients, rub in margarine. Stir in water and turn out onto a lightly floured board. Knead lightly until smooth. Roll from the centre outwards, cut in rounds. Cook in a very hot oven (250°C) for 12 to 15 minutes.

CHEESE SCONES

500 gr (1 lb.) Flour
125 gr (¼ lb.) cheese
1 level teaspoon carbonate soda
a pinch cayenne pepper
125 gr (¼ lb.) butter
2 eggs
1 level teaspoon cream tartar
a pinch salt
a little milk

Sift flour with soda and cream of tartar. Rub in the butter, grate in the cheese, and add cayenne and salt. Beat the eggs, add to dry ingredients and mix with sufficient milk to form a stiff paste. Turn on to a floured board, roll out, and cut into small round scones. Bake in a quick oven for 15 to 20 minutes.

CREAM SCONES

500 gr (1 lb.) Flour
½ cup milk
1 teaspoon carbonate soda
60 gr (2 oz.) butter
1 egg
2 teaspoons cream tartar
1½ tablespoons sugar

Cream butter and sugar, add egg, beat well together, and add flour and rising. Mix with milk to a soft dough. Bake as you would other scones.

GEM SCONES

1 Tablespoon Sugar
1 well-beaten egg
1½ cups flour
1 tablespoon butter
1 small cup milk
1 teaspoon carbonate soda
2 teaspoons cream tartar

Cream butter and sugar together, add egg, and milk with soda dissolved in it. Sift flour with cream of tartar, and add to mixture. Have gem irons so hot that the butter frizzles violently in them. Partly fill with the mixture and brown in the oven. Gem irons are like deep patty pans made of iron, and are bought in trays of half dozen, or dozen.

HOVIS SCONES

2 Cups Self-raising Flour
tablespoon butter
1 egg
1 tablespoon sugar
little salt
milk

Mix sugar and salt in the flour, rub in butter, then add well-beaten egg, and milk enough to make a soft dough that will nearly drop from the spoon. Dust the hands with flour, and drop one dessertspoonful of dough from one hand to the other and then drop lightly on to a floured oven shelf. Bake in a fairly hot oven, for 10 minutes. A very light scone. Sufficient to make 1½ dozen.

PUMPKIN SCONES

2 Cups Self-raising Flour
1 tablespoon butter
1 cup of cold mashed pumpkin
½ cup sugar
1 egg
1 tablespoon hot water
a pinch of salt

Cream the butter and sugar with hot water. Add the egg and beat well. Add the pumpkin, then the flour and salt. If too stiff, moisten with a little milk. Roll out, cut in shapes, and bake in a fairly hot oven for 10 minutes.

CINNAMON ROLL

2 Cups Self-raising Flour
½ teaspoon grated nutmeg
1 egg
½ cup sugar
1 tablespoon butter
1 cup milk

Mix dry ingredients, then melted butter, well-beaten egg, and milk. Bake in well-greased cocoa tins for ½ to ¾ hour. Turn out on stand, cool a little, then roll in a soup plate of milk, and then in a mixture made from ¼ cup coconut, ½ cup sugar, and 2 teaspoons cinnamon.

DAMPER

Self-raising Flour
salt
water

Mix ingredients into a stiff dough, mould into flat cakes, dust with dry flour, and cook in hot ashes, a camp oven or a brick oven. Test with a piece of wood (if it comes out clean the damper is done). If you have not self-raising flour, take to every pound of flour ½ a teaspoon of carbonate soda and 1 teaspoon of cream of tartar.

FRENCH LOAF

1 Large Cup Self-raising Flour
2 tablespoons melted butter
1 egg
½ cup milk
½ cup sugar
salt
cinnamon

Beat egg and sugar, add milk and sift in flour. Add melted butter and cook ½ hour in tin and, while hot, butter and sprinkle with cinnamon. Spread butter on slices.

HONEY BREAD

280 gr (9 oz.) Flour
140 gr (4½ oz.) sugar
1 tablespoon marmalade
1 cup milk
pinch salt
1 tablespoon honey
1 teaspoon carbonate soda

Mix flour, sugar, and milk and let stand for ½ an hour, then add honey, marmalade and soda. Bake in 2 round tins in a moderate oven for ½ to ¾ of an hour.

HONEY FRUIT LOAF

1 Breakfast Cup Plain Flour
¼ cup milk
1 egg
pinch of salt
½ cup honey
1 large tablespoon butter
½ cup chopped walnuts or mixed nuts
½ cup sultanas or raisins
1 heaped teaspoon baking powder

Cream butter and honey, add egg well beaten, beat again. Add the milk, and the flour, sifted with baking powder, then fruit and nuts. Bake in a moderate oven in an oblong baking tin size about 23 cm x 62 mm (9 in. x 2½ in.). Time to bake, 45 to 60 minutes. When cold, slice and serve plain or buttered.

HOT TEA CAKE

1 Cup of Flour
¾ cup milk
1 egg
¼ cup sugar
1 teaspoon cream tartar
½ teaspoon carbonate soda
1 tablespoon of butter

Mix butter and sugar together, add eggs and milk. Sift the flour with cream of tartar and soda and mix. Bake about 20 minutes in a hot oven. Cut cake in half and butter and sandwich it whilst hot. Serve for afternoon tea.

NUT BREAD

2 Cups Self-raising Flour	½ cup sugar
2 tablespoons butter	1 egg
a few nuts	a little milk

Beat sugar and egg together, add butter, melted, then flour and nuts. Make into a nice dough with just a little milk. Bake in 2 450 gr (1 lb.) bread tins, for about 35 minutes. Slices of this bread put into the open oven to brown, make delicious rusks.

NUT AND FRUIT LOAF

2 Cups Self-raising Flour	½ cup milk
250 gr (½ lb.) chopped walnuts	250 gr (½ lb.) sultanas
1 tablespoon treacle or golden syrup	2 eggs
2 tablespoons butter	½ cup sugar

Mix dry ingredients, then add eggs, sugar, butter, treacle and milk well beaten together. Mix well, and half fill 4 225 gr (½ lb.) cocoa tins. Put on lids. Bake in hot oven for 40 minutes.

POTATO LOAF

¾ Cup Cold Mashed Potatoes	1 cup sugar
2 cups self-raising flour	1 cup fruit (raisins, etc.)
1 cup milk	

Mix together potato, sugar, flour and fruit. Add milk. Mix well. Spoon into a loaf tin and bake in moderate oven for 35 minutes. When cold slice and butter. Will keep for weeks.

SALLY LUNN

2 Cups Flour	2 eggs
½ teaspoon salt	2 tablespoons butter
2 teaspoons baking powder	1 cup milk
1-3rd cup sugar	1 cup sultanas (if liked)

Mix and sift the dry ingredients, beat the eggs, and add the milk. Add gradually to the dry ingredients, beating to a smooth batter. Add the butter (melted) last. Put into a greased cake tin and bake in a hot oven.

SULTANA BUNS

2 Cups Buttermilk	1 cup sugar
3 cups self-raising flour	1 handful sultanas

Mix into a light scone dough and form into buns. Brush with egg and sprinkle on sugar. Bake in a brisk oven.

SULTANA LOAF

2 Cups Self-raising Flour
3 tablespoons sugar
1 egg
3 tablespoons butter
3 tablespoons sultanas
a pinch salt
milk

Rub butter into flour, add the salt and rest of dry ingredients. Beat egg and then add enough milk to make a fairly stiff dough. Divide into two, roll out about 25 mm (1 in.) thick, and form a cross, and brush with egg. Bake in hot oven for 20 minutes.

GIRDLE CAKES AND SCONES

The girdle is very useful and should be used more than it is for cooking. It is economical and very much quicker to heat up than is an oven. It is also very handy when scones or cakes are required for early breakfast. The girdle should be placed on the stove or over a clear open fire and allowed to become hot before commencing to mix dough. When hot, rub it over with a piece of fat or suet, and it is then ready to cook the scones or cakes.

When making drop scones, let the mixture stand for 5 minutes, then give two stirs, and cook. This makes the scones rise well, and they are very light.

DROP SCONES, No. 1 (SCOTTISH)

250 gr (½ lb.) Plain Flour
2 tablespoons sugar
½ teaspoon carbonate soda
1 egg
½ teaspoon cream of tartar
a pinch of salt
milk

Sieve dry ingredients into a basin and make a well in the centre. Add well-beaten egg, then enough milk to make a thick batter, beating all well together with a wooden spoon till the batter is full of air bubbles. Drop in spoonsful on hot, greased girdle. When surface is covered with bubbles, turn scones over. When both surfaces are nicely browned, the scones are ready. Buttermilk or sour milk may be used, but, in this case, use half quantity of cream of tartar.

DROP SCONES (No. 2)

8 Heaped Tablespoons Self-raising Flour
4 flat tablespoons sugar
a pinch of salt
2 eggs
1 cup milk

Mix together the flour, sugar, and salt. Then add the well-beaten eggs, and the milk. Mix well, and cook on a hot greased girdle. When cooked pile them on top of one another, and keep covered with a towel whilst cooling.

PIKELETS (No. 1)

1 Egg
2 tablespoons sugar
4 tablespoons self-raising flour
½ cup milk
a pinch salt

Beat egg well, add sugar, and beat well again. Add flour and milk and mix well. Drop in dessertspoons on hot greased pan. When they bubble turn with a knife. Lift on to a dry cloth and cover. When cold, butter, and serve.

PIKELETS (No. 2)

1 Egg
2 tablespoons cream
3 tablespoons sugar
about 1 cup milk
1 cup self-raising flour
a pinch of salt

Beat the egg well in a cup, and add milk to make a full cup. Add cream and sugar, and beat well. Add the self-raising flour with the salt. Drop from a dessertspoon on to a hot girdle that has been greased, and bake a light brown on both sides.

POTATO SCONES

500 gr (1 lb.) Flour
3 cold potatoes, mashed
pinch of salt
¼ teaspoon carbonate soda
15 gr (½ oz.) butter
buttermilk

Put flour into a basin with the cooked, mashed potatoes, the soda, butter, and salt. Make into a dough with buttermilk, and roll out very thin, using plenty of flour on baking board. Place on a very hot girdle. Turn when brown on one side, and brown the other.

RICE SCONES

1 Cup Boiled Rice
2 tablespoons flour
½ cup milk
3 eggs
a pinch of salt

Dry boil the rice, as for curry. Add to it the milk, and the yolks of the eggs, well beaten, then the flour, with salt. Beat whites of eggs to a stiff froth, add to other ingredients, and place in spoonsful on a hot buttered girdle immediately the mixture is ready.

SCOTCH OAT CAKE

500 gr (1 lb.) Fine Oatmeal
½ teaspoon carbonate soda
30 gr (1 oz.) butter or dripping
a pinch salt

Put half the above quantity of meal into a basin, and half the soda and shortening into a teacup, filling this half full with hot water. When the butter and soda are thoroughly melted, mix very quickly with the meal in the basin, with a knife. After mixing well, turn mixture on to a baking board, which has been

SCOTCH OAT CAKE—*continued*

well sprinkled with dry meal, mould it into a round, flat cake with the knuckles, spreading it very gradually so that it does not crack or break at the edges, strew with plenty of dry meal, and roll out very thin (this needs practice). Cut from the centre into 3 cakes and put cakes on to a hot girdle, moving the girdle round, and moving cakes from one spot to another, as they cook. When firm and dry, they are done. Move carefully from the girdle, as they are very brittle, and toast the unfired side to a pale biscuit colour in front of a clear fire. Mix the other half of the ingredients in the same manner. The quantity made is therefore 2 rounds, or 6 cakes. If dripping is used, add a pinch of salt to the oatmeal.

TREACLE SCONES

250 gr (½ lb.) Flour
½ teaspoon ground cinnamon
½ teaspoon carbonate soda
a pinch of salt
60 gr (2 oz.) butter
1 teaspoon sugar
1 large tablespoon treacle or golden syrup
buttermilk

Mix dry ingredients, rub in butter, mix treacle with the buttermilk (about ½ cup), and add, and drop in spoonsful on a hot, greased girdle. Cook a nice brown.

MADE WITHOUT COOKING

CAKES

8 gr (¼ oz.) Ground Almonds
60 gr (2 oz.) of thin lunch biscuits (grated)
8 gr (¼ oz.) castor sugar
whites of 2 eggs (whisked)

Mix these ingredients to a stiff paste. Roll out with castor sugar to about 13 mm (½ in.) in thickness. Cut in shapes and decorate with glace cherries.

DREAM SLICES

250 gr (½ lb.) Crushed Biscuits
90 gr (3 oz.) brown sugar
1 teaspoon vanilla
75 gr (2½ oz.) butter
1½ tablespoons cocoa
1 cup mixed fruit
1 dessertspoon milk
coconut
pinch salt

Cream butter and sugar together, add the crushed biscuit, then cocoa, vanilla, mixed fruit and salt. Mix all well together. Lastly add the milk. The mixture should not be too soft. Form into a roll and cover with coconut. Wrap in greaseproof paper, chill until firm. Cut into slices to serve.

FRUIT CAKE (UNCOOKED)

3 Cups All-Bran
2 tablespoons jam
1 cup chopped dates
1 teaspoon cinnamon
1 teaspoon vanilla
5 level tablespoons powdered milk
½ cup sherry or ginger ale
1½ cups mixed fruit
½ cup chopped cherries or nuts
¼ teaspoon nutmeg
½ cup lump-free icing sugar
125 gr (4 oz.) copha

Combine crushed All-Bran with sherry and jam in a large mixing bowl and set aside while you prepare other ingredients. Add other ingredients except copha and mix thoroughly. Add melted copha and mix again. Turn into an 18 cm or 20 cm (7 in. or 8 in.) tin lined with waxed paper. Press down firmly. Leave for several hours—better still until next day. Ice as desired. Chopped ginger or glace fruit can be used.

FRUIT CRUNCHES

185 gr (6 oz.) Icing Sugar
4 cups cornflakes
185 gr (6 oz.) copha
3 level tablespoons cocoa
1½ cups chopped fruit (sultanas, raisins, etc.)

Place in basin sifted icing sugar, cocoa, cornflakes and chopped fruit. Melt copha over gentle heat. It should be warm, not hot. Pour copha over dry ingredients and mix thoroughly. Press firmly into slab cake tin 26 cm x 18 cm (11 in. x 7 in.) lined with greaseproof paper, leave in a cool place to set. Remove from tin and cut into fingers before serving.

HEDGEHOG CAKE

250 gr (½ lb.) Milk Arrowroot Biscuits
1 teaspoon vanilla
1 egg
a little coconut
1 dessertspoon cocoa
125 gr (¼ lb.) butter
1 small cup sugar

Roll biscuits to fine crumbs. Melt butter and sugar. Add beaten egg, vanilla and cocoa. Pour mixture over crushed biscuits and mix well. Press into shallow cake tin well. When cold ice with chocolate icing. Sprinkle with coconut.

ICED NUT SQUARES

90 gr (3 oz.) Butter
½ cup brown sugar
2½ tablespoons milk
2 tablespoons cocoa
¼ cup chopped nuts
1 teaspoon vanilla
250 gr (½ lb.) milk arrowroot biscuits

Crush biscuits finely. Heat butter, sugar, milk and cocoa until boiling. Cool slightly, add to crumbs, add vanilla and nuts. Turn into well-greased tin, pressing down firmly with fingers. When cool and set, ice with chocolate icing. When icing sets cut into squares.

REFRIGERATOR CHRISTMAS CAKE

½ Cup Butter
½ teaspoon cinnamon
¾ teaspoon salt
1 teaspoon grated lemon rind
2 cups finely crushed breakfast cereal or plain biscuit crumbs
¼ cup dried apricots chopped
¾ cup dried dates chopped
¾ cup dried figs chopped
½ cup crystallised cherries
½ cup honey
pinch nutmeg
1 cup raisins
4 tablespoons sherry
½ cup crystallised pineapple
½ cup nuts

Combine honey and softened butter, spices and salt, mixing thoroughly. Add raisins, fruits, nuts, crumbs and sherry, blending well. Line an 18 cm (7 in.) square tin with greased paper and press mixture into it. Leave in refrigerator for several days. Keep in refrigerator and serve in finger lengths as required.

REFRIGERATOR PASTRY

3 Cups Cereal (rice bubbles, cornflakes, weeties, etc.)
¼ cup sugar
grated rind of lemon or orange
125 gr (4 oz.) shortening

Crush cereal finely and place in bowl with sugar, grated rind and melted shortening and mix well. Press the mixture into a 20 cm (8 in.) greased pie plate and leave in refrigerator for several hours until quite firm. For chocolate pastry, omit the lemon or orange rind and add 2 level tablespoons cocoa and one tablespoon hot milk.

RICE BUBBLE FANCY

125 gr (4 oz.) Chopped Dates
½ cup brown sugar
coconut
125 gr (4 oz.) butter
4 cups rice bubbles

Melt together butter, sugar and dates. When cool add rice bubbles. Grease swiss roll tin and line with coconut. Press in mixture and sprinkle with coconut. Allow to set, cut into pieces.

RICE BUBBLE SLICE

2 Cups Rice Bubbles
1 cup icing sugar
pinch salt
185 gr (6 oz.) copha
½ cup coconut
1 cup powdered milk
vanilla essence

Melt copha and mix well with other ingredients Press into a slab tin to set. Ice with chocolate icing.

SNOWBALLS

1 Packet Crushed Milk Arrowroot Biscuits
4 tablespoons icing sugar
1½ tablespoons cocoa
1 teaspoon vanilla
1 cup mixed fruits
90 gr (3 oz.) butter
3 tablespoons milk
coconut

Melt butter in milk and add vanilla. Combine other ingredients, roll into balls and toss in coconut. Leave to set.

WHITE CHRISTMAS

2 Cups Rice Bubbles
1 cup powdered milk
250 gr (½ lb.) copha
1 cup icing sugar
1 cup coconut
cherries, dates, walnuts (chopped but not too fine)

Melt copha, add to other ingredients. Flatten in pie-dish and leave to set. Very rich. Cut in small squares.

BISCUITS

AFGANS

185 gr (6 oz.) Butter
90 gr (3 oz.) brown sugar
1 tablespoon cocoa
185 gr (6 oz.) S.R. flour
60 gr (2 oz.) cornflakes or Fergies
1 egg
pinch salt

Cream butter and sugar, add egg, add dry ingredients and cornflakes and mix well. Place in small heaps on a cold greased oven slide. Bake in a moderate oven for 15 minutes. Ice with chocolate icing and walnuts.

ALMOND FINGERS

250 gr (½ lb.) Self-raising Flour
1 egg
125 gr (¼ lb.) icing sugar
125 gr (¼ lb.) butter
1 tablespoon sugar
chopped almonds
a little vanilla essence

Rub butter into flour, add sugar, and make into a stiff paste with the yolk of egg mixed with a little milk. Roll out thin. Take half the white of egg and beat to a stiff froth, add the icing sugar and mix well. Spread this icing thinly over the paste, sprinkle with chopped almonds, cut into fingers, and bake 15 to 20 minutes in a moderate oven. Desiccated coconut may be used instead of almonds.

ANZACS

½ Cup Sugar
1 cup flaked oatmeal
125 gr (¼ lb.) melted butter
1 tablespoon golden syrup
1 cup coconut
1 cup flour
1 level teaspoon carbonate soda
2 tablespoons boiling water

Mix all dry ingredients together, pour in melted butter, add soda and syrup dissolved in boiling water, and mix well. Drop in small pieces on oven slide and bake in a moderate oven 20 minutes.

ANZAC KISSES

125 gr ($\frac{1}{4}$ lb.) Butter
2 eggs
1 cup sugar
2 teaspoons cinnamon
2 cups self-raising flour

Beat butter and sugar to a cream, add eggs, flour, and cinnamon, and mix well. Roll out very thin and cut with a small round cutter. Bake 10 to 15 minutes in a moderate oven. Put two together with jam and ice on top.

BRANDY SNAPS

60 gr (2 oz.) Butter
60 gr (2 oz.) sugar (white or brown)
2 teaspoons ground ginger
60 gr (2 oz.) plain flour
2 tablespoons golden syrup
a little vanilla essence
a few drops of lemon juice

Put all ingredients except flour into an enamelled basin and warm. When melted stir in the flour slowly. Well grease an oven shelf or tin, and drop the mixture on in teaspoonsful, keeping them far apart. Bake 5 minutes, or till light brown.

Set aside till half cold, slide them off with a knife and roll up. Measure ingredients carefully and have a moderate oven.

BUBBLE BREAD (No. 1)

Butter
flour
water

To every 30 gr (1 oz.) butter allow 125 gr (4 oz.) flour. Mix with water to a stiff paste and roll out fairly thin. Cut into strips or squares and cook in a hot oven.

BUBBLE BREAD (No. 2)

310 gr (10 oz.) of Plain Flour
60 gr (2 oz.) butter
pinch of salt
60 gr (2 oz.) grated cheese
pinch of baking powder
pinch of cayenne pepper

Sift flour, cayenne, salt and baking powder, rub in the butter, add cheese. Make into a medium soft dough with water. Turn on to a floured board, and knead lightly. Roll out into a very thin sheet and cut in squares. Bake in a moderate oven till a pale brown. Leave on the oven shelf till cold.

BUTTER BISCUITS

375 gr ($\frac{3}{4}$ lb.) Flour
250 gr ($\frac{1}{2}$ lb.) butter
185 gr (6 oz.) sugar
1 egg
$\frac{1}{4}$ teaspoon baking powder

Mix flour, sugar, and powder together, and rub in the butter. Add the egg well beaten. Roll out very thin. Cut into shapes, and bake in a quick oven till a light golden brown.

CAIRO BISCUITS

185 gr (6 oz.) Butter
250 gr (8 oz.) flour
185 gr (6 oz.) sugar
vanilla essence

Cream butter in a basin with wooden spoon. Mix in the sugar, the flour, and a few drops of vanilla. Mix until paste leaves the sides of the basin quite clean. Turn out on a board, then mould with the hands into a long roll about 38 mm ($1\frac{1}{2}$ in.) deep. Cut in slanting slices about 25 mm (1 in.) thick and place on a buttered slide and bake in a moderate oven till a golden brown.

CHEESE BISCUITS (No. 1)

215 gr (7 oz.) Self-raising Flour
90 gr (3 oz.) butter
$\frac{1}{2}$ cup milk
125 gr (4 oz.) grated cheese
1 egg
salt and cayenne

Rub butter into flour, add cheese and mix like scone dough. Roll out about 13 mm ($\frac{1}{2}$ in.) thick. Bake in hot oven, take out, split and return to oven to crisp.

CHEESE BISCUITS (No. 2)

125 gr (4 oz.) Flour
$\frac{1}{4}$ teaspoon baking powder
$\frac{1}{2}$ teaspoon dry mustard
a squeeze lemon juice
60 gr (2 oz.) butter
60 gr (2 oz.) grated cheese
yolk 1 egg
a little water
cayenne pepper

Sift flour, baking powder, cayenne, and mustard. Rub in butter lightly add cheese, and mix well. Beat egg yolk, add lemon juice and water, then add to dry ingredients, and make into a stiff dough. Knead lightly, roll out thinly, and cut into small rounds. Bake in a moderate oven for 15 minutes. Garnish with sprigs of parsley.

CHOCOLATE DROPS

185 gr (6 oz.) Self-raising Flour
155 gr (5 oz.) soft shortening
$2\frac{1}{2}$ level tablespoons cocoa
1 cup sultanas or chopped dates
1 small egg
1 cup (tightly packed) brown sugar
1 teaspoon vanilla essence
2 cups rice bubbles

Combine all ingredients except fruit and rice bubbles. Beat 2 minutes, fold in fruit and rice bubbles. Drop in spoonsful on ungreased trays. Bake 10 minutes in moderate oven. Can be iced with chocolate or vanilla icing.

CINNAMON CURLS

2 Cups Flour
2 eggs
1 teaspoon baking powder
1 cup sugar
½ cup butter
cinnamon

Cream butter and sugar, add eggs, then flour with baking powder mixed through. Work into a dough, roll thin, sprinkle cinnamon over the surface, roll up like a swiss roll, and cut half an inch thick with a knife. Bake a pale brown in a moderate oven. When cooked these biscuits look like catherine wheels.

CINNAMON CURRANT ROLLS

2 Cups Flour
½ cup milk
4 teaspoons baking powder
cinnamon to taste
½ teaspoon salt
2 tablespoons butter
1 tablespoon sugar
currants

Sift flour, baking powder, salt and sugar into a basin, rub in butter, stir in milk, and then knead for a few minutes on a floured board. Roll out to 13 mm (½ in.) in thickness, spread with butter, sprinkle with sugar, cinnamon, and currants, roll up like a swiss roll, cut into 25 mm (1 in.) thick slices, and bake in a quick oven.

COCONUT BISCUITS

125 gr (¼ lb.) Butter
1 cup coconut
½ cup sugar
1 egg
1 cup self-raising flour

Beat butter and sugar to a cream, add eggs and mix well, then add coconut, and flour, and mix all together to form paste. Roll out thin and bake a light brown.

COCONUT DAINTIES

2 Eggs
a few drops cochineal
½ teaspoon baking powder
1 teaspoon vanilla essence
60 gr (2 oz.) coconut
weight of 2 eggs in sugar
flour and butter

Beat butter and sugar to a cream, add eggs well beaten, then flour gradually, then essence, coconut, baking powder and colouring. Put into flat tins. When baked cut into squares and sprinkle with castor sugar.

COOKIES

4 Tablespoons Sugar	3 tablespoons butter
2 tablespoons milk	1 egg
1 teaspoon baking powder	flour to make a stiff dough

Put sugar into a basin, melt the butter, pour over the sugar and beat well together. Beat the egg and add to it the milk and stir into the butter and sugar. Sift the baking powder with a little flour and add to the mixture, adding more flour to make it into a stiff dough. Well flour the baking board, turn out the dough and knead a little. Roll out to 13 mm (½ in.) thick, cut with biscuit cutter, roll each in sugar, place on greased oven shelf, and bake a golden brown. These require a hot oven.

CORNFLAKE BISCUITS

Whites of 2 Eggs	1 cup sugar
2 tablespoons melted butter	1 cup coconut
4 cups cornflakes	vanilla to taste

Beat whites of eggs with sugar, add melted butter, then coconut, cornflakes and essence. Drop on a cold slide. Bake in a moderate oven 10 to 15 minutes.

CORNFLAKE NUTTIES

2 Egg Whites	¾ cup castor sugar
1 teaspoon essence vanilla	1 tablespoon melted butter
4 breakfast cups cornflakes	½ cup walnuts or mixed nuts

Beat whites of eggs until stiff, add the castor sugar, then essence of vanilla, and melted butter. Stir in the nuts and cornflakes. Put heaped teaspoonsful on a warm buttered oven slide and bake in a moderate oven till a golden brown.

CRISP BISCUITS

250 gr (½ lb.) Butter	1 cup sugar
1 teaspoon treacle	3 tablespoons boiling water
1 small teaspoon carbonate soda	2 cups rolled oats
2 cups self-raising flour	1 teaspoon vanilla essence

Cream butter and sugar, add treacle (warmed) then the vanilla, the self-raising flour and oats, and lastly the soda, dissolved in the boiling water. Mix well. Drop on to a greased oven slide and bake a delicate brown in a moderate oven for about 10 minutes.

CRUSTIES

½ Cup Butter	¾ cup sugar
1 egg	2 cups flaked oatmeal
1 teaspoon baking powder	½ teaspoon salt

Beat together the butter and sugar, add the egg and beat well, stir in the flaked oatmeal, baking powder and salt. Mix well and put on oven shelf in spoonsful. Bake about ½ an hour in a slow oven.

CURRANT BISCUITS

250 gr (½ lb.) Flour
1 teaspoon baking powder
125 gr (¼ lb.) butter
1 egg
125 gr (4 oz.) sugar
125 gr (4 oz.) icing sugar
60 to 125 gr (2 to 4 oz.) currants
1 tablespoon milk

Sift flour and baking powder, add sugar, rub in butter, add currants and milk mixed with yolk of egg. Make into dough and roll out thinly. Beat whites of egg with icing sugar, spread on mixture cut into finger lengths 38 mm (1½ in.) wide and bake in a moderate oven 15 to 20 minutes. Coconut can be shaken over icing if liked.

CUSTARD CREAMS

125 gr (¼ lb.) Butter
4 tablespoons custard powder
2 teaspoons baking powder
1 cup plain flour
4 tablespoons sugar
essence vanilla
1 egg

Cream butter and sugar, add egg and vanilla essence. Sift all dry ingredients and combine with the mixture. Knead and leave 5 minutes—if hot weather, in the refrigerator. Cut into shapes or use biscuit forcer. Bake till a light colour in moderate oven. Join with vanilla flavour icing.

DATE LUNCHEONS

1 Cup Self-raising Flour
¾ cup sugar
1 egg
60 gr (2 oz.) cornflour
90 gr (3 oz.) butter
a little milk

Date Mixture: 500 gr (1 lb.) dates, ½ cup sugar, a little lemon juice, enough hot water to make like jam.

Beat butter and sugar to a cream, add egg and beat again, add flour, cornflour, and milk, and mix to a stiff dough. Cut in half, and roll out, put on greased papered oven shelf, cover with date mixture, and then cover with other half of dough. Cook about 15 minutes, and when cold cut into finger lengths.

GINGER NUTS (No. 1)

2 Tablespoons Butter
½ cup sugar
1 egg
1 teaspoon ground ginger
1 tablespoon treacle
1 large cup self-raising flour
¼ teaspoon carb. soda
½ teaspoon spice

Beat butter, treacle and sugar together and add egg. Sift in flour, spices, etc. Drop in teaspoonsful on greased oven slide and bake in slow oven 10-15 minutes, leaving spreading room. Cool on tray.

GINGER NUTS (No. 2)

1 Cup Dripping
1 cup golden syrup
1 teaspoon carbonate soda
1 cup sugar
1 dessertspoon ground ginger
a little boiling water
3 cups flour

Place in a saucepan the dripping, sugar, golden syrup, and ginger. Heat till nearly boiling, stir frequently and add the soda dissolved in a little boiling water. Beat in the flour and put scant teaspoonsful on a greased tray. Bake 10 minutes in a moderate oven. Do not remove until quite cold. This amount makes 9 dozen biscuits.

GOOD BISCUITS

8 Tablespoons Self-raising Flour
4 tablespoons butter
1 egg
3 tablespoons sugar

Mix. Roll out thinly and cut into shapes with a biscuit cutter, place on a cold oven slide and bake in a quick oven.

GUM BLOSSOMS

185 gr (6 oz.) Butter
310 gr (10 oz.) flour
185 gr (6 oz.) sugar
2 Eggs
1 teaspoon baking powder

Cream butter and sugar, add beaten egg, then flour with baking powder added. Roll out and cut into biscuits. Bake in a moderate oven. Ice when cold.

HONEY BISCUITS (RICH)

250 gr ($\frac{1}{2}$ lb.) Flour
90 gr (3 oz.) sugar
1 small egg (unbeaten)
lemon flavouring
155 gr (5 oz.) butter
90 gr (3 oz.) honey
pinch nutmeg
30 gr (1 oz.) extra flour for rolling out

Rub flour and butter together until very fine, add sugar, honey, egg and flavouring. This makes a very silky dough, and must be handled gently as the mixture is very short. Roll out carefully, using the extra flour sparingly. Cut into rounds with a cutter about the size of a 50c piece. Bake 20 to 25 minutes in a cool oven. Allow the biscuits to become cold then join two together with a little honey, sandwich fashion.

ICED BISCUITS

125 gr ($\frac{1}{4}$ lb.) Butter
essence
1 cup sugar
1 egg
2 cups self-raising **flour**

Cream butter and sugar, add beaten egg and sufficient sifted flour to make a stiff dough. Roll out and cut into shapes with a biscuit cutter. While still hot, fasten together with raspberry jam. When cool ice with passion fruit icing or with lemon icing sprinkled with chopped almonds.

INVERNESS BISCUITS

125 gr ($\frac{1}{4}$ lb.) Butter
1 teaspoon vanilla
2 teaspoons baking powder
1 cup sugar
1 egg
rolled oats

Beat butter and sugar to a cream, add egg and vanilla and enough rolled oats to make a dry mixture (baking powder to be added to the dry oats). Place in teaspoonsful on a well-buttered slide, not too close together. Bake 10 to 15 minutes. Allow to cool a minute or two before removing from the slide.

LIGHT BISCUITS

3 Cups Self-raising Flour
1 egg
$\frac{1}{2}$ cup currants or sultanas
1 cup butter
$1\frac{1}{4}$ cups sugar
milk

Mix the sugar with the flour, rub in the butter, add the fruit. Make into a firm paste with egg and milk, roll, and cut to shape. Bake in a moderate oven.

MACAROONS (No. 1)

Whites of 2 Eggs
125 gr ($\frac{1}{4}$ lb.) coconut
250 gr ($\frac{1}{2}$ lb.) sugar
essence

Beat whites of eggs to a very stiff froth. Stir in sugar and coconut. Mix well. Drop in teaspoonsful on greased paper. Bake 10 minutes in slow oven.

MACAROONS (No. 2)

Whites of 2 Eggs
$\frac{1}{2}$ teaspoon vanilla
1 cup of sugar
2 cups rice bubbles
$\frac{1}{2}$ cup shelled nuts (chopped)

Beat the egg whites until stiff, add sugar gradually, then add the vanilla, rice bubbles and nuts. Drop by spoonfuls on a buttered slide and bake in a moderate oven until the Macaroons are a delicate brown.

MACAROONS (CHOCOLATE)

125 gr (¼ lb.) Ground Almonds
30 gr (1 oz.) grated chocolate
3 whites of eggs
15 gr (½ oz.) ground rice
250 gr (½ lb.) castor sugar
½ teaspoonful vanilla
15 gr (½ oz.) shredded almonds

Put the ground almonds and half the whites of eggs into a basin and cream well together for 10 minutes, then add castor sugar and ground rice, vanilla, grated chocolate, and the remainder of the whites of eggs, and beat all together for 10 minutes. Put the mixture in a bag with a 13 mm (½ in.) plain pipe, and pipe the mixture out on to paper into rounds the size of a 20 cent piece. Put the shredded almonds on top, and bake in a moderate oven for about 20 minutes.

MALT BISCUITS

125 gr (¼ lb.) Butter
1 dessertspoon malt extract
185 gr (6 oz.) plain flour
90 gr (3 oz.) sultanas
60 gr (2 oz.) sugar
60 gr (2 oz.) condensed milk
1 teaspoon baking powder
salt

Cream butter and sugar, add malt and condensed milk, then flour. Form in balls and flatten with fork. Bake on greased slide.

MERINGUES

Whites of 4 Eggs
8 tablespoons sugar
flavouring
cream
sufficient cream of tartar to cover 5c

Beat whites stiffly, add sugar half tablespoon at a time, beating well. Add cream of tartar and flavouring, and beat well. Place in teaspoon heaps on greased paper. Bake about 2 hours in cool oven or they may be cooked for 1 hour, the soft centre removed, and shells filled with whipped cream.

MERINGUES (CORNFLAKE)

1 Large Cup Cornflakes or Weeties
½ cup sugar (icing for preference)
1 cup chopped nuts
white of 1 egg

Beat white of egg until stiff, then add sugar slowly. Add cornflakes and nuts, drop a teaspoonful on to buttered paper and bake in a moderate oven.

MONKEYS

250 gr ($\frac{1}{2}$ lb.) Self-raising Flour
1 egg
1 dessertspoon cinnamon
155 gr (5 oz.) butter
155 gr (5 oz.) sugar
1 teaspoon nutmeg
1 teaspoon ground ginger

Cream butter and sugar, add egg, and beat well. Sift flour with spices added, add to the rest, work into a dry dough, and roll out thinly. Cut into two sizes of rounds, one a little smaller than the other. Make a filling with 2 tablespoons currants, 3 tablespoons each of sultanas and raisins, 1 tablespoon lemon peel, cinnamon and spice to taste, lastly a little brandy if desired. Put a teaspoon of filling on each of the larger rounds, wet the edges and place smaller round on top, press edges together, decorate with an almond and bake in a moderate oven 25 minutes.

MUNCHIES

2 Cups of Flaked Oats
1 cup self-raising flour
1 cup butter
1 cup coconut
$\frac{1}{2}$ cup sugar
2 tablespoons golden syrup
4 tablespoons milk

Beat butter and sugar to a cream, add golden syrup, then other ingredients, which should be thoroughly mixed, and lastly, add the milk. Put teaspoonfuls on slide and cook in a slow oven.

NUTTIES (No. 1)

2 Cups Flour
2 cups coconut
2 tablespoons of golden syrup, treacle, or honey
250 gr ($\frac{1}{2}$ lb.) butter or fat
2 cups flaked oatmeal
1 cup sugar
4 tablespoons water
1$\frac{1}{2}$ level teaspoons carbonate soda

Place all dry ingredients in a basin. Melt butter and golden syrup, and put water, warmed, on soda, and pour into butter and syrup. Let boil a minute, add to the dry ingredients and mix well together. Place in pieces on a tray and press with fork to make them fancy. Bake a light brown. Nuts are an improvement.

NUTTIES (No. 2)

125 gr ($\frac{1}{4}$ lb.) Butter
$\frac{1}{2}$ teaspoon carbonate soda (small)
1 tablespoon boiling water
$\frac{1}{2}$ cup minced raisins
$\frac{3}{4}$ cup flour
$\frac{1}{2}$ teaspoon cinnamon
125 gr ($\frac{1}{4}$ lb.) sugar
1 egg
$\frac{1}{2}$ cup dates
$\frac{1}{2}$ cup walnuts
$\frac{1}{4}$ cup ground wheat
pinch salt

Beat butter and sugar to a cream, add egg and beat well. Add the soda dissolved in the boiling water, then the chopped fruit. Stir in flour and wheatmeal, cinnamon and salt. Make into balls about the size of a walnut. Bake 10 minutes in good oven.

NUTTIES (No. 3)

1 Tablespoon Treacle	**1 teaspoon essence coffee**
1 teaspoon carbonate soda	**2 cups flaked oatmeal**
1 cup sugar (white or brown)	**½ teaspoon baking powder**
1 cup flour	**125 gr (¼ lb.) butter**
2 tablespoons water	

Melt together the treacle, water, carbonate soda, essence, and butter, but do not boil. Mix together the oatmeal, flour, sugar, and baking powder, and add to the liquid. Drop on sandwich tins, or oven slide, and cook in good steady oven. They will spread very much, so use judgment in the dropping on slide.

OAT GEMS

2 Heaped Cups Rolled Oats	**1 cup sugar**
½ cup butter	**½ cup flour**
½ teaspoon carbonate soda	**1 tablespoon boiling water**

Mix oats, sugar and flour together. Melt butter and dissolve soda in water, and mix with dry ingredients. Drop on shelf in teaspoonfuls. Bake in moderate oven.

OATMEAL WAFERS

2 Cups Rolled Oats	**1 cup sugar**
1 teaspoon baking powder	**pinch of salt**
1 beaten egg	**2 tablespoons melted butter**

Put ingredients into a basin in the order given. Mix thoroughly. Place in small spoonfuls on greaseproof paper, allowing enough room for wafers to spread. Bake in a slow oven till pale brown. Leave till cold before removing from paper. This quantity makes 5 dozen wafers.

PEANUT BISCUITS

250 gr (½ lb.) Butter	**¾ cup sugar**
1 teaspoon vanilla essence	**1 tablespoon warmed golden syrup**
2 cups self-raising flour	**1 cup rolled oats**
1 cup peanuts	**1 teaspoon carb. soda**
3 tablespoons boiling water	

Cream butter and sugar, add golden syrup and vanilla. Mix well, add flour, oats, peanuts and carbonate soda dissolved in boiling water. Mix well. Put in teaspoon heaps on greased oven slide. Bake for 20 minutes in moderate oven.

PEANUT BUTTER FRUIT WHIRLS

1½ Cups Mixed Fruits	60 gr (2 oz.) butter
30 gr (1 oz.) sugar	1 egg
1 cup self-raising flour	pinch salt
2 tablespoons water	peanut butter

Cream shortening and sugar, add beaten egg and work in flour sifted with salt. Roll into an oblong shape 6 mm (¼ in.) thick, spread with softened peanut butter and cover with fruit softened with water over gentle heat. Roll up and chill 3-4 hours. Cut into slices 13 mm (½ in.) thick, bake on greased oven tray 15-20 minutes in moderate oven.

PEANUT COOKIES

60 gr (2 oz.) Butter	½ cup peanut paste
1 cup sugar	2 eggs
1 cup raw peanuts	2 cups plain flour
1 teaspoon baking powder	¼ teaspoon carb. soda
1 tablespoon cocoa	1 teaspoon cinnamon

Cream butter, peanut paste and sugar. Beat in eggs singly. Add peanuts chopped. Sift together then add gradually flour, baking powder, carbonate soda, cocoa and cinnamon. Roll dough into small balls, place on baking trays, flatten with fork, decorate with raw peanut halves. Bake in moderate oven 155° C (375° F.) till crisp. Yields 4 to 5 dozen delicious biscuits.

PUFFIES

155 gr (5 oz.) Flour	60 gr (2 oz.) butter
½ teaspoon salt	60 gr (2 oz.) grated cheese
cayenne pepper to taste	¼ cup of water

Rub butter into flour, add all the other ingredients and mix to a stiff paste with water. Roll out as thinly as paper, cut in long strips and place on slide. Then cut into 3-cornered pieces and bake in hot oven. Butter when serving.

RATAFIA BISCUITS

185 gr (6 oz.) Self-raising Flour	125 gr (4 oz.) sugar
90 gr (3 oz.) butter	almonds
1 teaspoon almond essence	1 egg

Beat butter and sugar, add egg, then essence, and lastly flour. Roll in little balls, pat with the hand, and place half an almond on top. Bake in a moderate oven.

RICE BISCUITS

125 gr (4 oz.) Butter
125 gr (4 oz.) flour
2 eggs
125 gr (4 oz.) sugar
125 gr (4 oz.) rice flour
½ teaspoon cream of tartar
¼ teaspoon carbonate soda

Cream the butter and sugar, add the eggs, and then the rice, flour and plain flour with cream of tartar and carbonate of soda added. Roll out to 3 mm (⅛ in.) thickness, place in rounds on a greased tray, and bake 10 to 15 minutes in a moderate oven.

RUSKS (No. 1)

500 gr (1 lb.) Self-raising Flour
½ teaspoon salt
about 1 cup of milk
1 tablespoon sugar
1 egg
60 gr (2 oz.) butter

Melt the butter and beat up the egg. Mix into already mixed flour, sugar, and salt till a nice consistency, about same as for pastry. Roll out 1½ mm ($\frac{1}{16}$ in.) thick. Cook in a moderate oven till a light brown. Then split in half and cook till brown and crisp. When put back the second time they burn easily, so it is a good idea to only half shut the oven door. These will keep 3 or 4 week if put in air-tight tin.

RUSKS (No. 2)

1 Cup Butter
2 cups self-raising flour
2 cups fine oatmeal
1 teaspoon carbonate soda
1 cup sugar
2 dessertspoons honey
pinch of salt
3 tablespoons boiling water

Beat the butter and sugar to a cream, add the honey, then the flour, oatmeal, and salt, and mix well. Lastly add the soda dissolved in the boiling water. Place spoonfuls on a greased slide, and bake 20 minutes in a cool oven.

RUSKS (No. 3)

90 gr (3 oz.) Butter or Lard
2 cups flour
2 teaspoons baking powder
2 eggs
1 teaspoon sugar
pinch salt

Beat eggs and butter together with sugar and salt. Add flour and enough milk to make a scone mixture. Cut into rounds and bake in a brisk oven. When cooked cut open with a sharp knife, and put back into oven and bake a nice brown.

SAONS

2 Cups Self-raising Flour
pinch salt
1 tablespoon butter

Rub butter into salt and flour. Mix to firm dough with water. Roll out very thinly, prick all over with a fork, cut into squares and bake quickly to light brown. This recipe makes 10 dozen.

SHORTBREAD BISCUITS

125 gr (4 oz.) Salt Butter
60 gr (2 oz.) castor sugar
2 tablespoons ground rice
185 gr (6 oz.) flour
(use ordinary flour, mixed with a dessertspoon of self-raising)

Beat butter and sugar to a cream. Work in flour and ground rice until it can be moulded into a cake. Roll out thinly. Cut into shapes, sprinkle with sugar. Bake in moderate oven until a light brown.

SHORTBREAD BISCUITS (FANCY)

375 gr (¾ lb.) Plain Flour
125 gr (¼ b.) icing sugar
125 gr (¼ lb.) custard powder
375 gr (¾ lb.) butter

Cream together the butter and sugar and add the flour and custard powder previously well sifted together. Make into small balls about the size of a walnut, place on cold oven slide and press with a four-pronged fork. Bake a pale brown in a moderate oven. Put two together with butter icing flavoured with vanilla. Roll in icing sugar. Allow the biscuits to become cold before joining together.

SUNBEAMS

2 Cups Self-raising Flour
2 tablespoons sugar
2 eggs
2 tablespoons butter

Make a dough and roll out like pastry. Spread with jam (thinly) and roll up like roly-poly. Cut into rounds 13 mm (½ in.) thick, roll in coconut, and bake in a quick oven.

SURRY BISCUITS

250 gr (8 oz.) Butter
310 gr (10 oz.) flour
essence of lemon or vanilla
250 gr (8 oz.) castor sugar
1 egg
salt
blanched almond kernels

Beat butter and sugar to a cream, add well-beaten egg and flavouring. Sift flour with salt and stir in carefully. Form into balls of dough and put away in cool place to chill it. This is very important, as chilling firms the butter and rolling becomes easier. Roll out chilled dough fairly thinly on floured board, if mixture is done in 2 pieces it will be easier. Cut out with sharp cutter, and place on cold slide. Put ½ blanched almond on each biscuit and bake in moderate oven. When cold store in airtight tins.

TEA BISCUITS

250 gr (½ lb.) Butter
2 teaspoons baking powder
125 gr (¼ lb.) coconut
250 gr (½ lb.) sugar
500 gr (1 lb.) flour
1 egg
juice of 1 small lemon and grated rind
pinch of salt

Cream butter and sugar, add egg and grated lemon rind. Sift flour with salt and baking powder and work into dough, then add coconut and lemon juice. Mix and knead well. Roll out and cut into fancy shapes, or put through a biscuit forcer.

VANITY BISCUITS

¾ Cup Sugar
2 cups self-raising flour
125 gr (¼ lb.) butter
3 eggs

Beat butter and sugar to a cream. Add the eggs and beat well together, then add the flour. Roll out thinly, cut into shapes and bake in a moderate oven.

WATER BISCUITS

1 Dessertspoon Butter
a pinch of salt
2 tablespoons plain flour
little milk

Roll out six or seven times, the last time as thin as possible. Dry on oven shelf in cool oven or on hob. Bake in a slow oven until golden brown. Very useful with butter or for savouries.

YORKSHIRE BISCUITS

250 gr (½ lb.) Self-raising Flour
1 egg
125 gr (¼ lb.) butter
125 gr (¼ lb.) sugar
pinch of salt

Divide into two pieces, roll or press one piece on to tin or oven tray, spread with raspberry jam and place remaining piece on top and bake in moderate oven for 20 minutes. Ice with butter icing when cold, and cut into shapes for biscuits. Or fill with 1 cup chopped dates, ½ cup sugar, ½ cup water boiled together.

ICINGS

ALMOND ICING (No. 1)

250 gr (½ lb.) Ground Almonds
4 egg yolks
500 gr (1 lb.) icing sugar
a little almond essence
some orange juice

Roll the sugar free from lumps, add ground almonds, and mix well. Beat yolks of egg, and add with the flavourings. Do not make it too soft. Roll out to size required, and press on cake.

ALMOND ICING (No. 2)

185 gr (6 oz.) Ground Almonds
2 egg yolks
435 gr (14 oz.) icing sugar
2 tablespoons sherry or orange juice
few drops lemon juice

Mix dry ingredients. Beat yolks, sherry and lemon juice together and add, making into a stiff paste. Brush cake well with white of egg before placing on almond paste.

BOILED ICING

White 1 Egg
boiling water
1 cup sugar
flavouring

Beat egg to a stiff froth. Put just enough boiling water on the sugar to melt it, then boil to a thick syrup. Pour the boiling syrup over the beaten egg, add flavouring as desired, and beat until thoroughly mixed. Pour over the cake while hot. If the frosting has a tendency to harden, add a few drops of hot water. It may have been over boiled.

CARAMEL ICING

1 Cup Brown Sugar
2 tablespoons milk
1 tablespoon butter

Place in a saucepan on fire. Allow to boil for about 10 minutes, or until a little dropped in cold water forms into a soft ball. Take from the fire, and whip until it becomes creamy. Spread on cake with a wet knife. Vanilla or lemon flavouring may be added before whipping.

CHOCOLATE ICING

1 Cup Icing Sugar
1 tablespoon cocoa
2 tablespoons boiling water
1 teaspoon butter

Melt the butter, mix in the cocoa, add the icing sugar, well sifted, and beat until smooth. Flavour with vanilla.

COFFEE ICING

185 gr (6 oz.) Icing Sugar
tablespoon coffee essence
a little warm water

Mix together the icing sugar and the coffee essence, and add a little warm water. Spread over cake, and decorate with chopped walnuts. This is the recipe for the Walnut Cream Cake.

PLASTIC ICING (No. 1)

1 kg (2 lb.) Icing Sugar
125 gr (4 oz.) liquid glucose
2 egg whites
flavouring

Sift icing sugar into basin. Soften glucose and add with egg whites. Beat well, gradually drawing in dry icing sugar to make a stiff paste. Knead till smooth.

PLASTIC ICING (No. 2)

250 gr (½ lb.) Icing Sugar
250 gr (½ lb.) glucose
3 level dessertspoons gelatine
½ cup water
30 gr (1 oz.) copha

Boil sugar, water and glucose for 3 minutes to 110° C (230° F.). Remove from heat and add copha and gelatine covered with cold water. Let cool a little and stir in some icing sugar until thick. Put icing sugar on to a board, make a well in centre and pour in cooled mixture. Knead in icing sugar till paste is the desired consistency. Flavour and colour as desired. Roll out and apply to cake, brushed with syrup, egg white or jam. This paste may be stored indefinitely in a screwtop jar. If it goes too stiff it can be broken down with a little water or copha.

PLASTIC ICING (No. 3)

4 Level Dessertspoons Gelatine
500 gr (1 lb.) sugar (not icing sugar)
125 gr (¼ lb.) copha
about 2½ kg (5 lb.) icing sugar
300 ml (12 oz.) cold water
4 tablespoons strained lemon juice

Soak gelatine in 100 ml (4 oz.) cold water. Put 200 ml (8 oz.) water into saucepan and add sugar and strained lemon juice. Boil with bulb of thermometer covered to 110° C (230° F.). Don't stir. Add soaked gelatine and stir with wooden spoon till dissolved. Then add 125 gr (¼ lb.) copha and dissolve. Add as much icing sugar as saucepan will take. You will need about 2½ kg (5 lb.) icing sugar. Put rest of icing sugar on table, make a well in the centre and pour contents into it. Mix and knead until pliable. The more you knead the whiter the icing. Roll out with rolling pin. (This will keep in a plastic bag for months.)

PLASTIC AND FONDANT ICING

A.
$\frac{1}{2}$ Cup Water
250 gr ($\frac{1}{2}$ lb.) white sugar
250 ml ($\frac{1}{2}$ lb.) liquid glucose

B.
30 gr (1 oz.) gelatine (4 level dessertspoons) stirred into 60 ml (2 oz.) cold water
60 gr (2 oz.) copha

C.
Approximately $1\frac{1}{4}$ kg ($2\frac{1}{2}$ lb.) icing sugar

Soak gelatine. Place A in a suitable saucepan and boil quickly to 110° C (230° F.). Remove from heat and add B. Let cool to 70° C (160° F.) and then stir in about 1 kg (2 lb.) sifted icing sugar (C). Sift remaining 250 gr ($\frac{1}{2}$ lb.) icing sugar on to table, forming a well. Pour mixture into well and leave until cold, then add 1 teaspoon orange essence to flavour. Knead until desired consistency and then add colouring if desired and knead in.

This mixture must be boiled quickly to achieve desired consistency suitable for modelling flowers and fruits, etc. Store in plastic bag until needed.

PLASTIC ICING (WITHOUT GLUCOSE)

A.
500 gr (1 lb.) Sugar
1 cup water
2 tablespoons lemon juice

B.
4 level dessertspoons gelatine
125 ml (4 oz.) water

C.
125 gr (4 oz.) copha

D.
Approximately 3 kg (6 lb.) icing sugar

Smaller quantities can be used in proportion. Place ingredients A in saucepan, boil to 110° C (230° F.) (or boil briskly for 4 minutes). Remove from heat and add ingredients B which have been soaking together. When dissolved add C.

Allow to cool a little, then commence adding sieved icing sugar. Continue until mixture is too thick to add any more.

On a table make a well with the remaining icing sugar and pour in the thick mixture. Allow to cool a little more, then knead in icing sugar until the right consistency is attained.

Store in a plastic bag and allow to stand 24 hours before using. When required to cover a cake, knead well again until pliable and able to be rolled out. This mixture keeps well if kept airtight in a plastic bag and stored in a cupboard.

For making moulded flowers, take several tablespoons of the above mixture, before the copha is added, and knead well into sieved icing sugar until the right consistency for modelling. Flower petals can be worked to paper thinness and will set hard.

ROYAL ICING

250 gr ($\frac{1}{2}$ lb.) Icing Sugar
1 teaspoon lemon juice
white of egg
1 teaspoon glucose

Roll the icing sugar well, and add the lemon juice, glucose and white of egg to form a stiff paste ($\frac{1}{2}$ or 1 white of a large egg will be found sufficient). Beat vigorously, and spread on cake with a wet, hot knife.

SOFT ICING

250 gr ($\frac{1}{2}$ lb.) Icing Sugar
1 teaspoon butter
1 tablespoon boiling water
flavouring as desired

Put the sugar in a saucepan, pour boiling water on to the butter, and add to the sugar. Mix over a slow fire till smooth, but do not let boil. Pour over sponge, or cakes to be decorated, and finish off with chopped nuts, coconut, cherries, etc., before the icing sets. Coffee essence makes a nice flavouring added to this icing. The icing sugar must be free from lumps.

VIENNA ICING

2 Tablespoons Butter
4 tablespoons icing sugar
1 dessertspoon sherry or orange juice

Warm butter, add icing sugar and sherry gradually, beating till creamy and fluffy. Can be used through a forcer.

FILLINGS

APPLE CHEESE

500 gr (1 lb.) Apples, stewed to a pulp
30 gr (1 oz.) butter
500 gr (1 lb.) powdered sugar
4 well-beaten eggs
grated rind and juice of 4 small lemons

Mix well all the ingredients except the butter. Melt the butter in a saucepan, add the other ingredients, and stir over a moderate fire till all the butter is thoroughly absorbed. Pour into pots and cover with paper. It keeps fairly well.

CHIFFON PIE FILLINGS

Lemon:

30 gr (1 oz.) Butter
½ cup cold water
½ cup sugar
5 tablespoons sugar
30 gr (1 oz.) plain flour
juice of a large lemon
2 eggs

Put butter in small saucepan and melt. Add flour and cook 3 minutes without browning. Remove from fire and add cold water and juice of lemon. Return to stove and bring to boil, stirring constantly until mixture thickens. Add ½ cup sugar, stir well and allow to cool slightly. Add egg yolks and cook 1 minute. Cool a little and pour into pastry case. Beat egg whites with 5 tablespoons sugar, pile on top of lemon filling and brown lightly in slow oven.

Orange:

Substitute orange for lemon.

Passionfruit:

Use lemon recipe adding ½ cup passionfruit pulp and 2 level teaspoons dissolved gelatine.

CREAM FILLING

1 Cup Milk
90 gr (3 oz.) butter
2 level dessertspoons cornflour
60 gr (2 oz.) sugar

Put the milk into a saucepan to warm, add the cornflour, blended with a little milk, stir until it boils, then stand aside until cold. Beat the butter and sugar to a cream, then add cornflour mixture, and whisk until white.

LEMON BUTTER

250 gr ($\frac{1}{2}$ lb.) Butter
4 eggs
500 gr (1 lb.) sugar
rind of 3 lemons
juice of 4 lemons

Put the butter and sugar in a saucepan, place on fire, and stir until clear. Add 4 yolks, and 2 whites of eggs, well beaten, juice and grated rind of lemons, and stir and cook till like honey.

LEMON CREAM

500 gr (1 lb.) Loaf Sugar (soft sugar will do)
250 gr ($\frac{1}{2}$ lb.) butter
4 eggs (the yolks of 2 others, unbeaten)
juice of 3 lemons

Grate rind of lemons and add with juice to other ingredients. Place all in a large jug, standing in boiling water on stove. Stir until consistency of honey, but do not allow to boil.

LEMON CHEESE

125 gr ($\frac{1}{4}$ lb.) Butter
6 eggs
500 gr (1 lb.) sugar
peel of 2 lemons
juice of 3 lemons

Put butter, sugar, well-beaten eggs (leaving out 2 whites), grated lemon rind, and juice into a pan, and let it simmer over the fire until dissolved, and it looks like honey. Stir all the time.

LEMON CHEESE FOR LEMON CHEESE CAKE

125 gr (4 oz.) Sugar
yolks of 2 eggs
60 gr (2 oz.) butter
white of 1 egg
juice and grated rind of 1 lemon

Beat all ingredients thoroughly together. Place in a saucepan and stir constantly over the fire until it thickens. Let cool, and use.

LEMON FILLING (ECONOMICAL)

500 gr (1 lb.) Sugar
1 egg
2 level tablespoons flour
125 gr (4 oz.) butter
3 lemons
1 breakfast cup water

Put sugar, butter, and water into a saucepan and make hot. Beat the egg and mix in the flour, using enough water to make it into a cream. Grate the rind of the lemons and add them together with the juice to the flour mixture. Pour the hot mixture on, stirring all the time, and boil until it thickens.

LEMON JELLY FILLING

1 lemon (grated rind and juice)
$\frac{3}{4}$ cup sugar
1 cup boiling water
1 tablespoon arrowroot or cornflour

Mix arrowroot to a smooth paste with a little cold water. Add rind and juice of lemon and blend well. Pour on 1 cup boiling water, stirring well. Stir over gentle heat till it thickens and clears. When nearly cold spread between layers of sponge cake.

MOCK CREAM FILLING (No. 1)

$\frac{1}{2}$ Cup Milk
1 teaspoon butter
2 dessertspoons cornflour
$1\frac{1}{2}$ tablespoons icing sugar
vanilla

Boil the milk and cornflour and let get cold. Then beat to a cream the other ingredients, and then beat both mixtures together well. Chopped nuts may be added if liked.

MOCK CREAM FILLING (No. 2)

60 gr (2 oz.) Butter
60 gr (2 oz.) sugar
2 dessertspoons boiling water
2 dessertspoons cold milk

Cream butter and sugar. Add one dessertspoon of boiling water, and beat for a few minutes, then add one dessertspoon of cold milk and beat for five minutes, now add the second dessertspoon of boiling water and beat for five minutes and finally the second dessertspoon of cold milk and beat thoroughly. This makes a delicious cream for tarts or filling for a cake, and can be served with sweets.

MOCK CREAM FILLING (No. 3)

3 Tablespoons Butter
1 tablespoon powdered milk
2 tablespoons cold water
3 tablespoons sugar
2 tablespoons hot water

Beat until light and fluffy. Excellent for small cakes and sponge fillings.

ORANGE FILLING FOR ORANGE CAKE

Grated Rind of $\frac{1}{2}$ an Orange
30 gr (1 oz.) sugar
juice of 1 orange
30 gr (1 oz.) butter
2 eggs

Mix all the ingredients together, put into a saucepan, and stir gently over the fire till the mixture thickens.

PASSIONFRUIT BUTTER

6 Passionfruit (8 if not very juicy)
2 dessertspoons butter
2 eggs
250 gr (½ lb.) sugar

Blend all ingredients together in a jug for 1 minute with a wooden spoon. Stand in a pan of boiling water and cook (stirring) till all the butter is melted. Cook gently another 15 to 20 minutes, stirring now and then. Do not let it boil. Seal down in small jars.

PASSIONFRUIT FILLING

1 Egg White
juice of 2 or 3 passionfruit
375 gr (¾ lb.) icing sugar

Beat the white of egg till stiff, and then add the icing sugar and the fruit juice.

WHEATMEAL COOKERY

ALL BRAN GINGER CAKE WITH SPICE TOPPING

¾ Cup Kellogg's All Bran
½ cup treacle or golden syrup
¼ cup butter or other shortening
½ level teaspoon bi-carbonate soda
1½ teaspoons ground ginger
½ cup brown sugar
½ cup milk or hot water
1½ cups sifted flour
1 egg
½ teaspoon cinnamon
pinch salt

Moisten All Bran with milk or water. Cream butter and sugar, add beaten egg, syrup, All Bran mixture, sifted flour, salt, soda, ginger, cinnamon. Mix evenly. Bake in a buttered cake tin 200 mm x 200 mm (8 in. x 8 in.) in a moderate oven 30 to 40 minutes. Lift out, spread surface with butter, sprinkle with 1 teaspoon cinnamon and 1 tablespoon icing sugar mixed together.

BRAN BISCUITS (No. 1)

1¼ Cups Self-raising Flour
125 gr (¼ lb.) butter
1 egg
2 cups bran
½ cup sugar
milk to mix

Cream butter and sugar, add egg, and beat well. Add flour and bran, and mix in a little milk. Mix and knead on a board. Roll out, cut into rounds or rectangles, and bake in a moderate oven until a light brown.

BRAN BISCUITS (No. 2)

2 Cups Bran
1 cup flour
1 teaspoon baking powder
1 teaspoon salt
2 cups wholemeal
125 gr (¼ lb.) butter or good dripping
1 egg
cold water to mix

Sift flour, baking powder, and salt. Add wholemeal and bran. Rub in butter, and mix with beaten egg and water to make a stiff biscuit dough. Roll thin, cut in squares, and bake in a moderate oven till light brown, dry, and crisp.

BRAN CAKES

60 gr (2 oz.) Bran
60 gr (2 oz.) sugar
1 teaspoon carbonate soda
1 breakfast cup flour
185 gr (6 oz.) butter
125 ml (1 gill) milk

Rub the butter into the flour and bran, add the sugar, warm the milk slightly, add the soda to the milk, then mix with dry ingredients. Roll out on a floured board to about 6 mm (¼ in.) in thickness. Cut into rounds. Bake in a slow oven about 20 minutes.

BRAN LOAF

2 Cups Bran
3 tablespoons brown sugar
1 cup milk
1 beaten egg
2 tablespoons melted butter
1 teaspoon carbonate soda
½ cup treacle
1 teaspoon salt
1 cup plain flour
¾ cup raisins
½ teaspoon cream of tartar

Mix butter, sugar, egg, milk, salt, add soda in treacle, then dry ingredients. Mix well, and bake in a flat tin in a moderate oven for 45 minutes.

BRAN RAISIN LOAF

1 Cup Bran
1½ cups self-raising flour
1 tablespoon melted butter
¼ cup sugar
1 handful sultanas or raisins
1½ cups milk
a pinch of salt

Mix all together and bake in a moderate oven.

BRAN SCONES

1 Cup Bran
1 teaspoon castor or icing sugar
1 cup self-raising flour
2 tablespoons cream or melted butter
milk to mix

Mix all to a soft dough with the milk. Cut in rounds and bake for 8 to 10 minutes in a hot oven.

BROWN BUNS

155 gr (5 oz.) Butter
1 egg
4 tablespoons boiling water
2 cups wholemeal
1 cup sultanas
1 cup brown sugar
1 dessertspoon treacle
1 teaspoon carbonate soda
1 cup dates
1 cup well-chopped almonds
½ teaspoon cinnamon

Cream together the butter and sugar, and add the well-beaten egg, and then the treacle dissolved in boiling water, with the soda. Add the wholemeal, dates, sultanas, almonds, and cinnamon. Mix well, and bake in a slow oven.

BROWN SCONES

90 gr (3 oz.) Butter
1 dessertspoon castor sugar
2 teaspoons baking powder
625 gr (1¼ lb.) wholemeal flour
½ teaspoon salt
milk to mix

Rub the butter into the wholemeal, add sugar, salt, baking powder, and mix into a light dough with the milk. Roll out, cut into scone-shaped pieces, brush over with milk, and bake in a moderate oven.

Tins used for baking wholemeal loaves or bread must be well greased before filling.

BROWN LOAF

- 1 Cup Self-raising Flour
- 1 teaspoon cream of tartar
- 3 teaspoons treacle
- 1 cup wheatmeal or bran
- ½ teaspoon carbonate soda
- a little milk

Mix flour, bran, cream of tartar, and soda. Dissolve treacle in milk, and add to flour to form a mixture not too stiff. Bake about ½ an hour in greased tins with lid on.

HEALTH LOAF

- 1 Cup Wheatmeal (fine)
- 1 cup flour
- 2 teaspoons cream of tartar
- 1 tablespoon honey
- 1 cup cooking bran
- 1 teaspoon salt
- 1 teaspoon carbonate soda
- small cup warmed milk

Mix together wheatmeal, bran, flour, salt, cream of tartar, and soda. Blend well, and make into a dough with the honey, mixed through the warm milk. Bake in a nut loaf tin for ¾ hour.

HONEY KISSES

- 90 gr (3 oz.) Butter
- 30 gr (1 oz.) sugar
- 1 egg
- a pinch of salt
- 90 gr (3 oz.) wholemeal self-raising flour
- 90 gr (3 oz.) cornflour
- 1 dessertspoon water

Beat butter and sugar together, add beaten egg, and then other ingredients. Put in small teaspoon heaps, and bake for 6 minutes in a moderate oven. Stick together with honey, and sprinkle with icing sugar.

HONEY SPONGE

- 1 Tablespoon Butter
- 1 egg
- 1 cup wheatmeal
- 1 teaspoon cream of tartar
- 1 cup honey
- ½ cup milk
- ½ teaspoon carbonate soda
- 1 dessertspoon ground ginger
- a few grains of salt

Cream the butter and honey. Beat the egg well, and add the milk slowly. Stir in the sifted meal, soda, ginger, and cream of tartar, and a few grains of salt. Pour into a greased tin and bake for 15 minutes. Cut in halves and fold together with mock or fresh cream.

LUNCHEON CAKE

- 500 gr (1 lb.) Self-raising Flour
- 250 gr (½ lb.) butter or good dripping
- 185 gr (6 oz.) currants
- 15 gr (½ oz.) mixed spice
- 250 gr (½ lb.) wholemeal
- 250 gr (½ lb.) sugar
- 185 gr (6 oz.) sultanas
- 2 eggs
- 250 ml (2 gills) milk

Rub the shortening into the flour, together with sugar and spice. Add fruit, and lastly the well-beaten eggs and the milk. Bake in a moderate oven until firm.

MELTING MOMENTS

- 250 gr (8 oz.) Butter
- 155 gr (5 oz.) wholemeal flour
- 60 ml (2 oz.) honey
- 125 gr (4 oz.) cornflour

Beat butter and honey, add flour and cornflour. Drop portions on cold tray and bake in a slow oven. When cooked place aside to cool, then put together with honey between.

NUT CAKE

- 1 Teacup Flour
- ½ teacup butter
- 1 teaspoon baking powder
- ½ cup sugar
- 2 teacups wheatmeal
- ½ teacup milk
- 3 eggs
- ½ cup chopped walnuts
- ½ cup chopped raisins

Cream the butter and sugar, and add the eggs, then milk, walnuts, and raisins. Add wheatmeal and flour with baking powder sifted through. Bake on a flat tin on greased paper, for about 1 hour in a moderate oven. When cool, make an icing with 60 gr (2 oz.) butter and 155 gr (5 oz.) icing sugar, flavoured with almond and vanilla, and ice the cake. Sprinkle chopped walnuts over icing and press lightly down.

WALNUT BROWNIES

- 125 gr (¼ lb.) Butter
- 1 cup brown sugar
- 4 teaspoons cocoa
- 1 cup wholemeal flour
- 1 egg
- ½ cup chopped walnuts

Cream butter and sugar, add egg, then add other ingredients. Press out about 6 mm (¼ in.) thick on a greased tray, and bake in a moderate oven for 20 minutes. Cut into fingers whilst hot.

WALNUT AND WHOLEMEAL BRITTLES

- 2 Cups Wholemeal (coarse)
- 1 cup fine ground wholemeal
- 1 cup sugar
- 2 tablespoons golden syrup
- 1 cup desiccated coconut
- ½ cup chopped walnuts
- ½ cup good dripping
- 3 tablespoons water
- 1 teaspoon carbonate soda

Put on the fire the dripping, syrup, and water, bring to the boil, and quickly add the soda. Mix with dry ingredients, pinch into small pieces, and put on cold, floured tray in a warm oven. Do not have the oven too hot, as they burn easily. Cook 15 minutes.

WHEATEN LOAF

- 3 Cups Wheatmeal
- 1 teaspoon carbonate soda
- 2 heaped tablespoons golden syrup
- 1 cup self-raising flour
- a pinch of salt
- 2 small teaspoons cream of tartar
- milk

Mix all together, and add sufficient milk to make a fairly stiff dough. Bake in nut or loaf tins in a hot oven for ½ hour.

WHEATMEAL APPLE FRITTERS

1 Cup Wheatmeal	**½ cup plain flour**
1 tablespoon sugar	**1 small teaspoon cream tartar**
½ teaspoon carbonate soda	**1 egg**
milk	**apples**

Mix flour, wheatmeal, and sugar. Add well-beaten egg, and enough milk to make a stiff batter. Slice peeled and cored apples. Dip into batter, and fry in deep fat. Before serving, dust with icing sugar.

WHEATMEAL BISCUITS (No. 1)

1 Cup fairly coarse Wholemeal	**1 cup fine wholemeal**
1 level teaspoon carbonate soda	**2 level teaspoons cream of tartar**
125 gr (4 oz.) butter	**½ cup sugar**
2 eggs	**2 tablespoons milk**

Cream butter and sugar, add beaten eggs, milk, and flour, with cream of tartar and soda added. If dough is not firm enough, add more flour. Turn on to a floured board, roll out thinly, and cut into rounds. Bake in a moderate oven from 15 to 20 minutes.

WHEATMEAL BISCUITS (No. 2)

3 Cups Wheatmeal	**3 cups self-raising flour**
250 gr (½ lb.) butter	**2 large cups sugar**
2 or 3 eggs	**milk or water to mix**

Melt butter and beat in the sugar, then the eggs one at a time. Add flour, and milk or water to mix to a stiff dough. Put in teaspoonfuls on a greased oven tray, and bake a nice brown in a good oven. Fruit may be added if liked. The eggs may be omitted.

WHEATMEAL BISCUITS (No. 3)

½ Cup Butter	**½ cup milk**
1 cup sugar	**1 egg**
2 teaspoons cream of tartar	**plain flour**
1 teaspoon carbonate soda	**wheaten flour**

Beat butter and sugar, add egg, then cream of tartar, and soda dissolved in milk. Add flour and wheaten flour, half and half to make a stiff dough. Roll out, stamp in rounds, and bake.

WHEATMEAL PUDDING

1 Cup Wheatmeal
1 cup sugar
2 tablespoons treacle
1 cup fruit (dates, etc.)
1 cup self-raising flour
1 teaspoon cinnamon
90 gr (3 oz.) dripping or butter
1 egg
milk to mix

Mix dry ingredients. Melt dripping and treacle in a saucepan. Beat egg, and mix all together. Steam for 3 hours.

WHOLEMEAL CHRISTMAS CAKE

500 gr (1 lb.) Butter
500 gr (1 lb.) each sultanas, currants, raisins
250 gr (½ lb.) almonds (shelled)
juice of 1 orange or lemon (about 2 tablespoons juice)
2 teaspoons baking powder
8 or 9 eggs according to size
1 teaspoon cinnamon
500 gr (1 lb.) brown sugar
625 gr (1¼ lb.) fine wholemeal flour
125 gr (¼ lb.) each lemon peel, cherries, figs
2 tablespoons treacle
½ teaspoon salt (scant)
¼ grated nutmeg
½ teaspoon mixed spice

Cream the butter and sugar, beat the eggs and add gradually. Sift the flour, baking powder and spices; add alternately to the mixture with spoonful of fruit. Add the fruit juice last. Bake in a tin (lined with two or three layers of paper), in a moderate oven 2 to 2½ hours. This cake improves with keeping.

WHOLEMEAL COCONUT GINGER GEMS

½ Cup Butter
2 eggs
1 breakfast cup coconut
½ teaspoon cinnamon
¼ cup tepid milk
¼ cup sugar
1 breakfast cup wholemeal
1 teaspoon ginger
½ cup golden syrup
½ teaspoon carbonate soda

Rub butter into the flour, and add all dry ingredients, except soda, which should be dissolved in milk and added last. Add the other ingredients, then the dissolved soda. Have gem rings hot, so that the butter boils when you butter them. Cook a few minutes. Finest wholemeal must be used.

WHOLEMEAL DATE LOAF

2 Cups Wholemeal Self-raising Flour
¾ cup sugar
1 cup chopped dates
1 egg
1 tablespoon butter
½ teaspoon salt
1 small teaspoon cinnamon
1 cup milk

Place dry ingredients in a mixing bowl, and rub butter through, then add sugar, and dates, and beat egg well, and add to milk. Pour on dry ingredients, and mix thoroughly to a firm consistency. Bake in loaf tin for 1 hour in a moderate oven, or divide mixture and bake in small tins for ¾ hour.

WHOLEMEAL LOAF

1 Cup Self-raising Flour
1 tablespoon sugar
1 pinch carbonate soda
1 egg
1 cup wholemeal
1 tablespoon treacle
1 cup milk
1 tablespoon butter

Mix flour, wholemeal, soda, sugar, and butter together. Beat egg, and add milk, then treacle, and mix well. Bake in tins with lid on for 1 hour, in a moderate oven.

BREAD, BUNS, RAISED CAKES AND YEAST

ACID YEAST

1 Medium Sized Potato
2 dessertspoons flour
2½ dessertspoons sugar
1½ cups warm water
enough tartaric acid to cover 5c piece

Grate the potato, and mix it with the other ingredients. Bottle in an old yeast bottle, cork tightly, and tie. This will be ready for use in about 12 hours.

HOPLESS YEAST AND BREAD

Yeast:

1 Good Sized Potato
flour
2 dessertspoons sugar
salt

Cut potato into small pieces, and boil without salt. When cooked, pour off potato water into a jug, and mash potato well, adding sugar. Beat well, and add to potato water. Put aside to cool, and when cool, add enough flour to thicken to consistency of good separated cream, and add to old yeast. Add 2 teaspoons salt to old yeast immediately after it has worked a second time.

Bread:

2 Sifters of Flour
500 ml (1 pint) of yeast
2 teaspoons salt
750 ml (1½ pints) tepid water

Sift the salt into the flour, and mix well. Make a cavity in the flour, add yeast and water, and knead well. Keep warm till risen twice its size (about 3½ to 4 hours). Knead again, and make into loaves. Allow to rise to tops of tins. Put into a hot oven, allowing the heat of fire to slowly decrease. Cook 1 hour.

LEMON YEAST

3 Tablespoons Flour
2 tablespoons lemon juice
1 tablespoon sugar
½ large cup warm water

Beat all well together, bottle, and cork.

YEAST (No. 1)

1 Small Dessertspoon Hops
water
1 small potato
a piece of dough
sugar

Put the hops into a basin or billy can (enamel), and pour 1 litre (1 quart) of boiling water on them. Boil the potato, put it and the water it was boiled in on to the hops, let these cool, and then mix the dough in, and add a tablespoon of sugar. Leave with cover over till morning, strain, and add hot water to yeast till lukewarm. This quantity will be sufficient for 5 kg (10 lb.) of flour. The dough is a piece kept from previous batch of bread.

YEAST (No. 2)

750 ml (1½ pints) Water
2 heaped tablespoons sugar
¾ cup old yeast
½ cup hops
2 heaped tablespoons salt
½ cup flour

Boil together the water, hops, sugar, and salt, and then let simmer for 20 minutes. Let stand till warm, strain into earthenware jar, and then add old yeast mixed with flour. Mix well and let stand overnight in a warm place till yeast looks bubbly. This makes sufficient for 3 bakings.

YEAST AND BREAD

1 Medium Sized Potato
about 375 gr (¾ lb.) flour (for sponge)
3 kg (6 lb.) flour
750 ml (1½ pints) water
1¼ cups yeast
a handful of sugar and salt

Boil the potato in the water till quite soft, then mash, and when lukewarm, mix in with the hand the flour, and add the yeast. (Stir yeast in earthenware jar well before taking out yeast for sponge.) Mix well, put lid on saucepan, cover with a piece of blanket, and put in a warm place overnight. By morning it should be risen right up. Sift the flour with the sugar and salt, make a well in the centre, and pour in sponge, to which you have added some warm water, and add more warm water as you require it to mix the bread. Knead for 15 minutes and then leave to rise till quite double its size. When risen, turn bread out on tables, and cut into loaves. Knead well and put loaves into a warmed, greased tin to rise for 1 hour, then bake 1 hour in a good oven.

GERMAN COFFEE CAKE

500 gr (1 lb.) Flour
3 eggs
1 cup milk
¼ teaspoon salt
1 cup yeast
a little ground mace
125 gr (¼ lb.) sugar
125 gr (¼ lb.) butter
¼ teaspoon cinnamon
a few currants and sultanas
essence lemon

Mix the flour, sugar, cinnamon, salt and mace together then add melted butter, milk (slightly warm) the essence and well-beaten eggs. Add the fruit (cleaned and dry) and lastly, the yeast. Knead well and put away to rise. When risen to double the size, roll out to about 13 mm (½ in.) thick on a greased baking sheet and let rise again. When well risen, brush over with melted butter, and put on the following: 250 gr (½ lb.) flour, 125 gr (¼ lb.) sugar, 125 gr (¼ lb.) butter, ½ teaspoon cinnamon, a little mace. Rub all together with the hands till quite crumbly. Sprinkle thickly on the cake and bake for 20 minutes in a good oven.

LIGHT BUNS

2 Tablespoons Currants
2 tablespoons sugar
500 gr (1 lb.) flour
a little lemon peel if liked
2 tablespoons butter
3 tablespoons yeast
about 2 cups milk
a pinch of salt

Put currants, sugar, and butter into a saucepan, add the milk, and set at the side of stove until warm enough to melt the butter (do not allow to get hot). Sift the flour into a vessel, make a well in the centre, pour in the yeast, and then add the salt and peel. Beat in the warm milk, previously stirred to dissolve the sugar. Set to rise overnight, in a warm place. Early next morning have two sandwich tins greased. Make dough into small buns. It will be soft, but do not use much extra flour. 7 will fit into a tin, 6 around the sides, and 1 in the middle. Bake in a moderate oven for 20 minutes. For glazing buns, put into a cup, 1 dessertspoon of sugar and 2 tablespoons milk. Have it very hot and brush over the buns as soon as they are cooked. ½ teaspoon of essence of lemon or ½ a grated nutmeg is an improvement added to the dough.

MALT BREAD

1 Cup Bran
6 cups plain flour
½ cup yeast
2 tablespoons treacle
1 cup wholemeal
½ handful salt
warm water
1 tablespoon malt
1 cup potato water

Make a sponge by mixing together with the warm water, the bran, wholemeal, 2 cups plain flour, salt, and yeast, and let rise all night in a warm place. Next morning, add 3 to 4 cups flour, the treacle, and the malt, all dissolved in the potato water. Knead well, and form into loaves, let rise, and then bake for 1 hour in a moderate oven.

RAISED BREAD CAKE

60 gr (2 oz.) Sugar
250 gr ($\frac{1}{2}$ lb.) currants
60 gr (2 oz.) butter
1 cup new milk
bread dough sufficient for a 1 kg (2 lb.) loaf

Take the risen bread dough. Knead well into it the sugar and currants, warm the butter in the milk, and knead well into the dough. Form into a loaf (a little extra flour may be required). Place in a greased tin, allow to rise to double its size, and then bake in a good oven.

WHOLEMEAL YEAST BREAD

7 Large Cups Wholemeal
1 tablespoon butter or dripping
1 dessertspoon sugar
1 large cup potato water
$\frac{1}{2}$ cup yeast
1 tablespoon treacle or golden syrup
salt to taste
water or milk to mix

Put wholemeal in a basin, place salt and sugar in the centre, and then yeast and butter, treacle, and potato water, which have been warmed together. Mix and add enough warm water or warm milk to make a moist dough. Bake longer than white bread.

DRI-BALM OR COMPRESSED YEAST BREAD

Compressed Yeast:

1 Dessertspoon Yeast
1 dessertspoon salt
6 cups flour
1 dessertspoon sugar
500 ml (1 pint) tepid water (use cold in hot weather)

Cream yeast and sugar and add 1 cup water. Leave 5 minutes till yeast works, then add 1 cup flour and leave to rise to top of basin, about 30 minutes. Sift flour and salt into large bowl and make well in centre. Turn in yeast mixture, add remaining water and knead to a smooth elastic dough, about 10 minutes. Leave to rise in warm place covered with clean cloth. In hot weather, wring cloth out in water. When doubled in bulk (about 2 hours) knead into 2 loaves and put into well-greased tins and leave to rise till doubled in bulk again, and up to top of tin. Bake in hot oven 1 hour.

Dri-balm Yeast:

Use same proportions, using 1 heaped dessertspoon dri-balm. Leave yeast, sugar and water to work until it froths before adding flour.

Both these recipes can be made without mixing sponge first, but should be knocked back once before being kneaded into loaves. The sponge is a "tester" for the yeast. Both dri-balm and compressed yeast should be kept in refrigerator when opened.

YEAST BUNS (No. 1)

1 Heaped Dessertspoon Dri-Balm
1 dessertspoon sugar
1 scant cup sugar
1 cup water
juice of lemon
1 teaspoon salt
1 cup lukewarm water
4 cups flour
1 tablespoon butter
1 egg
$\frac{1}{2}$ cup mixed fruit
1 teaspoon allspice

Take dri-balm, lukewarm water, and 1 dessertspoon sugar and stir well. Let stand 10 minutes (till it froths). Add 1 cup flour and let stand till it doubles in bulk. While this is rising put the cup of sugar, butter and 1 cup water into saucepan and melt together. Cool and add beaten egg and juice of lemon. Add 3 cups flour, mixed fruit, allspice and salt. Stir in yeast sponge and mix to a soft dough. Let rise until doubled in bulk, about 2 hours. Knead into buns and put on well-greased tray and leave to rise double size. Bake in hot oven 20 minutes. Glaze tops with boiled sugar and water.

YEAST BUNS (No. 2)

500 gr (1 lb.) Flour
60 gr (2 oz.) butter
$1\frac{1}{2}$ cups milk
250 gr ($\frac{1}{2}$ lb.) mixed fruit
1 teaspoon salt
1 level tablespoon compressed yeast
1 egg
$\frac{1}{2}$ cup sugar
1 teaspoon spice

Cream yeast with 1 teaspoon sugar. Melt butter in milk and add beaten egg. Add warmed liquid to yeast, stir in flour sifted with spices and salt. Add sugar and beat till smooth. Allow to rise until doubled in bulk. Knead on floured board and make into 18 buns. Leave to rise on well-greased tray until double in size. Bake 20 minutes in hot oven and glaze with boiled sugar and water.

PEANUT BUTTER BREAD

1 Cup Milk
1 tablespoon sugar
$\frac{2}{3}$ cup peanut butter
$\frac{1}{4}$ cup lukewarm water
$\frac{3}{4}$ cup boiling water
1 teaspoon salt
45 gr ($1\frac{1}{2}$ oz.) compressed yeast
$5\frac{1}{2}$-6 cups flour

Mix together sugar, salt and peanut butter, milk and boiling water. Cool to lukewarm. Soften yeast in lukewarm water and add. Stir in flour enough to make it kneadable. Turn on to floured board and knead until smooth (about 8-10 minutes). Leave to rise until double in bulk. Knead into two loaves and leave until double in size. Bake in hot oven 20 minutes, reduce heat to moderate and bake a further 30 minutes.

POTATO BREAD

6 Cups Flour
$\frac{1}{2}$ cup lukewarm water
30 gr (1 oz.) yeast (compressed)
$1\frac{1}{2}$ cups cooked potato
1 egg
$\frac{1}{2}$ cup butter
1 teaspoon salt
1 cup cream
$\frac{1}{4}$ cup raisins

Dissolve yeast in lukewarm water and let it stand 10 minutes. Put sieved flour and salt into basin and rub in butter, add mashed potatoes, raisins and cream and yeast mixture. Knead until smooth and leave to rise until double in bulk. Knead into loaves and put into well-greased tins. Leave to rise until double in bulk and bake 10 minutes in hot oven, reducing heat to moderate for another 50 minutes.

NEVER FAIL WHOLEMEAL BREAD

Measure three cups warm water—pour one cup over yeast and sugar which has been crumbled together, and let work for ten minutes—it rises and bubbles. Sift flour together and make a well in flour and pour in yeast mixture and remaining warm water (salt has been added to sifted flour). Mix. Knead.

Have prepared well greased orange cake tins—make into loaves or rolls—cover with teatowel in warm place and leave 20 minutes. Bake in hot oven for 20 minutes. Turn out.

500 gr (1 lb.) wholemeal flour
500 gr (1 lb.) white flour
2 dessertspoons salt (may be warmed in oven in cold weather)
60 gr (2 oz.) compressed yeast
2 teaspoons sugar or honey

Note: When wishing to substitute compressed yeast for any other yeast, the equivalent is 30 gr (1 oz.) compressed yeast to each 500 gr (1 lb.) of flour included in the recipe.

HERE AND THERE

AMERICA

AMERICAN CHICKEN CHOP SUEY

2 Cups Cold Cooked Chicken
1½ cups boiled rice
⅛th teaspoon pepper
2 tablespoons flour
1 cup boiled celery
1 teaspoon salt
1 tablespoon butter or fat
1½ cups chicken stock

Cut chicken and celery in thin strips. Mix them with rice, salt and pepper. Melt butter and make into smooth paste with flour. Add stock slowly, stirring constantly. Bring to boil, continuing stirring. Add the chicken and rice mixture and heat thoroughly. A cup of sauteed mushrooms will add to this dish. Thin noodles, sauteed until crisp in a little fat, make an appropriate addition. Arrange them on top of mixture.

Chicken noodle soup is a good substitute for stock and also for noodles.

AMERICAN HAMBURGERS

375 gr (¾ lb.) Minced Beef
1 teaspoon salt
cream or milk to moisten
125 gr (¼ lb.) minced pork
2 tablespoons Worcestershire sauce or pickles
¼ teaspoon pepper
½ cup finely minced onion

Mix minced meat with seasoning and cream. Press into small flat cakes. Put two together with a filling made from onions mixed with sauce or pickles. Press edges together firmly. Brown on both sides on very hot skillet, then reduce heat and turn meat often till cooked.

AMERICAN RICE (4-6 serves)

1½ Cups Rice
500 gr (1 lb.) mince
1 tin tomato soup
sippets of toast
2 diced onions
1 tin green peas
1 cup grated cheese

Boil rice in plenty of water till tender, then wash thoroughly and drain. Fry diced onions and mince. Add rice, green peas, tomato soup and grated cheese. Stir well and serve with sippets of toast.

BEETROOT (Hot, with Pink Sauce)

500 gr (1 lb.) Beetroot
30 gr (1 oz.) flour
pepper and salt
30 gr (1 oz.) butter
250 ml ($\frac{1}{2}$ pint) milk

Peel beetroot and cut into cubes. Cook in very little water, lightly salted until tender. Melt butter in another saucepan, stir in flour, add liquid from cooked beetroot, then add milk, stirring until thick. Check seasoning. Serve beetroot hot with pink sauce poured over it.

CALIFORNIA PLUM PUDDING

$\frac{1}{4}$ Cup Butter
1 egg
1 teaspoon soda
$\frac{1}{2}$ teaspoon salt
$\frac{1}{2}$ cup raisins
$\frac{1}{4}$ cup peel
$\frac{1}{4}$ cup currants
$1\frac{1}{2}$ cups flour
1 cup brown sugar
1 cup crushed tinned pineapple
$\frac{1}{4}$ teaspoon each ground cloves, cinnamon and nutmeg
$\frac{1}{2}$ cup dates
$\frac{1}{2}$ cup nuts

Cream butter and brown sugar and add egg. Heat crushed pineapple and add soda, ground cloves, cinnamon, nutmeg and salt. Chop raisins and dates, and add peel, nuts and currants. Mix fruit with flour and add alternately with pineapple to creamed mixture and mix well. Steam 3 hours in well-greased basin.

HAWAIIAN CURRY

$1\frac{1}{2}$ kg (3 lb.) Lean Diced Meat
1 cup chopped onion
salt and pepper
$1\frac{1}{2}$ tablespoons curry
2 tablespoons lemon juice
$\frac{1}{4}$ cup shortening
$\frac{1}{2}$ cup shredded pineapple
$1\frac{1}{2}$ cups coconut
$\frac{1}{2}$ cup diced apple
2 cups rice

Boil coconut in 2 cups of water and strain. Fry onions lightly, add meat, diced apple and curry and cook till meat is well browned. Stir in coconut water and simmer 2 hours. Stir in lemon juice and pineapple. Boil rice in salted water and serve curry ringed with rice.

SAVOURY RELISH

1 Small Tin Salmon
2 tablespoons margarine (rounded)
500 ml (1 pint) milk
1 small tin sweetcorn kernels
2 tablespoons plain flour (heaped)
grated cheese
1 small tin peas
pepper and salt

Melt margarine, add flour, mixing to smooth paste. Add milk and bring to boil. Add little grated cheese. Add sweetcorn, peas and shredded salmon. If sauce is thin leave out liquid from salmon. Place in greased fire-proof dish. Sprinkle with bread-crumbs and grated cheese and dot with margarine. Bake 20 minutes in moderate oven. Serve hot with fingers of buttered toast.

SAVOURY SPREAD

1 Bottle Cream Cheese
2 cloves crushed garlic
few drops anchovy sauce
1 small bottle horseradish sauce
mayonnaise
½ cup cream
pepper and salt to taste

Mix all together with mayonnaise and serve in small bowl with biscuits on platter.

WALDORF SALAD

1 Tart Apple
mayonnaise
lettuce

Dice apple and crisp white lettuce. Take equal portions of both and mix with plenty of mayonnaise.

ARABIA

ARABIAN BAKED APPLES (SWEET)

4 Red Apples
2 tablespoons water
1 dessertspoon lemon juice
3 tablespoons sugar
4 marshmallows
¾ cup chopped dates
1 teaspoon butter
2 tablespoons chopped peanuts
½ cup water

Slit skin around centre of each apple and peel off skin above the slit. Brush peeled portion with a little lemon juice. Remove cores. Put dates in saucepan with 2 tablespoons water, butter and lemon juice. Cook on low heat till soft, beat till smooth and add peanuts. Fill core cavity and put apples in a dish with sugar and ½ cup water. Bake till tender, basting frequently. When cooked, place marshmallow on top, leave a few minutes to melt and then serve.

CHERVAH

1 Neck Mutton
500 gr (1 lb.) onions
pepper and salt
500 gr (1 lb.) tomatoes
1 small handful chopped mint
spaghetti

Trim neck of mutton, cut off fat, slash the meat. Cut up tomatoes, onions and mint. Place all together with salt in a minimum of water and simmer until flesh falls from bone (2½ hours). Lift bone from saucepan. Boil spaghetti and add to above and serve promptly (green peas make an excellent addition). Thicken if desired.

AUSTRIA

AUSTRIAN FISH FILLETS

4 Fish Fillets (schnapper, bream or king fish)
2 tablespoons stale breadcrumbs
2 tablespoons chopped parsley
2 tablespoons melted margarine
¼ cup wine and water
2 tablespoons Worcestershire sauce
2 tablespoons chopped pickles
2 tablespoons chopped onion
1 cup stoned chopped prunes
½ teaspoon salt, pepper
sliced lemon

Place fish in greased ovenproof dish and sprinkle with salt and pepper. Mix breadcrumbs, sauce, pickles, parsley, onion, prunes and margarine. Blend with wine and water and spread over fish. Bake uncovered in hot oven. To be eaten with sliced lemon.

VIENNESE FINGERS

125 gr (4 oz.) Butter
30 gr (1 oz.) icing sugar
½ teaspoon vanilla
pinch salt
125 gr (4 oz.) plain flour

Sift flour and icing sugar. Cream butter well, add dry ingredients and vanilla. Pipe on to greased tray with star pipe in finger lengths. Bake in moderate oven 20-25 minutes. When cool, sandwich with chocolate butter icing and dip one end in warm melted chocolate.

VIENNESE PINEAPPLE CAKE

1½ Cups Self-raising Flour
¾ cup crushed or grated pineapple
2 eggs
2 tablespoons butter
¾ cup sugar
vanilla
1 cup chopped nuts

Beat butter with sugar till creamy. Add vanilla essence and beaten egg yolks and stir in sifted flour. Put into two well-greased sandwich tins and chill. Beat egg whites stiffly with 2 tablespoons sugar and spread on cake mixture. Press chopped nuts and pineapple into meringue and bake in slow oven 30-35 minutes. Decorate with whipped cream if desired.

BELGIUM

BELGIAN PUDDING

250 gr (½ lb.) Prunes
250 gr (½ lb.) flour
60 gr (2 oz.) mixed peel
½ teaspoon spice
pinch of salt
250 gr (½ lb.) currants
90 gr (3 oz.) suet
½ teaspoon carb. soda
1 egg
little milk

Scald prunes and stone. Chop suet finely and mix dry ingredients together. Dissolve soda in warm milk, add beaten egg and blend into dry ingredients. Pour into well-greased mould and steam 4 hours.

BELGIAN SHORTCAKE

1 Cup Self-raising Flour
60 gr (2 oz.) custard powder
1 egg
2 tablespoons cherries
½ cup sugar
125 gr (4 oz.) shortening
2 tablespoons peanuts

Cream shortening and sugar, add egg. Sift flour and custard powder and blend in. Add nuts and cherries. Press into greased shallow tin. Sprinkle top with more chopped nuts and cherries and bake in slow oven until pale brown—about 20 minutes.

BELGIAN STEW

500 gr (1 lb.) Breast of Veal
dripping
1 teaspoon vinegar
2 dessertspoons grated cheese
2 small onions
6 potatoes
2 dessertspoons flour
seasoning

Cut meat into small squares, roll in flour and fry in boiling fat to which vinegar has been added. Drain off fat, add 250 ml (½ pint) water and simmer for 45 minutes. Peel potatoes and chop onions and add. Simmer another 45 minutes. Just before serving add seasoning, sprinkle with grated cheese and brown in hot oven for 3 minutes.

BRAZIL

BRAZILIAN ICED CHOCOLATE (Beverage)

60 gr (2 oz.) Unsweetened Chocolate
3 dessertspoons sugar
3 cups milk
cinnamon
1 cup freshly made strong coffee
pinch salt
cracked ice
whipped cream

Add grated chocolate to hot coffee and stir over low heat till melted. Add sugar and salt and cook for 4 minutes, stirring constantly. Add milk. Chill and pour into glasses containing cracked ice. Top with cream and dust with cinnamon.

CHINA

DARN FAR LONG

125 gr (¼ lb.) Lean Pork
250 gr (½ lb.) tomatoes
750 ml (1½ pints) stock
spring onions
½ cup shelled peas
2 eggs
1 dessertspoon oil or fat
salt and pepper

Mince the meat finely and fry in smoking hot oil, stirring until mince falls apart easily. Add stock and peas and simmer for 10 minutes. Cut tomatoes into small chunks, add and bring to the boil and boil 2 minutes. Beat eggs lightly, add to soup and stir well. Add salt and pepper to taste and serve sprinkled with chopped spring onions.

DIM SIMS

500 gr (1 lb.) Pork
250 gr ($\frac{1}{2}$ lb.) cooked mashed cabbage
$\frac{1}{2}$ teaspoon pepper
90 gr (3 oz.) finely minced shallots
2 cups plain flour
125 gr (4 oz.) peeled cooked prawns
1 egg
2 tablespoons cornflour
1 teaspoon salt
1 egg

Mince the pork and mash the cabbage to a paste and add egg, pepper, salt, shallots and cornflour to make a stiff paste. Make pastry of 2 cups plain flour and egg and enough water to make a pliable dough. Roll out to paper thinness and cut into 8 cm (3 in.) squares. Place a small spoonful of pork mixture on each square, roll up and seal and put a prawn on each. Put into a dish or basin and put over another dish of water and steam 25-30 minutes.

FRIED RICE

$\frac{1}{2}$ Cup Oil
3 slices bacon diced finely (with rind removed)
bunch eschalots
4 cups boiling water
2 eggs
2 cups dry rice
500 gr (1 lb.) prawns
salt to taste

Heat oil, add dry rice, bacon and eschalot (white portion) and stir till evenly browned. Continue to add small quantity of boiling water, stirring constantly, until all water is absorbed. Put lid on pan and simmer for 10 minutes, stirring occasionally. Add prawns, chopped greens from eschalots and cook another 5 minutes, stirring continually. Take pan from stove and leave to stand at least 2 hours. Reheat to serve. Scramble 2 eggs and add to rice when ready to serve. Extra pork may be used instead of prawns.

DENMARK

DANISH PATTIES (with Onion)

750 gr ($1\frac{1}{2}$ lb.) Minced Steak
3 onions
$\frac{3}{4}$ cup soft white breadcrumbs
1 teaspoon horseradish
6 bacon rashers
parsley
2 tablespoons shortening
1 tablespoon chopped parsley
1 egg
tomato wedges
seasoning to taste

Peel onions, cut into thick slices and arrange in casserole. Pour over melted shortening and season to taste. Combine steak, breadcrumbs, parsley, horseradish and seasoning and bind with egg. Shape into 6 cakes and wrap each in a rasher of bacon and put on top of onions. Cover and bake 35-40 minutes. Serve garnished with tomato wedges and parsley.

EGYPT

EGYPTIAN SPONGE

1 Cup Flour
1 tablespoon melted butter
2 eggs
1 tablespoon cinnamon
1 cup sugar
6 tablespoons warm milk
1 teaspoon carb. soda
2 teaspoons cream of tartar

Beat all together for 3 minutes (cake-mixer) or 10 minutes by hand beater. Bake in moderate oven 15-20 minutes and join with whipped cream.

FRANCE

DUCHESS POTATOES

1 kg (2 lb.) Peeled Potatoes
butter
olive oil
3 egg yolks
flour

Boil the potatoes. Drain well. Dry mash them enough to break up well. Add the yolks of three eggs, mashing between each yolk. Add just enough butter to bring them to frothy creaminess. Add salt and a little pepper. (On no account use milk.) Roll the mashed potato quickly and lightly into small balls, about 19 mm ($\frac{3}{4}$ in.) diameter. Roll lightly in flour. Place in refrigerator or cool place for at least two hours. Five minutes before you are ready to serve, drop them into very hot "deep oil". Be sure it is at least 8 cm (3 in.) deep, but not smoking hot. Do not crowd saucepan. Balls will pop to the surface. When brown remove from oil and drain.

FRENCH SALAD (Serve With Steak Diane)

1 Lettuce
3 parts best olive oil to 1 part vinegar
tomatoes
mint finely chopped
1 clove of garlic
onion
pepper and salt

Using a wooden salad bowl mix 3 parts of best olive oil to 1 part vinegar (preferably tarragon). Add a little pepper and salt and crush clove of garlic. Tear crisp lettuce leaves into pieces about 52 mm (2 in.) square. Toss in salad bowl until each piece is coated with oil and vinegar. Serve immediately. Quarters of firm tomatoes, thin slices of onion and finely chopped mint all make agreeable additions.

LA FONDUE

500 gr (1 lb.) Gruyere Cheese
1 teaspoon salt
1 clove garlic
crusty bread
250 ml ($\frac{1}{2}$ pint) light wine
pepper
1 tablespoon cornflour
little Kirsch, or other spirit

Grate cheese and put in large saucepan with wine. Heat slowly until melted. Add salt, pepper, crushed garlic, and cornflour mixed with spirit to a smooth paste. Cook gently and stir well to produce smooth gently bubbling mash. Cut bread into cubes. With individual forks impale cube, dip in bubbling fondue, and eat immediately.

PATE A FRIRE (French Batter)

2 Eggs
155 to 185 ml (5-6 oz.) fresh or sour milk
125 gr (4 oz.) flour
30 ml (1 oz.) olive oil

Separate yolks from whites of eggs. Sieve flour into basin, beat in slowly about $\frac{3}{4}$ of the milk. Add egg yolks and beat well. Add olive oil slowly, beat well. Beat in milk until smooth coating consistency is obtained. Leave for 1 hour. When ready to use, beat egg whites to stiff snow and fold rapidly and evenly into batter.

QUICHE LORRAINE

One 25 cm (9 Inch) Diameter Pie-dish lined with pastry dough $\frac{1}{8}$ inch thick
grated cheese
4 eggs
pinch salt and nutmeg
250 gr ($\frac{1}{2}$ lb.) melted butter
bacon
1 tablespoon flour
250 ml ($\frac{1}{2}$ pint) cream

Fill shell with a layer of grated cheese (mild), then a layer of grilled bacon and so on, finishing with cheese on top. Over this pour a very rich custard made by beating together eggs, flour, salt and nutmeg. Stir in 250 ml ($\frac{1}{2}$ pint) cream and 250 gr ($\frac{1}{2}$ lb.) melted butter. Pour over bacon and cheese until custard almost reaches rim of tart. Bake in moderate oven about 45 minutes.

STEAK DIANE

Fillet Steak
parsley
butter
garlic
Worcestershire sauce
salt and pepper

Remove all fat from fillet (no other cut will do), cut and hammer into pancake size pieces 6 mm ($\frac{1}{4}$ in.) thick. Rub lightly with salt and minimum of pepper. Put at least 60 gr (2 oz.) butter in the pan and be prepared to renew liberally. When butter is sizzling drop in first piece of steak, giving it a quick move to prevent sticking. Cook 40 seconds for underdone, 1 minute for medium. Turn steak, sprinkle liberally with finely chopped parsley and garlic. Turn again, sprinkle again. A moderate dash of Worcestershire with the butter reacting with a sizzle. Quickly move steak, distributing sauce. Serve immediately.

GERMANY

COLESLAW SALAD

1 Young Cabbage
¼ cup chopped celery
½ cup vinegar
pepper to taste
½ cucumber
1 tablespoon minced onion
1 teaspoon salt
½ cup light cream

Soak leaves of cabbage in very cold water. Dry between towels, wrap and crisp in refrigerator. Mix 3 cups crisped and finely shredded cabbage with diced cucumber, celery and minced onion. Add mixture of vinegar, salt, pepper and mix lightly with fork. Leave in refrigerator for 1 hour. Just before serving add light cream.

GERMAN BISCUITS

125 gr (¼ lb.) Butter
1 large egg or 2 small
2 cups self-raising flour
¼ cup sugar
1 tablespoon treacle
½ packet mixed spice

Beat butter and sugar to a cream and add egg and treacle. Stir in flour sifted with spice. Roll out and cut into shapes and bake in slow oven 10-15 minutes. Leave to cool on tray. Join with jam and ice tops. Keep several days before eating.

GERMAN APPLE PIE

Pie Crust (for bottom of dish)
2 eggs
1 teaspoon cinnamon
1 tablespoon butter
4 medium sized apples
1 cup sugar
½ cup plain flour

Make a rich pie crust for the bottom of dish only. Peel and slice apples lengthwise. Place slices of apple on pastry, lapping over like shingles. Sprinkle with cinnamon and sugar. Beat eggs and add flour. Spread carefully over apple mixture. Cut butter into small squares and dot over top. Bake ¾-1 hour in slow oven.

SOUR SWEET STEW

500 gr (1 lb.) Lean Chops (stewing)
500 gr (1 lb.) french beans
1 onion
plain flour
vinegar

Stew chops and onion. About ¾ hour before chops are done add sliced beans. When cooked, thicken stew with a mixture of plain flour and vinegar.

HOLLAND

DUTCH BUTTER BISCUITS

250 gr (½ lb.) Butter
1 egg
1 teaspoon cinnamon
almonds
185 gr (6 oz.) sugar
375 gr (12 oz.) flour
pinch salt

Beat butter to a cream with sugar and egg yolk. Sift in flour, cinnamon, salt and nuts. Press mixture into swiss roll tin, mark into squares and decorate each square with a split almond. Brush over with unbeaten egg white to glaze and bake in moderate oven 20 minutes.

HUNGARY

GOULASH CONTINENTALE

1 packet Spaghetti
2 teaspoons olive oil
750 gr (1½ lb.) mince
½ teaspoon herbs
½ cup grated cheese
2 cloves garlic
1 dessertspoon Worcestershire sauce
1 tablespoon butter
1 large tin tomato soup
little tomato sauce, salt, cayenne

Cook spaghetti in boiling salted water until tender. Drain. Fry butter, mince, garlic, olive oil and salt until brown. Add soup plus ½ tin water. Add spaghetti, herbs, Worcestershire sauce, tomato sauce, and cayenne. Cheese can be stirred in or used as a garnish.

Note: Has a better flavour if made the day before it is required for use.

HUNGARIAN GOULASH

1 kg (2 lb.) Veal
750 ml (1½ pints) brown stock
12 small onions (whole)
1 cup diced turnips
flour
4 onions (sliced)
1 cup diced carrots
2 cups mashed potato
seasoning

Cut veal into cubes and fry in bacon fat with sliced onion until brown. Place in casserole, cover with stock, season to taste and cover and cook in moderate oven for 1½ hours. Shape potato into balls with enough flour to bind. Brown balls, whole onions, turnips and carrots, and add to casserole and cook another 30-45 minutes till all are tender. Thicken gravy before serving.

HUNGARIAN RICE PUDDING

1⅔ Cups Rice
1 teaspoon salt
¾ cup sugar
juice of 1 orange and 1 lemon
preserved fruit, stewed fruit (apricots, apples or quince)
2 egg whites
4 cups milk
1 tablespoon butter
3 tablespoons hot water
2 tablespoons rum (optional)
2 tablespoons sugar

Add rice to boiling milk and salt. Cover and simmer till rice is soft. In another saucepan put butter and sugar and brown lightly. Add hot water and fruit juices and bring to the boil. Pour into rice and simmer for 3 minutes. Remove from heat and add rum. Cool. Spread alternate layers of rice and fruit until all ingredients are used. Top with meringue made by beating egg whites and sugar until stiff. Bake in slow oven till lightly browned.

INDIA

KARACHI CURRY

750 gr (1½ lb.) Cooked Lamb (diced)
1 tablespoon curry powder (less if desired)
4 peeled thickly sliced potatoes
2 cups chopped skinned tomatoes
3 carrots peeled and sliced
1 bay leaf
½ cup peas
3 dessertspoons butter
1 cup sliced beans
½ cup stock
1 clove garlic (crushed)
¼ cup raisins
salt and pepper
bananas
boiled rice

Heat butter in large saucepan, add curry powder and mix well. Add potatoes, beans, tomatoes, stock, crushed garlic, bay leaf, salt and pepper. Simmer gently 30 minutes or until potatoes are nearly cooked. Add lamb, peas and raisins. Continue cooking another 20 minutes. Serve on bed of hot rice, garnish with fried bananas and extra raisins.

CHICKEN PILAU

(Indian Recipe used on Festive Occasions)

- 1 Fowl
- 2 tablespoons ghee (butter)
- 16-18 almonds (blanched and sliced)
- 3-4 onions sliced
- 10 cm (4 inches) cinnamon
- 8-9 hard boiled eggs ("Bullets")
- 500 gr (1 lb.) rice
- 1 tablespoon sultanas
- 6 cloves
- ½ dozen cardamom seeds

Put fowl with onions to boil until tender. Fry sultanas in ghee and set aside, then almonds, then onions. Keep each separate. When fowl is boiled, brown and keep aside. Fry rice in ghee and add to boiling broth 2½ fingers above rice. While rice is boiling add heaped teaspoonful salt and spices. Stir to prevent burning, allow to simmer until perfectly cooked.

Serve in a flat dish. Place layer of rice then fowl, then cover over with rice. Cut hardboiled eggs ("Bullets") in halves. Arrange over rice. Strew over the whole the fried onions, almonds and sultanas.

Note: Mutton may be used instead of fowl.

ITALY

ITALIAN CREAM

- 30 gr (1 oz.) Gelatine
- 250 ml (½ pint) cream
- 1 dessertspoon brandy
- sugar to taste
- 250 ml (½ pint) milk
- 3 egg yolks
- few drops of vanilla
- 60 ml (½ gill) water

Soak gelatine in water for 1 hour. Make a custard of egg yolks and milk and sugar. When cooled, stir in brandy, vanilla and dissolved gelatine. Add whipped cream and pour into glasses or wetted mould and chill.

MILANAISE SPAGHETTI

- 3 Cups Cooked Spaghetti
- ¾ cup tomato puree
- 2 rashers bacon cooked and chopped
- 1½ cups grated cheese
- 1 tablespoon chopped parsley
- 1½ cups white sauce (medium thick)
- 6 sheep's tongues (cooked, skinned and chopped)
- 2 tablespoons grated onion
- 3 tomatoes
- seasoning to taste

Mix spaghetti with white sauce, fold in tomato puree, add tongues, bacon, onion and half the cheese, seasoning and chopped parsley. Fill greased dish and cover with sliced tomatoes and grated cheese. Bake in moderate oven until thoroughly heated and the cheese is golden brown.

NEAPOLITAN RICE

125 gr (¼ lb.) Rice
60 gr (2 oz.) grated cheese
seasoning to taste
3 large tomatoes (skinned)
30 gr (1 oz.) butter
60 gr (2 oz.) bacon

Boil rice as for curry, and drain. Fry diced bacon in butter, add rice, tomatoes (chopped finely), cheese and seasoning. Simmer gently till tomatoes are absorbed. Serve very hot.

NEAPOLITAN TRIPE

625 gr (1¼ lb.) Tripe
1 tablespoon chopped onions
3 tomatoes
grating of nutmeg
2 bacon rashers
1 level dessertspoon shortening
1 clove garlic
pinch herbs
seasoning to taste

Cook tripe until tender and cut into thin strips. Melt shortening and add chopped onion, crushed garlic and peeled and sliced tomatoes. Cook until tomatoes are soft. Dice bacon and put half in bottom of dish, cover with tripe, tomato mixture and top with remaining bacon. Grate nutmeg over and bake uncovered for 15 minutes in moderate oven.

SCALLOPINI

500 gr (1 lb.) Veal
1 medium onion
½ cup cooked peas
250 gr (½ lb.) spaghetti
250 gr (½ lb.) ripe tomatoes
250 gr (8 oz.) tin mushrooms or 90 gr (3 oz.) mushrooms fried and added to 1 small cup white sauce
1 slice bacon
1 tablespoon sherry

Slice onion, fry in fat until golden brown. Put aside into large saucepan removed from fire. Cut veal into small thin slices and fry on both sides. It must not go dry. Add to onion. Fry bacon which has been cut into small pieces and add to veal and onion. Drain all fat from saucepan. Cut tomatoes into small chunks and fry. Add to veal, etc. Add mushrooms and sherry. Simmer gently for approximately ½ hour. Add peas. Place cooked spaghetti on large platter and pour scallopini over it.

SPAGHETTI WITH ITALIAN SAUCE

250 gr (½ lb.) Ground Veal
250 gr (½ lb.) ground beef
250 gr (½ lb.) ground pork
250 gr (½ lb.) sausage
125 gr (¼ lb.) butter
¼ clove garlic
2 sprigs chopped parsley
2½ cups tomato puree
½ teaspoon Worcestershire sauce
625 gr (1¼ lb.) chopped onions
1 green pepper
250 gr (½ lb.) mushrooms
1 cup ketchup
2 teaspoons salt
½ teaspoon pepper
2 teaspoons lemon juice
250 gr (8 oz.) spaghetti
grated parmesan cheese

Brown meats in butter, add onions, garlic, pepper, parsley. Add mushrooms, tomato puree, ketchup and ½ cup water, Worcestershire sauce, lemon juice, pepper and salt. Simmer for 1½ hours. Boil spaghetti in salted water until soft. Drain. Pour sauce over spaghetti and serve. Sprinkle generously with cheese.

JAMAICA

JAMAICAN FRUIT CAKE

125 gr (4 oz.) Sultanas
125 gr (4 oz.) raisins
60 gr (2 oz.) cherries
90 gr (3 oz.) chopped dates
125 gr (4 oz.) currants
125 gr (4 oz.) peel
90 gr (3 oz.) chopped prunes
90 gr (3 oz.) dried apricots
2 tablespoons rum
2 tablespoons port wine
1 tablespoon orange juice
250 gr (½ lb.) sugar
250 gr (½ lb.) butter
4 eggs
60 gr (2 oz.) self-raising flour
250 gr (½ lb.) plain flour
1 teaspoon ground cloves
2 teaspoons cinnamon
pinch salt
1 teaspoon nutmeg
2 teaspoons spice
90 gr (3 oz.) blanched almonds

Combine sultanas, currants, raisins, peel, cherries, prunes, dates, rum and wine and allow to stand 3 hours. Cream butter and sugar and add eggs, one at a time, and beat well. Add sifted dry ingredients alternately with prepared fruits and chopped almonds. Turn into paper-lined 20 cm (8 in.) cake tin and bake in slow oven 3-3½ hours. Allow to cool in tin.

JEWISH

FISH CUSTARD

500 gr (1 lb.) Small Fish (herring or mullet)
1 lemon
2 eggs
1½ cups water
2 bay leaves
1 onion
pepper and salt to taste

Stew fish with sliced lemon, sliced onion and water. When cooked, remove slices of lemon. Lift out fish. Beat eggs well and add to liquid. Place fish in serving dish. Pour over liquid and place in refrigerator.

MALAYA

MALAYAN VEAL HOT POT

500 gr (1 lb.) Minced Veal
125 gr (¼ lb.) minced bacon
1 small onion
1 egg
½ cabbage
1 cup stock
½ cup breadcrumbs
1 tablespoon butter
1 red chilli
flour
nutmeg, salt, pepper

Combine veal, onion, bacon and breadcrumbs. Bind with egg and shape into rolls and flour well. Separate cabbage leaves and parboil for 2 minutes and drain. Wrap each roll in a leaf and secure with toothpick. Shred remainder of cabbage and chilli and put into casserole. Sprinkle lightly with nutmeg, pepper and salt. Place rolls on top and dot with butter. Pour over sufficient hot stock to cover shredded cabbage, but not rolls. Cover and bake in moderate oven 1 hour.

MEXICO

MEXICAN CHICKEN

1 Small Young Chicken
250 gr (½ lb.) tomatoes
1 tablespoon flour
½ cup stock
1 chopped onion
2 tablespoons oil
1 tablespoon tomato puree
¼ cup white wine
1 green pepper
1 tablespoon shortening
1 tablespoon chopped shallot
salt and pepper

Joint prepared chicken, brown well in hot oil in heavy saucepan. When well browned, pour off excess oil. Add skinned chopped tomatoes and puree. Sprinkle with flour and stir to mix, add wine and stock. Cook onion and sliced pepper in shortening until onion begins to brown. Add to chicken with shallot and seasoning. Cover and simmer 1-1¼ hours till chicken is tender.

MEXICAN RAISIN RICE

½ Cup Dry Rice
¼ cup salad oil or bacon fat
500 gr (1 lb.) minced beef
1 finely minced clove of garlic
2 cups water
¾ cup seeded raisins
1 medium onion
1 cup chopped tomatoes
2 teaspoons salt
pepper to taste

Wash rice and add to hot salad oil in large saucepan, stirring frequently and cooking slowly until lightly browned. Add chopped onion, garlic and beef and cook slowly till meat is lightly browned. Add remaining ingredients and cook 5 minutes, stirring occasionally. Pour into casserole, cover and bake 45 minutes; uncover and bake 15 minutes till browned on top. This may be simmered on stove top, adding more water if necessary.

PORTUGAL

VINHADALHOS

Fish or Chops
1 dessertspoon pepper
1 large clove crushed garlic
1 dessertspoon allspice
small bay leaf
white wine if fish used
red wine if chops used

Blend pepper, allspice, garlic with as little water as possible, add enough white wine to cover fish (red wine if chops used) and add bay leaf. Cover with lid and put in refrigerator for at least 24 hours. Lift from liquid immediately into heated pan and fry as usual.

RUSSIA

BORSCH (Russian Soup)

500 gr (1 lb.) Beetroot
4 cups water
250 gr (½ lb.) beef
¼ cup sugar
4 eggs
1 cup tomatoes
1 small onion
1 tablespoon lemon juice
¼ teaspoon salt

Peel and cut beetroot into strips. Place in water with onion and meat cut small and simmer for ½ hour. Add lemon juice, sugar and salt. Boil another ½ hour. Beat eggs with salt and add to hot soup a little at a time, stirring well. Serve very hot.

RUSSIAN FRUIT GINGER BREAD (CAKE)

½ Cup Sultanas
½ cup preserved ginger
½ cup candied peel
60 gr (2 oz.) brown sugar
2 tablespoons treacle
pinch salt
½ teaspoon cinnamon
½ teaspoon mixed spice
½ teaspoon ginger
½ teaspoon carb. soda
½ cup currants
½ cup chopped nuts
60 gr (2 oz.) butter
1 egg
2 tablespoons milk
155 gr (5 oz.) plain flour

Cream butter and sugar, add beaten egg, treacle, milk, fruit and chopped nuts. Sift in dry ingredients and mix. Bake in moderate oven 35 minutes.

BEEF STROGANOFF

1 kg (2 lb.) Fillet Steak
2½ tablespoons butter
¼ cup stock
1 cup sour cream
1 finely chopped onion
1 tablespoon Worcestershire sauce
salt, pepper and flour
parsley

Slice meat into small thin pieces, salt, pepper and flour the meat. Fry in butter the finely chopped onion and add meat. Add stock, Worcestershire sauce and sour cream. Mix well, cook until deep yellow brown (do not cook dry). Put in deep dish and sprinkle with chopped parsley.

SPAIN

CHICKEN JAMBALAYA (Creole Spanish)

2½ Cups Rice
3 slices ham finely chopped
2 large onions finely chopped
2 cloves minced garlic
2 glasses sherry
¼ teaspoon ground cloves
1 teaspoon chopped green pepper
1½ kg (3 lb.) chicken
125 gr (¼ lb.) pork sausage meat
3 tablespoons butter
2 bay leaves
2 sprigs thyme and parsley chopped
4 litres (4 quarts) chicken broth or stock
salt, pepper and cayenne to taste

Cut chicken into small pieces. Put butter into saucepan, add onion and chicken and brown slowly. Add sherry, stirring frequently, then add ham, garlic, minced herbs, thyme and parsley, bay leaf, cloves, and brown all for 5 minutes longer. Add sausage meat and let cook another 5 minutes. Add 4 litres (4 quarts) of broth or stock, let cook 10 minutes, then add washed rice. Add green pepper, salt and pepper and cayenne, simmer for 30 minutes and serve very hot.

SPANISH POTATO SALAD

6 Medium Sized Cooked Potatoes
2 tablespoons chopped green pepper or pimento
½ tablespoon chives or spring onions
3 chopped hard boiled eggs
½ teaspoon salt
1 clove garlic
1 tablespoon mayonnaise
1 tablespoon wine vinegar
pepper to taste

Rub salad bowl with garlic. Mix diced pototoes, lightly with pimento, onion, egg and vinegar mixed with 1 tablespoon mayonnaise, salt and pepper. Cover and chill for 1 hour. Serve on lettuce leaves sprinkled with chopped chives or parsley.

SWEDEN

SWEDISH RICE (SWEET)

250 gr (½ lb.) Rice
1 teaspoon butter
2 teaspoons cinnamon
1 teaspoon lemon rind
¼ cup fruit juice or sherry
250 ml (½ pint) milk
4 apples
2 tablespoons sugar
125 gr (¼ lb.) raisins

Boil rice for a few minutes in deep water and pour off water. Add milk, grated apple, raisins, sugar, cinnamon, juice or sherry, and simmer together for ½ hour till apples are cooked, raisins puffy, and rice soft. Serve hot or cold.

SWITZERLAND

SWISS STEAK WITH PUMPKIN PUFFS

500 gr (1 lb.) Round or Topside Steak
1 teaspoon mustard
2 tablespoons tomato sauce
375 ml ($\frac{3}{4}$ pint) stock or water
2 tablespoons flour
1 dessertspoon brown sugar
1 small onion
1 dessertspoon vinegar
seasoning to taste

Mix dry ingredients together and coat steak, cut into small cubes. Put into casserole and sprinkle with remaining flour. Add chopped onion. Combine liquids and pour over meat. Cover and bake in moderate oven till tender, $1\frac{1}{2}$-2 hours.

Puffs

$1\frac{1}{2}$ Cups Self-raising flour
$\frac{1}{2}$ teaspoon celery salt
30 gr (1 oz.) butter
1 egg
1 cup cold mashed pumpkin
little milk
$\frac{1}{2}$ teaspoon salt
pinch pepper

Sift dry ingredients, rub in butter and add pumpkin. Mix to a soft dough with beaten egg and a little milk. Pat out 19 mm ($\frac{3}{4}$ in.) thick and cut into rounds. Remove lid from casserole and place puffs on meat. If desired, they may be glazed with egg and milk. Bake in hot oven 15 minutes.

TURKEY

TURKISH PILAF

1 Cup Rice
1 cup chopped celery
$\frac{1}{2}$ cup chopped almonds or peanuts
salt, pepper and cinnamon to taste
1 tablespoon shortening
1 cup chopped raisins
$\frac{1}{2}$ cup apricots (canned or fresh) cut in small pieces
1 egg
1 onion
$\frac{1}{2}$ cup stock

Boil rice with $1\frac{1}{2}$ cups water and 1 teaspoon salt. Bring to boil, cover lightly and simmer for 20 minutes. Mix rice, raisins, apricots, celery, nuts in large bowl. Add beaten egg, cinnamon and seasoning. Chop onion finely and brown in shortening. Add to rice mixture with stock. Put mixture in greased casserole and bake in moderate oven for 15-20 minutes.

JAMS, JELLIES, MARMALADES AND PRESERVES

When your fruit is in the pan, ready to place on the stove for the first boiling, try placing a cover on the pan. You will find that the fruit cooks thoroughly and in a fraction of the time necessary in an open pan. It is seldom necessary to stir before adding the sugar.

Pressure Cooker Hint: Cut up fruit and leave stand 3 hours. This makes enough juice to start. Pressure cook about 5 minutes for soft fruits, 10 minutes for hard fruits. Leave lid off, add sugar, and proceed as usual boiling until it jells.

Try placing a bowl of lime on the shelf where your jams and preserves are stored, and it will prevent mould from gathering on them.

When jam or jellies ferment, it is an indication of under-cooking. Re-cook the jam to evaporate the water that has been left in it. If jam is sticky or syrupy, too much sugar has been used, or maybe the fruit was over ripe, or cooked beyond jell stage.

When pasting paper lids on jams, etc., instead of using paste just dip papers in white of egg. Press over jars firmly.

Remember to always heat your jam jars before pouring in your jam. This will prevent cracking. Label your jars with the kind of jam and the date filled, and store in a cool, dry place.

When bottling jams, jellies, pickles, etc., stand the jars or bottles on a thick, wet cloth. They will seldom crack.

When making plum or other jam on which an amount of scum rises, do not remove scum as it is the best of the colouring, after jam has cooked for a while add one tablespoon of butter to every lb. of fruit, this will send the scum back into the jam and prevent the sugar from crystallising.

APRICOT JAM

$3\frac{1}{2}$ kg (7 lb.) Apricots
1 cup cold water
$2\frac{3}{4}$ kg ($5\frac{1}{2}$ lb.) sugar
1 dozen kernels

Wipe your fruit carefully, cut in halves, and remove stones. Crack about 1 dozen of the stones, and remove kernels. Pour boiling water on kernels, and remove the skins. Put the water into the preserving pan, add prepared fruit, and kernels. Bring slowly to the boil, and simmer gently for 20 minutes. While fruit is cooking, place the sugar in a dish in the oven, and heat thoroughly. Then stir the sugar gradually into the fruit. Boil till the jam sets, when you test a little on a cold plate. The time is about 1 hour in all.

BANANA JAM

$1\frac{1}{2}$ kg (3 lb.) Bananas
juice of 1 lemon
500 gr (1 lb.) pears
$1\frac{1}{4}$ kg ($2\frac{1}{2}$ lb.) sugar

Put the pears (nice juicy ones), pared and cut into small pieces, lemon juice, and 500 gr (1 lb.) sugar, into a preserving pan. When the mixture boils, add bananas and 750 gr ($1\frac{1}{2}$ lb.) sugar. Stir quietly till it boils, and then boil quickly for 1 hour. Skim and put into jars while still hot.

CAPE GOOSEBERRY JAM

3 kg (6 lb.) Cape Gooseberries
$2\frac{1}{4}$ kg ($4\frac{1}{2}$ lb.) sugar
500 ml (1 pint) cold water

Remove the husks from the berries and weigh. Prick with a darning needle and place in alternate layers, fruit and sugar, in a preserving pan. Add water and boil gently until a little of the syrup will jell, when poured on to a cold plate. The juice of the lemon may be added, or a small teaspoon of tartaric acid, just before the jam is ready.

CAPE GOOSEBERRY AND MELON JAM

3 kg (6 lb.) Piemelon
$4\frac{1}{2}$ kg (9 lb.) sugar
3 kg (6 lb.) cape gooseberries
2 lemons

Peel the melon, remove the seeds, and weigh. Put into a preserving pan, and sprinkle over about 2 kg (4 lb.) of sugar, and leave all night. In the morning bring to the boil, and add remainder of sugar. Boil until the melon begins to look clear, then add the cape gooseberries, which have been cleared of husks, and weighed. Prick each berry with a darning needle before adding. Add the lemon juice, and boil till jell point—about 4 hours.

DRIED APRICOT JAM

1 kg (2 lb.) Apricots (dried)
1 teaspoon citric acid
2½ kg (5 lb.) sugar
1 teaspoon almond essence

Well wash apricots in hot water, then soak 12 hours in 2 litres (2 quarts) of fresh cold water. Drain water into pan, add sugar, bring to boil, and add fruit. Boil briskly for ½ an hour, stirring briskly for the last ten minutes. Add acid 10 minutes before removing from the fire, essence after removing.

FIG JAM (No. 1)

4½ kg (9 lb.) Sugar
6 kg (12 lb.) figs
2 teaspoons citric or tartaric acid

Pick the figs before they are ripe, when only the flower end is at all soft. Top and tail, and cut into slices. Place in pan with a cup of water to prevent burning, place a lid or fitting cover over the pan, and bring gently to boiling point. Boil until the fruit is soft—about 20 minutes if the fruit was picked at the right time. Keep lid on the pan all the time. Add sugar and acid, stir well to dissolve the sugar, replace the lid, bring to the boil, remove the lid, and boil gently till thick and clear, stirring occasionally.

FIG JAM (No. 2)

3 kg (6 lb.) Figs
juice of 3 lemons
250 ml (½ pint) water
2⅛ kg (4¼ lb.) sugar

Cut up the figs, and boil all together for 3 or 4 hours. Leave rinds of lemons whole and cook in jam. When done, take out rinds and bottle jam while hot. Seal next day.

FIG JAM (No. 3)

3 kg (6 lb.) Figs
250 ml (½ pint) water
1 cup vinegar
2 kg (4 lb.) sugar

Skin and stem the fruit. Make a syrup of sugar, water, and vinegar. When boiling, drop in the cut up figs. If conserve is desired, put the figs in whole. Simmer slowly for 3 hours.

GRAPE JAM

3 kg (6 lb.) Grapes
1 kg (2 lb.) cooking apples
2 kg (4 lb.) sugar
1 litre (2 pints) water

Remove the grapes from the stalks, and prick with a needle. Boil the sugar and water to a syrup, and put in the grapes, and the pared and sliced apples. Boil gently until the syrup jells on testing. The seeds will float to the top and must be removed.

GRAPEFRUIT JAM

2 kg (4 lb.) Grapefruit
4 litres (8 pints) water
6 kg (12 lb.) sugar

Cut fruit in quarters, remove the pips and white centres, and put the latter into a jug with 500 ml (1 pint) of the water. Slice the fruit very thinly and put into a basin with the remainder of the water. Let all stand overnight. In the morning, strain liquid from the seeds, and add to the fruit. Boil for 1 hour, then add the sugar which has been previously warmed in the oven, and boil all together for another hour, or until a little, when tested on a saucer, jells.

MARROW JAM

500 gr (1 lb.) Marrow
25 gr ($\frac{3}{4}$ oz.) lump ginger
500 gr (1 lb.) sugar
rind and juice of 1 lemon

Cut the marrow into small dice, weigh, put in preserving pan, allowing an equal amount of sugar. Add the sugar, and leave it to stand for 24 hours when the sugar will have drawn out the water. Now grate the rinds of the lemons, and squeeze out the juice. Bruise the ginger by banging it with a heavy weight. Tie in a bag, add it to the marrow with the juice of the lemons, and cook slowly until the sugar is dissolved, then bring it to the boil. Remove the scum, add the grated rinds of lemon, and boil all together until the preserve will jell when tested.

MELON AND DRIED APRICOT JAM

2 kg (4 lb.) Melon (peeled and seeded)
3 kg (6 lb.) sugar
500 gr (1 lb.) dried apricots
$1\frac{3}{4}$ litres ($3\frac{1}{2}$ pints) boiling water
juice of 1 lemon

Quarter the apricots, pour boiling water over them, and soak for 24 hours. Add cut up melon, and boil for 2 hours, then add the sugar gradually, and boil for $1\frac{1}{2}$ hours longer. Add lemon juice last.

MELON AND GINGER JAM

6 kg (12 lb.) Melon
250 gr ($\frac{1}{2}$ lb.) preserved ginger
$4\frac{1}{2}$ kg (9 lb.) sugar
3 lemons

Cut up melon into little squares, cover with sugar, and leave overnight. Next morning, add cut up lemons and ginger, and boil all together for from 5 to 6 hours.

MELON AND PINEAPPLE JAM

2 kg (4 lb.) Firm Sugar Melon in cubes
1 kg (2 lb.) pineapple
$1\frac{1}{2}$ kg (3 lb.) sugar

Cut melon overnight, put in pan, and sprinkle with half of the sugar. In the morning, add pineapple and boil for 3 hours. Then add rest of sugar, and boil for 1 hour. Bottle while hot, and seal next day.

MELON AND PRUNE JAM

3 kg (6 lb.) Melon
3 kg (6 lb.) sugar
500 gr (1 lb.) dried prunes
6 to 8 cloves

Peel and seed melon, cut into small dice, and put into a dish. Cut and stone prunes, lay over melon, sprinkle with about 250 gr ($\frac{1}{2}$ lb.) sugar, and leave to stand overnight. Next day, put on to cook, gradually adding remainder of sugar, while boiling. Cook until melon is clear and prunes well broken up, then try a little on a saucer.

MELON JAM

5 kg (10 lb.) Melon
juice and rind of 2 lemons
$3\frac{3}{4}$ kg ($7\frac{1}{2}$ lb.) sugar
60 gr (2 oz.) green ginger

Cut melon and lemon and allow to stand overnight, sprinkled with 2 cups sugar. Next morning boil until clear, then add remaining sugar, and boil until it jells.

MOCK GINGER

6 kg (12 lb.) Melon
500 gr (1 lb.) whole ginger
6 kg (12 lb.) sugar
4 litres (1 gallon) water
lime water

Make some lime water, by mixing a large basin of fresh lime in a bucket of water. Let lime settle, skim, and pour off the clear liquid. Cut the melon into dice, and allow to lie in the lime water for 24 hours. Drain, and make a syrup by boiling the sugar and ginger in 4 litres (1 gallon) of water for 20 minutes. Add the melon to the syrup and boil for 4 or 5 hours.

MOCK RASPBERRY JAM (No. 1)

3 kg (6 lb.) Ripe Tomatoes
juice of 1 lemon
1 bottle essence of raspberry
$2\frac{1}{4}$ kg ($4\frac{1}{2}$ lb.) sugar
15 gr ($\frac{1}{2}$ oz.) powdered orris root
cochineal

Pour boiling water over tomatoes, and peel them. Put them into a preserving pan and add sugar, orris root, and lemon juice. Boil until thick, then add raspberry essence. Remove from the fire, and colour to desired colour with cochineal.

MOCK RASPBERRY JAM (No. 2)

2 Large Quinces
$1\frac{1}{2}$ kg (3 lb.) tomatoes
$2\frac{1}{2}$ kg (5 lb.) sugar

Peel the quinces, and put through the mincer. Peel the tomatoes by placing in boiling water, when the skins will come off readily, add the sugar to the fruit, and boil for about 3 hours.

MULBERRY AND FIG JAM

Mulberries
water
figs
sugar

Put 1 kg (2 lb.) mulberries into a preserving pan with $\frac{1}{2}$ cup water. Simmer slowly till the mulberries are soft, strain, and add $2\frac{1}{2}$ kg (5 lb.) sugar to 4 cups of juice. Boil up and skim well, then add 1 kg (2 lb.) mulberries, 1 kg (2 lb.) ripe figs, thinly sliced. Boil slowly for $\frac{1}{4}$ of an hour, turn into a crockery bowl, and allow to stand till next day. Boil up until thick, and will set when tried in a saucer, put into jelly glasses and seal.

NECTARINE JAM

3 kg (6 lb.) Nectarines (stoned)
2 cups water
few kernels
$2\frac{1}{4}$ kg ($4\frac{1}{2}$ lb.) sugar
1 dessertspoon butter

Wash nectarines, do not peel, cut up. Place in pan with butter, water and kernels, and boil until soft. Add sugar gradually, boil well, about 2 hours, until thick. Bottle hot.

ORANGE AND MELON JAM

$4\frac{1}{2}$ kg (9 lb.) Preserving Melon
3 lemons
18 oranges
2 cups water
375 gr ($\frac{3}{4}$ lb.) of sugar to each 500 gr (1 lb.) of fruit

Cut up or mince the melon very finely. Shred the rind of the oranges and lemons, cut up the pulp, and put in a muslin bag, and squeeze well with a spoon while boiling in a preserving pan. Keep well stirred, and have an asbestos mat to prevent burning. Boil for 3 hours, then add 375 gr ($\frac{3}{4}$ lb.) sugar to each 500 gr (1 lb.) of fruit, and boil until cooked (2 or 3 hours). Bottle while still hot, and seal. Weigh after first three hours of boiling. Weight of pan should be known. Take the pulp and drain in a sieve before adding the sugar.

PASSIONFRUIT JAM

Passionfruit
$\frac{1}{2}$ teaspoon lemon juice
1 cup sugar to each cup of pulp

Wipe the fruit well, cut into halves, and scoop out the seeds and the juice. Put the skins into a saucepan, add sufficient water to cover, and boil until the skins are quite tender. Then remove the fleshy part from the skins, and place in a pan with the seeds, juice, lemon juice, and sugar. Boil slowly till the jam sets. Bottle while hot, and cover closely.

PEAR AND PASSIONFRUIT JAM

2 kg (4 lb.) Pears
1 litre (2 pints) water
1½ kg (3 lb.) sugar
6 passionfruit

Boil sugar and water for 15 minutes. Peel and slice pears and add to syrup. Boil for 1 hour. Add passionfruit pulp and continue boiling until jam will set when tested. Bottle hot.

PEAR GINGER (No. 1)

3 kg (6 lb.) Hard Pears
2½ kg (5 lb.) sugar
2½ litres (5 pints) water
250 gr (½ lb.) preserved ginger

Boil the water and sugar for 20 minutes. Keep well skimmed, add 250 gr (½ lb.) preserved ginger, cut into small squares, and the pears, peeled and cut into quarters (3 kg (6 lb.) pears after peeling). Boil 4 to 5 hours. The syrup should be of the consistency of honey, and a nice clear colour.

PEAR GINGER (No. 2)

3 kg (6 lb.) Pears
2¼ kg (4½ lb.) sugar
250 gr (½ lb.) preserved ginger
250 ml (½ pint) water

Peel and quarter the pears, add ginger, cut in cubes, and then add sugar and water. Stand 24 hours. Boil until a deep red colour, bottle, and cover and label when cold. Make apple ginger the same recipe.

PEACH AND GINGER JAM

2 kg (4 lb.) Peeled and Stoned Peaches
125 gr (¼ lb.) green ginger
2 kg (4 lb.) sugar
juice 1 lemon
1 dessertspoon glycerine

Place the cut up peaches in the preserving pan, and cover with the sugar. Cut the ginger into small pieces, and add to peaches. Boil the peach stones and skins for about an hour, in just enough water to cover, then strain off the liquid, and add it to the peaches. Boil for about 2½ hours, or until the syrup jells, adding the glycerine and lemon juice about 15 minutes before removing from the fire.

PEAR JAM

1¾ kg (3½ lb.) Pears
14 cloves
nearly 250 ml (½ pint) vinegar
1½ kg (2¾ lb.) sugar
1 small stick cinnamon
a few drops cochineal

Boil spice in vinegar for 10 minutes, then add sugar and pears, and boil gently till a nice pink colour. If you like it a little darker, add a few drops of cochineal. Boil till it jells.

PLUM JAM

6 kg (12 lb.) Plums
4½ kg (9 lb.) sugar
½ cup water

Prick or cut plums and add water. Boil until tender, add sugar and boil quickly until jell point.

To vary add 1 kg (2 lb.) apples to 4 kg (8 lb.) plums; 1½ kg (3 lb.) peaches to 3 kg (6 lb.) plums; 2 kg (4 lb.) mulberries to 2½ kg (5 lb.) plums.

Use 375 gr (¾ lb.) sugar to each 500 gr (1 lb.) fruit used.

QUINCE HONEY

5 Large Quinces
2½ kg (5 lb.) sugar
500 ml (1 pint) water

Peel and grate the quinces, or cut in very small dice. Put sugar and water on the fire, and when it boils, put in the grated quinces, and boil for ½ an hour, keeping it well stirred.

QUINCE JAM

Quinces
sugar
water

Wipe quinces with a damp cloth to remove the down, and boil whole in water until tender. Let cool, peel, and cut into dices. To every 500 gr (1 lb.) of fruit allow 500 gr (1 lb.) of sugar, and 500 ml (1 pint) of water. Boil until a rich pink colour. The pips can be boiled separately, and the juice added to the jam to make it jell better.

RASPBERRY JAM (ECONOMICAL)

Grapes
sugar
1 tin raspberry jam

Boil any quantity of grapes, on the green side, to a pulp for 3 hours. Strain this through an enamel colander, which will keep back both skins and pips. Mash well, and get all the fleshy parts as well as the juice. Then measure 1 cup of pulp to 1 cup of sugar, and to every 4 cups of pulp add 1 tin of raspberry jam. Do not put jam in until ½ an hour before taking off the stove. Boil the sugar and pulp hard for about 2 hours, add citric acid to taste, then the jam. Then bottle. It is quite nice without the jam. Black currant may be added instead of raspberry.

RHUBARB JAM

3 kg (6 lb.) Rhubarb
60 gr (2 oz.) whole ginger
1 small piece cinnamon
2½ kg (5 lb.) sugar
4 cloves
1 juicy lemon

Cut rhubarb into small pieces, cover with sugar, and leave till next day. Add spices tied in a muslin bag, the strained juice of lemon, grated rind, and a litre (1 quart) of water. Boil until jam sets when tested, remove scum, and take out spices.

STRAWBERRY JAM

$1\frac{3}{4}$ kg ($3\frac{1}{2}$ lb.) Sugar
2 kg (4 lb.) fruit
juice of 4 lemons

Put fruit in pan with lemon juice and simmer for 30 to 45 minutes. Add sugar and continue stirring until dissolved. Boil briskly for 15 minutes and test for setting. When it sets readily allow to cool a little, stirring occasionally. Bottle and seal.

TINNED BLACK CURRANT AND MELON JAM

1 kg (2 lb.) Tin Black Currants
1 tablespoon citric acid
3 kg (6 lb.) melon, peeled and seeded
$2\frac{1}{2}$ kg (5 lb.) sugar
1 tablespoon cochineal

Mince the melon, using the large cutter, and place in a pan overnight, having sprinkled it with half the sugar. In the morning, boil for 2 hours, then add black currants, acid, and cochineal, and boil 1 hour longer. Bottle while hot, and seal next day.

TOMATO JAM (GREEN)

$7\frac{1}{2}$ kg (15 lb.) Green Tomatoes
6 lemons
6 kg (12 lb.) sugar
125 gr ($\frac{1}{4}$ lb.) green ginger
1 tablespoon vanilla essence

Dice the tomatoes, cover with half the sugar, and allow to stand for 24 hours. Squeeze the juice from the lemons, then slice the fruit finely, and cover with water for 24 hours. Bring all to the boil, and cook until the mixture begins to thicken; then add the rest of the sugar, and cook for 25 to 30 minutes. Test, then remove from the fire, and add the essence. Bottle hot and seal when cold.

TOMATO JAM (RIPE)

Tomatoes
sugar
orris root or tartaric acid

Scald, and skin the tomatoes, add 500 gr (1 lb.) of sugar to each 500 gr (1 lb.) of fruit, and boil together until it will jell, stirring well. Five minutes before removing from the fire, add 1 teaspoon of powdered orris root or 1 teaspoon of tartaric acid, first mixing it well in a little of the jam. This quantity of acid would be sufficient for 3 kg (6 lb.) of fruit. Put jam in airtight bottles.

JELLIES

APPLE JELLY

Green Apples **water**
sugar

Select small green apples, cut in quarters, and cover with water. Simmer over fire for ½ an hour, then strain the liquid. Measure juice, and put into a preserving pan. Bring to the boil, boil 5 minutes, skim, and add a bare 500 gr (1 lb.) of sugar to each 500 ml (1 pint) of juice. Boil smartly for 20 or 30 minutes, till it jells. Bottle and seal.

GRAPE JELLY

Grapes **sugar**

Any kind of grapes will do for this jelly. String the grapes, and put as many into the preserving pan as will allow them to be shaken. Stand on the fire without any water, and boil gently for 2 hours, shaking the pan constantly for the first 5 minutes. Strain, squeezing as much juice through as possible. Allow 375 gr (¾ lb.) sugar to every 500 ml (1 pint) of juice, and boil for 1½ hours. Bottle hot.

GUAVA JELLY

Guavas **water**
sugar **lemon or lime juice**

Take ripe guavas, pare, quarter, and drop the sections into cold water. Simmer them till tender in water enough to nearly cover them; strain by hanging in a jelly bag overnight. Do not squeeze the bag; boil the juice for 1 hour, uncovered, skim, and add 1 scant 500 ml (1 pint) of white sugar to each 500 ml (1 pint) of juice. Let simmer till the jelly is clear, add lemon or lime juice to taste, and let simmer ½ an hour more, skimming frequently. Pour into jars and seal when cold.

MELON, LEMON AND ORANGE JELLY

7½ kg (15 lb.) Melon **6 lemons**
6 oranges **sugar (to measure)**

Cut up *whole* melon, cover with water. Cut lemons and oranges roughly. Place in separate basin and cover with boiling water. Next day boil all together until soft. Strain. Measure and allow 1 cup sugar to 1 cup liquid.

Boil until it reaches jell point. Bottle at once.

PARSLEY JELLY

Parsley
lemon
sugar
gelatine
essence lemon

Wash a quantity of parsley, cover with water, and press firmly down in the pan. Add juice of a lemon, and boil gently for 1 hour. Strain through a jelly bag, then add to every 1 litre (1 quart) of juice, 250 gr ($\frac{1}{2}$ lb.) of sugar. Boil for 20 minutes, and add 30 gr (1 oz.) of gelatine (previously soaked) to every 1 litre (1 quart) of juice. Skim well, and boil another 10 minutes. Remove from the fire, and add a few drops of essence of lemon. Bottle while hot.

PASSIONFRUIT AND APPLE JELLY

1½ kg (3 lb.) Cooking Apples
1 litre (1 quart) of passionfruit juice
1 litre (1 quart) water
1 large lemon
2 kg (4 lb.) sugar

Boil the apples in the water till well broken down, but not pulped. Put a sieve over a preserving pan, and turn the apples into it, and allow the liquid to drain through. Take sufficient passionfruit to give 1 litre (1 quart) of juice. Cut fruit in halves, and drain contents through a sieve, so as to keep back the seeds. Add the juice to the apple water. Simmer for 10 minutes, and add the lemon juice, and pour through a jelly bag. Return to pan again and bring to the boil. Heat the sugar till quite hot, and stir gradually into the boiling fruit juice. Boil rapidly for 20 minutes. Test to see if it jellies. If not, boil until it does. Watch carefully. Pour into jars and cover down.

QUINCE JELLY (No. 1)

8 Large or 12 Medium Sized Quinces
2¼ kg (4½ lb.) sugar
4 litres (8 pints) cold water

Rub the fluff from the quinces, put them (uncut) into the preserving pan, and add water and sugar. Boil all together for 4 hours. After 4 hours, the jelly should go into a lot of small bubbles (this indicates that it will set well). Strain off into jelly jars. The fruit remaining is delicious with cream or custard.

QUINCE JELLY (No. 2)

Quinces
water
sugar

Rub fluff from quinces and cut up roughly. Cover with water and simmer until thoroughly soft (4-5 hours). Strain through jelly bag or tea towel. Measure liquid and put in clean pan to boil. When boiling add 1 cup sugar to each cup liquid and boil fast until it jells.

MARMALADE

APPLE MARMALADE

6 Lemons
3 kg (6 lb.) apples
3 litre (6 pints) water
3 kg (6 lb.) sugar

Slice lemons thinly, soak overnight in the water (boiling when put on), and cook gently until the rind is tender–about ½ an hour. Meanwhile, peel and cut up the apples, add to cooked lemon, and cook quickly until soft, then add sugar, and cook quickly for ½ an hour.

FRENCH MARMALADE

3 Large Carrots
2½ kg (5 lb.) sugar
4 lemons
8 breakfast cups water

Grate the carrots, put the lemons through the mincer, and leave all in a basin overnight with half the water. In the morning, add the rest of the water, and boil for ½ an hour, then add the sugar, and cook for 2½ hours.

FOUR FRUIT MARMALADE

1 Orange
1 grape fruit
1 lemon
1 apple
sugar

Choose good sized fruit in each case. Wash the fruit carefully. Peel and core the apple, cut orange, lemon, and grapefruit into halves, squeeze out the juice, and remove the seeds. Cut the skins in pieces, and put them through a mincing machine along with the apple. Combine with the fruit juice, and measure. Allow 3 times this amount of water. Combine, and let stand overnight. Next morning, boil all together for 1 hour. Let stand until next day, then cook with an equal measure of sugar, added hot, for about 1 hour, or until it will set. Put into jars, and cover when cold.

MARMALADE

7 Seville Oranges
4½ litres (9 pints) water
2 lemons
4½ kg (9 lb.) sugar

Cut up oranges and lemons very thinly. Add the water, and allow to stand for 36 hours. Bring it to the boil, and let boil for 2 hours. Allow to stand for 20 hours. Bring it to the boil and add the sugar, and then stir as little as possible. Let it boil for 1 hour. Make the bottles hot, and fill them while the marmalade is hot.

ORANGE MARMALADE

12 Seville Oranges	**6 lemons**
water	**sugar**

Wash fruit and take off rind with a carrot grater. Peel off all white pith, and cut up the fruit finely. Let stand overnight with 4 cups cold water to 1 cup fruit. Next day, boil up, then let stand overnight again. Then boil up and allow 1 cup of sugar to 1 cup of fruit. Boil until it jells when tried on a cold saucer.

ORANGE AND PINEAPPLE MARMALADE

6 Oranges	**2 pineapples**
2 kg (4 lb.) sugar	**$1\frac{1}{2}$ litres ($1\frac{1}{2}$ quarts) water**

Wash the oranges and soak them in the water overnight. Boil them in the same water in the morning until tender, then cut them into small pieces, and return to pan with the sugar added, and the pineapple (cut fine). Boil the marmalade, stirring all the time till it jells.

RHUBARB MARMALADE

2 kg (4 lb.) Rhubarb	**2 kg (4 lb.) sugar**
3 oranges	**500 gr (1 lb.) walnuts**

Wash and peel the rhubarb. Cut into 26 mm (1 in.) pieces, add orange juice, rind, and sugar, and boil gently for 30 minutes. Add walnuts broken into small pieces, and cook 10 to 15 minutes longer or until thick.

PRESERVES

It is better for fruit to be under ripe than over ripe for preserving. If one has her own home garden, the fruit can be selected just at the right time. Fruit for preserving must be perfectly sound, and free from blemishes. Select fruit of an even size. It packs and looks better, and cooks more evenly. Stone fruit is better cut in half and the stones removed.

Choose wide-necked jars for preserving. They are much easier to fill. Various kinds are on the market. It is necessary to replace the rubber rings at each preserving. The covers can, with care, be used for several seasons.

A copper or large boiler makes an excellent sterilizer. A kerosene tin cut lengthwise is also good. A strip or two of wood should be placed in the bottom of the boiler for the bottles to stand on, and to keep them from direct contact with the heat.

It is also a good plan to place some straw under and between the bottles.

To bottle successfully a thermometer is required.

A nice preserving syrup is made from 3 kg (6 lb.) of sugar to 4 litres (1 gallon) of water. Place in a preserving pan, and bring to the boil slowly. Boil for 3 minutes. Have your bottles ready packed with the prepared fruit. They must be full. Pour over the syrup, filling to the neck. The fruit must be completely covered. Put on the lid, but do not screw tightly. Allow for a little expansion. Put the packed bottles into the prepared boiler. Fill with cold water right up to the neck of the bottles. Gradually heat the water to 75° C (165° F.), and allow bottles to remain at that temperature from 10 to 15 minutes. It should take from 1¼ to 1½ hours for the water to reach the above degree. Remove the bottles one at a time, and fill quite full with boiling syrup (surplus boiling syrup should be ready), screw the lids tightly, return to boiler, which should be removed from the fire, and leave to cool in the water. 75° C (165° F.) is a good standard to follow when preserving. It suits most fruits.

Canned fruits and vegetables should always be stored in a cool dry cupboard.

Apples, pears, and quinces for preserving, should be prepared by peeling and coring. The sections as they are cut should be thrown into a weak solution of salt and water. This hardens the fruit, and prevents it discolouring.

Peaches should be prepared for preserving by dipping in scalding hot water for just a minute, then into cold water. The skins will slip away easily. Peach kernels may be cooked in the syrup, and greatly improve the preserve.

When canning pears, add a little tartaric acid to each jar. Dissolve the acid in a little water. The acid relieves the otherwise very sweet flavour.

Nectarines and apricots are prepared by cutting in halves. The time to cook after reaching 75° C (165° F.), is about 12 minutes.

Pineapple should be sliced or cut into dice. The time is 15 minutes.

Plums should be cooked for 10 minutes. Greengage plums should be cooked for 8 minutes. These can be preserved in large crocks, and keep excellently. A squeeze of lemon juice to each 500 ml (1 pint) of syrup is a pleasant addition. All fruit cooked in this way has kept good for 2 years.

BOTTLING FRUIT

Cut a kerosene tin lengthwise to cook the fruit in, and put a piece of wood in the bottom of the tin to stand the bottles on. Be sure the bottles do not touch each other or they will crack. Put a pan on the stove with $1\frac{1}{2}$ kg (3 lb.) sugar and 24 cups water, to boil for the syrup, then wipe, peel, and stone the fruit. Pack them, cut side facing downwards into clean dry bottles, stand the bottles on a damp cloth, and fill with the boiling syrup. Put covers on bottles lightly while cooking in tin. Do not screw them down, or put the rubber rings on until cooked. For peaches, plums, etc., cook about 25 minutes. Pears take much longer. Put bottles in lukewarm water to start and bring to the boil. When cooked screw down the lids tightly, and seal with white wax, or melt mutton fat and beeswax together and seal. Fruit keeps for 2 years splendidly preserved in this way. When the bottles are in the tin, pieces of rag or paper should be placed in between them to keep them from touching.

BOTTLED STEWED FRUIT

Have clean warm preserving bottles with rubbers in place ready. Stew fruit in syrup ready for serving. Put in jars as near to boiling as possible. Fill jar to overflowing. Place on lid and clamp and allow to stand 48 hours or until cold (24 hours in winter). Remove clamp and test for sealing. Fruit done this way keeps well. It is an easy way for a busy housewife, but it tastes as stewed fruit distinct from preserved fruit.

CANDIED PEEL (No. 1)

6 Lemon or Orange Rinds	**3 cups sugar**
salt	**water**

Soak rinds in slightly salted water for 3 days. Drain, and rinse. Boil slowly in fresh water until tender. Make a syrup by boiling the sugar, and $1\frac{1}{2}$ cups water together for 5 minutes, keeping the pan uncovered. Put rinds into a basin, and cover with syrup. Leave for 2 days. Strain off the syrup, and boil up again. Put in rinds and boil until semi-transparent—about 20 minutes. Take out the rinds, and lay them on flat tins. Put a little syrup in the centre of each, and sprinkle with castor sugar. Dry a little in a cool oven.

CANDIED PEEL (No. 2)

Orange or Lemon Peel
sugar
water

This is a simple method. Remove the skin in quarters, put into a brine consisting of 1 tablespoon salt to 1 cup cold water, and allow to stand for 3 days. Remove from the brine, put into clean water, place on stove, and allow to boil quickly for 10 minutes. Prepare a syrup of 1 cup water, and 2 cups sugar. Let it boil until the sugar is dissolved. Remove peel from boiling water, and place in the syrup. Let it simmer quietly on the side of the stove for about 3 hours, or until it is a clear, amber colour. Store in wide-mouthed jars, and it will keep indefinitely.

MARROW PRESERVE

6 kg (12 lb.) Marrow
185 gr (6 oz.) root ginger
1 dozen chillies
rind and juice 4 lemons
6 kg (12 lb.) sugar

Cut marrow into pieces, put a little sugar over it and leave overnight. In morning put all in pan with remainder of sugar and lemon rind. Bruise ginger, tie chillies in a bag and remove when cooked. Boil for 3 or 4 hours or until quite clear. Bottle.

PRESERVING PASSIONFRUIT

This is one of the most useful of our fruits, but most people make the mistake when using passionfruit in cooking, of boiling the seeds and juice. To retain the distinctive flavour of the passionfruit, these should never be raised to a temperature higher than 32° C (90° F.)—to bring them to boiling point kills the special flavour and hardens the seeds. Remove pulp from skins, adding sugar (which, of course, is in itself a preservative) in the proportion of 500 gr (1 lb.) of sugar to 6 dozen passion fruit. Stir over heat till sugar is dissolved, fill jars, and seal as with all bottled fruit.

PRESERVED PASSIONFRUIT (UNCOOKED)

To 1 cup passionfruit pulp stir in $\frac{3}{4}$ cup sugar. Stir frequently until all sugar is dissolved. Fill small jars and cover with plastic and screw on top securely. This will keep on the shelf for 12 months. (It usually takes time to dissolve sugar—leave overnight.)

PEARS IN SYRUP

3 kg (6 lb.) Sugar | **750 ml ($1\frac{1}{2}$ pints) vinegar**
pears

Make a syrup of sugar and vinegar. Boil, stirring occasionally. When boiling, place in as many peeled, cored, and quartered pears as the syrup will cover. Boil gently until the pears are a deep red. Lift out carefully with as little syrup as possible, and pack into jars. Place another lot of pears in the syrup, cook, and remove as before. When all pears are done, pour remaining syrup over the pears in the jars. Cover, and store. A little ginger or spice may be added when making the syrup, if liked.

PRESERVED CUMQUATS

Cumquats | **water**
sugar

Prick the cumquats with a darning needle, and boil gently in plenty of water till tender. Then make a syrup of 625 gr ($1\frac{1}{4}$ lb.) sugar and 250 ml ($\frac{1}{2}$ pint) water to each 500 gr (1 lb.) of fruit, boil it for 20 minutes then add fruit and boil 15 minutes longer. Turn into bottles and seal securely.

PRESERVED FIGS (No. 1)

Figs | **water**
sugar

Prepare figs by cutting a little off each end. Put in a preserving pan, and cover well with water, and boil for $2\frac{1}{2}$ hours. Add 500 gr (1 lb.) of sugar to 500 gr (1 lb.) of fruit and water, and cook until well browned. Remove from the fire, and place in bottles. Small brown figs are preferred.

PRESERVED FIGS (No. 2)

9 kg (18 lb.) Figs | **2 dessertspoons cayenne pepper**
2 litres (2 quarts) water | **125 gr ($\frac{1}{4}$ lb.) dry ginger**
6 kg (12 lb.) sugar

Bruise the ginger, tie in a muslin bag with the pepper, and put in the sugar and water. Boil quickly for $\frac{1}{2}$ an hour. Prick the figs, and wash them, leaving the stalks on. Place in syrup. Boil until the syrup is thick and a dark brown. Bottle and seal.

CHUTNEYS, PICKLES, SAUCES AND RELISHES

APPLE CHUTNEY (No. 1)

$1\frac{1}{2}$ kg (3 lb.) Sour Apples
2 lemons
750 gr ($1\frac{1}{2}$ lb.) brown sugar
1 dessertspoon ground ginger
500 gr (1 lb.) seedless raisins
1 kg (2 lb.) onions
1 tablespoon mustard
pepper and salt
500 ml (1 pint) brown malt vinegar

Peel the apples and onions, cut them in pieces, and mince them with the raisins. Put the mixture into a saucepan with the grated rind and strained juice of the lemons, and all the other ingredients, bring to the boil, and simmer gently till tender, stirring often. When cold, bottle and seal down. Keep for six weeks before using.

APPLE CHUTNEY (No. 2)

10 Large Cooking Apples
3 cups stoned raisins
1 tablespoon mustard
1 tablespoon salt
5 large onions
1 kg (2 lb.) dark sugar
1 tablespoon black pepper
1 teaspoon cayenne pepper
$1\frac{1}{2}$ bottles vinegar

Chop the apples and onions finely, mix with all the other ingredients, and boil gently for 2 hours. Bottle, and make air tight. A few chopped almonds improve all apple chutneys.

FIG CHUTNEY

3 kg (6 lb.) Figs
750 gr ($1\frac{1}{2}$ lb.) onions
1 bottle vinegar
125 gr ($\frac{1}{4}$ lb.) salt
500 gr (1 lb.) apples
30 gr (1 oz.) garlic
500 gr (1 lb.) sugar
spices

Slice all up small, and add the vinegar, sugar, and salt. Tie in a muslin bag 45 gr ($1\frac{1}{2}$ oz.) cloves and allspice, 15 gr ($\frac{1}{2}$ oz.) whole ginger, a few chillies, or $\frac{1}{2}$ a teaspoon cayenne pepper, and boil all for 3 hours.

FIG AND TOMATO CHUTNEY

1½ kg (3 lb.) Ripe Tomatoes
1½ kg (3 lb.) onions
500 gr (1 lb.) sultanas
15 gr (½ oz.) chillies
1 tablespoon ginger
2 kg (4 lb.) ripe figs
1½ kg (3 lb.) brown sugar
30 gr (1 oz.) garlic
2 tablespoons salt

Cut up, cover with vinegar and stand overnight. Next day add spices (in a bag) and boil 2 hours.

FRUIT CHUTNEY

1 kg (2 lb.) Figs
1 kg (2 lb.) peaches
1 kg (2 lb.) onions
2 bottles vinegar
1 kg (2 lb.) sugar
1 kg (2 lb.) apples
500 gr (1 lb.) sultanas
salt and spices to taste

Boil all together till fairly thick. Ground mace is nice in this chutney, and cayenne if liked hot. Any other fruits may be used.

INDIAN CHUTNEY

250 gr (½ lb.) Brown Sugar
1 kg (2 lb.) apples
125 gr (4 oz.) salt
90 gr (3 oz.) almonds
90 gr (3 oz.) onions
1½ kg (3 lb.) raisins
500 gr (1 lb.) dried figs
125 gr (4 oz.) ground ginger
45 gr (1½ oz.) garlic
30 gr (1 oz.) cayenne pepper
1¼ litre (2½ pints) best vinegar

Put all ingredients through the mincer, and mix thoroughly. Allow to stand for 2 or 3 hours before bottling as it swells a little. No boiling required.

MELON CHUTNEY (No. 1)

2½ kg (5 lb.) Minced Melon
2 tablespoons salt
2½ cups brown sugar
a few cloves
1 cup currants
2 apples
1 tablespoon turmeric
500 ml (1 pint) vinegar
1½ kg (3 lb.) sliced onions
1 tablespoon spice
1 dessertspoon pepper
1 cup sultanas
1 tablespoon flour
1 tablespoon curry powder

Put the melon into a pan with the vinegar, onions, salt and brown sugar, and bring to the boil. Then add the spice, cloves, pepper, currants, sultanas, and apples, and boil for 3 hours. Just before taking off, make a paste with a little vinegar, flour, turmeric, and the curry powder. Blend well, stir into the chutney, and boil for a few minutes.

MELON CHUTNEY (No. 2)

1½ kg (3 lb.) Minced Melons
1 kg (2 lb.) sugar
1 dessertspoon cloves
1 teaspoon cayenne pepper
1 tablespoon plain flour
1 kg (2 lb.) onions
1 teaspoon mixed spice
1 dessertspoon salt
1 tablespoon turmeric
1 tablespoon mustard
vinegar

Just cover the minced melon with cold vinegar, and let stand all night. In the morning, add the onions minced, the sugar, and spices. Boil for 2 hours. Then mix the plain flour, mustard, and turmeric with a little cold vinegar. Add this to the boiling mixture, and cook a little longer.

TASTY CHUTNEY

1½ kg (3 lb.) Apples
1½ kg (3 lb.) tomatoes
500 gr (1 lb.) brown sugar
2 tablespoons golden syrup
1 tablespoon whole pepper
1½ kg (3 lb.) onions
500 gr (1 lb.) stoned raisins
750 ml (1½ pints) vinegar
1 tablespoon salt
1 tablespoon allspice

Cut up the apples, onions, and tomatoes into thin slices. Chop the raisins, and add all other ingredients. Place in a saucepan and boil for 3 hours. Put spices in a muslin bag.

TOMATO CHUTNEY (No. 1)

6 kg (12 lb.) Tomatoes
250 gr (½ lb.) salt
3 kg (6 lb.) apples
750 ml (1½ pints) vinegar
4 small knobs garlic
8 gr (¼ oz.) cayenne pepper
1½ kg (3 lb.) sugar
1½ kg (3 lb.) onions
750 gr (1½ lb.) sultanas
2 level tablespoons grated horse radish
15 gr (½ oz.) cloves
15 gr (½ oz.) allspice

Boil the tomatoes until soft, then press the pulp through a colander. Add sugar, salt, onions (cut very fine), apples, sultanas, vinegar, horse radish, and garlic. Put the spices into a muslin bag, and add. Let the whole simmer for 3 hours. Lift out the spices and bottle. *Note*: A small handful of almonds cut up is an improvement.

TOMATO CHUTNEY (No. 2)

6 kg (12 lb.) Ripe Tomatoes
750 gr (1½ lb.) onions
3 kg (6 lb.) apples
750 gr (1½ lb.) sultanas
15 gr (½ oz.) cloves
1½ kg (3 lb.) sugar
125 gr (¼ lb.) salt
750 ml (1½ pints) vinegar
15 gr (½ oz.) cayenne pepper
15 gr (½ oz.) allspice

Boil tomatoes to a pulp, then strain. Add to the liquid, the vinegar, and spices in a cloth. Boil for ½ an hour, then add all ingredients, and boil about 4 hours.

TOMATO CHUTNEY (GREEN)

10 kg (20 lb.) Green Tomatoes
3 green apples
6 chillies
15 gr (½ oz.) cloves
1 tin treacle
2 litres (2 quarts) vinegar
4 tablespoons cinnamon
750 gr (1½ lb.) onions
3 large peaches
½ teaspoon cayenne
2 tablespoons salt
500 gr (1 lb.) dark sugar
4 pieces green ginger

Cut all up small and boil together until like jam.

TOMATO AND APPLE CHUTNEY

2 kg (4 lb.) Ripe Tomatoes (scald and peel)
1 kg (2 lb.) sugar
500 gr (1 lb.) onions
¾ cup sultanas
garlic to taste
a few cloves
1 kg (2 lb.) cooking apples (sliced)
60 gr (2 oz.) salt
500 ml (1 pint) vinegar
¾ cup currants
cayenne pepper
2 teaspoons ground ginger

Mix all together and stand overnight. Cook three hours.

PICKLES

BEETROOT (PICKLED)

Beetroot
30 gr (1 oz.) whole spice
1 dessertspoon salt
30 gr (1 oz.) whole pepper
1 dozen cloves
½ cup sugar
1 litre (1 quart) of vinegar

Cook enough beetroot to fill a large earthenware jar, when peeled and sliced. Prepare sufficient vinegar to cover, by boiling with spices and sugar. Boil 10 minutes slowly, strain, and pour while hot over the beetroot. When cold, seal with 13 mm (¼ in.) melted fat. This is essential. When this cools, tie down tightly with greaseproof and brown paper. Will keep 4 months.

CUCUMBERS (PICKLED)

3 litres (3 Quarts) Water
1 dozen bay leaves
½ stick celery
some vine and peach leaves
2 handfuls salt
a few blades of mace
500 ml (1 pint) vinegar
cucumbers
some pepper corns, or ½ dozen chillies
dill seed

Select firm, green cucumbers, about 15 cm-20 cm (6-8 in.) long. Wash and wipe them, and into the bottom of a large glazed crock, or clean cask, put a layer of leaves and spices, then a layer of cucumbers, and so on alternately until it is nearly full. Mix the vinegar with the salted water, and pour over all. Place a weighted plate on top to keep the cucumbers submerged. Store in a cool place, and as a white froth or film arises, skim off once or twice. They are ready for use in two or three weeks. Remove cucumbers as required, wash, and peel, cut into strips a few inches long, and serve in glass dishes. They are delicious with cold meat. *Note*: The dill flavour is essential. The seeds can be obtained from seedmen, and sown in the garden at the same time as you sow cucumber seed. Stalks, leaves, and seeds can then be used.

CAULIFLOWER PICKLE (No. 1)

Cauliflowers
1 teaspoon peppercorns
vinegar
1 teaspoon allspice
6 cloves

Take firm white cauliflowers and sufficient vinegar to cover them. To each 1 litre (1 quart) of vinegar allow the above amount of spices. Break the cauliflower into small sprays, place them on a dish, sprinkle liberally with salt, and let them remain for 3 to 6 hours. Meanwhile, tie the seasoning ingredients in muslin, and boil them in vinegar for ½ an hour, and allow to become quite cold. Drain the cauliflower well from the salt, place in wide necked bottles, and pour the prepared vinegar over them. Cover closely.

CAULIFLOWER PICKLE (No. 2)

1 Large Cauliflower
1¾ litres (3½ pints) vinegar
2 tablespoons mustard
¾ cup flour
2 cups salt
500 gr (1 lb.) onions
1 tablespoon turmeric
4 cups sugar

Put the cauliflower, broken in sections, into a pan of boiling water, to which the salt has been added. Boil for 1 minute and then strain. Boil the vinegar with the onions (minced), and while boiling, mix the mustard, tumeric, flour and sugar well together. Blend with 1 cup cold vinegar to a smooth paste, and add to the boiling vinegar and onions. Boil 1 minute, add the drained cauliflower, and bring again to the boil. Remove from the fire and bottle. An excellent pickle.

CABBAGE AND MUSTARD PICKLE

1 Large Cabbage
1 cup salt
1 cup flour
1 teaspoon curry powder
4 large onions
1 litre (1 quart) vinegar
2 cups sugar
2 tablespoons mustard
500 ml (1 pint) vinegar (to mix)

Cut the cabbage up finely, also the onions, sprinkle with the salt, and allow to stand for 24 hours. Drain well and boil slowly in 1 litre (1 quart) vinegar for 20 minutes. Mix together the flour, sugar, curry powder, mustard, and blend with the 500 ml (1 pint) of vinegar. Add to cabbage, and boil for 5 minutes longer. Put into jars, and seal tightly.

EGG PICKLES

2 Dozen Eggs
vinegar
a pinch cayenne pepper
water
a pinch mace
or 4 cloves

Boil the eggs for ½ an hour in plenty of water. Remove the shells, and place eggs in wide mouthed glass jam jars. Bring to the boil enough vinegar to cover the eggs, and add a pinch of mace, cayenne pepper, and 3 or 4 cloves. Pour over the eggs, and when cold screw the top on the jars. These are ready to use in 10 days.

FIGS (PICKLED)

6 Dozen Figs
1 kg (2 lb.) sugar
3 litres (3 quarts) vinegar
30 gr (1 oz.) allspice
60 gr (2 oz.) cloves
60 gr (2 oz.) whole ginger
30 gr (1 oz.) whole pepper
250 gr (½ lb.) salt
½ teaspoon cayenne pepper

Place the whole figs into a large pan, cover with all the ingredients, and leave for 3 days. Then draw off the liquid Put figs into a large jar, bring liquid to the boil, and pour it over the figs. Allow to remain for 1 month before using.

GRAPES OR FIGS (PICKLED)

1 litre (1 Quart) Vinegar
30 gr (1 oz.) salt
30 gr (1 oz.) cloves
30 gr (1 oz.) peppercorns
750 gr (1½ lb.) sugar
30 gr (1 oz.) allspice
30 gr (1 oz.) ginger
fruit

Soak the fruit in the above ingredients for 3 days, and then place fruit in jars. Boil the liquid for 10 minutes, and add, boiling, to the fruit. When cold, cork tightly. This recipe is enough for 4 dozen figs, or 2½ kg (5 lb.) grapes.

GHERKINS (PICKLED)

4 Cups Small Green Gherkins
1 litre (1 quart) vinegar
$\frac{1}{2}$ cup white mustard seed
1 teaspoon whole cloves
8 gr ($\frac{1}{4}$ oz.) ginger root
500 gr (1 lb.) brown sugar
1 litre (1 quart) boiling water
1 cup salt
1 teaspoon powdered alum
8 gr ($\frac{1}{4}$ oz.) stick cinnamon
8 gr ($\frac{1}{4}$ oz.) allspice
1 cup green pepper

Dissolve salt in water and pour (boiling hot) over the gherkins. Allow to stand for 24 hours, drain, wipe dry, and cover with boiling vinegar, in which other ingredients have been boiled. Place in jars, and seal tightly. Small green cucumbers may be used for this pickle.

MELON PICKLE

3-4 kg (6-8 lb.) Melon
$\frac{1}{2}$ cup treacle
1 cup plain flour
1 tablespoon mustard
1 kg (2 lb.) onions
$\frac{1}{2}$ cup sugar
1 tablespoon turmeric
$1\frac{1}{4}$-$1\frac{1}{2}$ litre ($2\frac{1}{2}$ to 3 pints) vinegar
salt and spice to taste

Cut up melon and onions, and put on to boil with all the other ingredients except mustard and flour. When the melon and onions are well cooked, mix the flour and mustard with a little water, and add to the pickle. Let simmer for 15 minutes, then take off to cool.

MUSTARD PICKLE

1 litre (1 Quart) Green Tomatoes
1 litre (1 quart) onions
a few peppercorns or chillies
salt
6 tablespoons mustard
1 cup flour
1 litre (1 quart) cauliflower
1 litre (1 quart) cucumbers
2 litres (2 quarts) vinegar
water
1 tablespoon turmeric
1 cup sugar

Make a brine of salt and water, strong enough to float an egg. Cut up vegetables, and lay in the brine overnight. Put brine and vegetables on the fire, and bring to scalding point. Take off the fire and strain. Put vinegar in a pan with the spices, boil, and thicken with the mustard, turmeric, flour, sugar, mixed to a smooth paste with cold vinegar. Put in the vegetables, mix well, and heat through. Bottle while hot.

ONIONS (PICKLED), No. 1

Onions
2 litre (2 quarts) vinegar
1 tablespoon cloves
salt
1 tablespoon whole pepper
1 tablespoon mace
1 tablespoon allspice

Peel a quantity of small onions, put them into salt and water, and leave for 12 hours. Boil together the vinegar, spices and a little salt for 1 hour. Drain the onions, and pour the hot liquid on to them.

ONIONS (PICKLED), No. 2

12 kg (24 lb.) Onions
$4\frac{1}{2}$ bottles vinegar
2 tablespoons ground mace
2 tablespoons pepper
1 kg (2 lb.) salt
1 kg (2 lb.) sugar
2 tablespoons allspice
2 tablespoons coriander seed

With the salt, make a boiling brine, and cover the onions. Leave 24 hours, drain, pour cold water over them, then drain again. Wipe onions dry, and place in dry jars. Boil together the vinegar and other ingredients for $\frac{1}{4}$ of an hour. Strain, and pour over onions boiling hot, and seal.

PICKLED OLIVES

The olives must be gathered with care so as not to bruise the fruit. (A good idea is to pick them into a bucket half filled with water.) Cover the olives with a brine made of 292 gr ($9\frac{3}{4}$ oz.) salt to 4 litres (1 gallon) water, stand for eight (8) days, then drain.

Cover the olives with a fresh brine made of 500 gr (1 lb.) salt to 4 litres (1 gallon) water, stand for eight (8) days, then drain.

Cover the olives with a solution made of 75 gr ($2\frac{1}{2}$ oz.) Caustic Soda to 4 litres (1 gallon) water.

Allow to stand for 24 hours, *taking great care*. Use rubber gloves, and keep well out of the reach of children. Drain the olives and wash well. Continue to wash and rinse frequently for 2-3 days, or until the water turns reasonably clear. Pack the olives in jars and cover with a brine made of 240-300 gr (8-10 oz.) salt to 4 litres (1 gal.) water (depending on taste). Sterilize at 75° C (180° F.) for $\frac{1}{2}$ an hour. If not desired to sterilize pack in jars with a slightly stronger salt solution 375-425 gr (12-14 oz.). A scum will form on the top, but this will not affect the olives. It is a good idea to keep the olives away from strong light. If using glass jars, wrap around with dark paper. Dark plastic buckets are ideal to use during the processing, if only small quantities of olives for home use are being preserved.

PEAR PICKLE

3 kg (6 lb.) Firm Pears
3 bottles vinegar
1 teaspoon cayenne pepper
$1\frac{1}{2}$ tablespoons curry powder
salt
2 large onions
750 gr ($1\frac{1}{2}$ lb.) sugar
$1\frac{1}{2}$ tablespoons mustard
4 tablespoons flour

Cut up onions, sprinkle with salt and leave overnight. Peel and cut pears into small pieces, drain brine off onions and add. Then add vinegar and sugar. Boil until tender.

Dissolve curry powder, mustard, cayenne and flour with a little vinegar. Add to fruit mixture and boil about 5 minutes.

PEARS (PICKLED)

- 3½ kg (7 lb.) Pears
- 750 ml (1½ pints) vinegar
- 1½ kg (3 lb.) sugar
- 1 dozen whole cloves
- 3 sticks cinnamon

Put all ingredients into a pan, and boil until pears are tender. Lift out, and boil vinegar until the syrup is thick. Pour over pears, and bottle.

PICCALILLI PICKLES (No. 1)

- 3 kg (6 lb.) Marrow
- 1 large cucumber
- 750 gr (1½ lb.) French beans
- 1 dozen peppercorns
- 1 dozen or more chillies
- 375 gr (12 oz.) castor sugar
- 60 gr (2 oz.) turmeric
- 1 kg (2 lb.) cauliflower
- 500 gr (1 lb.) onions
- 4 litre (1 gallon) vinegar
- 2 teaspoons mustard seeds
- 90 gr (3 oz.) mustard
- 45 gr (1½ oz.) flour
- vinegar to mix

Peel the onions, which should be on the small side. If large, cut in two. Break the cauliflower into small sprigs, removing all hard stalks. Peel and remove seeds from the marrow and cut into pieces. Peel the cucumber and cut into pieces the same size. If beans are small they will only need the ends removed, if big, cut down the centre. Cover all the ingredients with salt and leave for 24 hours, then put them into a preserving pan with sufficient vinegar to cover. To every 4 litres (1 gallon) of vinegar allow the given amount of peppercorns, mustard seeds, and chillies. Add more or less chillies, according to how hot you like your pickle. Bring all to the boil and boil for 10 to 15 minutes, then mix to a paste with a little vinegar, the mustard, sugar, flour, turmeric (these quantities are also for 4 litres (1 gallon) of vinegar). Add to the boiling pickle, boil for another 2 minutes, and then put into jars while hot. Tie down next day.

PICCALILLI PICKLES (No. 2)

- 500 gr (1 lb.) Very Young Kidney Beans
- 2 large cauliflowers
- a few gherkins
- 4 tablespoons ground rice (rice flour)
- 1 tablespoon turmeric
- 1½ kg (3 lb.) onions (or less)
- 3 good sized cucumbers
- 375 gr (¾ lb.) mustard
- 2½ litres (2½ quarts) vinegar
- 60 gr (2 oz.) spices
- salt
- 6 chillies

Peel onions (dry), place in a bowl, and cover with a good handful of salt. Cut up the cauliflower and other vegetables, place on onions, and cover these with two good handfuls of salt. Mix mustard, turmeric, and ground rice to a smooth paste with 500 ml (1 pint) of vinegar, and stand for 12 hours or more. Boil balance of vinegar in a pan with the spices tied in muslin, then put in the vegetables, and boil up. Add mustard mixture and boil all together for 5 minutes. When cold, put into jars.

PLUMS (PICKLED)

2½ kg (5 lb.) Plums
500 gr (1 lb.) sugar
60 gr (2 oz.) cloves
1 litre (1 quart) vinegar
1 cup treacle
3 chillies

Use Orleans, Grand Duke or Angelina plums. Wipe and prick the plums carefully with the prongs of a small fork, and place them in earthenware jars. Tie the cloves and chillies in a piece of butter muslin and boil with the sugar, vinegar and treacle. Boil for 15 minutes, pour the boiling liquid over the plums, cover at once, and leave for a week before using.

SPICED TOMATOES

2½ kg (5 lb.) Small Tomatoes
1 tablespoon salt
1 tablespoon peppercorns
1 teaspoon ground cinnamon
1 kg (2 lb.) sugar
½ small teaspoon cayenne pepper
1 tablespoon cloves
22 gr packet mixed spice
vinegar

Put the tomatoes whole into a preserving pan with sugar, salt, and spices, add enough vinegar to cover, and boil until skins begin to break. Take out tomatoes, boil vinegar for 1 hour, put tomatoes back, and boil for ½ an hour.

TOMATO CHOW-CHOW

3 kg (6 lb.) Green Tomatoes
3 apples
4 litres (4 quarts) water
2 teaspoons allspice
½ cup plain flour
1 teaspoon cayenne pepper
4 or 5 medium sized onions
500 gr (1 lb.) salt
2 bottles good vinegar
3 cups sugar
2 teaspoons curry powder
2 tablespoons mustard
2 tablespoons turmeric

Put the tomatoes, onions, and apples into a brine made of the salt and water, and let them stand overnight. Next day, put all on the fire, allow to come to the boil, then remove, and drain. Now put into a pan the vinegar and allspice. While this is coming to the boil, prepare the sugar, flour, curry powder, pepper, mustard, and turmeric, by mixing with about 500 ml (1 pint) cold water until smooth. Add to the boiling vinegar, stir well, then add tomatoes, etc. Boil for ½ an hour, and bottle and seal when cold.

TOMATO PICKLE (GREEN)

4 kg (8 lb.) Green Tomatoes
salt
1 litre (2 pints) vinegar
1 heaped teaspoon allspice
½ cup sugar
5 or 6 onions
cayenne pepper
3 tablespoons mustard
1 heaped teaspoon cloves
1 cup treacle

TOMATO PICKLE (GREEN)—*continued*

Slice the tomatoes, and sprinkle with salt. Let stand for 12 hours. Strain off the liquid, and sprinkle with the cayenne. Add the onions, sliced, the vinegar, mustard, spices, sugar, and treacle. Boil for 1 hour. Bottle when cold.

WALNUTS (PICKLED)

Green Walnuts
30 gr (1 oz.) allspice
125 gr (4 oz.) salt
1 litre (1 quart) vinegar
1 teaspoon salt
1 litre (1 quart) water

Use green walnuts, sufficiently soft to allow a darning needle to penetrate easily. Prick the walnuts well, and place in an earthenware vessel. Cover with the cold brine made from 125 gr (4 oz.) salt to 1 litre (1 quart) water. Stir walnuts two or three times a day for 6 days. Drain and cover with fresh brine, in which let them remain for 3 days, drain again, and spread on large flat dishes. Place in the sun until quite black, then three-quarter fill with walnuts some wide necked bottles, which have previously been sterilised. Boil together the vinegar, salt, and allspice, and when quite cold, pour over the walnuts in the bottles. Cover and store in a cool, dry cupboard.

SAUCES

APRICOT SAUCE

3 kg (6 lb.) Apricots (stoned weight)
60 gr (2 oz.) ground cloves
125 gr (4 oz.) garlic
60 gr (2 oz.) salt
1½ litres (3 pints) light vinegar
500 gr (1 lb.) onions
1 kg (2 lb.) sugar
½ teaspoon cayenne pepper
1 teaspoon ground mace
juice of 2 or 3 lemons

Boil all 3 hours, strain and bottle.

FRENCH MUSTARD

1 Tablespoon Curry Powder
1 teaspoon mustard
1 teaspoon sugar
a pinch of salt
some strong cold tea

Mix dry ingredients with the the tea, bottle and seal.

GRAPE SAUCE

2½ kg (5 lb.) Muscatel or Centennial Grapes
1 tablespoon cloves
1 tablespoon salt
1 kg (2 lb.) brown sugar
1 tablespoon cinnamon
1 tablespoon allspice
1 tablespoon cayenne pepper
2 cups vinegar

Put the grapes on to boil in just sufficient water to keep them from burning. Simmer gently until they are soft enough to rub through a sieve, return pulp to preserving pan, and add spices, sugar, salt, and vinegar. Boil till it thickens. Bottle and seal securely.

GRAPE VINEGAR

12½ kg (25 lb.) Grapes
6 litres (1½ gallons) water

Crush the grapes and put them into an earthenware crock or a wooden barrel. Add the water, cover the mouth of the crock with a piece of close cheese cloth or muslin, and place in a dark warm place for 10 or 14 days. Remove the scum that forms on top, strain, and allow the liquid to stand for a few weeks longer. Strain through fine muslin and bring to the boil. Boil gently for 10 minutes, and bottle when cool. The vinegar matures in about two months. For a dark vinegar use dark grapes. Light grapes make a light coloured vinegar.

HOME MADE TASTY SAUCE

4 litres (4 Quarts) Vinegar
15 gr (½ oz.) mace
1 cup sugar
8 gr (¼ oz.) spice
60 gr (2 oz.) ground ginger
30 gr (1 oz.) cayenne pepper
60 gr (2 oz.) garlic
8 gr (¼ oz.) cloves
8 gr (¼ oz.) pepper
250 gr (½ lb.) salt
1 kg (2 lb.) treacle

Let all come to the boil, burn sugar, and add slowly to the boiling vinegar. Don't add treacle until the vinegar is hot. Simmer for ½ an hour. Add 2 tablespoons flour, mixed with cold vinegar just before taking off the fire.

PLUM SAUCE

3 kg (6 lb.) Dark Plums
1½ kg (3 lb.) sugar
15 gr (½ oz.) allspice
2 dessertspoons salt
½ teaspoon cinnamon
1½ litre (3 pints) vinegar
15 gr (½ oz.) whole pepper
15 gr (½ oz.) cloves
½ teaspoon cayenne pepper
125 gr (4 oz.) whole ginger

Bruise the ginger, and boil all slowly together until the stones leave the fruit, then strain through a colander, and bottle.

SPICED VINEGAR

(For Pickling Vegetables)

1 litre (1 Quart) Vinegar
15 gr (½ oz.) peppercorns
15 gr (½ oz.) cloves
15 gr (½ oz.) bruised ginger
15 gr (½ oz.) mace
15 gr (½ oz.) salt

Boil all well, and use as required. It is useful for red cabbage, beetroot, mixed vegetables, etc. If required for pickling plums, grapes, figs, etc., add 1 cup of brown sugar to above quantities. White sugar and a little treacle may be used in place of brown sugar.

TOMATO SAUCE (No. 1)

6 kg (12 lb.) Tomatoes
4 cups sugar
½ cup salt
½ cup garlic (chopped)
2 teaspoons ground ginger
1 dessertspoon ground cloves
1 kg (2 lb.) apples (not peeled or cored)
6 cups vinegar
1 large onion
1 teaspoon cayenne pepper
1 dessertspoon allspice

Put all ingredients together and boil 4 hours. Strain through a fine sieve. Cork and seal down when cold. Crown seals instead of corks are excellent. It makes about 14 large bottles of sauce.

TOMATO SAUCE (No. 2)

6 kg (12 lb.) Ripe Tomatoes
1½ litre (2¼ bottles) vinegar
1 large tablespoon salt
2 large tablespoons peppercorns
7 large onions
1 small teaspoon cayenne
1¼ kg (2½ lb.) sugar
2 large tablespoons allspice

Boil tomatoes and onions for two hours. Strain. Add other ingredients (tie peppercorns and allspice in muslin bag). Boil 2½ hours. Bottle, and seal when cold.

TOMATO SAUCE (No. 3)

2½ kg (5 lb.) Tomatoes
15 gr (½ oz.) garlic
8 gr (¼ oz.) whole pepper
185 gr (6 oz.) sugar
8 gr (¼ oz.) whole spice
90 gr (3 oz.) salt
8 gr (¼ oz.) cloves
250 ml (½ pint) vinegar
15 gr (½ oz.) whole ginger

Place tomatoes in boiling water to skin, then cut up roughly. Tie other ingredients in muslin, add sugar and salt and boil all together 3 or 4 hours. Bottle. Do not add vinegar until nearly cooked.

TOMATO SAUCE (Hot), No. 4

4 kg (8 lb.) Tomatoes
1 kg (2 lb.) sugar
30 gr (1 oz.) white pepper
60 gr (2 oz.) garlic
30 gr (1 oz.) whole pepper
125 gr (¼ lb.) salt
1 litre (1 quart) vinegar
30 gr (1 oz.) cloves
60 gr (2 oz.) chillies
4 apples
6 onions

Boil all thoroughly for 3 hours, strain through a sieve, and bottle while hot. For a mild sauce halve all peppers.

W.A. SAUCE

2 litre (2 Quarts) Vinegar
250 gr (½ lb.) salt
1 dessertspoon mace
1 dessertspoon cloves
1 kg (2 lb.) brown sugar
1 dessertspoon cayenne pepper
1 dessertspoon whole spice
1 garlic

Place all in a saucepan on the stove, and boil gently for 1 hour. Strain and bottle. This is good with meats or fish.

RELISHES

CUCUMBER RELISH

500 gr (1 lb.) Apples
500 gr (1 lb.) onions
60 gr (2 oz.) salt
750 gr (1½ lb.) cucumbers
250 gr (½ lb.) sugar
1 teaspoon cayenne pepper
500 ml (1 pint) vinegar

Peel, core, and slice the apples, add the vinegar, and boil till soft. Mince the onions, and cucumbers, add other ingredients and mix well into apples and vinegar. No further cooking is necessary.

GREEN TOMATO RELISH

5 kg (10 lb.) Green Tomatoes
1 kg (2 lb.) sugar
2 dessertspoons turmeric
2 teaspoons cayenne pepper
1½ teaspoons allspice
2 kg (4 lb.) onions
2 dessertspoons mustard
4 dessertspoons flour
1½ teaspoons ground cloves
12 pieces garlic
2 large, green apples
salt

Slice the tomatoes, onions and apples, put salt between the layers, and stand overnight. Drain off next morning, cover with vinegar and boil for ¾ of an hour with the spices, then add the flour, turmeric, and mustard, mixed with a little cold vinegar, and boil for another ¾ of an hour. Bottle and seal when cold.

TOMATO RELISH (No. 1)

2½ kg (5 lb.) Nearly Ripe Tomatoes (sliced)
500 gr (1 lb.) sugar
30 gr (1 oz.) salt
2 teaspoons ground ginger
1 tablespoon curry powder
1 kg (2 lb.) onions (sliced)
1 kg (2 lb.) apples (sliced)
1 tablespoon cloves
1 tablespoon allspice
¾ litre (1 bottle) vinegar
1 tablespoon mustard

Tie the cloves, allspice and curry powder in a bag, and put all ingredients, except the vinegar and mustard, in a pan, and let stand overnight. Boil for 1 hour with a bottle of vinegar. Then mix the mustard with a little cold vinegar, add to the pickle, and boil for another ½ an hour. Bottle and seal when cold.

TOMATO RELISH (No. 2)

1½ kg (3 lb.) Tomatoes (ripe)
500 gr (1 lb.) sugar
2 large tablespoons plain flour
1 tablespoon salt
500 gr (1 lb.) onions
1½ tablespoons mustard
1 large tablespoon curry
vinegar

Cut up tomatoes and onions finely and sprinkle with salt. Leave overnight. Next day drain well and put in pan with sugar. Almost cover with vinegar and boil 5 minutes. Mix flour, mustard and curry to a paste with vinegar and add. Mix well and boil for 1 hour. If a sweeter pickle is needed add more sugar. Bottle and seal when cold.

CONFECTIONERY

ALMOND SWEETS

3 Cups Sugar
¼ teaspoon cream of tartar
1 cup water
125 gr (¼ lb.) chopped almonds

Boil sugar and cream of tartar in the water till it breaks crisp when a little is dropped into cold water. Add the chopped almonds, and when cool enough to handle, pull till the mixture is white and set. Twist just before the mixture sets, and mark into suitable pieces for eating. Break up, and keep in a closed tin.

ALMOND NOUGAT

125 gr (¼ lb.) Almonds
butter the size of a walnut
250 gr (½ lb.) granulated sugar
2 tablespoons water
1 white of egg

Drop the almonds into hot water for a moment, and then remove the skins. Dry them in a cloth, cut into slices, and put on a plate in the oven until they are dry and warm. Put the sugar into a saucepan with the butter and the water. Stir slowly till the sugar has melted and become a syrup, but do not let it boil. Have ready the white of an egg, beaten till the fork will stand up in it. Take the saucepan from the fire, and stir in the egg white, and the warmed almonds. Mix well, and turn into a lightly buttered tin. Press down with a hot, wet knife, and when dry, cut into cubes.

APRICOT BALLS

250 gr (½ lb.) Dried Apricots (minced)
½ cup coconut
rind of an orange
½ tin condensed milk
250 gr (½ lb.) brown sugar

Mix all dry ingredients with condensed milk, roll into small balls, cover with coconut and leave to set.

BUTTER SCOTCH (No. 1)

500 gr (1 lb.) Loaf Sugar
250 gr (½ lb.) butter
250 ml (½ pint) water
a pinch of cream of tartar

Place the sugar and water in a saucepan and stir over a gentle heat until the sugar is melted. Add the butter by degrees, then the cream of tartar. Stir well, and boil gently. Try a little in cold water, and if crisp, pour on a buttered dish, and cut into shapes before it hardens.

BUTTER SCOTCH (No. 2)

3 Cups Sugar | **$\frac{3}{4}$ cup boiling water**
$\frac{1}{4}$ cup butter | **$\frac{1}{2}$ teaspoon vanilla**

Combine the butter, sugar, and water, and boil until a little tried in cold water is brittle—about $\frac{3}{4}$ of an hour. Add the essence, and pour into a shallow, buttered dish. Before the mixture gets cold, mark into squares with a buttered knife. Nuts may be added if wished.

CHOCOLATE

250 gr ($\frac{1}{2}$ lb.) Gelatine
1 kg (2 lb.) cocoa
$2\frac{1}{2}$ kg (5 lb.) honey
500 ml (1 pint) water
vanilla flavouring

Melt the gelatine in a pint of water, add the honey, and warm thoroughly, then add the cocoa. Flavour with vanilla after it is taken off the fire. Pour into greased dishes or moulds.

CHOCOLATE CARAMEL

22 gr ($\frac{3}{4}$ oz.) Gelatine
$2\frac{1}{2}$ cups sugar
2/3 cup milk
$1\frac{1}{2}$ squares of chocolate
$\frac{1}{2}$ cup chopped nuts

Soak the gelatine in the milk for 10 minutes. Put the sugar on the stove, and when dissolved add the chocolate. Add the gelatine, and boil for 15 minutes. Allow to cool a little, stir till it thickens, add the nuts, and pour into a wet dish. When set immerse dish in hot water, loosen the edges, and turn out. Cut into squares, and roll in powdered sugar.

CHOCOLATE FUDGE (No. 1)

60 gr (2 oz.) Good Cocoa
2 cups granulated sugar
1/3 cup golden syrup
$\frac{1}{2}$ cup cold milk
2 tablespoons butter
1 teaspoon vanilla

Put all except vanilla into a pan, and cook slowly, stirring once in a while. Cook until it makes a soft ball in cold water Remove from the fire, add the vanilla, and beat until it begins to granulate. Pour at once into a buttered dish. Mark deeply in cakes when nearly cold.

CHOCOLATE FUDGE (No. 2)

2 Cups Sugar
1 teaspoon butter (large)
1 cup milk
1 teaspoon vanilla essence
30 gr (1 oz.) of chocolate

Grate the chocolate. Mix the sugar and milk thoroughly, then place it on the stove and add the butter, and stir continually. This is necessary. When it comes to the boil add the chocolate; allow it to boil until a little dropped into cold water forms a soft lump (about 10 minutes). Remove from the fire. Add the essence and keep stirring until the mixture becomes stiff. Pour into plates and cut into squares before it gets quite cold. Nuts or fruit may be added when the fudge is removed from the fire.

CHOCOLATE ROUGHS

500 gr (1 lb.) Sugar
60 gr (2 oz.) chocolate
2 egg whites

Pound the sugar and chocolate till very fine, then sift. Mix with the stiffly beaten whites of egg, and drop in small heaps on buttered paper. Dry in a slow oven.

COCONUT ICE

2 Cups Sugar
a pinch cream of tartar
½ cup water or milk
1 cup coconut
flavouring

Boil all together for 5 to 10 minutes, beat well, and pour out on to a wet dish. Repeat, colour part pink and pour over the white.

CREAM DATES (No. 1)

Dates
white of 1 egg
250 gr (½ lb.) ground almonds
250 gr (½ lb.) castor sugar
flavouring

Open the dates lengthways and remove the stone. Put the almonds on a flat slab or board, mix with the sugar, and moisten with the white of an egg, and any desired flavouring. Knead well till it forms a paste. Place a piece of filling in each date and close. Put on plates and let dry.

CREAM DATES (No. 2)

Dates
1 white of egg
625 gr (1¼ lb.) icing sugar
1 dessertspoon cold water
a few drops vanilla essence

Halve the dates carefully and remove the stones. Beat the white of egg with the water, to which has been added a few drops of vanilla essence. Add the icing sugar and beat well until it forms a paste thick enough to roll easily between the hands. If too moist, add a little more icing sugar. Roll into long narrow pieces, and press the halved fruit on either side. Leave to set for about ½ an hour.

CREAM TOFFEE

2 Cups Sugar
1 teaspoon cream of tartar
2 tablespoons butter
1 teaspoon essence vanilla
¾ cup boiling water

Boil sugar, cream of tartar, butter and water until a little dropped in cold water breaks brittle. Remove from the fire, and add the vanilla. Pour into a buttered dish. Keep turning up the edges to prevent hardening. Pull with the hands until white and creamy. Cut into pieces with scissors. Put a little butter or flour on the hands when pulling, as it is very hot to handle. Roll in waxed paper.

FRENCH JUBES

¾ Cup Cold Water
60 gr (2 oz.) gelatine
1½ teaspoon tartaric acid
icing sugar
¾ cup boiling water
1 kg (2 lb.) sugar
flavouring
coconut
colouring

Soak the gelatine in the cold water for 1 hour. Put into a saucepan, and pour on to it the boiling water. When melted, add the sugar. Place over the fire, and bring to the boil, and boil for 8 minutes, stirring all the time. Draw aside from fire, and add the acid gradually (dissolved in a little water), then add the flavouring. Pour into wet flat dishes, and leave for 48 hours. Cut into squares with a wet knife, and roll in icing sugar, coconut or nonpareils. These jubes may be coloured pink, yellow, green, etc., or they may be made two or three toned colours.

FRENCH ROCKS

500 gr (1 lb.) Loaf Sugar
a little cream of tartar
1 breakfast cup water
essence desired

Place ingredients in a clean saucepan, omitting the essence. Stir constantly until the mixture boils, and then for 5 minutes longer. Turn out on to a large meat dish (greased), sprinkle over a few drops of flavouring, and fold over and over with a wooden spoon. When cool enough to handle, keep pulling it out until it is white and firm. Form into a long roll and cut into pieces with a pair of scissors. Many varieties can be made by varying the flavourings, and some can be coloured.

FONDANT (No. 1)

2 Teaspoons Gelatine
½ teaspoon cream of tartar
250 gr (½ lb.) sugar
125 ml (¼ pint) water
flavouring

Place all ingredients except flavouring in a saucepan on the fire. When dissolved, bring to the boil, and boil for 5 minutes. Remove from the fire and leave to cool. Then add flavouring, and beat until thick and creamy. Place aside, and when firm cut into desired shapes, and dip in chocolate covering or fill prepared dates, prunes, etc.

FONDANT (No. 2)

750 gr ($1\frac{1}{2}$ lb.) Granulated Sugar
a pinch cream of tartar
250 ml ($\frac{1}{2}$ pint) water
flavouring
colouring

Dissolve the sugar in the water, and boil quickly till the thermometer registers 115° C (240° F.) or when a little tested in cold water will form into a soft ball. Take off the fire, and when the air bubbles have ceased, pour into a wet basin. Let it stand till nearly cold, then stir until it is creamy and thick enough to handle. Knead well on a sugared board, then wrap in a damp cloth and lay aside for an hour or more. Then knead again till it is very soft and creamy. Divide into two or three parts and colour and flavour each portion differently.

HONEYCOMB TOFFEE

2 Tablespoons Golden Syrup
1 teaspoon carbonate soda
2 tablespoons sugar
butter

Boil sugar, butter and syrup for 10 minutes, lift off the fire, and stir in the soda quickly. Pour on a buttered dish to set.

MARSHMALLOWS

1 Cup Sugar
3 dessertspoons gelatine
juice of 1 lemon
coconut
1 cup water
$\frac{1}{2}$ teaspoon cream of tartar
1 dessertspoon rose water
icing sugar
chopped dates or nuts

Mix together the sugar, water, gelatine, and cream of tartar, simmer for 10 minutes, allow to cool, and add the lemon juice and rose water, and also the nuts. Beat the mixture till white and thick, pour into a greased tin, and leave for a few hours. Cut into squares and roll in coconut or icing sugar. The marshmallow can be coloured with green or red colouring, and some colouring can be mixed in with the coconut in which the sweets are rolled.

MARZIPAN EGGS FOR EASTER

500 gr (1 lb.) Icing Sugar
flavouring
250 gr ($\frac{1}{2}$ lb.) ground almonds
eggs to mix

Rub the icing sugar through a sieve and mix with the ground almonds. Add whatever flavouring you prefer, and colour either with a little coffee, cocoa, cochineal, etc., and add sufficient beaten egg to make a stiff paste. Divide into portions and make into egg shapes, then set aside to harden. This will take a few hours. These eggs can be varied in many ways. Rub some stale cake through a sieve, mix to a paste with sherry

MARZIPAN EGGS FOR EASTER—*continued*

or milk, shape into small eggs, and coat the outside with jam. Then cover with a marzipan coat, or make the marzipan eggs plain, and give a coating of hundreds and thousands or chocolate shavings before setting to dry. Make surprise eggs by putting a chocolate button, a jelly baby, or some other sweet in the centre when moulding. These eggs are a delight to the small folk.

MILK CHOCOLATE

30 gr (1 oz.) Rock Chocolate
milk
500 gr (1 lb.) castor sugar
coconut

Scrape the chocolate to a powder, and mix with the sugar. Mix this into a thick paste with milk, stirring until smooth, then add a little more milk. Let it simmer for 5 minutes, stirring all the time, then spread layers in a greased tin, or drop small lumps on to greased paper, and let stand to cool. Coconut may be added.

NOUGAT

1 kg (2 lb.) Sugar
2 tablespoons cream of tartar
whites of 2 eggs
250 gr ($\frac{1}{2}$ lb.) honey
1 cup water
500 gr (1 lb.) almonds
icing sugar

Boil water and sugar together, and when beginning to boil, add honey and cream of tartar. Boil for 10 minutes, or until a little when stirred in a cup forms a cream. Take off the fire, and add the white of egg, beaten stiff with a little icing sugar. Work in the almonds, previously blanched and sliced and 125 gr ($\frac{1}{4}$ lb.) icing sugar. Smooth out into a flat slab, and cut in squares. Raisins, dates, or walnuts may be used instead of almonds.

OLD ENGLISH TOFFEE (No. 1)

2 Tablespoons Honey
1 teacup sugar
125 gr ($\frac{1}{4}$ lb.) butter
$\frac{1}{2}$ tin condensed milk
a few nuts, dates, and raisins

Put into a saucepan the honey, butter, and sugar, and boil for 13 minutes, add the milk, and boil for 20 to 30 minutes. Pour into a greased tin after adding the fruit.

OLD ENGLISH TOFFEE (No. 2)

1 Tablespoon Vinegar
250 gr ($\frac{1}{2}$ lb.) brown sugar
60 gr (2 oz.) butter
a few drops vanilla

Place all ingredients in a saucepan and boil for about 20 minutes, or until it sets when tried, stirring occasionally. Pour on to a buttered dish, and leave to harden.

PEPPERMINT STICK

3 Cups Granulated Sugar
$\frac{1}{4}$ teaspoon tartaric acid
$1\frac{1}{2}$ cups water
1 teaspoon extract peppermint

Boil together the sugar, water and acid until on trying in cold water it will almost crack, but if held a moment can be rolled into a hard ball. Do not stir, but pour into a buttered dish to cool. As soon as it can be handled add the extract of peppermint, and pull until it is white, then cut into sticks.

RUSSIAN TOFFEE

1 kg (2 lb.) Sugar
1 cup water
125 gr ($\frac{1}{4}$ lb.) butter
1 tin condensed milk
2 teaspoons essence vanilla

Boil all well together for $\frac{1}{2}$ an hour, then turn out into a greased plate and cut into squares. This needs a lot of stirring, as it burns easily.

SNOWBALLS

4 Dessertspoons Gelatine
2 bare cups water
chocolate or cocoa
500 gr (1 lb.) sugar
2 teaspoons lemon juice
coconut

Soak the gelatine in 1 cup water. Boil the sugar in the remaining water for 10 minutes. Add the gelatine, and boil for 20 minutes. Cool a little, and flavour with lemon juice. Turn into a basin and beat until stiff. While the mixture is still warm, form into balls with the hands, then dip into melted chocolate, and roll in coconut. The mixture may be poured into wet gem irons to shape, or moulds may be made as follows. Put a 5 cm (2 in.) layer of cornflour into a box or deep cake tin. Using four eggs to make impressions, press them into the flour, leaving two set in the flour while next two shapes are made. This prevents the moulds losing their shape. Pour the mixture into these moulds after carefully removing the eggs. When the snowballs are cold, brush off the surplus flour and proceed as directed. Coat with chocolate, etc.

TOFFEE

8 Tablespoons Sugar
2 tablespoons water
2 tablespoons vinegar
2 tablespoons butter

Put the sugar, vinegar, water, and butter on to boil, and boil until it becomes hard when dropped into cold water. Pour on to a deep buttered plate, and when cool cut into squares.

TOFFEE APPLES

500 gr (1 lb.) Sugar
½ cup water
2 teaspoons vinegar
½ teaspoon cream of tartar

Boil all ingredients together and when toffee "crackles" remove from heat. Test by dropping a few drops in cold water. Dip apples in toffee and leave to set on a greased tray.

500 gr (1 lb.) sugar makes approximately 20 toffee apples.

TURKISH DELIGHT (No. 1)

30 gr (1 oz.) Gelatine
500 gr (1 lb.) sugar
colouring
250 ml (½ pint) water
1 lemon
cornflour
icing sugar

Soak the gelatine in a little cold water, then dissolve over the fire. Put the sugar, water, and a strip of lemon rind into a saucepan, and bring to the boil. Add dissolved gelatine, and boil for 15 to 20 minutes. Add the lemon juice, and strain half into a wet dish. Colour the other half a very pale pink, and strain into another dish. When cold and set, cut into squares with a knife dipped into boiling water, and quickly dried. Dip into cornflour, leave on a wire sieve for 24 hours, then roll in icing sugar, and pack in waxed paper and store in airtight tins.

TURKISH DELIGHT (No. 2)

250 gr (½ lb.) Granulated Sugar
30 gr (1 oz.) honey
105 gr (3½ oz.) icing sugar
a few drops rosewater
45 gr (1½ oz.) cornflour
435 ml (3½ gills) water
⅛ teaspoon tartaric acid
lemon essence

Put the sugar and 125 ml (1 gill) of water into a saucepan, and bring to a temperature of 115° C (240° F.). Add the tartaric acid, and stand aside for a short time. Mix the cornflour and icing sugar with a little of the cold water, boil the rest, and when boiling pour on to the blended cornflour and sugar, stirring hard to prevent lumps. Return to the saucepan, boil, and beat vigorously until clear and thick. Then add the syrup gradually, beating over the fire. Continue to boil for 20 minutes, at the end of which time the mixture should be a very pale straw colour, and transparent. Add the honey and flavouring, and blend thoroughly. Pour half the contents of the pan into a buttered tin, colour the remainder pale pink, and pour it on the top of the mixture already in the tin. Stand aside until quite cold. Put a sharp knife into icing sugar, cut into neat pieces, and toss in icing sugar. Stand aside in the sugar for at least 24 hours.

WALNUT CARAMELS

250 gr (½ lb.) Walnuts
250 gr (½ lb.) icing sugar
250 gr (½ lb.) sugar
125 gr (¼ lb.) ground almonds
1 white of egg
½ teacup water
½ teaspoon cream of tartar

Break the walnut shells carefully, and remove the skins from the walnuts. Put the icing sugar and almonds into a bowl, then the stiffly-beaten white of an egg. The mixture must be barely moistened. Now take a piece of the mixture and work it round in a ball. Put half a walnut on one side of it, and a half on the other side. Leave for a day, and then put the ordinary sugar, the water, and cream of tartar into a small saucepan and let it boil till it thickens like toffee. Dip the walnuts one by one into this, and put them on buttered plates till cold.

WALNUT CREAMS

1 Egg White
icing sugar
water
vanilla
walnuts

Put the unbeaten white of egg into a basin, add half its quantity of cold water, and stir well to mix the two together. Put in enough icing sugar to make it stiff enough to handle. Flavour with vanilla, and mould into small rounds. Place a piece of walnut on each. Peppermint creams can be made by omitting vanilla, and adding essence of peppermint.

BEVERAGES

BARLEY WATER

4 Tablespoons Barley (well washed)
4 cups boiling water
1 lemon
60 gr (2 oz.) castor sugar

Place the barley in a jug, add the sugar and lemon juice, and the thin yellow rind of the lemon. Pour over all the boiling water, and leave till cold. Ice is an improvement. If an effervescing drink is liked, take $\frac{1}{2}$ glass of the barley water and fill up with soda water. Refreshing summer drink.

BOSTON CREAM

1 kg (2 lb.) Sugar
$2\frac{1}{2}$ litres (5 pints) boiling water
whites of 2 or 3 eggs
60 gr (2 oz.) tartaric acid
1 tablespoon lemon essence
carbonate soda

Mix the sugar and acid, pour over the boiling water, and allow to cool. When quite cold, add the essence, and the stiffly beaten egg whites. Strain through muslin and bottle. When drinking, place 2 tablespoons of the syrup in a glass, and fill up with water. Stir in quickly a small teaspoonful of carbonate of soda.

CHILLI BEER

4 Cups Sugar
2 teaspoons citric acid
$\frac{1}{2}$ teaspoon cayenne pepper
4 teaspoons chillies
1 teaspoon cloves
$\frac{1}{2}$ bottle essence lemon
3 litres (6 pints) water

Boil sugar, chillies, acid, cloves, and cayenne together for $\frac{1}{4}$ hour, strain, and add essence of lemon and cochineal to colour. Then bottle. Use 1 to 2 tablespoons to a glass of water.

CHILLI SYRUP

2 kg (4 lb.) Sugar
2 litres (2 quarts) boiling water
18 chillies
2 teaspoons citric acid
2 teaspoons essence lemon

Put sugar, chillies, and acid into an earthenware vessel, pour on the boiling water, colour with a little burnt sugar, and stir well. When cold, put in the essence, strain, and bottle. Dilute with water. The chillies must be broken up, and more can be added if liked hotter.

CHILLI WINE

8 Small Dried Chillies
750 gr ($1\frac{1}{2}$ lb.) sugar
1 teaspoon essence lemon
4 cups boiling water
15 gr ($\frac{1}{2}$ oz.) citric acid
1 tablespoon burnt sugar

Pour the boiling water over the sugar, add the chillies, well crushed, and boil for 10 minutes. Add the acid and burnt sugar. When cool, strain and add essence, and bottle. Add a small quantity of the wine to a tumbler of water.

CLARET CUP

1 Bottle Claret
1 cup water
1 orange
125 gr ($\frac{1}{4}$ lb.) castor sugar
1 wineglass sherry
2 bottles soda water
2 lemons
a few slices cucumber
ice

Take the sugar and the thinly peeled rind of 1 orange, cut the lemon into slices, and add these to the water. Work with a spoon to draw out the flavour. Add the squeezed juice from the orange, and 1 lemon, and stir well. Allow to stand for 30 minutes, then strain into a large jug and add the claret and cucumber. Add the sherry, soda water, and ice just before serving, and stir well.

COFFEE ESSENCE (SWEETENED)

4 Cups Water
250 gr ($\frac{1}{2}$ lb.) pure coffee
250 gr ($\frac{1}{2}$ lb.) sugar

Bring water to the boil and pour it on to the coffee (in a jug). Stir well. Cover the jug and stand it in a pan of water (the water should come half way up the jug). Bring to the boil, and let boil for an hour. Pour the coffee into a saucepan and add the sugar. Simmer until it thickens to a syrup. Bottle. Use 1 teaspoon of this essence for each cup of coffee.

COFFEE ESSENCE (UNSWEETENED)

125 gr ($\frac{1}{4}$ lb.) Coffee
2 cups boiling water
a pinch salt

Place the coffee in a jug, pour on the boiling water, stir well, and add the salt. Allow to become cold, strain through muslin, and put away in an uncorked bottle. A tablespoon of essence to a cup of boiling milk and water is required. This essence will keep over a week. The flavour of the coffee will be improved if a few grains of salt are sprinkled over it before the boiling water is added.

WHEAT COFFEE

750 gr ($1\frac{1}{2}$ lb.) Whole Wheat	2 tablespoons black sugar
$\frac{1}{2}$ teaspoon salt	$\frac{1}{2}$ cup water

Dissolve sugar and salt in water, and dampen the wheat. Bake slowly till almost black, stirring occasionally. Grind and store.

CREAM SODA

$1\frac{1}{4}$ kg ($2\frac{1}{2}$ lb.) Sugar	2 tablespoons flour
whites of 4 eggs	60 gr (2 oz.) cream of tartar
60 gr (2 oz.) tartaric acid	flavouring
1 litre (1 quart) water	

Put into a saucepan the water, acid, cream of tartar, sugar. Melt the flour with a little water into a smooth paste, and add. Then add the whites of eggs well-beaten. Place on the fire and heat, but do not allow it to boil, and then add lemon essence or other flavouring. Bottle, and when required for use, put 3 tablespoons of syrup in a tumbler two-thirds full of water, add a pinch of carbonate of soda, and drink immediately.

FRUIT CUP

6 Lemons	a few mint leaves
$\frac{3}{4}$ litre ($1\frac{1}{2}$ pints) boiling water	1 bottle ginger ale or lime and soda
1 tin pineapple juice	
1 cup sugar	

Put the juice of the lemons and the rind of 2 with the sugar and cover with boiling water and mint leaves. Let cool and strain. Add the pineapple juice and a bottle of ginger ale or lime and soda just before using. Sherry or gin may be added if liked. Serve cold.

FRUIT DRINK

2 Lemons	1 teaspoon chopped barley
2 tablespoons sugar	1 orange
a little chopped pineapple	a few strawberries

Pare the lemons very finely, leaving no white pith on the yellow rind. Put the pared rind on to boil in 500 ml (1 pint) of water, and boil for 5 minutes. Mix the barley with a little water to the consistency of cream, add to the boiling water, and cook for 4 or 5 minutes, stirring all the time. Squeeze the juice of the lemons and orange into a large jug or bowl, sweeten with sugar, and pour the boiling barley water straight on to it. Add cold water to make 2 litres (2 quarts). Serve very cold, plain as above, or with additional fruits added before pouring on the hot barley water. This lemon and orange alone makes a very refreshing drink.

FRUIT SALTS (No. 1)

60 grs (2 oz.) Epsom Salts
125 gr ($\frac{1}{4}$ lb.) cream of tartar
125 gr ($\frac{1}{4}$ lb.) carbonate soda
500 gr (1 lb.) icing sugar
125 gr ($\frac{1}{4}$ lb.) tartaric acid

Mix all together and sift several times. Place in a glass jar, and cork tightly. Use 1 large teaspoon to $\frac{3}{4}$ glass of water.

FRUIT SALTS (No. 2)

60 gr (2 oz.) Carbonate Soda
60 gr (2 oz.) tartaric acid
15 gr ($\frac{1}{2}$ oz.) carbonate magnesia
60 gr (2 oz.) cream of tartar
60 gr (2 oz.) Epsom salts
125 gr (4 oz.) icing sugar

Mix all together and roll thoroughly. Keep in a dry place.

GINGER BEER PLANT

In a screw top jar put 8 sultanas, juice of 2 lemons, teaspoon lemon pulp, 4 teaspoons sugar, 2 teaspoons ground ginger and 2 cups cold water. Leave for 2 or 3 days to ferment. Each day for one week add 2 teaspoons ground ginger and 4 teaspoons sugar. Pour 4 cups of boiling water onto 4 cups sugar, stir till dissolved and add juice of 4 lemons. Strain into ginger beer plant in a fine muslin and squeeze cloth dry, add 28 cups cold water and bottle. Keep for three days before using.

To keep plant alive, halve sediment in muslin, put in jar with cups cold water and for one week feed with 4 teaspoons sugar and 2 teaspoons ginger.

GINGER BEER (No. 1)

4 litres (1 Gallon) Cold Water
1 teaspoon cream of tartar
1 tablespoon ground ginger
500 gr (1 lb.) sugar
½ teaspoon tartaric acid
2 tablespoons yeast (or 1 teaspoon compressed yeast)

Mix all together in a pan, and allow to stand for 6 hours. Bottle and cork.

GINGER BEER (No. 2)

2 kg (4 lb.) Sugar
60 gr (2 oz.) cream of tartar
1 cup yeast (or 1 dessertspoon compressed yeast)
2 lemons
125 gr (4 oz.) bruised ginger
1 kerosene tin water

Boil the tin of water, and put in the sugar, lemons, cream of tartar, and ginger. When warm stir in the yeast, and stand for 24 hours. Strain and bottle.

GINGER CORDIAL

$1\frac{1}{2}$ kg (3 lb.) Sugar
4 good teaspoons ginger essence
30 gr (1 oz.) tartaric acid
scant half teaspoon cayenne
4 teaspoons essence of lemon
3 litres (3 quarts) boiling water

Place ingredients in basin and pour boiling water over. Strain, and bottle when cold.

GINGER LEMONADE

½ Cup Good Vinegar
2 teaspoons ground ginger
1 cup sugar
iced water

Place the vinegar, sugar, and ginger in a 1 litre (1 quart) jug, and fill up with iced water.

HEBE'S CUP

Cucumber
3 tablespoons sugar
6 tablespoons sherry
rind of 1 lemon
3 tablespoons brandy
2 bottles soda water
1 bottle claret

Take about 5 cm (2 in.) of fine, fresh, cucumber, and slice it very thin. Put the slices into a bowl with the thin rind of lemon, and the sugar. Work them well together with a wooden spoon for a few minutes, then add the brandy, sherry, soda water (1 bottle), and the claret. Mix all thoroughly and let stand for 1 hour. Before serving add the other bottle of soda water.

HOP BEER (No. 1)

125 gr (¼ lb.) Hops
125 gr (¼ lb.) raisins
20 litres (5 gallons) water
500 gr (1 lb.) wheat, or barley
125 gr (¼ lb.) whole ginger (crushed)
2½ kg (5 lb.) sugar
1 teaspoon salt
1 cup yeast

Put all ingredients except the yeast into a vessel, and boil well for 1 hour, then strain and put into a barrel. When cool, put in the yeast and let it work for 2 days, then close down to settle. Bottle. It is ready for use in a day or so.

HOP BEER (No. 2)

125 gr (¼ lb.) Hops
1¼ kg (2½ lb.) sugar
white 1 egg
125 gr (¼ lb.) raisins
1 bottle yeast
water

Boil the hops and raisins in a kerosene tin of water for 10 minutes, add the sugar, and boil for 15 minutes. Take off the fire, and when cool put in the yeast. 20 minutes before bottling add the whisked white of egg.

LEMON SYRUP

1½ kg (3 lb.) Loaf Sugar
60 gr (2 oz.) essence lemon
105 gr (3½ oz.) citric acid
¾ litre (1½ pints) boiling water

Dissolve the sugar in 500 ml (1 pint) of boiling water, and the acid in 250 ml (½ pint) of boiling water. When quite dissolved, put the two together. Leave standing till quite cold, then add the essence and stir up well. Bottle, and when required for use, take a tablespoonful to a tumbler of water.

LIGHT ORANGE COCKTAIL

4 Large Oranges
2 tablespoons sherry
½ cup water
1 cup sugar
a few cherries
mint sprigs

Make a syrup using the sugar and water. Boil for five minutes, then leave until cold. Add the sherry. Peel the oranges and dice or cut into sections. Place in cocktail glasses. Pour over the chilled syrup. Decorate with cherries. Garnish with sprigs of mint. Serve very cold.

MALTED MILK

Wheat
water
milk

Wash some wheat, put it into a thin muslin bag, and put to soak in water for 24 hours. Winter time is best for this, as it is liable to turn sour if soaked in summer. When soaked, lay on a damp bag on the ground, with another wheat bag on top. Keep the bags damp, and as soon as the wheat begins to shoot (the young shoots will show through the muslin bag) take out and dry, and bake a pale brown in the oven. Put through a grist mill, and boil a little in milk as required. You will then have a delicious malted milk. The wheat may be gristed very finely, added to a little flour, and made into very nice malt biscuits.

MULBERRY WATER

500 gr (1 lb.) Ripe Mulberries
500 ml (1 pint) boiling water
sugar to taste

Crush the mulberries, and place in a vessel with the boiling water, and sugar to taste. Allow to stand until cold, strain, ice, and serve.

MULBERRY WINE

Ripe Mulberries
water
sugar

Pick the mulberries, crush out the juice, and strain through double net. Add 1 cup water to each cup juice, and strain again through double cheese cloth. For every cup of the prepared liquid use 1 cup sugar. Put the mixture into a barrel. The barrel must be full, and about 1 litre (1 quart) or so of the juice must be kept back to fill up the barrel as the wine ferments and flows over the top. Keep it open for six weeks, filling up each day. Fill up the barrel when working is done, bung down, and keep for 12 months. The longer the wine is kept the better it is.

ORANGE AND LEMON CORDIAL

2 Oranges	15 gr ($\frac{1}{2}$ oz.) tartaric acid
2 lemons	15 gr ($\frac{1}{2}$ oz.) citric acid
875 gr ($1\frac{3}{4}$ lb.) sugar	1 litre (2 pints) cold water

Grate rinds finely, avoiding the white pith. Add juices, acids, sugar and water. Stir well and stand overnight. Stir again and bottle. Store in refrigerator, but it will keep about 10-12 days without refrigeration. Use with water added.

PASSIONFRUIT CORDIAL

1 Dozen Passionfruit	2 cups sugar
2 teaspoons citric acid	500 ml (1 pint) boiling water

Stir until dissolved. Strain, bottle and cork when cold. Use with water added.

PLUM VINEGAR

Satsuma Plums	water
vinegar	sugar

Cover plums well with water, and simmer until plums are soft. Strain the juice through a jelly bag, and to each cup of juice, add one-third cup of vinegar. Heat, and add 1 cup of sugar to each cup of syrup. Boil for 3 minutes. If boiled any longer it will jell. A small quantity added to a tumbler of water makes a delicious summer drink. Raspberries, black currants, or other well flavoured fruit can also be used.

RASPBERRY VINEGAR

2 kg (4 lb.) Sugar	2 litres (2 quarts) boiling water
1 tablespoon tartaric acid	2 cups vinegar
30 gr (1 oz.) bottle raspberry essence	1 bottle cochineal

Pour boiling water on the sugar, acid, vinegar, and cochineal, and stir well. Add essence when cool.

SUMMER CUP

3 Oranges	2 lemons
500 ml. (1 pint) water	3 tablespoons sugar
500 ml (1 pint) tea	$\frac{1}{2}$ wineglass brandy or sherry

Grate the rind of the oranges into the water, add the sugar, and boil gently for 5 minutes. Add the juice of the oranges, and the lemons, strain, and add the tea, which was strained directly after infusion. The brandy or sherry may be added if desired.

SIMPLE HOME REMEDIES

TO CURE HICCOUGHS—

To cure hiccoughs, take one teaspoon of vinegar. This remedy has never been known to fail.

Half a teaspoonful of sugar, dissolved in the mouth, will cure hiccoughs. They may also be stopped by pressing the thumb of the right hand into the palm of the left hand, at the same time holding the breath for several seconds.

TO CURE CHILBLAINS—

The following is a very effective cure for chilblains. Mix ½ a teaspoon of carbonate of soda with a small teaspoon of vinegar, stir till dissolved, and put on the chilblains.

TO REMOVE FISH BONE FROM THROAT—

To remove a fish bone from the throat, swallow a raw egg, and follow, if possible, by eating plenty of mashed potatoes or bread. The egg will carry the bone to the stomach, and the potatoes will prevent it from doing any harm there.

FOR TIRED FEELING—

If feeling very tired, warm the soles of the feet before the fire.

When very tired take a warm bath with a tablespoon of cloudy ammonia added to the water. The tired feeling will vanish as if by magic.

REMEDIES FOR COLDS—

An excellent remedy for children's coughs and colds is made in the following way. Mix well together 1 tablespoon of glycerine, 1 tablespoon of orange juice, and 1 teaspoon of ipecacuanha wine. Give ½ a teaspoonful when necessary.

A tablespoon of honey mixed with the same quantity of strained lemon juice, is recommended to relieve sore throats or colds.

CROUP–

To relieve croup in a young child in an emergency cover the cot with a blanket and have steam from a boiling kettle or electric jug filtering under the blanket, with the kettle standing on a stool or chair situated behind the pillows at the back of the bed. This requires much caution as there is a danger of fire or scalds. Cover the child's upper bedclothes with plastic to catch drips.

FIRST AID TREATMENT FOR SNAKE BITE–

[*Reproduced with the kind permission* of St John Ambulance Australia, W.A. Ambulance Service Inc.]

Assume all snakes are poisonous.
Always believe someone when they say they have been bitten by a snake, even though you may not see any puncture marks.

Management–pressure immobilisation method
Rest the casualty
Do not panic
Apply direct pressure over the bitten area
Apply a broad bandage over the bite area first, then bandage down the limb and continue to bandage up the full length of the limb
Immobilise the limb with a splint
Call for medical aid

Remember–
Do not wash the bitten area
Do not remove the bandage
Do not elevate the limb
Do not walk or run – get help to the casualty

TO SETTLE A CHILD'S STOMACH WHEN UPSET–

When children's stomachs are upset and they can't keep food down, give them the following mixture. Mix together 1 level dessertspoon cornflour, a pinch of sugar, and ¼ cup cool, boiled water.

CURES FOR BOILS–

The following is a remedy for boils, abscesses, and carbuncles, prescribed by a doctor. Put some Epsom salts on a saucer in the oven until it powders, then add a very little drop of glycerine—just enough to mix it into an ointment. If this is applied about every eight hours the affected part will soon be well.

Starch Poultice: Mix together 1 tablespoon starch,½ teaspoon boracic acid, and 5 tablespoons cold water. Mix well, and boil till thick, stirring constantly. Rub vaseline round the part to be poulticed, and apply the poultice cold. Renew every six hours. This is splendid for boils, splinters, festering sores and eczema.

INSECT BITES–

Dampened salt applied to insect bites will relieve the itching at once. It should be applied quickly and bound tightly over the spot.

For insect bites, apply liquid ammonia or a little vinegar and glycerine.

EMBROCATIONS–

Embrocation: To make a quick embrocation for strained or tired muscles, mix equal parts of olive oil and ammonia, and rub the affected parts well.

To make a good liniment for general use, put in a fair sized bottle 125 ml ($\frac{1}{4}$ pint) each of turpentine, vinegar, and methylated spirits. Beat an egg well and add to the bottle. Shake well. Should this, in keeping, become thick so that it will not pour, add a little more vinegar.

The following is an excellent remedy for chilblains, or for rubbing the body after strenuous exercise, also for colds on the chest. Shake together 2 eggs, $\frac{1}{2}$ cup turpentine, and 1 cup vinegar. Bottle, and shake before using. This keeps indefinitely. For colds on the chest, a few teaspoonsful rubbed on the chest and back will give relief.

INVALID COOKING

APPLE SOUFFLE

2 Large Cooking Apples
1 dessertspoon sugar
1 small teaspoon lemon juice
white of 1 egg
lemon rind

Bake the apples until quite soft, scrape out the pulp, and press through a sieve. Add about $\frac{1}{4}$ of a grated lemon rind, lemon juice, sugar, and the white of egg, beaten to a very stiff froth. Bake in a small pie-dish at once, let it rise, sprinkle with sugar, and serve with a light sponge cake.

ARROWROOT JELLY

2 Heaped Teaspoons Arrowroot
1 teaspoon sugar
250 ml ($\frac{1}{2}$ pint) boiling water
3 teaspoons sherry wine
cold water

Blend the arrowroot with a little cold water, pour on the boiling water, stirring all the time, and put into a saucepan. Stir over the fire till it becomes thick and clear. Remove from the fire, add wine and sugar, and pour into dainty sweet dishes or custard glasses. Grate over a little nutmeg and set aside to cool.

BARLEY WATER

60 gr (2 oz.) Pearl Barley
500 ml (1 pint) cold water
2 litres (2 quarts) boiling water
sugar to taste
rind and juice of 1 lemon

Wash the barley thoroughly, put it in a saucepan with the cold water, and simmer for $\frac{1}{4}$ of an hour. Then strain off the water and throw it away. Pour the boiling water on to the barley, and boil till the liquid is reduced to one half, then strain, add the lemon juice and rind, sweeten, and set aside to cool. Remove the rind and serve. This is very nourishing and cooling.

BEEF TEA

500 gr (1 lb.) Beef
500 ml (1 pint) water

Shred the beef, add 250 ml ($\frac{1}{2}$ pint) cold water, put in a jar, and stand in a saucepan of cold water. Bring the water to the boil and simmer for 2 or 3 hours, then strain off the beef tea, and add 250 ml ($\frac{1}{2}$ pint) of boiling water to the beef. Stand in boiling water again and simmer for 3 hours. Then add to first straining, let stand and skim before heating up again for use.

BEEF TEA CUSTARD

125 ml ($\frac{1}{4}$ Pint) Beef Tea
a little pepper and salt
the yolks of two eggs and the white of one

Beat up the eggs slightly, putting aside the white. Add the beef tea, and season slightly. Butter a large cup, pour the custard into it, and twist a piece of buttered paper round the top. Put it into a saucepan with as much boiling water as will come half-way up. Draw the pan to the side of the fire, and allow the custard to remain in it till firm (about 20 minutes). The water must not be allowed to boil while the custard is steaming, or it will be full of holes. When the custard is firm, turn it out, and serve either hot or cold. This is very nourishing.

CHICKEN BROTH

½ a Fowl or a Small Chicken
1 small onion
1 teaspoon arrowroot
a small piece of mace
a shake of pepper
water

Skin the fowl, cut in pieces, place in a jar with onion, mace and pepper, cover with cold water, and set in a pan of boiling water. Let it simmer for 5 hours, skim, strain, and set aside till cold. Remove the fat, heat up, add salt, and thicken with arrowroot blended with a little water.

EGG FLIP

1 Cup Milk
1 egg
sugar to taste

Warm the milk slightly. Beat the yolk of egg, and add it to the milk, mixing well, then beat the white of egg till stiff and add to the milk. Add sugar to taste.

LEMON WHEY

1 Lemon
½ cup water
1 cup new milk
1 dessertspoon sugar

Grate the lemon rind, squeeze out the juice, put both in a saucepan with the milk and water, and boil up. Strain, sweeten, and drink as hot as possible. This is excellent for a cold. Take on retiring at night.

MUTTON BROTH

3 Shanks Mutton or 1 kg (2 lb.) Shoulder
1 litre (2 pints) water
a little salt

Simmer slowly for several hours, set to cool, remove fat, re-heat, and serve. A little boiled rice or barley can be added and heated in the broth.

OLIVE OIL TONIC

Whip one tablespoonful of olive oil with the juice of half a lemon, pour over a cupful of boiling water, and sip slowly. This is particularly good for cold night work, or when physically exhausted.

RAW BEEF JUICE

125 gr (¼ lb.) Top Side Steak
a pinch salt

Warm the steak until a light brown on the griller, slash well with a sharp knife, squeeze between two saucers, or with a metal lemon squeezer, and strain.

RAW LIVER JUICE

250 gr (8 oz.) Fresh Liver — **water, or orange or lemon juice, according to doctor's orders**

Pass liver twice through the mincer, catching every drop of juice. Then rub through a wire sieve, scraping the under part of the sieve well. Put pulp so obtained into a vessel, and if possible, set it on ice for an hour or two, to chill it thoroughly. Serve the quantity ordered in a ruby glass with orange or lemon juice added, or a little cold water.

RAW LIVER SANDWICHES

Brown Bread and Butter
185 gr (6 oz.) liver puree (250 gr (½ lb.) liver)
lettuce, tomato, mustard or cress
pepper and salt

Pass liver twice through the mincer, and rub through a wire sieve. Weigh after sieving. Season lightly with made mustard, pepper, and salt. Cut some thin bread and butter, spread thickly with liver, sprinkle with some tomato, lettuce or cress with a drop or two of vinegar, place a piece of bread and butter on top to form a sandwich, press, and cut neatly. The bread may first be spread with anchovy paste.

STEAMED FISH

1 or 2 Fillets of Fish or Cutlets
lemon juice
butter
salt

Butter two plates, place fish on one of them, squeeze over them some lemon juice, add a pinch of salt, cover with the second plate, and set the plates over a saucepan of boiling water. Steam for about 25 minutes. Fish cooked in this manner is delicious.

STRENGTHENING BROTH

125 ml (¼ Pint) Mutton Broth
3 tablespoons thin cream or milk
yolk of egg

Strain the meat from the broth, and put it into a saucepan. Make it quite hot, but not boiling, beat the yolk of egg, add the cream, and strain this into the broth. Mix well, and let the egg barely set. Be sure it does not boil. Season delicately with pepper and salt and serve with tiny dices of toast.

WHEY

500 ml (1 Pint) Fresh Milk
1 tablespoon cold water
1 to 2 junket tablets

Stand jug containing milk in a saucepan of boiling water, and bring just to blood heat. Then add junket tablet, which has been dissolved in the cold water. When the curd has become solid, break with a fork, and bring to the boil, stirring all the time. Strain through butter-muslin into a clean jug.

BUTTER MAKING AND CHEESE

All utensils used in butter making should be scalded after having been thoroughly washed in the usual way.

The cream should be kept away from strong smells.

Never mix fresh cream with old cream directly after separating. First allow it to cool.

When mixing two lots of cream make sure each lot is quite cool, and then mix thoroughly so that a uniform ripening will result. Cream is ready to churn when it has developed a certain amount of acid. The acid can be detected by taste and smell. Acid cream appears much thicker than fresh cream, and has a shiny surface. Cream should be stirred morning, noon, and evening every day during the ripening process. This is the only way to obtain an even development. An evenly ripened cream gives a good butter.

BUTTER MAKING

Keep your cream well stirred. It should be sour but not bitter or over ripe. Scald the churn with boiling water, then rinse with cold water to prevent the butter sticking. Do not turn the churn too quickly, and keep the cream scraped off the lid and sides from time to time, or a good deal of cream will be wasted. When the butter has come, pour off the buttermilk and cover the butter with clean, cold water. Wash it several times before putting in the salt, allowing 15 gr (½ oz.) of salt to every 500 gr (1 lb.) of butter, and work the salt in well. To remove any strong flavour of clover, etc., put 1 teaspoon of carbonate of soda in the first washing water.

CHEESE

8 litres (2 Gallons) New Milk
salt
2½ kg (5 lb.) jam tin (which will hold the cheese from 6 gallons of milk)
1 teaspoon cheese colouring
1 dessertspoon rennet or 9 rennet tablets

Warm the milk to blood heat, add the cheese colouring and rennet, and stir well. Cover with a cloth to keep in the heat. When the curd is set and firm, cut through and through with a

CHEESE—*continued*

large knife to release the whey. Dip the whey off with a saucer, pressing the curd while doing so. Drain off all whey, and when fairly dry crumble the curd and add salt to taste—about 2 teaspoons should be about sufficient. Line a cheese press with cheese cloth, pack the curd into it, and fold the cloth well over the top. Put on lid—a saucer that will fit in the tin will do very well—place a 3 kg (6 lb.) weight on top, and press for 12 hours. Then take out cheese, trim edges, and replace the cheese cloth with a dry one. Repeat this every day for 7 days increasing the pressure every day. The cheese should then be fairly dry. Wipe and rub well, roll in butter muslin, and place in a cool place, turning every day, for a fortnight. The cheese will be ready in about 6 weeks, but is better if kept for 3 months. (A press may be made out of a 2½ kg (5 lb.) jam tin. The bottom must be punctured, and holes punched round the tin.) A wooden press is best.

CREAM CHEESE (No. 1)

500 ml (1 Pint) Milk

Set the milk in a warm place, and when quite thick and sour, turn into a piece of muslin. Tie up loosely, and hang up to drain for several hours. When drained, tighten the muslin around the curd as much as possible, and press between two plates for an hour. A small cream cheese of delicious flavour is the result.

CREAM CHEESE (No. 2)

1 Cup Separated Cream **salt to taste**

Tie up the cream in a piece of muslin, and hang up to drain for 24 hours. Take out of the muslin, salt to taste, and press into jars. Celery salt may be used if liked. This cheese will keep only about five days. It is nice for savouries or lunch.

CROWDY (SCOTTISH CREAM CHEESE)

Sour Milk **salt**

Put some sour milk into an enamel saucepan, and heat very slowly until it is quite hot. Remove to a cooler part of the stove for a short time, then take off the stove, and cool slowly. Strain through a very fine sieve, and when the curd looks dry, turn into a basin, add salt to taste, and knead into a compact mass. This is greatly improved by the addition of some cream.

CURING OF MEATS

CURING OF HAM AND BACON

$7\frac{1}{2}$ kg (15 lb.) Leg or Side
60 gr (2 oz.) saltpetre
30 gr (1 oz.) black pepper
500 gr (1 lb.) bay salt
500 gr (1 lb.) common salt
750 gr ($1\frac{1}{2}$ lb.) treacle

Allow the above ingredients to a $7\frac{1}{2}$ kg (15 lb.) leg or side. Powder well the salt, saltpetre, common salt, and black pepper. Lay the meat in the mixture for 4 days, turning, and rubbing every day. Add the treacle, and let meat remain in this for 1 month, turning every day. When you remove from the mixture, soak in water for 24 hours and hang up to dry.

KEEPING HAMS THROUGH THE HOT WEATHER

Make a thick paste of flour and water, and cover the hams with a coating at least 13 mm ($\frac{1}{2}$ in.) thick. Lay the floured meat to dry in an airy place, and hang up. The paste will set hard, and may be soaked or chipped off.

PICKLED MUTTON

8 litres (2 Gallons) Water
1 dessertspoon saltpetre
$\frac{1}{2}$ cup sugar
salt

Use sufficient salt to float a fresh egg. Mix all ingredients together, and place on the stove, cut the mutton into handy joints, and place in the liquid. Bring to the boil, then remove from the fire. Cover with a piece of muslin, and stand in a cool place.

PORK AND BEEF SAUSAGES

For every 375 gr ($\frac{3}{4}$ lb.) of lean meat allow 125 gr ($\frac{1}{4}$ lb.) of fat, and for every 5 kg (10 lb.) of meat, season with 125 gr (4 oz.) salt, 30 gr (1 oz.) of black pepper, and about 1 tablespoon of sage. Mix thoroughly, and fill into small skins. The sausage meat can be packed in stone jars, and hot lard poured on top of it. It will keep for several days in a cool place. It can be cut into slices, rolled in flour, and cooked.

SPICED BEEF

About 4 kg (8 lb.) Skirt Beef
45 gr ($1\frac{1}{2}$ oz.) ground white pepper
brine pickle
22 gr ($\frac{3}{4}$ oz.) allspice

Cut the beef rather longer than broad, and place in a moderately strong pickle for 1 or 2 days, then take out and drain. Place it on a clean board, and strew the pepper and allspice all over the top surface of the beef, then roll up as tightly as possible, and tie very firmly to prevent spices from boiling out. Plunge into boiling water, and boil slowly for $2\frac{1}{2}$ hours. Remove the saucepan from the fire, allow meat to remain in the liquid until cold, and serve in thinly cut slices.

FRUIT DRYING

The general principle involved is the removal by evaporation without injury to the fruit, of sufficient moisture to ensure its preservation. Little equipment is necessary.

The methods are simple and equipment incxpensive.

(1) By exposing fruit to sun's rays.

(2) By artificial heat, such as oven or radiator.

A tray on which to spread the fruit is necessary. This could be a wooden rack, a wire cake rack or oven rack out of gas stove where the mesh or slat is wide enough. Cover with a layer of muslin.

For sun drying, either rack system or trays may be used.

Trays for this may be made by joining together four boards 15 cm (6 in.) wide by 13 mm (½ in.) deep by 7½ cm (3 in.) long. Nail with a cleat 5 cm (2 in.) long by 25 mm (1 in.) wide and deep. This gives a tray 91 cm x 61 cm (36 in. x 24 in.) approx.

Any size may do, but all trays are better to be uniform in size for convenience of packing.

Racks may be made. A wooden rack with cross pieces at convenient distances, over each tier are stretched sheets of hessian and the prepared fruit is left thereon until sufficiently dried.

HOME EVAPORATOR

A size that will fit on a range or in fireplace or be suspended over or hung in the vicinity of the kitchen range where currents of warm air will dry it.

A useful size–61 cm (24 in.) high x 61 cm (24 in.) wide x 46 cm (18 in.) deep.

It should be fitted with wire trays placed as shelves.

Can be stood at night after dinner on kitchen wood range or any time when fire is low.

Oven Drying–With door partly open for wood stove, very low heat, preferably after dinner cooking.

For Gas or Electricity–Oven temperature about 45° C (120° F.) to 65° C (150° F.).

Place fruit in and then light the oven and heat slowly to prevent outside hardening or, in the case of plums, the skin from bursting.

Storing–When removed from the oven, fruit should be exposed to ordinary room temperature for 12 hours to cool.

Pack in wooden or cardboard boxes lined with greaseproof paper. Put away in a dry place.

Drying in the Sun—The period required for drying depends largely on weather conditions, etc., varying from 2½ days to 6 days —in some cases longer.

All pieces on the one tray do not dry alike and some are collected from trays before others. Examine trays occasionally.

The appearance and texture of fruit is a guide. When ready, the pieces will be somewhat pliable, yet will show no sign of juice or be mushy on twisting. When this stage is reached they are ready to be conditioned.

If there be any rain or dew, the trays should be stacked one over the other and a cover thrown over the whole as a protection from dampness. Fruit should be equally dried before packing.

Preparation of Fruit—Some fruits dried whole—grapes, prunes, figs—usually dipped in a solution of lye to cut the bloom and cause minute cracks, just visible to the eye, to open on the surface of the skin, thus hastening the drying process.

Lye—500 gr (1 lb.) caustic soda to 64-80 litres (16-20 gallons) water. If too strong or fruit left too long in solution skin will probably burst.

Time—about 10-15 seconds.

Then rinse in clear cold water.

For dipping—Use a wire fry basket or a perforated tin with a handle. Make the perforation from the inside.

Sulphuring—This process is not necessary for "home use" fruits, but it acts as a bleach and keeps the natural colour of the fruit, i.e., prevents darkening.

The amount of suphur used is proportionately 500 gr (1 lb.) to every 12 litres (cubic foot).

The sulphur is placed in a receptacle, placed on the floor of the tray box and ignited by a few live coals. Close or well cover the box and subject the fruit to the fumes for required time.

After sulphuring—dry the fruit.

Apricots—Fruit should be ripe but not mushy—dried whole or in halves.

If cut, place fruit cut side up in sulphur box. Length of time differs—from 4 to 5 hours or overnight—anything from 1 to 12 hours.

Some determine the time for removing fruit by the depression of the apricot filling with juice.

Apples—Any kind may be used. Best are the cooking and white fleshed variety for good looks when dried.

Apples should be fully matured but not mealy. Apples are

peeled, cored and sliced. May be peeled, cored and dried whole.

To prevent discoloration during preparation the fruit may be dropped into weak solution (2 tablespoons to 4 litres (1 gallon)) of salt water. Do not leave too long in solution.

Use a stainless knife for peeling.

Sulphur for a few minutes—then dry until the slices or rings are velvet to the touch and a pliable texture, or test by taking a handful of slices, close hand tightly pressing—when released the fruit should separate at once and will be ready for removal.

If drying apple rings in oven, thread them on skewer or stick. Balance over a tart dish which should take several sticks.

Pears—Pears may or may not be skinned, halved, spread on trays cut side up, well sulphured and dried.

When finished should be somewhat doughy and stretchy if worked between the fingers.

Peaches—Use firm yellow fleshed variety. Treat as for apricots. Usually require longer time.

Prunes—Prunes do not need sulphuring. Selected when fully ripe and treated with lye. When ready should have shrunken skin —texture firm, springy and pliable if pressed in hand.

Grapes—Grapes should be ripe "Coorde" variety, or a good Lexia selection.

Dip in lye and spread to dry.

Currants are best exposed to gentle, hot wind without the glare of sunlight.

Bunches of currants may be tied in small bags and hung in shade where air moves.

Muscatel or Dessert Raisins—Grapes left on stem, carefully handled. Do not dip.

Take care in packing as the retention of colour and bloom is important for appearance.

Figs—Ripe figs used. Dip in lye, then sulphur and dry.

When dried, to prevent them becoming unduly hard and to destroy insect life, it is considered advisable to dip them in to a boiling solution of rock salt and water (about 90 gr (3 oz.) salt to 4 litres (1 gallon)), then place in heaps for a few hours.

Salt counteracts excessive sweetness of the fig. The salty taste is most pronounced at first but is unnoticeable after a few days.

Herbs—Gather on a dry day after dew has dispersed. They are best gathered prior to flowering stage. Cleanse. Spread on butter muslin on tray or sieve.

Dry in an airy room or a cool oven with door slightly ajar.

Raise the temperature from 43° C (110° F.) to 50° C (130° F.).

They should dry quickly, so that colour and flavour are protected.

Leaves then stripped and sieved and stored in clean dry bottles and corked.

May be tied in bags and hung up to dry in warm place.

Parsley—(1) As for others. (2) Wash under running water.

Remove coarse stalks, place in butter muslin and dip quickly into slightly salted boiling water for two minutes. Drain and shake, then dry as for other herbs.

Can be stored in small sprig form so as to be useful in garnishing, then just soak in warm water for a few minutes.

Mushrooms—Must be very fresh. Remove coarse part of stem, peel if necessary, dry in a cool oven (43° C (110° F.) to 45° C (120° F.)) until leathery in texture or thread on a fine string and hang in the air to dry. Store in a dry place.

DAIRY PRODUCTS MARKETING BOARD
CHEESE ADVERTISING CAMPAIGN—1955-56

CHEESE ENTREE RECIPE COMPETITION—PRIZE WINNING ENTRIES

1st Prize:

CHEESE AND FRUIT CASSEROLE

250 gr (8 oz.) cheddar cheese, diced small
3 cups breadcrumbs
½ cup melted butter or margarine
4 cups sliced raw apples
½ cup honey
Juice of two oranges
1 orange (peeled or unpeeled) sliced very thin
2 tablespoons sherry (optional)

Mix crumbs with melted butter, place half in a casserole, and alternate layers of cheddar cheese (keeping back a little for top) and sliced apples. Blend honey, orange juice and sherry, pour into dish, cover with remaining crumbs and cheddar cheese. Bake in moderate oven 180° C (375° F.) until apples are done—about 30 minutes. Garnish with orange slices.

2nd Prize:

VEGETARIAN CHEESE MINCE

250 gr (8 oz.) grated cheese
4-5 slices brown bread
1 egg
1 tablespoon butter
2 teaspoons meat extract (or Marmite)
1 small onion
Salt and pepper
1 tomato
1 teaspoon chopped parsley
1 rounded tablespoon breadcrumbs

Soak the sliced bread in milk or water. Chop onion and cook lightly in butter. Mix with the bread, cheese, breadcrumbs, meat extract, salt and pepper. Work all together with the egg and form into balls. Fry brown. In the same butter fry the sliced and peeled tomato. On each cheese ball place a slice of fried tomato, sprinkle with chopped parsley. Serve with a butter sauce.

3rd Prize:

CHEESOTTO

1 onion (chopped)
60 gr (2 oz.) butter or margarine
4 heaped tablespoons rice
10 tomatoes (4 peeled)
750 ml (1½ pints) stock or water
Salt, pepper, nutmeg and made mustard
390 gr (13 oz.) cheddar cheese (150 gr (5 oz.) grated)
185 gr (6 oz.) sliced ham

CHEESOTTO—*continued*

Fry onion in fat and add the uncooked rice. Cook for a few minutes, stirring. Add 4 peeled tomatoes 750 ml (1½ pints) stock or water and bring to boil. Add salt and cook gently for about 30 minutes until rice is soft and liquid almost absorbed. Season with nutmeg, salt and pepper. Remove from heat and stir in 125 gr (4 oz.) grated cheese and turn into greased fireproof dish. Cut 250 gr (8 oz.) cheese into a dozen 5 cm (2 in.) squares. Spread a little mustard on ham slices, cut and fold over to make 12 neat pieces. Cut each of remaining tomatoes into three slices and sprinkle with pepper and salt. Take 4 skewers and put pieces of tomato, cheese and ham alternately on each one, beginning and ending with tomato. Place the prepared skewers on top of the cheese risotto, sprinkle with remaining cheese and put into hot oven 240° C (450° F.) for 5-8 minutes until cheese slices begin to melt. Serve hot.

Note: If desired the above ingredients may be prepared in smaller proportions and arranged on smaller skewers.

Special Mention

CHEESE FROSTED HAM SALAD LOAF

1 loaf day-old bread (preferably sandwich shape)
¾ cup mayonnaise
¾ cup milk
1½ tablespoons mixed mustard
1 tablespoon vinegar
3 cups finely chopped cooked ham (or any finely diced cold meat)
Salt and pepper to taste
2 tablespoons gelatine
½ cup cold water
500 gr (1 lb.) cheddar cheese (softened to spreading consistency with warm milk)
1 doz. stuffed olives
1 doz. radish roses
Lettuce leaves and celery curls

Trim all crust from loaf, cut a slice lengthwise from top and remove inside of loaf, leaving walls 13 mm (½ in.) thick. Combine mayonnaise, milk, mustard, vinegar, cold meat, salt and pepper. Soften gelatine in cold water and dissolve over boiling water. Stir gradually into meat mixture, mix well. When beginning to thicken, fill in prepared bread case. Replace top slice and secure with cocktail sticks. Chill until filling is set. Remove cocktail sticks. Pipe or spread softened cheddar cheese over entire surface of loaf. Chill. Place on lettuce leaves on serving platter. Garnish with stuffed olives, radish roses and celery curls. Serve in slices.

AS FROM Dr G. L. Sutton, Chairman, Dairy Products Marketing Board, 135 St. George's Terrace, PERTH.

SELF-RAISING FLOUR AND BAKING POWDER

SELF-RAISING FLOUR

5 kg (10 lb.) Flour
60 gr (2 oz.) carbonate soda
125 gr (4 oz.) cream of tartar
1 teaspoon tartaric acid

Mix all well together, and put through the sifter. Keep in a tin or bag ready for use.

BAKING POWDER

125 gr (4 oz.) Carbonate Soda
125 gr (4 oz.) ground rice
250 gr (8 oz.) cream of tartar

Roll the soda thoroughly, add the cream of tartar, and roll again. Add the ground rice, and roll again. Sift mixture three or four times, and put away in airtight tins or screw-top bottles.

Contents

Microwave Hints & Recipes

Continued over....

O O O O

USING THE MICROWAVE OVEN FOR EVERY-DAY MEALS

GENERAL HINTS

All food should be allowed to stand for the time it has taken to defrost before it is either cooked or served, ie: a piece of meat for roasting will take 8-10 mins.per 500g (lb) to defrost and should stand for the same length of time before being put in the oven. An average sized cake, which has been frozen, will take from 5-7 mins. to defrost and should stand for the same length of time before it is served. In some cases defrosting and reheating can be done in one operation. Take care with bread as it is one of the easiest foods to overheat and dry out.

The more food you put into the microwave oven the longer it takes to cook. The temperature of the food to be cooked will also make a difference. Food from the refrigerator will take a little longer than food at room temperature.

Cover foods in the microwave oven if you normally covered them when using conventional methods. This will retain moisture and speed cooking.

When reheating plates of food, always place the larger pieces of food around the outer edges of the plate, eg: cauliflower, potatoes or meat outside with peas or beans in the centre.

Remember — like your conventional oven, open the door now and then, stir and test. Opening the door during cooking will not affect the time clock.

* * * * * *

Stale biscuits will freshen in oven when warmed 1 min., then cooled on rack. Barbeque snack biscuits and potato chips will also refreshen 1 min. in microwave and then cooled.

To liquify honey that has crystallised, heat in microwave on high for 30-40 secs. (Remove lid first).

Refrigerate fresh percolated coffee and reheat by the cupful in microwave for 2 mins. on high. Coffee doesn't get "cooked up" bitter flavour.

Get more juice from lemons, oranges or grapefruit by warming on high 30 secs. Let stand for 3 mins. before squeezing.

Dry all herbs quickly in microwave. Place a few sprigs or half cup of leaves between paper towels and heat 3-4 mins. on high. (Time may vary for different herbs).

If any smell lingers in the oven (ie: fish, onions etc). Boil some water and lemon juice in oven for 2 mins.

Blanch nuts by heating in boiling water on high for about 1 min. Drain and slip skins off by rubbing between paper towels. Toast nuts in small glass bowl in microwave on high. 1½ cups takes 3-5 mins. Stir twice.

Melt chocolate for cooking on medium. 30 gr. will take 2 mins. Chocolate does not lose its shape when melted, so check and stir before adding extra time.

Toast coconut in small glass bowl in microwave on high. heat ⅓ cup-1¼ to 2 mins. or until golden brown. Stir twice.

To dry damp salt or sugar — heat in microwave for 20-45 secs. depending on amount.

To peel peaches, tomatoes, plums etc. — Place 4 pieces of fruit at a time into oven. Cook on high for 30 secs. stand for 25 seconds, then peel.

* * * * * *

HINTS FOR BREAD, ROLLS etc.

To dry bread for croutons or breadcrumbs, place 120 gr. of bread cubes in glass dish in microwave and set on HIGH for 4-5 mins. Stir occasionally.

For quick Garlic Bread — cut a french loaf in slices, almost through, and spread with butter, pinch of mixed herbs and a teaspoon of garlic salt (or fresh garlic if you have it), wrap in paper towel and microwave for 1-3 mins.

Reheat Croissants or Danish Pastries in seconds — stand on sheet of kitchen paper towel.

Reheat Bread Rolls in a bread basket lined with a serviette for a few seconds before serving.

Breakfast:

PORRIDGE

Combine 1 cup milk and ½ cup oatmeal in cereal bowl. Cook on HIGH 1½-2 minutes. Stir during cooking. Add a little more liquid, if required. Water may be used in place of milk if desired.

OMELETTES

Preheat browning dish for 6 minutes on Full Power. Beat together 2 eggs, 1 tablespoon water and pepper to taste. Add 1 teaspoon butter to browning dish, allow butter to melt, then pour in egg mixture and microwave for 1½-2 minutes on HIGH, stirring occasionally with fork to ensure even cooking. When set, roll and serve. If using a glass plate, sprinkle with paprika and chopped parsley to give extra colour.

Grated cheese, cooked bacon, mushrooms etc. may be added when omelette is almost set.

POACHED EGGS

Melt 1 teaspoon butter in a cup or small receptacle. Add egg and cook on DEFROST or LOW 2-2½ minutes per egg.

SCRAMBLED EGGS

Combine 2 eggs and ¼ cup milk. Beat well in a plastic bowl or jug. Cook on HIGH 2 minutes. Beat after with a fork (Chopped tomato, onion or parsley may be added if desired).

BACON

Place 2 rashers of bacon in between a paper towel. Cook on HIGH 1-1½ minutes per rasher.

Soups

CELERY & ONION SOUP

Slice 2 sticks celery and 1 onion finely. Cook in 1 tablespoon butter for 5 minutes covered. Add 2 cups chicken stock and cook on HIGH, 5 minutes. Blend in 1 cup milk and cook 2 minutes on HIGH. Beat 2 egg yolks, add 1 or 2 tablespoons hot soup to beaten egg, then stir gently into soup. Reheat on HIGH 2 minutes.

OLD-FASHIONED BEEF AND VEGETABLE SOUP

750 gr (1½ lb.) shin beef, cut into small cubes
1½ cups water, approximately
1 large onion)
3 medium size carrots,) Peeled and
2 parsnips) finely
1 swede turnip) chopped
1 turnip)
4 sticks celery, washed and finely sliced
500 gr (1lb.) tomatoes, peeled and chopped, or 1 can (440 gr) tomatoes drained and chopped.
1 tablespoon butter
few drops Tabasco
6 cups beef stock

Mixed vegetable soups are better made the day before as the flavour improves with standing.

Place the cubed beef into a casserole dish and pour the 1½ cups of water over. Microwave on Full Power for 8 minutes, or until the liquid has come to the boil. Reduce heat to simmer setting (50% power) and microwave for 40 to 60 minutes or until the meat is tender, adding a little more water if necessary.

Place the prepared vegetables and butter in a microwave oven safe dish, cover dish with plastic wrap and microwave on Full Power for 12 minutes or until the vegetables are soft. Stir once or twice during cooking. Add stock, cooked beef, chopped tomatoes and tabasco. Microwave on Full Power for approximately 12 to 15 minutes, or until boiling. Reduce heat to simmer setting (50%) and microwave for 15 minutes.

Serve with bread croutons.

PUMPKIN or POTATO SOUP

1 kg (2lb) pumpkin or potatoes
1 teaspoon sugar
2 cups chicken stock
1 teaspoon tarragon.
1 teaspoon basil or dill
¼ cup fresh or sour cream
Chopped chives or parsley to garnish

This soup does not need a sauce to thicken it. It is made by cooking and pureeing a large quantity of vegetables, then thinning the soup down with stock.

Microwave the potatoes in their jackets for 12-14 minutes on Full Power, or cut pumpkin into wedges, remove seeds and microwave for 12-14 minutes on Full Power. Allow the potatoes or pumpkin to cool then peel. Puree in a blender or food processor and place in a microwave oven safe dish, add chicken stock and herbs, stir well and combine.

Microwave on Full Power for 10 minutes to heat through and blend the flavours. Add the cream and garnish with chopped chives or parsley.

DUMPLINGS

60 gr (2oz.) suet, finely chopped
125 gr (4oz.) self-raising flour.
pinch mixed herbs
¼ teaspoon salt
cold water to mix.

Mix all ingredients to a soft pliable dough. Shape into balls and add to soups or stews 7 to 8 minutes before the end of cooking time.

Vegetables

ROAST VEGETABLES

Baste roasting vegetables in fat your roast provided. Remove excess — place vegetables in and cook uncovered. They will not dehydrate as the fat stops this. This takes approximately 10-15 minutes extra than boiled vegetables.

Most vegetables take 5-7 minutes on Full Power per 500 gr (1lb.) to cook — 8 mins. on Full Power will give a softer vegetable.

1-2 tablespoons water is all that is needed to steam vegetables. Extra water slows down the cooking time. If cooking vegetables together, make sure they are of similar size and density, as thickness and size make a difference to cooking times.

As vegetables carry on cooking and rapidly discolour, they should always be taken out before they seem fully cooked. They may look raw and taste a bit tough and it is easy to be tempted to cook them a bit longer. DON'T. They will complete cooking in the standing time, which is approx. half cooking time.

All vegetables should be stirred occasionally during cooking to distribute the microwave energy evenly.

Most vegetables give better results if cooked in a plastic bag. This keeps heat from the steam in, so you use little or no water and cut cooking time even further and add to nutritional value.

BLANCHING

Vegetables can also be blanched in your microwave oven, if you have a surplus at any time. The blanching time is half the cooking time for the same vegetable, and they must then be placed into cold water before placing in bags for freezing.

All vegetables should be cooked to a fork tenderness. Overcooking will not generally give a soft or mushy result but a tougher drier one.

* * * * * *

ASPARAGUS (Fresh)

8th cup water, salted | **500 gr fresh asparagus**

Melt salt in water, cook about 6 mins. on HIGH — covered. When cooked add knobs of butter and sprinkle with lemon pepper — serve.

CARROTS

Peel (cut as desired) and place in plastic bag. Wash, pour off water, seal bag, cook 3 minutes per cup full on HIGH.

CABBAGE

Shred cabbage, place in bag, rinse and drain. Using half average size cabbage cook 6 minutes on HIGH. Alternate method — cut cabbage in half and wash. Spread 1 dessert spoon butter or margarine over surface and sprinkle with a little garlic. Put in bag and cook 6 mins. per half cabbage.

CAULIFLOWER OR BROCCOLI

Cut into flowerets, cut stems as short as possible and put a cross into stems. This will help them to cook better. A little butter may be added if desired. Cook in bag 3 mins. per cup on HIGH.

PEAS

Cook frozen peas in bag, with just a little water, for 3 mins. per cup. (It is best to take out of the freezer for a time prior to cooking).

POTATOES BAKED STUFFED

4 med. potatoes, baked
½ cup shredded cheddar cheese
¼ cup milk
60 gr butter or marg.
1 egg
salt and pepper to taste
paprika

Cut a thin slice (lengthwise) from each potato. Scoop out potato, leaving a thin shell. Combine potato, cheese, milk, butter, egg, salt and pepper, mash until smooth. Spoon potato mixture into shell; sprinkle with paprika. Cook on paper towel lined glass oven tray 5-6 mins. on HIGH or until heated through. Adjust heating time as necessary. Serves 4.

POTATOES (Jacket)

4 Potatoes — prick skins all over. Microwave 3-4 minutes on HIGH. Turn over — microwave another 3 minutes. Cut to serve with butter or sour cream. (Time may vary 1 minute with size of potato).

POTATOES.....JAZZED UP

6 peeled potatoes
2 tblspns. breadcrumbs
1 oz. butter
paprika

Melt butter. Cut the potatoes into thin slices, but not all the way through, leaving an uncut base. Pour the butter over potatoes and cook uncovered on HIGH for 12 mins. Sprinkle paprika and breadcrumbs over the potatoes and cook a further 4 mins. on HIGH or until they are ready.

POTATOES (Mashed)

Peel and place in bag whole, wash in bag, pour off all water. Cook for 3 minutes per potato on HIGH, eg., 1 potato-3 minutes: 3 potatoes-9 minutes. Potatoes may be cut in smaller pieces if desired.

PUMPKIN

Peel, cut into large pieces, place in bag etc. cook 8 mins. on HIGH (approx 1 lb.).

For baked pumpkin, choose small whole butternut, cut in half lengthwise. Remove seeds, stuff with mixture of vegetables and herbs, wrap in plastic wrap. Cook 12 mins. (1½ lbs.) on HIGH.

PUMPKIN STUFFED

1 med. pumpkin (butternut)
carrot straws
zucchini
parsley
peas
potatoes
butter
mushrooms

Wash pumpkin and poke a few holes into the skin. Halve the pumpkin. Scoop out the centre. Mix with chopped vegetables and arrange in shell. Cover and cook 10-12 mins. on HIGH. Add parsley.

* Meat may be added to this recipe to make it a full meal.

ZUCCHINI CASSEROLE

2 onions (sliced)
1 or 2 zucchini (washed and sliced)
2 tomatoes (sliced)
2 tblspns. butter
cheese for topping

Place onion in dish with butter. Cook covered 2 mins. on HIGH. Stir in zucchini and tomatoes. Cover, cook further 5 mins. Sprinkle cheese on top and allow to melt.

Meat and Poultry

Meat should always be roasted on a rack so that it does not 'sit' in the fat and become soggy. Do not roast meat on a rack intended for reheating food, as these sit too high. A roasting rack should be about 1 in. high.

To keep oven clean, cover meat loosely with paper towel, which will catch the spattering fat. A roast can be cooked in an oven bag, but be sure to secure it with string or an elastic band and NOT a metal tie.

The crackling on pork acts as a barrier to microwave energy, so cut crackling off and then grill.

Do not add extra time if food is stuffed, just add an extra 2 tblspns. water to the usual mixture to give the stuffing a softer consistency. Meat can be roasted successfully on Full Power allowing from 8-12 mins. per 500 gr (1lb.) depending on its tenderness. Some shrinkage is likely to occur, therefore 70% power is preferable, though it may take a little longer.

Liquid for a pot roast should simmer gently, not boil.

If Simmer Setting (50%) power is too high, use a lower setting. Allow meat to stand for ⅓, or preferably ⅔ cooking time to allow it to finish cooking. If you have a microwave oven with a Warm setting (10% power) casseroles and pot roasts can be cooked for 8 to 10 hrs., the same as if using a crock pot. The energy output and running cost at this level is the same in both cases.

Do not cook meat to perfection. Remove it before it is cooked right through. It will finish cooking while it is 'standing' (approx. 15-20 mins.). The roast will stay at the same temp. for approx. 15-20 mins. so there is no need to reheat afterwards.

TENDER CUTS TIME: Double weight, eg: 1.5 kg + 1.5 kg. = 3.0 kg. = 30 mins.
TOUGH CUTS TIME: Cook on HIGH 10 mins. then 3 times its weight on LOW: eg: 1.5 kg. + 1.5 kg + 1.5 kg. = 4.5 kg. = 45 mins.

* * * * * *

HINTS

When reheating Meat Pies. Place pie upside down at start and heat for approx. 2 mins. then with egg slice (or similar) turn over and heat pastry top. This way the pastry on top will not go hard.

Put Frankfurts into buttered hot dog rolls, spread on a little mustard and sprinkle with grated cheese. Wrap in paper towel or serviette. 2 rolls, 2 mins — 4 rolls, 3-4 mins.

ROASTING CHART

	OVEN SETTING	TIME PER 500 g (1 lb)	INTERNAL TEMPERATURE BY THERMOMETER PROBE	HINTS
BEEF	Full Power followed by Roast Setting (70%)	10 minutes 12 to 14 minutes	80°C (180°F)	Place thin end of meat to centre of dish.
LAMB	Full Power followed by Roast Setting (70%)	10 minutes 10 to 12 minutes	80°C (180°F)	Remove shank from leg or shoulder after 10 to 14 minutes.
VEAL	Full Power followed by Roast Setting (70%)	6 to 8 minutes 10 to 12 minutes	75°C (165°F)	Rub with butter before cooking to make surface crisp and keep meat moist.
CHICKEN	Full Power followed by Roast Setting (70%)	8 to 10 minutes 12 to 14 minutes	94°C (200°C)	Brush with oil and sprinkle with paprika to obtain crispness and natural colour. Put thermometer probe into thickest part of thigh, checking that it is not touching bone or a false reading will be given.
TURKEY	Simmer Setting (50%)	15 to 20 minutes	94°C (200°C)	See chicken.
TURKEY HINDQUARTER	Simmer Setting (50% power)	15 to 20 minutes	94°C (200°F)	See chicken.
DUCK	Roast Setting (70%)	12 to 14 minutes	94°C (200°F)	See chicken.
PORK	Full Power followed by Roast Setting (70%)	8 to 10 minutes 12 to 14 minutes	94°C (200°F)	Remove crackling before roasting; cook separately.
BOILING FOWL, RABBIT	Simmer Setting (50% power)	15 to 20 minutes	94°C (200°F)	Cook with a little liquid, herbs and butter. See French Roasting instructions.

COUNTRY POT ROAST

1.5 kg. (3 lb.) piece fresh topside, silverside or round beef
2 med. sized onions, peeled and sliced
2 sticks celery, sliced
4 med. sized carrots, peeled and sliced
1 bayleaf
125 gr (4 oz.) bacon
1 tbspn. butter
1 tbspn. plain flour
1 cup water
1 beef stock cube (optional)

Place bacon on paper towelling and microwave on HIGH for 1 min. per rasher, or until crisp. Crumble bacon when cooled. Microwave onions, in a dish covered with plastic wrap, for 4 mins. on HIGH. Microwave carrots and celery, with 1 tbspn. water in a dish covered with plastic wrap, for 5 mins. on HIGH. Melt butter in a jug for approx 10 secs. in the microwave oven. Add flour to butter and mix well. Add hot water gradually and microwave on HIGH until sauce comes to the boil. Add crumbled stock cube, if desired. Mix the vegetables and bacon, and place in a casserole dish. Place meat on top of vegetables and pour sauce over. Add bayleaf. Cover and microwave on HIGH for approx. 5 mins. or until sauce reaches a full boil. Reduce heat to simmer setting (50% power) and microwave for 20 mins. per 500 gr (1 lb.), turning meat over once during cooking.

INDIENNE LAMB ROAST

1.5 kg (3 lb.) leg lamb
MARINADE:
1 clove garlic, crushed
2.5 cm (1 in.) piece green ginger, finely chopped
1 tbspn. oil
1 tblspn. soy sauce
2 tspns. lemon juice
1 tspn. curry powder
½ tspn. turmeric
½ cup water
pepper to taste

Make diagonal cuts, about 5mm (¼ in.) apart across leg of lamb in both directions to make a diamond pattern. Mix the marinade ingredients together, pour over the meat and allow to stand for at least ½ hour. Place meat, fat side down, on roasting rack in dish and microwave for 10 mins. on HIGH. Turn meat fat side up and spoon marinade back over it. Add ½ cup water to the dish, reduce heat to roast setting (70% power) and microwave for 12-14 mins. per 500 gr (1 lb.) or, if using a probe, until the internal temp. of the meat registers 80°C (180°F). Stand for 15-20 mins. tented in foil, before carving. Serve with fried rice or roast vegetables.

ROAST CHICKEN WITH STUFFING

1.5 kg. chicken
pkt. stuffing mix
Season-All
gravy browning

Wash chicken and place stuffing into bird. Place browning on to bird. Cook in dish, breast down for 15 mins. Turn over and cook for further 15 mins.

Casseroles and Stews

Casseroles and stews take only ⅓ of the usual time when cooked in a microwave oven, this would be about 40 to 60 mins. depending on quality of meat used. The food should be cooked on HIGH for approx. 10 mins. or until the liquid comes to the boil. The heat should then be reduced to Simmer Setting (50% power), or even lower if the liquid is bubbling too fast, to complete the cooking.

It is a matter of choice whether or not the meat is browned first. If you have a casserole browning dish, preheat it in the microwave oven on HIGH, then brown the meat on all sides. If you do not have a browning dish, the meat can be browned in a frying pan on top of the stove, then transfer it to a casserole dish to complete cooking in the microwave oven.

The liquid added should just cover the meat; if too much is added, the microwave energy will heat the liquid but not the food and the process will be slowed down. Extra gravy can be made by adding more liquid when the meat is cooked.

Always cook the vegetables separately. If cooked with meat, the salt from the stock will make them tough. Add them to the meat in the last 10-15 mins. of cooking time to blend the flavours. Stir from the edges to the centre several times during cooking to distribute the microwave energy through the food and maintain even cooking. Oven bags and heavy-duty freezer bags can be used for freezing and reheating casserole dishes, as they stand up to heat as well as to cold.

Foods cook from the outside to the centre, so stir casseroles always once or twice during cooking, spooning the outside towards the centre so that contents cook uniformly.

ALL-IN-ONE CHICKEN CASSEROLE

4 chicken breast fillets
2 lge. potatoes, thinly sliced
2 tspns. grated green ginger
2 tbspns. dry sherry
1 tbspn. soy sauce
1 tspn. sugar
2 tbspns. cornflour
1 cup chicken stock
185 gr mushrooms, sliced
4 green shallots, chopped

Chop chicken into bite-sized pieces. Combine with potatoes, ginger, sherry, soy sauce and sugar. Stir in blended cornflour and stock, cook on HIGH 20 mins. or until potatoes are tender, stirring occasionally. Add mushrooms and shallots. Cook on HIGH 10 mins. Serves 4.

CHUNKY CASSEROLE

750 gr topside or round steak
1 tbspn. br. sugar
½ tspn. mustard
1 cup hot water
1 tbspn. tomato sauce
1 tspn. worcestershire sauce
2 tbspns. flour
1 tspn. salt
¼ tspn. pepper
2 beef stock cubes
1 tbspn. vinegar
500 gr chunky vegetables of your choice

Cut meat into small cubes. Combine all dry ingredients in a plastic bag. Coat meat well with this mixture. Place meat into deep casserole dish. Combine water, stock cubes and sauces and pour over meat. Heat, covered on HIGH 10 min. reduce to SIMMER for 25 mins. Add chunky vegetables and cook for an additional 25 mins. or until meat is tender. Meat must be kept under liquid. Serves 4.

CREAM OF MUSHROOM AND CHICKEN CASSEROLE

Size 15 chicken
2 onions, sliced
125 gr mushrooms, sliced
15 gr butter
440 gr can cr. of mushroom soup
⅓ cup mayonnaise
2 tspns. french mustard
¾ cup sour cream
3 zucchini, sliced
2 tbspns. grated parmesan cheese
2 tbspns. chopped parsley

Cut chicken into serving sized pieces, remove skin and fat. Place butter in large dish, add onions and mushrooms, cook on HIGH 3 mins. Stir in undiluted soup, mayonnaise, mustard and cream; add chicken pieces. Cover. Cook on HIGH 20 mins. stirring occasionally. Stir in zucchini, sprinkle with cheese and parsley, cook on HIGH 5 mins. Cover dish, stand 15 mins. before serving. Serves 4.

HEARTY FAMILY CHICKEN CASSEROLE

8 chicken thigh fillets
2 lge. carrots, thinly sliced
2 bay leaves
1 cup chicken stock
¼ cup plain flour
2 tbspns. water
1 cup frozen peas
125 gr mushrooms, sliced

Cut fillets in half, place in dish, add carrots, bay leaves and stock. Cover, cook on HIGH 10 mins. Blend flour with water, add to chicken with peas and mushrooms. Cook on HIGH 10 mins. or until chicken is tender; remove bay leaves before serving. Serves 4 to 6.

HERBED LAMB CASSEROLE

Medium High cooking allows time for the fresh herb flavours to develop. Dried herbs can be used if necessary in the proportion of 1 tspn. dried to 2 tbspn. fresh. Ask the butcher to remove the bone from the leg of lamb.

1 sml. leg of lamb boned (about 1kg.)
2 bacon rashers, chopped
1 onion, quartered
1 clove garlic, crushed
2 med. potatoes, chopped
2 med. carrots, sliced
1 tbspn. chopped thyme
2 tbspns. ea. chopped mint and basil
½ cup chicken stock
1 tbspn. plain flour
1 tbspn. tomato paste
1 cup frozen (or fresh) peas

Remove fat from lamb, cut into 2.5cm pieces. Combine bacon, onion and garlic in bowl, cook on HIGH 5 mins. or until onion is tender; add lamb, potatoes, carrots and herbs. Blend flour with stock, stir in tomato paste, stir into meat mixture. Cook, covered on MEDIUM HIGH 20 mins. stirring occasionally. Stir in peas, cook on HIGH 5 mins. Serves 6.

CHICKEN CHOW MEIN

3 chicken breasts (sliced)
2 tbspns. cornflour
½ cup chicken stock
1½ tbspns. soy sauce
1 cup celery (sliced thinly)
1 onion (diced)
1 tin baby corn
250 gr sliced mushrooms
chow mein noodles

Place chicken pieces into a casserole. Cover and cook on HIGH for 5-6 mins. Stir once. Blend cornflour to boiling stock and soy sauce. Add vegetables to chicken and pour stock over. Cover and cook on HIGH 10 mins. Stir once.

Serve surrounded by noodles.

TURMERIC CHICKEN WITH CORN

4 chicken breast fillets
½ tspn. turmeric
2 tspns. grated green ginger
1 tbspn. soy sauce
1 red pepper
1 tspn. cornflour
2 tbspns. water
425 gr can corn, drained

Cut chicken fillets into 1 cm. strips, combine with turmeric, ginger and soy sauce, mix well, stand 15 mins. Cut pepper in strips. Place chicken in shallow dish, cook on HIGH 3 mins. Add blended cornflour and water, pepper and corn, cook on HIGH 4 mins. or until mixture boils and thickens. Stir once during cooking. Serves 4.

CHICKEN IN TANGY TOMATO SAUCE

1 kg. chicken pieces
1 onion, finely chopped
1 stick celery, chopped
4 med. ripe tomatoes, peeled and chopped
1 tbspns. cornflour
2 tbspns. vinegar
1 clove garlic, crushed
¼ cup tomato sauce
1 tbspn. worcestershire sauce
½ cup water
1 tbspn. tomato paste
1 tbspn. sugar
1 tbspn. chopped parsley

Combine onion and celery in shallow dish, cook on HIGH 3 mins. Add tomatoes, cook on HIGH 2 mins. Blend cornflour and vinegar in bowl, stir in garlic, sauces, water, tomato paste and sugar. Add to tomato mixture, cook on HIGH 5 mins. stirring once. Add chicken, mix well, cook on HIGH 10 mins. Sprinkle with parsley. Serves 4.

CHICKEN POTATO SLICE

1 BBQ'd chicken
750 gr potatoes, thickly sliced
15 gr butter
6 green shallots, chopped
1 sml. red pepper, chopped
30 gr butter, extra
1 clove garlic, crushed
2 tbspns. plain flour
⅓ cup water
1 chicken stock cube
⅓ cup dry white wine
½ cup cream
2 tspns. french mustard
1 tbspn. mayonnaise
grated tasty cheese
paprika
2 tbspns. chopped parsley

Remove chicken meat from bones, break into bite-sized pieces. Place potatoes in shallow dish, dot with butter, cover, cook on HIGH 9 mins. or until tender, top with chicken and shallots. Melt extra butter with garlic in bowl on HIGH 30 secs. Stir in flour, water, crumbled stock cube, wine and cream, cook on HIGH 3 mins. Stir in mustard and mayonnaise, pour over chicken, sprinkle with cheese and paprika. Cook on HIGH 5 mins. or until heated through. Sprinkle with parsley before serving. Serves 6.

CREAMY CHICKEN CURRY

4 chicken breast fillets
30 gr butter
1 onion, finely sliced
2 tspns. curry powder
1 tspn turmeric
2 tbspns. Benedictine
1 cup chicken stock
2 tbspns. plain flour
2 tbspns. water
¼ cup cream

Cut chicken into thin strips. Combine butter, onion, curry powder and turmeric in dish. Cook on HIGH 5 mins. Stir in chicken, Benedictine and stock. Cook on HIGH 8 mins. or until chicken is tender. Remove chicken to serving plate. Blend flour with cold water, stir into liquid in dish with cream. Cook on HIGH 3 mins. or until sauce boils and thickens. Pour over chicken. Serves 4.

Benedictine adds an unusual flavour...brandy is quite a good substitute. Adjust the amount of curry powder according to type used and personal tastes. This is nice served with mango chutney, sliced banana dipped in lemon juice, coconut and chopped tomatoes and cucumbers tossed in yoghurt with chopped parsley and mint. Can serve with boiled rice.

DEVILLED LAMB CHOPS

4 lamb chump chops
2 tbspns. fruit chutney
1 tspn. curry powder
1 tbspn. br. sugar
2 tbspns. soy sauce
1 tspn. vinegar

Remove fat from chops, place chops in single layer in shallow dish, top with combined chutney, curry powder, sugar, soy sauce and vinegar. Cook on HIGH 5 mins. or until chops are tender. Serves 4.

Seafood

Fish cooks quickly in the microwave oven, therefore the flavour is 'locked in'.

Never overcook fish, 4-6 mins. per 500 gr (lb.) on Full Power, followed by 2 mins. standing time per 500 gr (1lb.) is all that is needed. If the eyes have been left in the fish, they will become opaque or milky-white, when the fish is cooked; otherwise test by inserting a sharp knife into the flesh. It should be just beginning to flake. After standing time, it will flake easily. Always place the thin parts of fish fillets to the centre as they will overcook if placed on the edge.

Slash and brush fish skin with melted butter before cooking to stop skin toughening.

GARLIC PRAWNS

Heat 1 clove garlic with 2 tablespoons of butter for 30 secs. Add 250 grams raw (deveined) prawns and heat for 60 secs. stirring after 30 seconds.

FISH FILLETS ALMONDINE

½ cup blanched almonds
500 gr flounder fillets
2 tspns chopped parsley
125 gr butter
salt and pepper
lemon juice

Sliver almonds — heat butter in large shallow dish for 1 min. Add almonds and cook about 4 mins. HIGH, stir occasionally until lightly browned. Remove nuts with slotted spoon and set aside. Place fish in same dish — turning to coat with butter. Season to taste and sprinkle with parsley and lemon juice. Cover and cook 4 mins. Sprinkle nuts evenly over fish — re-cover and cook 30 secs. Allow to stand 4 mins. then test with fork, — if fish flakes easily, reheat a few secs. and serve. Otherwise cover and return to oven for 1 min. Serve with lemon and parsley.

FISH WITH LEMON SAUCE

4 white fish fillets
1 lemon
2 tspns. dry sherry
1 red pepper

SAUCE:

3 tspns cornflour
¼ cup lemon juice
1 tspn. soy sauce
1 tspn. tomato sauce
1½ tbspns. sugar
½ cup water

Remove skin and bones from fish; place fish in single layer in shallow dish. Cut two strips from lemon using vegetable peeler; shred lemon rind finely. Cut pepper into thin strips. Sprinkle sherry over fish, cook on HIGH 6 mins. Sprinkle pepper strips and lemon rind over fish, pour sauce over, cook on HIGH 1 min. or until heated through.

SAUCE: Blend cornflour with lemon juice in bowl, add remaining ingredients. Cook on HIGH 2 mins. stirring after 1 min. Serves 4.

HIGH FIBRE SALMON & VEGETABLE CASSEROLE

Cook about 2/3 cup brown rice for this recipe; drain well before using.

15 gr butter
1 onion, chopped
1 carrot, chopped
1 stick celery, chopped
1½ cups cooked brown rice
1 egg
90 gr mushrooms, sliced
1 small red pepper, chopped
220 gr can salmon
130 gr can whole kernel corn, drained
1 tbspn. chopped chives
½ cup grated tasty cheese

Combine butter, onion, carrot and celery in dish, cover, cook on HIGH 5 mins; add rice, lightly beaten egg, tomato paste, mushrooms, red pepper, undrained salmon, corn and chives, mix until well combined. Sprinkle with cheese, cook on HIGH 8 mins. Serves 4.

TUNA RISOTTO

440 gr can tuna
60 gr butter
2 onions, chopped
2 tspns. curry powder
1 cup long grain rice
3 cups chicken stock
4 hardboiled eggs, quartered
1 tblspn. chopped parsley
1 sml. red pepper, chopped
2 tblspns. lemon juice

Drain tuna, reserve liquid. Melt butter, saute onions on HIGH about 4 mins. Add curry powder, cook 1 min. Add rice, stock and reserved liquid, cook on HIGH about 15 mins. Stir in flaked tuna, eggs, pepper, lemon juice and parsley, reheat, stirring gently.

TUNA TETRAZINNI

440 gr tuna
90 gr butter
125 gr baby mushrooms, sliced
1 sml. red pepper, chopped
½ cup plain flour
2 cups chicken stock
¼ cup dry sherry
¾ cup cream
45 gr can anchovies, drained
375 gr pasta
½ cup grated tasty cheese
30 gr butter, extra
½ cup stale breadcrumbs
2 tblspns. chopped parsley

Drain tuna, reserving liquid. Melt butter, cook mushrooms and pepper 2 mins. on HIGH, stir in flour, cook 1 min. on HIGH. Gradually add stock and reserved liquid, stir, cook on HIGH 4 mins. Cook pasta in large pan boiling water until tender; drain. Combine pasta with half sauce, pour into ovenproof dish. Combine remaining sauce with tuna and place in centre of pasta, sprinkle with cheese. Melt extra butter, add crumbs, bake uncovered 10 mins. on HIGH. Sprinkle with parsley.

Cakes and Slices

Cakes and pastries should be cooked on a low rack which gives more air under the cake dish and stops the sticky 'steamed' effect that often occurs, particularly when using a glass turntable.

Cakes should be slightly sticky or moist on top when cooked, but a skewer inserted into the centre of the cake should come out cleanly.

The cake surface will dry during standing time.

Butter, chocolate and icing can be softened or melted in the microwave oven to save time. Allow 10-20 secs. on HIGH for 1-2 tbspns.

* * * * * *

HINTS

Do NOT grease cooking containers used for baking cakes or the cake will stick. Use a little non-stick spray or line the container with ungreased greaseproof paper.

Soften dried fruits (raisins, sultanas, etc.) by adding 1 tbspn. water to 1 cup of fruit — Cook on HIGH for 1 min. allow to stand 3-4 mins. drain and use.

* * * * * *

COOKING TIMES

Average-sized cake — 125 gr to 185 gr (4 to 6 oz.) flour — 5-7 mins. on HIGH.
Larger cake — 250 gr (8 oz.) flour — 7-9 mins. on HIGH.
Very large or very rich cakes — 9-12 mins. on Roast setting (70% power).

Cakes should be cooked in a round dish, as square dishes are subject to microwave penetration at the corners, creating uneven cooking. Microwave safe plastic containers, unlike glass ones, do not retain the heat, so there is less chance of overcooking or sticking.

* * * * * *

CUP CAKES

Just for fun try making children's cakes in icecream cones. If they are iced nicely, children won't notice they are a bit tough in the corners.

Polystyrene cups can be cut into rings, place paper patty pans inside them, fill them with mixture and microwave for 20-40 secs. per cup cake, depending on size.

Place cakes in a circle and do not put any in the centre. Try 6 at a time in patty pans for 1½-2 mins. on HIGH.

BANANA CAKE

125 gr butter
1 tspn. vanilla essence
3-4 ripe bananas, mashed
½ tspn. Bicarb soda
4 tspns. milk
1 cup castor sugar
2 eggs
2 cups sifted S.R. flour
pinch salt

Cream butter, sugar and vanilla and beat in eggs. Fold in mashed bananas and combine well. Dissolve soda in milk and add to creamed mixture alternatively with flour and salt. Grease and line with buttered brown paper in an oblong pyrex dish 26 x 16 cm. extending paper 1 in. above dish. Pour in mixture and cook on HIGH 8 mins. Allow to stand 5 mins. before turning out. Peel off paper. ice with lemon icing if desired.

CHOCOLATE CAKE

125 gr butter
1 tbspn. cocoa
small cup milk
2 eggs
1 cup sugar
1 lge. cup S.R. flour
pinch salt

Melt butter with milk and cocoa. Froth eggs and sugar. Sift flour and sprinkle some into egg mixture. Then add liquid and flour. Mix well. Cook 3 mins. HIGH then 2 mins. 2 secs. on MED. HIGH. Stand 5 mins. before turning out.

DATE AND WALNUT CAKE

125 gr dates, chopped
½ cup hot water
½ cup br. sugar
60 gr walnuts, chopped
pinch salt
½ tspn. bi-carb soda
125 gr butter
1 egg
1 cup S.R. flour

Soak dates with bi-carb. soda and water, cover and leave to soften. Cream butter and sugar, add egg and beat well. Fold in walnuts, date mixture and lastly sifted flour and salt. Grease and line with brown paper a ring pan. Place mixture into prepared pan and bake on HIGH 3 mins. then on MED. HIGH 3 mins. When cold ice with mocha icing.

HAZELNUT AND CHOCOLATE TORTE

2 egg whites
½ cup castor sugar
125 gr roasted hazelnuts
2 tbspns. plain flour

Chocolate Cream:

4 egg yolks
⅔ cup castor sugar
2 tbspns. cornflour
2 cups milk
100 gr dark cooking choc. chopped
2 tspns vanilla

Beat egg whites in small bowl, on elec. mixer until firm peaks form, gradually beat in sugar, until dissolved. Finely grind hazelnuts in processor or blender, combine with flour, fold gently into egg white mixture. Grease and flour 2 x 23 cm bases of springform pans, spread mixture evenly over the two bases, smooth tops. Cook on two levels in pre-heated 180°C CONVECTION oven for 10 mins. Change position of cakes, cook further 10 mins. or until light golden brown and firm to touch. Cool 5 mins. loosen gently from bases with knife, turn onto wire rack to cool.

Cream: Combine egg yolks, sugar and cornflour in bowl, gradually whisk in milk, cook on HIGH 6 mins. or until sauce boils and thickens, stirring several times during cooking. Stir in chocolate and vanilla, beat until smooth, cover, refrigerate until cold. Then place between layers of cake and decorate with icing sugar or as desired.

PINEAPPLE FRUIT CAKE

1 medium tin crushed pineapple
4 tbspns. butter
1 cup br. sugar
250 gr mixed fruit
1 tspn. bi-carb. soda
2 eggs
1 cup S.R. flour
1 cup plain flour

Place fruit, butter, sugar and pineapple into bowl and bring to boil on HIGH 5 mins. Lower power to LOW 10 mins. Add bi-carb. When cool beat eggs, mix in flour and put into plastic or glass container. Cook on ROAST or MED/HIGH 10 to 12 mins.

Note: If a darker cake is required, 1 tspn. parisian essence can be added.

POPPYSEED HAZELNUT TORTE WITH CHOCOLATE ROUGH GLAZE

⅓ cup poppy seeds
⅓ cup roasted hazelnuts
2 tbspns. S.R. flour
4 eggs separated
⅓ cup br. sugar
300 ml. ctn. thickened cream
250 gr punnet strawberries

Chocolate Rough Glaze:

125 gr dark cooking choc. chopped
15 gr butter

Grind poppy seeds, nuts and flour in blender until fine. Beat egg yolks with 2 tbspns. of the sugar on electric mixer until thick and creamy. Beat egg whites until soft peaks form, add remaining sugar, beat until dissolved. Fold poppyseed mixture into egg yolk mixture, fold in egg white mixture. Spoon into lightly greased, base lined 20 cm. ring pan. Cook on HIGH 3½ mins., stand 5 mins. before turning out onto wire rack to cool. Reserve ¼ cup of cream for Chocolate Rough Glaze. Split cake, fill with remaining whipped cream and sliced strawberries, place on serving plate. Top with Chocolate Rough Glaze.

Glaze: Combine hazelnuts, reserved cream, chocolate and butter in bowl, cook on HIGH 3 mins. or until chocolate has melted. Stir well.

CHOC DROP COOKIES

125 gr butter
¾ cup sugar
½ pkt. choc. drops*
1 tspn. vanilla
1 egg
1½ cups S.R. flour

***2 dstspns. drinking chocolate may be used.**

Place sugar and butter in microwave bowl, cook on HIGH 2½ mins. Mix in ½ pkt. choc. bits and vanilla. Allow to cool, add egg and then S.R. flour. Place 1 tspn. mixture into a ball, press 2 choc. drops on top of biscuits. Cook on HIGH 3 mins. (10-12 biscuits.).

OATY FRUIT SQUARES

1 cup chopped dried apricots
1 cup chopped pitted dates
⅔ cup water
1 cup chopped walnuts or pecans
2 tspns. grated lemon peel
2 tspns. lemon juice
1¼ cups plain flour
½ tspn. bi-carb. soda
½ tspn. salt
1½ cups quick oats
¾ cup packed br. sugar
155 gr (5 oz.) margarine

Combine fruits and water in a 6 cup heatproof bowl. Microwave uncovered on HIGH 4-5 mins. stirring every min. (Water should be absorbed and mixture fairly smooth). Stir in nuts, peel and juice. Set aside.

Combine flour, soda and salt, stir in oats and br. sugar. Set aside. Cut butter into pieces, place in 23 cm. (9 in.) heatproof baking dish. Microwave 1 min. until melted. Add flour mixture to butter, mix thoroughly with fork until crumbly. **Remove 1 cup** of crumbs and reserve. Press remainder evenly over bottom of dish. Spread filling evenly over crust. Sprinkle with reserved crumbs. Place dish on inverted saucer in microwave. Cook uncovered, on HIGH until puffed and set (about 6 mins.) rotating dish ¼ turn each 2 mins. Place dish on bench top to cool. Cut into squares.

ROCK BUNS

1½ cups S.R. flour
120 gr (4 oz.) margarine
⅓ cup sugar
½ cup sultanas
⅓ cup mixed peel
1 lge egg
milk

Sift flour and rub in margarine until it is like breadcrumbs. Stir in sugar, sultanas and peel, then bind ingredients with egg and enough milk to make stiff mixture. Divide evenly into 18 little buns and cook 6 at a time for 3 mins. on HIGH. Leave to cool.

SCONES

450 gr S.R. flour
55 gr butter
½ tspn. salt
280 ml. milk (¼ cup)

Melt butter, add flour, salt and milk to make fairly moist dough. Knead lightly, roll out and cut into shapes. Heat browning dish for 5 mins. Place 1 tbspn. butter on browning dish and place scones onto dish. Cook on HIGH 2 mins. Turn over and cook further 1 min. (approx. 8-9 scones). Serve with jam.

Desserts

HINTS

Make any Custards, Cornflour or Chocolate Sauces by mixing all dry ingredients together with a little milk. Heat remaining milk, add and microwave on HIGH 2 mins. Stir — then microwave 2 more minutes. Ready to serve.

* * * * * * * * * * * *

APPLES BAKED

If apples are microwaved in their skins, skins remain tough, so peel and core them, or leave ⅓ of skin at base of fruit.

Fill centre of each apple with either mixed dried fruit, chopped dates or apricots and chopped nuts. Top with knob of butter, ¼ tspn. soft br. sugar and a sprinkling of cinnamon or mixed spice. Microwave for 1½-2 mins. per apple on HIGH, depending on size. Apples DO NOT need to be covered during cooking. Stand for 3-4 mins. before serving.

APPLE CRUMBLE

6 apples (sliced)
1 cup plain flour
¼ cup br. sugar
½ cup toasted coconut
½ cup muesli
½ cup melted butter

Place sliced apples into dish. Cover with plastic. Cook 1 min. per apple, ie: 6 mins. Stir. Melt butter. Mix all dry ingredients together and stir in butter. Spread over cooked apples and then add toasted coconut on top. Cook on HIGH 3 mins.

To toast coconut — Place in small heatproof container and cook on HIGH 2½ mins. It will appear white. Stir and the centre will be toasted and brown.

BAKED RICE CUSTARD

3 cups milk
1 cup cooked rice
2 eggs, beaten
¼ cup sugar
½ cup sultanas or raisins
¼ tspn. cinnamon

Heat milk in large bowl on HIGH 2-3 mins. until almost boiling. Stir in rice, then add remaining ingredients and mix well. Cook on MEDIUM for 5 mins. or until custard is set. In first 2-3 mins. stir custard several times for more even cooking. Let stand 10 mins. before serving.

CUSTARD BAKED

1 ½ cups milk
¼ cup sugar
⅛ tspn. salt
1 tspn. vanilla
2 eggs, slightly beaten
nutmeg or mace

Scald milk in 1 qt. casserole. Whisk other ingredients and add to scalded milk. Microwave at 50% (MEDIUM) 8-14 mins. rotating ¼ every 3 mins. Centre will not be set, but will firm up while cooking. Serves 4.

BUTTERSCOTCH BANANAS

100 gr brown sugar
50 gr butter
20 ml. rum
50 ml. cream
3 bananas

In a small jug place brown sugar and butter. Cook on HIGH 3 mins. Stir, sugar, should be all dissolved, add cream and rum. Peel and slice each banana into three pieces. Place into 3 dishes, pour the sauce over, cook on MED/LOW 5-6 mins. Stir after 2 mins. to coat bananas with sauce. Serve with ice cream. Serves 3.

CHOCOLATE SELF-SAUCING PUDDING

60 gr butter
1½ cups S.R. flour
1 cup castor sugar
¼ cup cocoa
¾ cup milk
2 tspns. vanilla
1 cup br. sugar packed
⅓ cup cocoa, extra
2 cups boiling water

Place butter in dish, melt on HIGH 1 min. stir in flour, sugar and cocoa, milk and vanilla. Beat until smooth with wooden spoon. Sprinkle with combined br. sugar and extra cocoa. Pour boiling water over mixture carefully. Cook on HIGH 12 mins. or until just cooked in centre. Stand 5 mins. before serving with cream or ice cream. Serves 4 to 6.

GOLDEN SYRUP DUMPLINGS

1¼ cups S.R. flour
¼ cup golden syrup
30 gr butter
⅓ cup milk

SAUCE:

30 gr butter extra
½ cup br. sugar lightly packed
½ cup golden syrup extra
1½ cups water
2 tspns. grated lemon rind

Sift flour into basin, rub in butter. Combine golden syrup and milk. make well in centre of dry ingredients gradually stir in milk mixture. Stir mixture until combined thoroughly. Do not overbeat. Mixture should be moist and sticky. Make sauce by combining extra butter, sugar, extra golden syrup, water and lemon rind in heatproof dish. Cover with tight-fitting lid. Microwave sauce on HIGH 6 mins. stirring occasionally to dissolve sugar. With floured hands, roll the dumpling mixture into walnut sized balls, place into boiling sauce. Cover the mixture loosely with plastic food wrap, microwave on HIGH 3-4 mins. or until dumplings are well risen and firm. Serve immediately. Serves 6. Cost approx $1.

PEARS IN RED WINE

6 ripe pears
½ cup dry red wine
1 tblspn. sugar
2 tspns. arrowroot
2 tbspns. toasted almonds
1 small piece cinnamon stick
strip lemon rind

Peel pears. Remove core, taking it out through bottom of pear, leaving stalk intact. Place pears, sideways down in dish, add cinnamon stick, sugar and lemon rind and pour wine over. Microwave on HIGH 6-8 mins. depending on firmness of pears. Turn pears once during cooking. Take out and place each pear in individual dish. Strain liquid. Mix arrowroot with 2 tspns. cold water and carefully add strained liquid. Reheat on HIGH 1-2 mins. or until sauce comes to boil, stirring once or twice with wooden spoon. When sauce becomes clear and of a coating consistency, spoon over pears. Sprinkle with toasted almonds and serve cold with whipped cream.

QUICK BREAD PUDDING

1½ cups bread
2 eggs
½ cup sugar
1 tspn. vanilla
1½ cups milk
½ cup sultanas

Cut bread into small pieces and put in dish. Sprinkle with sultanas. Mix other ingredients together and pour onto bread. Sprinkle with nutmeg and cook for 10 mins.

STEAM PUDDING

A quick steam pudding can be made by covering the bottom of an ice-cream dish with a good thick layer of honey or jam. Make a 1 egg steam pudding mixture and place on top. Microwave uncovered for 6-7 mins. and when removed from oven will be 'tacky' on top, but when turned out onto plate, jam or money runs down sides and makes very presentable.

YUMMY PUDDING

4 thick slices bread
80 gr brown sugar
1½ tspn. mixed spice
1 egg
50 ml golden syrup
250 gr mixed fruit or sultanas
110 gr butter
200 ml. water

Break bread into pieces and soak in the water till well moistened. Strain water out, so bread is wet but not soggy, then mix together fruit, syrup, spices, egg, sugar and butter, beat well. pour into dish 25 x 15 cm. and cook on MED/LOW 15 mins. Serve hot or cold cut into slices.

Tip: Sprinkle top with a little brown sugar and cinnamon before cooking. Serves 4-6.

Jams

STRAWBERRY JAM

500 gr fruit — cut up evenly
1½ cups sugar
2 tbspns. lemon juice.

Microwave fruit and lemon juice for 6 mins. — covered — on HIGH. Add sugar, stir well. Microwave in two 10 min. phases on HIGH. Stir half way through each phase.

FIG JAM

This may be made as per above recipe.

HINTS THAT HELP IN THE HOME AND PRESERVE THE TEMPER

TO TEST EGGS FOR FRESHNESS

Fill a basin with water and put the eggs in one by one. A fresh egg sinks to the bottom and lies flat. If it rises slightly it is not perfectly fresh, and if it floats, it is bad.

TO CLEAN EGGS THAT ARE STAINED

Wet some baking soda, and wipe the eggs with it. This will remove all stains.

TO BANISH COCKROACHES–

Boracic acid sprinkled in sink cupboards, and around fire-places will banish cockroaches.

TO CLEAN COPPER PANS–

To clean copper pans, rub the pans with a mixture made by mixing together 2 tablespoons strong vinegar or old lemon skins, and 1 handful of salt. Rub with a piece of flannel, and wash in clean hot water. Dry thoroughly.

TO SHARPEN BLADES OF MINCER–

Blades of a mincing machine become blunt after a time, but if two or three small pieces of bath brick are ground through the machine it will sharpen them.

TO REMOVE MARKS FROM POLISHED TABLE–

Nothing ruins the polished surface of a dining-room table more quickly than hot plates, which leave a very noticeable mark wherever they are put down. The use of mats will avoid this, but when a polished surface does become marked, it can be remedied with spirits of camphor. Apply to the marked spot with a soft rag, rubbing lightly. When the stain disappears, polish well with a chamois duster.

To remove marks from a polished table caused by placing hot articles upon it, rub well with equal parts of olive oil and salt. Finish with a soft duster.

KNIFE HANDLES, TO CLEAN–

If ivory handles of knives are discoloured, rub them with lemon and salt.

TO IMPROVE STOVE POLISH–

If you add a little methylated spirits to your favourite stove polish you will get a greater gloss in about half the usual time.

TO CLEAN WINDOWS, ETC.–

To clean windows, mirrors, and lamp glasses, wipe over with damp newspaper and dry and polish with dry newspaper. A little rubbing is needed, but a brilliant polish is the result.

To clean windows quickly, rub dust off, then dip a clean soft rag in methylated spirits and rub thoroughly over the glass. Finally polish with a duster. By this method windows are cleaned better and quicker.

TO PREPARE A DUSTER–

To make an oiled duster, take a piece of old soft cloth, soak in paraffin, and then wring out and dry. This duster will gather up the dust, and give a brilliant polish to mirrors and lamp globes.

A TEA COSY HINT–

Chamois leather is a great retainer of heat. If you have any spare pieces, join them together and use to line your tea cosy. You will find your tea will keep warm much longer.

WHEN THE WINDOWS OR DOORS STICK–

If a window or doors stick, rub the sides of the jambs with soap or a little paraffin.

TO PREVENT CASTORS ON FURNITURE FROM RUSTING–

All locks and hinges and the castors on chairs and sofas should be oiled at least once a year. This prevents rusting and makes them run easily. Include this in your spring cleaning.

CRACKS IN ROOMS, TO STOP–

The following is a method of filling cracks in rooms. Soak for two or three days pieces of newspaper. Then tear to shreds. Mix a basin of starch as done for starching clothes, and mix the starch with the paper. Then take the pulp little by little and press and smooth into the crack. It will harden like brick.

TO SAVE FIRE WOOD–

When not actually cooking, put on a piece of wood such as white gum, jam, or anything, that burns to a white ash, and close the doors of the stove, and the flue. The fire will stay in for hours, and be easily lighted up again with a few chips. This keeps the kitchen cooler, and saves wood chopping.

TO CLEAN SILVER–

To clean silver like new, put a tablespoon of washing soda in a vessel of boiling water. Use anything aluminium, such as an egg slice, etc., and place the silver in. Polish with a soft cloth.

TO KEEP LEMONS FRESH–

Keep lemons fresh by packing them in salt and keeping them from touching each other.

SCISSORS IN THE KITCHEN–

Instead of using a knife, use scissors for cutting orange rind for marmalade, tripe, pastry, dates, parsley, steak, etc. Scissors are very useful in the kitchen.

TO MAKE COSY INNER SOLES FOR SLIPPERS–

Cosy fur inner soles can be made from discarded fur collars and cuffs.

TO MAKE A BEDSIDE MAT–

A good bedside mat can be made out of old silk stockings, cut into strips and crocheted up.

AN EASY WAY TO DRAW THREADS–

Before drawing threads in linen for hemstitching, make a thick lather of soap and apply it with a shaving brush to the fabric. When the linen dries the threads draw easily.

RENEWING WORN PILLOWSLIPS–

When pillowslips are beginning to show signs of wear, cut off the bottom seam, put side seam to middle, and sew bottom up again. The tape should not need altering.

USE FOR OLD FELT HATS–

Old felt hats make cosy insoles for shoes.

CARE OF NEW KID GLOVES—

Before putting on a pair of new kid gloves, hold them over a bowl of boiling water for a minute. The steam will soften them so that they are easily pulled on without fear of the kid splitting.

TO MAKE A PILLOW—

When making a pillow, pack the filling into a bag made of double mosquito net. Cut to fit the pillow ticking. The filling is then easily removed for airing or the ticking for washing.

TO MAKE A FEATHER PILLOW—

If you want a feather pillow, try this way: Make your pillow covering from a good strong ticking—linen for preference. Rub the inside well with common household soap, and turn to the right side. Each time you pluck poultry (and of course you will scald before plucking) put your fine breast feathers into a paper bag and hang out in the sun to dry. When dry, pop them into your pillow case and secure the top with a safety pin. Cover your case with an old pillow slip to keep it clean and hang up anywhere out of the way. You will be surprised just how soon your pillow will be ready for sewing up. Of course, if time permits you can strip your pen feathers and use also. If you put them at each plucking into a paper bag it is a nice wet day job for the children, and a good lesson for them as well.

KNITTING HINT—

When knitting, instead of knotting wool, take a darning needle and thread with wool one end. Darn along the other end for about three inches. It will not come undone or show the join. Also, if there is a space at the end of the needles, instead of putting needle in front at the beginning, put it behind the one just knitted, and there will be no space. This last hint applies when knitting sox.

TO WASH GLASSWARE—

A few drops of lemon juice in the rinsing water will give lustre to glassware.

TO CLEAN PIANO KEYS—

To clean the white keys of a piano, rub with a paste of lemon juice and whiting.

CARE OF LAMP GLASSES—

To prevent lamp glasses from cracking, put them into cold water, bring them to the boil, and let them cool gently. Then see that they are perfectly dried and polished.

TO CLEAN MARBLE–

Common salt is one of the best things you can use for cleaning marble. It will remove tarnish and stains and leave the marble bright and clean.

CARE OF FOODS–

Never put foods away in tins. Fully one half of the cases of poisoning from the use of tinned goods arise from the food having been put back into the tin and kept over for another meal.

SMOKY CEILINGS, TO CLEAN–

Ceilings which have become blackened with smoke may be cleaned with a cloth damped in warm water and soda.

BORAX IN THE KITCHEN–

In the kitchen a little borax in the washing up water is a splendid grease and stain remover, and it should always be added to the water in which tea-cloths are washed.

TO PURIFY RAIN WATER–

Rain water that has drained over roofs is rarely clean, but the supply may be easily purified in this way. From a piece of strong coarse cloth make a bag which can be fitted over the end of the pipe leading from the roofs. Fill the bag with small pebbles and then tie it over the mouth of the pipe to act as a filter.

THREAD FOR BEADS–

If the thread used to string beads is well waxed with beeswax it will wear much longer than otherwise, as the wax prevents the beads cutting into the fibres of the thread.

CLEANING CARPETS–

Sawdust is excellent for cleaning carpets. Damp the sawdust and sprinkle over the carpet. Then brush off with a carpet brush. Sawdust used instead of soap on kitchen tables, pastry boards, etc., will make them beautifully white and clean.

TO CLEAN SMELL OF TOBACCO–

If a saucer of water is placed at night in the room where people have been smoking, the smell of stale tobacco will be gone in the morning.

TO CLEAN IRON OR TIN UTENSILS–

The right time to clean any utensil made of iron or tin is when it is hot. A gas stove, iron, or tin kettle, etc., can be rubbed clean while hot in half the time they would take to clean if cold.

TO CLEAN PHOTOGRAPHS–

Cotton wool dipped in methylated spirits will clean photographs without destroying their polished surface.

TO FROST GLASS–

A simple method of making imitation frosted glass is to dissolve 60 gr (2 oz.) of epsom salts in a teacupful of warm beer. When the mixture is cold apply to the glass with soft muslin.

TO PREVENT SILVER FROM TARNISHING–

Olive oil rubbed over silver before it is put away will prevent it from tarnishing. When required wash in warm soapy water and dry thoroughly.

TO CLEAN GREASY SAUCEPANS–

Greasy frying pans or saucepans should be well rubbed with plenty of soft paper while still hot. The paper will absorb every particle of grease and will be found useful for lighting the fire next morning.

TO CLEAN SINK PIPES–

To clean sink pipes, dissolve a teaspoonful of common soda in a cupful of strong vinegar, and pour down the sink. This will clean the pipes of all grease.

TO REMOVE WHITEWASH STAINS–

A few drops of hot vinegar will remove the most obstinate whitewash or distemper splashes.

TO WASH A FLEECE

Take 60 gr (2 oz.) soap, a small cupful of washing soda, 4 kerosene tins (buckets) of warm water, shred the soap and boil it with the soda in a small saucepan of water. Divide in three, and put one-third in each of three tins of water. Take 500 gr (1 lb.) of fleece and shake out, cutting off any very dirty pieces. Put the fleece wool into the first water, stir about with the hands, lift it out, and place in the second water, and repeat, lift into third water and repeat. Rinse in the fourth tin of clear warm water, and place wool on some fine wire netting to dry. Turn it about for several days until thoroughly dry. Shake the wool from time to time as it dries and tease with the fingers. Do not squeeze or wring. It is advisable to wash only 500 gr (1 lb.) of wool at a time. About 2 kg (4 lb.) of fleece is required for a single bed quilt.

SHEEPSKIN MATS

Take a sheep skin immediately it has been removed from a sheep, and sprinkle the skin side with 250 gr ($\frac{1}{2}$ lb.) of alum and salt mixed together. Fold over skin to skin, roll up, and lay aside for two days. Unroll and wipe with a cloth. Have ready a supply of water. First put the skin in a bath of cold water, then into several baths of warm water, with plenty of soap and a little washing soda. Rinse in cold water, and hang on the clothes line for two days, skin side out. Spread on a board and scrape all fat off with the back of a knife. To dye the mat 5 packets of dye will be required. For a golden brown use 3 packets of yellow and 2 of dark brown dye. Boil quickly in a small quantity of water, add it to enough water to just cover the skin, and leave skin in dye for about seven hours, working it about occasionally. Take out skin and tack it on a flat board or box. Before it is quite dry (about 24 hours after taking out of the dye bath), rub into the skin side 250 gr ($\frac{1}{2}$ lb.) alum and 250 gr ($\frac{1}{2}$ lb.) saltpetre, crushed to a powder, and mix well together. Work it up well with a smooth brick. When thoroughly dry, comb the hair with a hair comb. Condys crystals will dye a skin a dull brown. These mats are very serviceable.

DRY TANNING MIXTURE FOR SKINS

Use 1 part of alum to 2 parts of saltpetre. Pulverise and mix. Tack skins on a board, fur side in, and rub the mixture in daily till tanned. Then, if necessary, soften with a little neats-foot oil, well rubbed in.

A COUNTRY RADIATOR

Get a round plough disc (one that has been cast aside). Take an oil drum or petrol tin, and punch holes all round the sides, and put a fire in it, and when it has finished smoking, and only clear red coals remain, put the tin on the disc and place it in the room or hall where it is required. Mallee roots make lovely coals, and throw out a lot of heat. This is an excellent way of heating a cold hall on a winter's night.

DOOR MAT FROM MOTOR TUBE

Cut a tube into long strips one inch wide. Tack each end on a table or board, and then lay another strip across it as right angles, tacking the ends as before. Put the next under the first strip and as close to the second as possible. Do this until you have the width you require. Punch holes in the last strip with a leather punch, and when the mat is the required size, lace with a leather thong or narrow strip of tubing. The ends may be finished by cutting and punching. A good effect may also be obtained by laying the strips diagonally and using black and red tubes.

QUILT MADE FROM WOOL

The following directions for the making of a quilt from wool are issued by the C.W.A. of Victoria:—

For a quilt double bed size you will require $7\frac{1}{2}$ m ($8\frac{1}{2}$ yds.) of $\frac{3}{4}$ m (30 in.) wide material (sateen or similar material), $5\frac{1}{2}$ m (6 yds.) of butter muslin, and $1\frac{3}{4}$ kg ($3\frac{1}{2}$ lb.) of scoured prepared wool. (Scour wool, beat on a wooden floor with cane, and tease with ordinary comb.)

Cut and stitch the butter muslin required size. Mark the design you wish to carry out in pencil or chalk. (For a design copy an eiderdown.) Place muslin on table, and, beginning at the centre, place the wool on it, and stitch down with long tacking stitches, taking care not to cover pencil marks. Take other piece of muslin, and pin down to correspond with piece on which wool is stitched. Tack together, and then tack on the sateen, still keeping the divisions for the design. When all is firmly together, stitch with the machine. Work five eyelet holes in the centre of the quilt for ventilation.

For a simpler quilt omit the butter muslin. Machine the outer covers in long straight lines 20-30 cm (8-10 in.) apart and stuff each division lightly with wool. For a single-bed quilt, 1 kg (2 lb.) of wool should be sufficient.

LAUNDRY HINTS, SOAPS AND PASTES

SOAP HINTS–

Mutton fat is best for soap, and whatever fat is used must be free from salt.

Press the little tin capsules used for bottles instead of corks, on to your cakes of soap, and allow the soap to rest on the capsule. It will keep the soap dry.

Always keep soap a while before using. The harder it is the farther it goes.

TO IRON TUSSORE SILK–

Do not iron tussore and assam silk articles wet. It is hard to iron them evenly, and very often the seams and thick parts are not a success. Dry the articles, then lay them between other dampened down clothes, and they will iron easily and evenly.

CARE OF WOOLLENS–

Woollens shrink and become hard through various causes:–

1. Washing in water too hot or too cold.
2. Steeping them.
3. Using hard instead of soft water.
4. Using soap instead of soap jelly.
5. Rubbing soap on instead of squeezing.
6. Leaving them lying about wet.
7. Drying in too great heat.
8. Drying too slowly.
9. Ironing while wet with a very hot iron.

Washing powders containing lime are very injurious to fabrics.

TO WASH BLANKETS—

To wash blankets, fill the copper with rain water. Bring to the boil, then put in 250 gr (½ lb.) of block ammonia and stir well. Put one blanket at a time into the boiling water, stir well for about 5 minutes, then rinse well in two tubs of water. Shake and hang in the air to dry. They will become soft and white and look like new. Don't use any soap, and don't be alarmed at putting the blankets into boiling water. They will not spoil or shrink.

TO WASH CHAMOIS GLOVES—

When washing chamois gloves, add a few drops of glycerine to the last rinsing water. This will make them dry without harshness, and they will not wear out so quickly.

TO WHITEN HANDKERCHIEFS—

If, when washed, your white handkerchiefs are not a good colour, add a little peroxide of hydrogen to the last rinsing water. It will remove fruit stains, and make the fabric snowy white.

TO PREVENT COLOURS FADING—

Zephyrs and cambrics of delicate hues are apt to run. This may be prevented by soaking in cold water for ½ an hour with half a packet of epsom salts. Lift out the article without wringing, and hang it dripping wet in the shade. When perfectly dry, wash in the usual way.

STAINS

GENERAL PRINCIPLES FOR THEIR REMOVAL

The removal of a stain from frock, table linen, or carpet, is an almost every-day problem met with by the housewife. The following rules for their removal should be studied, and the methods described adopted:—

(1) Treat immediately if circumstances allow.

(2) Whenever possible, employ organic solvents (methylated spirits, turpentine, acetone), as these seldom affect the dye, and have no deleterious action on the fabric.

(3) Always try the simplest method first.

(4) Wherever a strongly re-acting substance has been used, such as bleaching acid, always wash out thoroughly all traces with cold water.

(5) When convenient, stretch the fabric to be treated over a bowl, or between embroidery hoops.

(6) Use as little solvent as is practicable.

STAINS—*continued*

(7) Rub dry with a clean cloth, rubbing from the outside, inwards, in order to minimise the risk of leaving a "ring".

(8) Always experiment beforehand on an unimportant piece of material.

COFFEE STAINS—

Boiling water, then a weak solution of ammonia in water.

Coffee stains can be removed in the same manner as tea stains, by pouring boiling water through them, provided the coffee has not had time to be thoroughly absorbed into the cloth. If the stain is not treated at once, equal parts of yolk of egg and glycerine spread over the spot and left to dry, will remove it. When the mixture has dried, wash the cloth in the usual way.

FRUIT, TEA, COFFEE, WINE OR BEERS—

Use water, followed by hydrogen peroxide, or warm borax solution. On coloured material which is known to be fast dye, use peroxide, otherwise use water, followed by methylated spirits and soap.

FRUIT STAINS—

Borax and boiling water poured from a height.

Fruit stains can be removed if salt is rubbed in at once, and boiling water is poured through the mark.

Fruit stains on linen can be removed if the spot is wet with a little camphor before washing.

MOST FOODS—

Water (no soap) or if greasy, detergent

IRON MOULD—

Salts of lemon, oxalic acid or citric acid solution.

SEALING WAX—

Methylated spirits.

SUGAR, GLUE, ETC.—

Water.

OIL VARNISH—

Treat as paint.

SHELLAC VARNISH—

Mixture of carbon tetrachloride and methylated spirits.

IRON RUST—

Rust may be removed from linen by tying a little cream of tartar in the affected part, and boiling in the usual way.

Iron rust may be removed by rubbing the spot with a ripe tomato, covering it with salt, and letting it dry in the sunlight. Finally wash the garment in warm water.

Iron rust may be removed effectively by soaking the rusty spots in the water in which rice has been boiled, for 4 or 5 hours, and then rinsing in clean water.

INK STAINS—

Dip the stained part in pure tomato juice, and let it dry before washing. If the first application does not remove the stain, repeat. This removes ink stains from linen or silk.

Cover spot with salt, then dip in hot milk, and allow to soak for some time. Wash out thoroughly.

To remove ink stains from white materials, place the stained parts in a dish, and sprinkle with tartaric acid. Pour hot water over the stains, and allow to stand for an hour or more. Rinse, and boil in the usual manner. You will find the stains will have disappeared.

To remove red ink stain from a tablecloth or linen, spread freshly made mustard over the stain, and leave for ½ an hour, then sponge off, and all trace of the ink stain will have gone.

Fresh ink stains can be removed if washed out at once in butter milk, or even fresh milk.

Salts of lemon will remove rust or ink stains from white cloths. Put a little on the stained part, pour boiling water over, then rinse well to remove the salts.

WINE OR FRUIT STAINS—

Tomato juice will remove wine or fruit stains.

IODINE STAINS—

To remove iodine stains, soak in methylated spirits.

CHOCOLATE STAINS—

A little yolk of raw egg will remove chocolate stains from most materials. Rub it gently on the stain with a clean piece of linen, and afterwards, wash in clean soap suds. Rinse thoroughly.

GRASS STAINS—

No soap, cold water only.

TO REMOVE GRASS STAINS—

Soak in pure alcohol, and rub briskly.

TO REMOVE PAINT—

Hot vinegar will remove paint from cotton fabrics. Equal parts of ammonia and spirits of turpentine will take paint spots out of clothing, no matter how hard and dry the paint has become. Saturate the spots several times if necessary, and then wash out in soap suds.

BLOOD STAINS—

Use soap and water or strong soda water.

PERSPIRATION STAINS—

Place the garment in a soap solution, and set in sunshine. It is difficult to remove.

GREASE STAINS, TO REMOVE—

Eucalyptus oil will remove grease stains from any kind of material. Apply with a clean piece of flannel, and rub gently until the stains disappear.

AXLE GREASE, TO REMOVE—

To remove axle grease stains from materials such as white serge or silk, apply a liberal application of shaving soap. For best results, moisten the article with a thick lather made with hot water, and then rub the soap itself vigorously on the stain. Let it stand for an hour or two, and then wash off with clear, tepid water.

MOTOR GREASE, TO REMOVE—

To remove motor car grease spots from shirts or wash dresses, first rub well into marks while dry some fat or dripping. Use as with soap, then wash in the usual way, and the marks will all come out.

Salt dissolved in ammonia will remove grease spots.

DYE STAINS—

If dye comes out of your coat, and your blouse is discoloured, put your blouse in milk, and let it stand in it overnight. It will remove all stains.

SCORCH MARKS–

To remove scorch marks proceed in the following manner: Chop an onion small and put it with 60 gr (2 oz.) of Fuller's Earth and 250 ml ($\frac{1}{2}$ pint) of vinegar into a saucepan. Boil the mixture until it becomes thick and pasty. Stir well, and allow to cool, Spread some of the paste on the scorch mark and leave it to dry. Then brush off the paste, and wash the article in cold water.

To remove scorch marks damp them and expose to the sun.

If a scorched article of any kind is immediately put into boiling water and left for a while, the marks will fade out.

To remove scorch marks on linen, rub with a raw lemon, and allow to dry in the sun. To remove scorch marks from woollens and silks, smear with borax and glycerine, and leave for an hour. Wash carefully.

USES FOR LEMON JUICE–

The juice of a lemon placed in the water when boiling white clothes removes stains and makes the clothes beautifully white.

To remove perspiration marks from white clothes, dampen the article with a little lemon juice and salt before it is put in the soap and water.

TO REMOVE LETTERS FROM FLOUR BAGS, ETC.–

To remove letters from sugar, flour, and salt bags, proceed in the following way. The night before washing sprinkle with kerosene and let this remain all night. In the morning boil the sack in strong soap suds, and the lettering will disappear. There are many uses for these bags, and they look much better with the letters and printing erased.

MILDEW, TO REMOVE–

Mildew can be removed by damping the damaged part; rub with soap, and sprinkle with fine chalk. Expose to the sun It may be necessary to repeat this process several times as mildew is a difficult stain to remove.

Mildew spots should be rubbed with laundry soap, then put salt and lemon on both sides of the cloth, and lay out in the hot sun. Repeat the process if necessary.

TO REMOVE MILDEW FROM LACE–

The following is a means of removing mildew from lace: Mix an ounce each of soft soap and powdered starch, half an ounce of salt, and a dessertspoonful of lemon juice with a little water to a smooth paste. Spread on the mildew spots, leave for 12 hours, and then rinse in tepid water. If the marks are not entirely removed, repeat the operation.

HOUSEHOLD SOAP (No. 1)

8 litres (2 Gallons) Cold Water
375 gr ($\frac{3}{4}$ lb.) resin
1 tablespoon borax
3 kg (6 lb.) clarified fat
500 gr (1 lb.) caustic soda
1 large packet Lux
$\frac{1}{2}$ bottle cloudy ammonia

Put into a kerosene tin the cold water, fat, resin, caustic soda and borax. Boil all together slowly. If boiling over add a tablespoon of cold water to check it. Boil until it thickens (about $\frac{1}{2}$ an hour or a little longer), then add the Lux and ammonia. Remove from the fire, and leave until next morning, when you can turn the tin upside down, and the mould of soap will slip out. Cut into bars, and allow a month to dry. This soap does not hurt the hands as some home made soaps do.

HOUSEHOLD SOAP (No. 2)

3 kg (6 lb.) Clarified Fat
500 gr (1 lb.) caustic soda
8 litres (2 gallons) cold water
250 gr ($\frac{1}{2}$ lb.) resin

Put the fat and water into a kerosene tin, and put over the fire till dissolved, then add the soda, a teaspoonful at a time, stirring the mixture all the while. Add the resin, which has been ground to a powder, and let the whole boil very slowly for an hour and 20 minutes. It boils over if you don't boil slowly. Have ready a kerosene tin with one side cut out and no holes in it. Pour the soap into it, and leave till next day, then turn out and cut into blocks. In a month it is nice and firm.

HOUSEHOLD SOAP (No. 3)

8 litres (2 Gallons) Rain Water
125 gr ($\frac{1}{4}$ lb.) borax
500 gr (1 lb.) caustic soda
$2\frac{1}{2}$ kg (5lb.) clarified dripping
250 gr ($\frac{1}{2}$ lb.) resin
$\frac{1}{4}$ beer bottle machinery castor oil

Put all ingredients together in a kerosene tin with a handle, place on a small fire, and bring to the boil. It runs over very easily, so watch carefully and remove to the side of stove, or have only a few chips burning to keep it just simmering for about 2 hours. When finished, add the castor oil, and turn the mixture into suitable vessels. Leave a day or two, then turn out and cut into bars. Keep for a short time to allow the moisture to dry out.

WASHING FLUID

2 litres (½ Gallon) Water
4 litres (1 gallon) clear lime water
1 litre (2 pints) boiling water
500 gr (1 lb.) washing soda
90 gr (3 oz.) borax
90 gr (3 oz.) pulverised carbonate ammonia

Dissolve the soda in the 2 litres (½ gallon) of water, and add the lime water (made from freshly slaked lime). Stir together, let it settle, and pour off the clear liquid. To this add the borax, dissolved in the boiling water. Let it get cold, and add the carbonate of ammonia. When fully dissolved, pour off into bottles and cork securely. 1 cup of this to 24 litres (6 gallons) of water will be found sufficient. Soak the clothes in it overnight. In the morning wring out the water, rubbing where any soiled places remain, put into the copper (little or no soap necessary), boil up, rinse well, and hang out. This does not injure the clothes.

GLUEING PASTE (No. 1)

1 Tablespoon Plain Flour
½ tablespoon starch
1 tablespoon sugar
1 teaspoon powdered alum
water

Mix all together with a little cold water, making sure there are no lumps, then add sufficent boiling water to make a thick, transparent paste. Be sure the water is boiling, and stir continuously as in making starch. This paste will keep.

GLUEING PASTE (No. 2)

15 gr (½ oz.) Alum
15 gr (½ oz.) flour
500 ml (1 pint) boiling water
a few drops of oil of cloves

Dissolve the alum in the boiling water, and add to this the flour which has been mixed to a smooth paste, and then add a few drops of oil of cloves. Let the whole come to boiling point again.

TOILET HINTS

TO SOFTEN WATER FOR HAIR WASH–

A squeeze of lemon juice added to the water with which the head is washed will soften the water, and remove the soap from the hair.

BAKING SODA IN THE BATH–

Baking soda if used at the rate of 250 gr (½ lb.) to a bath of water is very refreshing. It banishes body odour, and allays irritation.

TO CURE WARTS–

The following is a tried remedy for warts. Take a small quantity of ordinary lime, say a teaspoonful, moisten with water to a paste, and then place a little of the mixture on the wart. Allow to dry, and repeat daily, oftener if convenient, and in a few days the warts will dry out and disappear. This is a particularly good remedy, and may be used with safety on the skin of quite small children without injury, pain, or burning.

FLOOR AND FURNITURE POLISHES

A good mop for polishing floors can be made with an old hair broom covered with sheep skin nailed on at the top.

Linoleum that has become shabby can be varnished by taking equal parts of carriage varnish and turpentine. It takes about two days to dry. When dry it can be polished.

When washing linoleum, add to the water any left over cold boiled starch. It makes the linoleum shine.

Keep your mop oil in a fly tox spray pump, and spray the floor. Then polish with the mop. The oil goes twice as far, and the work is much lighter.

A few drops of paraffin in the water when washing paint will dissolve the dirt.

The juice of a ripe tomato will remove ink stains from furniture.

White of egg will give new life to old leather furniture. Rub first some vaseline into the leather, and when well rubbed in and dry, rub with white of egg. This treatment is very useful for saddles, harness, etc. Rub until a good polish is obtained.

FLOOR STAIN

60 gr (2 oz.) Shellac
2 cups methylated spirit
60 gr (2 oz.) ground resin

Put ingredients into a bottle, shake well, and cork. Let stand for 24 hours and apply to the floor with a brush.

FLOOR POLISH

125 gr ($\frac{1}{4}$ lb.) Beeswax
250 ml ($\frac{1}{2}$ pint) turpentine
250 ml ($\frac{1}{2}$ pint) cold water
5 tablespoons ammonia

Melt the beeswax in the water by placing both in a tin and standing in a pan of boiling water over the fire. Allow to melt gradually, take off the fire, and add the turpentine. Stir well, and then add the ammonia.

FURNITURE POLISH

Raw Linseed Oil
methylated spirits
turpentine
vinegar

Take equal parts of the above ingredients, mix well, and apply with a soft cloth. Rub well in, and polish with a clean soft cloth.

MOP OIL

210 ml (7 oz.) Linseed Oil
15 gr (½ oz.) camphor
45 ml (1½ oz.) turpentine
30 ml (1 oz.) kerosene

Dissolve the camphor in the kerosene and put all into a bottle and shake well.

HOME MAKING, GARDENING AND OUTDOOR HINTS

HINTS FOR HOME MAKING ON THE LAND

Select the site for the home with first regard to water, suitability of ground for garden, and as a convenient working centre for the farm.

Leave timber around the house for shade, shelter, and beauty.

Build stables and out-houses so that drainage will not go to the house, but don't build such in front of house. Don't build out-houses too near the home.

Don't build of iron. It is too hot in summer, and too cold in winter. Cement bricks are as cheap as wood.

However small the house don't have a flat roof. A high roof and verandahs mean coolness and comfort.

Pay particular attention to ventilation.

Fly doors and screens are a necessity.

When planting trees or creepers, plant fruit-bearing ones. Even with waste water, one good grape vine and fig tree can be grown if half kerosene tins are embedded, one on each of the four sides of the plant, and the water put in these, and the surface soil often turned over. The Adam Fig, and the Ladies' Finger Grape Vine are very suitable for dry areas, being quick growers and prolific bearers.

When fencing the garden make it rabbit proof. Raise early seedlings for winter and spring garden.

THE HOME GARDEN

Home is not a Home without a garden. Plant one, and it will repay you.

Every wise housewife knows the value of the kitchen garden. It is a money saver, and a pleasure at all times. Nearly all vegetables are of easy culture. All soup vegetables should be grown at home. It is a great comfort to slip out and cut your own home requirements in your own back yard. Some at least of our vegetables are available all the year round.

Celery, parsley, onions, carrots, and parsnips should find a place in the home garden. A grated carrot added to soup stock gives body and richness. A grated carrot added to a fruit or plum pudding is a decided improvement.

Reserve a plot for beans and peas in the garden. Sow some garlic. Lettuce is a health giver–grow it in the home garden. You will enjoy the flavour of a freshly cut lettuce.

Cabbage, cauliflower, beet, turnips, and artichokes are very easily grown. Find a spacc for them.

There should be a herb bed in every garden. Lavender is a delightful herb, and it will grow anywhere. The flowers are the valuable part, and they should be cut, tied in bundles, and dried in the sun, mixed with rosemary, thyme, and mint leaves in the proportion of one part each of these to ten parts of lavender, and with just a sprinkling of ground cloves, you have a moth preventative superior to any of the patents you can buy.

Thyme is another very useful herb, and very valuable for flavouring soups, seasoning, etc. Marjoram and mint need little recommendation. No garden should be without a bed of these old-fashioned herbs.

Plant tomatoes, pumpkins, melons, cucumbers, and gherkins. The runner beans, French beans and the useful Tongan bean are well worth growing.

Own your own vine and fig tree, and don't forget the useful lemon. This tree will flourish almost anywhere in this State. If space permits, plant other fruits suitable to the soil and the locality in which you live. A few shrubs and flowers are easily managed.

Remember to give back to your soil as liberally as you take from it. Every garden should have a compost heap. Refuse of all kinds should be saved–stable and fowl manure, bones, green cuttings, weeds, leaves, ashes, soot, paper–in fact, waste of every kind. All these should be thrown on the heap, and house slops thrown over all. The whole can be turned occasionally, and a shovelful of lime added from time to time to hasten decay. Soil can also be mixed in. A dressing from this heap is a valuable addition to the garden plot.

Don't throw away onions that are shot and decaying, and unfit for use. Plant them in your kitchen garden and watch the results.

Bury the potato peelings in your garden and later on gather in the harvest.

The life of cut flowers depends on several things.

The most important of these is to cut your blooms before they are too old. Do your cutting early in the morning, or late in the evening, the morning for preference. Each bloom should be placed into water immediately it is cut. Poppies should be cut just before the buds open, and the ends of the stems should be burnt.

TO KEEP CUT FLOWERS FRESH—

A pinch of alum in water will lengthen the life of cut flowers.

GERBERAS

Gerberas should be cut early in the morning and ends burnt.

CARE OF FERNS—

Ferns and palms that have lost their glossy appearance may be considerably improved and freshened by sponging over occasionally with a mixture of milk and lukewarm water in equal parts. Sponging with a solution of soap flakes and water is also found beneficial to the health and appearance of palms and aspidistras.

CARE OF GRAPE VINES—

Grape vines require dusting with sulphur just at the flowering stage. A handy duster can be made from cocoa, coffee, or dried milk tins. Punch holes in the bottom of the tin, fill $\frac{3}{4}$ full with sulphur, put the lid on, and the dusting can be well and quickly done.

FOR YOUR ROSE BED—

If you are not requiring it for soup, pour the water in which fish have been boiled (when cold) on to your rose bed. It will improve your roses wonderfully.

MANURE FOR TREES (FRUIT, CITRUS, ETC.)—

The following is a quickly acting manure for stone fruit trees:—

1 kg (2 lb.) Nitrate of Soda
2 kg (4 lb.) superphosphate
250 gr ($\frac{1}{2}$ lb.) sulphate potash

Mix all together and allow $3\frac{1}{4}$ kg ($6\frac{1}{2}$ lb.) to each tree. Sprinkle round the tree by hand, and then dig in. This manuring should be carried out in the early spring before the blossoms appear. In addition to this fertilizer, the soil should be abundantly supplied with decaying vegetable matter. Vegetable matter of all kinds improves the soil, and is a great aid in the conservation and better distribution of water. Trees should be well watered after the fertiliser is used.

The following is a good manure for citrus fruit trees and roses:—

6 kg (12 lb.) Blood and Bone Manure	6 kg (12 lb.) superphosphate
1 kg (2 lb.) sulphate potash	1 kg (2 lb.) sulphate ammonia
	1 kg (2 lb.) nitrate of soda

Mix all well together, and give about 500-750 gr (1-1½ lb.) to each tree, according to size of tree, dig well in, and give a liberal watering. This manure is excellent for carnations. Sprinkle round the plants, dig and water.

CALF FOOD

Linseed Cake Meal	fine oatmeal
ground linseed	5 litres (5 quarts) boiling water
60 gr (2 oz.) sugar	a little salt

Boil together two parts each of linseed cake meal and fine oatmeal, one part ground linseed, and the boiling water. Boil mixture 10 minutes. Add the sugar, and a little salt, before feeding.

SCALY LEGS IN POULTRY

½ Cup Unsalted Fat	1 teaspoon kerosene
2 tablespoons sulphur	

Mix together the fat (lard is good), sulphur, and kerosene, and rub well over the legs of the affected birds. If only mild cases, one application is sufficient, but bad cases require two or even three applications. The disease is caused by a parasite that works under the scales of the legs. It is infectious. The perches should be fumigated.

COLD IN FOWLS

To cure cold in fowls, dip a feather in stockholm tar and touch their drinking water with it. This forms a film on the top and adheres to the beak. If this is done several times a day, the epidemic will be checked and all cases cured within a week.

INDEX

C.W.A OF W.A. DIVISIONS

AVON HILLS
Aldersyde
Bakers Hill
Beverley
Bolgart
Brookton
Calingiri
Cunderdin
Jennacubbine
Meckering
Mt Helena/Parkerville
Mundaring
Northam
Quairading
Tammin
Toodyay
Wooroloo
York

BANKSIA
Bayswater
Bullsbrook
Caversham
City of Perth
Doubleview
Gidgegannup
Greenmount/Darlington
Karrinyup
Kings Park
Metropolitan
Midland
Morley/Bedford
Tuart Hill & Districts
Wanneroo
Western Suburbs

CAPRICORNIA
Broome
Carnarvon
Derby/West Kimberley Air
Karratha
Kununurra
Newman
Port Hedland
Wittenoom
Wyndham

CENTRAL GREAT SOUTHERN
Arthur River
Badgebup/Rockwell
Broomehill
Darkan
Dumbleyung
Duranillin/Moodiarrup
Jingalup/Mobrup
Katanning
Kojonup
Kukerin
Lake Grace
Lake Varley
Muradup
Newdegate
Nyabing
Tambellup
Wagin
Woodanilling

EASTERN WHEATBELT
Bodallin
Bullfinch
Kellerberrin
Korbelka
Kununoppin
Merredin
Narembeen
Nukarni
Nungarin
Shackleton
Southern Cross
Trayning
Westonia

ENDEAVOUR
Applecross/Mt Pleasant
Armadale
Bentley
Claremont
Cloverdale
Cockburn
Cottesloe
Gooseberry Hill/Kalamunda
Gosnells
Kelmscott
Lynwood/Ferndale
Melville
Richmond
Roleystone
South Perth/Como
Thornlie
Victoria Park
Walliston
Wattle Grove
Willetton/Leeming
Yangebup

GEOGRAPHE
Acton Park
Alexandra Bridge
Augusta
Bunbury
Burekup/Brunswick
Busselton
Capel
Collie
Cowaramup
Dunsborough
Eaton
Leschenault
Margaret River
Rosa Brook
Rosa Glen/Witchcliffe
Ruabon

GOLDEN WAVE
Bullaring
Bulyee
Corrigin
Cuballing
Dudinin
Highbury
Hyden
Karlgarin
Kulin
Narrogin
Nomans Lake
Pingaring
Pingelly
Popanyinning
Pumphreys Bridge
Quindanning/Boddington
Wandering
Wickepin

KARINGA FIELDS

Boulder
Condingup
Esperance
Gibson
Grass Patch
Hopetoun
Kalgoorlie
Mt Madden
Munglinup
Norseman
Postal
Ravensthorpe
Salmon Gums

LOWER SOUTHERN

Albany
Cranbrook
Denmark
Forest Hill/Denbarker
Frankland
Gairdner
Gnowangerup
Jerramungup
Lower King
Mt Barker
Mt Manypeaks
Ongerup
Rock Gully
Wellstead

MERINDA

Coolup
Dwellingup
Harvey
Keysbrook
Kwinana Districts
Mandurah
Pinjarra
Rockingham
Safety Bay
Serpentine & Districts
Wellard/Baldivis
Yarloop
Yunderup

MID WEST MURCHISON

Ajana/Binnu
Bluff Point
Chapman Valley
Denison/Dongara
Meekatharra
Mingenew
Moonyoonooka/ East Chapman
Morawa
Mt Magnet
Mullewa
Northampton
Port Gregory
Sandstone
Shark Bay
Useless Loop
Walkaway
Wiluna
Wonthella
Yandanooka
Yuna

SOUTHERN VALLEYS

Balingup
Boyanup
Boyup Brook
Bridgetown
Donnybrook
Greenbushes
Manjimup
Manjimup Evening
Mayanup
Nannup
Northcliffe

WEST COAST PLAINS

Badgingarra
Cervantes
Chittering/Bindoon
Dandaragan
Gingin
Greenhead/Leeman
Jurien
Koorunga
Lancelin
Moora
Ocean Farm
Quinns Rocks
Yanchep Districts

WHEATLANDS

Ballidu
Beacon
Bencubbin
Cadoux
Carnamah
Coorow
Dalwallinu/Pithara
Dowerin
Dowerin Evening
Jibberding
Kalannie
Kondut
Konnongorring/Goomalling
Koorda
Latham/Caron-Bunjil
Perenjori
West Ballidu
Wongan Hills

Angus&Robertson
An imprint of HarperCollins*Publishers,* Australia

First published in Australia by E. S. Wigg & Son Pty Limited in 1936
Angus & Robertson (forty second) edition first published in 1992
by HarperCollins*Publishers* Australia Pty Limited
ABN 36 009 913 517
A member of the HarperCollins*Publishers* (Australia) Pty Limited Group
www.harpercollins.com.au

HarperCollins*Publishers*
25 Ryde Road, Pymble, Sydney, NSW 2073, Australia
31 View Road, Glenfield, Auckland 10, New Zealand
77–85 Fulham Palace Road, London W6 8JB, United Kingdom
2 Bloor Street East, 20th floor, Toronto, Ontario M4W 1A8, Canada
10 East 53rd Street, New York NY 10022, USA

ISBN 0 207 18071 7

Printed and bound in Australia by Griffin Press on 80gsm UPM Fine Offset

60 59 58 57 56 55 05 06 07 08